Also by America's Test Kitchen

More Mediterranean

The Complete Plant-Based Cookbook

Cooking with Plant-Based Meat

Desserts Illustrated

Modern Bistro

Boards

The Savory Baker

The New Cooking School Cookbook:
Fundamentals

The Complete Autumn and
Winter Cookbook

One-Hour Comfort

The Everyday Athlete Cookbook

Cook for Your Gut Health

Foolproof Fish

Five-Ingredient Dinners

The Ultimate Meal-Prep Cookbook

The Complete Salad Cookbook

The Chicken Bible

Meat Illustrated

Vegetables Illustrated

Bread Illustrated

Cooking for One

The Complete One Pot

How Can It Be Gluten-Free
Cookbook Collection

The Complete Summer Cookbook

Bowls

The Side Dish Bible

100 Techniques

Easy Everyday Keto

Everything Chocolate

The Perfect Cookie

The Perfect Pie

The Perfect Cake

How to Cocktail

Spiced

The Ultimate Burger

The New Essentials Cookbook

Dinner Illustrated

America's Test Kitchen Menu Cookbook

Cook's Illustrated Revolutionary Recipes

Tasting Italy: A Culinary Journey

Cooking at Home with Bridget and Julia

The Complete Mediterranean Cookbook

The Complete Vegetarian Cookbook

The Complete Cooking for Two
Cookbook

The Complete Diabetes Cookbook

The Complete Slow Cooker

The Complete Make-Ahead Cookbook

Just Add Sauce

How to Braise Everything

How to Roast Everything

Nutritious Delicious

What Good Cooks Know

Cook's Science

The Science of Good Cooking

Master of the Grill

Kitchen Smarts

Kitchen Hacks

100 Recipes

The New Family Cookbook

The Cook's Illustrated Baking Book

The Cook's Illustrated Cookbook

The America's Test Kitchen Family
Baking Book

America's Test Kitchen Twentieth
Anniversary TV Show Cookbook

The Best of America's Test Kitchen
(2007–2023 Editions)

The Complete America's Test Kitchen
TV Show Cookbook 2001–2023

Healthy Air Fryer

Healthy and Delicious Instant Pot

Toaster Oven Perfection

Mediterranean Instant Pot

Cook It in Your Dutch Oven

Vegan for Everybody

Sous Vide for Everybody

Air Fryer Perfection

Multicooker Perfection

Food Processor Perfection

Pressure Cooker Perfection

Instant Pot Ace Blender Cookbook

Naturally Sweet

Foolproof Preserving

Paleo Perfected

The Best Mexican Recipes

Slow Cooker Revolution Volume 2:
The Easy-Prep Edition

Slow Cooker Revolution

The America's Test Kitchen D.I.Y.
Cookbook

The Cook's Illustrated All-Time Best Series

All-Time Best Brunch

All-Time Best Dinners for Two

All-Time Best Sunday Suppers

All-Time Best Holiday Entertaining

All-Time Best Soups

Cook's Country Titles

Big Flavors from Italian America

One-Pan Wonders

Cook It in Cast Iron

Cook's Country Eats Local

The Complete Cook's Country TV Show
Cookbook

For a Full Listing of All Our Books

CooksIllustrated.com

AmericasTestKitchen.com

Praise for America's Test Kitchen Titles

"An exhaustive but approachable primer for those looking for a 'flexible' diet. Chock-full of tips, you can dive into the science of plant-based cooking or just sit back and enjoy the 500 recipes."
Minneapolis Star Tribune on *The Complete Plant-Based Cookbook*

"Here are the words just about any vegan would be happy to read: 'Why This Recipe Works.' Fans of America's Test Kitchen are used to seeing the phrase, and now it applies to the growing collection of plant-based creations in Vegan for Everybody."
The Washington Post on *Vegan for Everybody*

"The go-to gift book for newlyweds, small families, or empty nesters."
Orlando Sentinel on *The Complete Cooking for Two Cookbook*

"A mood board for one's food board is served up in this excellent guide . . . This has instant classic written all over it."
Publishers Weekly (starred review) on *Boards: Stylish Spreads for Casual Gatherings*

"In this latest offering from the fertile minds at America's Test Kitchen the recipes focus on savory baked goods. Pizzas, flatbreads, crackers, and stuffed breads all shine here . . . Introductory essays for each recipe give background information and tips for making things come out perfectly."
Booklist (starred review) on *The Savory Baker*

"Reassuringly hefty and comprehensive, *The Complete Autumn and Winter Cookbook* by America's Test Kitchen has you covered with a seemingly endless array of seasonal fare . . . This overstuffed compendium is guaranteed to warm you from the inside out."
NPR on *The Complete Autumn and Winter Cookbook*

"The book's depth, breadth, and practicality makes it a must-have for seafood lovers."
Publishers Weekly (starred review) on *Foolproof Fish*

"Another flawless entry in the America's Test Kitchen canon, *Bowls* guides readers of all culinary skill levels in composing one-bowl meals from a variety of cuisines."
BuzzFeed Books on *Bowls*

"*The Perfect Cookie* . . . is, in a word, perfect. This is an important and substantial cookbook . . . If you love cookies, but have been a tad shy to bake on your own, all your fears will be dissipated. This is one book you can use for years with magnificently happy results."
Huffpost on *The Perfect Cookie*

"The book offers an impressive education for curious cake makers, new and experienced alike. A summation of 25 years of cake making at ATK, there are cakes for every taste."
The Wall Street Journal on *The Perfect Cake*

"If you're one of the 30 million Americans with diabetes, *The Complete Diabetes Cookbook* by America's Test Kitchen belongs on your kitchen shelf."
Parade.com on *The Complete Diabetes Cookbook*

"True to its name, this smart and endlessly enlightening cookbook is about as definitive as it's possible to get in the modern vegetarian realm."
Men's Journal on *The Complete Vegetarian Cookbook*

VEGAN COOKING *for* TWO

200+ Recipes for Everything You Love to Eat

AMERICA'S TEST KITCHEN

Library of Congress Cataloging-in-Publication Data

Names: America's Test Kitchen (Firm), author.
Title: Vegan cooking for two : 200+ recipes for everything you love to eat /
America's Test Kitchen.
Description: Boston, MA : America's Test Kitchen, [2022] | Includes index.
Identifiers: LCCN 2022021759 (print) | LCCN 2022021760 (ebook) | ISBN 9781954210189 (paperback) | ISBN 9781954210196 (ebook)
Subjects: LCSH: Vegan cooking. | Cooking for two. | LCGFT: Cookbooks.
Classification: LCC TX837 .A44 2022 (print) | LCC TX837 (ebook) | DDC 641.5/6362--dc23/eng/20220521
LC record available at https://lccn.loc.gov/2022021759
LC ebook record available at https://lccn.loc.gov/2022021760
ISBN 978-1-954210-18-9

America's Test Kitchen
21 Drydock Avenue, Boston, MA 02210

Printed in Canada
10 9 8 7 6 5 4 3 2 1

Distributed by
Penguin Random House Publisher Services
Tel: 800.733.3000

Pictured on front cover **Stuffed Eggplant with Lentils, Pomegranate, and Cashew Ricotta (page 230)**

Pictured on back cover (clockwise from top left) **Carrot Soup with Thai Curry Paste and Tofu Croutons (page 76), Green Fried Rice with Green Beans and Spinach (page 236), Garam Masala–Spiced Mango Crisp (page 344), Not-from-a-Box Weeknight Tacos (page 120)**

Editorial Director, Books **Adam Kowit**

Executive Food Editor **Dan Zuccarello**

Deputy Food Editor **Stephanie Pixley**

Executive Managing Editor **Debra Hudak**

Book Editor **Sara Zatopek**

Senior Editors **Camila Chaparro, Valerie Cimino, Nicole Konstantinakos, Sara Mayer, and Russell Selander**

Test Cooks **Sāsha Coleman, Olivia Counter, Carmen Dongo, Jacqueline Gochenouer, Eric Haessler, Hisham Hassam, Jamal Salaam, and Patricia Suarez**

Assistant Editor **Emily Rahravan**

Design Director **Lindsey Timko Chandler**

Deputy Art Director **Katie Barranger**

Associate Art Directors **Molly Gillespie and Ashley Tenn**

Photography Director **Julie Bozzo Cote**

Senior Photography Producer **Meredith Mulcahy**

Senior Staff Photographers **Steve Klise and Daniel J. van Ackere**

Staff Photographer **Kevin White**

Additional Photography **Joseph Keller and Carl Tremblay**

Food Styling **Joy Howard, Sheila Jarnes, Catrine Kelty, Chantal Lambeth, Gina McCreadie, Kendra McNight, Ashley Moore, Christie Morrison, Marie Piraino, Elle Simone Scott, Kendra Smith, and Sally Staub**

Project Manager, Creative Operations **Katie Kimmerer**

Senior Print Production Specialist **Lauren Robbins**

Production and Imaging Coordinator **Amanda Yong**

Production and Imaging Specialists **Tricia Neumyer and Dennis Noble**

Copy Editor **Cheryl Redmond**

Proofreader **Kelly Gauthier**

Indexer **Elizabeth Parson**

Chief Creative Officer **Jack Bishop**

Executive Editorial Directors **Julia Collin Davison and Bridget Lancaster**

Contents

ix Welcome to America's Test Kitchen

x   The Veg-inner's Guide to Cooking for Two

28 Breakfast

62 Soups, Stews, and Chilis

100 Sandwiches, Burgers, and Flatbreads

136 Salads

178 Pasta and Noodles

214 Grain, Bean, and Vegetable Mains

266 Small Plates

316 Desserts

352 Nutritional Information for Our Recipes

360 Conversions and Equivalents

362 Index

Welcome to America's Test Kitchen

This book has been tested, written, and edited by the folks at America's Test Kitchen, where curious cooks become confident cooks. Located in Boston's Seaport District in the historic Innovation and Design Building, it features 15,000 square feet of kitchen space including multiple photography and video studios. It is the home of *Cook's Illustrated* magazine and *Cook's Country* magazine and is the workday destination for more than 60 test cooks, editors, and cookware specialists. Our mission is to empower and inspire confidence, community, and creativity in the kitchen.

We start the process of testing a recipe with a complete lack of preconceptions, which means that we accept no claim, no technique, and no recipe at face value. We simply assemble as many variations as possible, test a half-dozen of the most promising, and taste the results blind. We then construct our own recipe and continue to test it, varying ingredients, techniques, and cooking times until we reach a consensus. As we like to say in the test kitchen, "We make the mistakes so you don't have to." The result, we hope, is the best version of a particular recipe, but we realize that only you can be the final judge of our success (or failure). We use the same rigorous approach when we test equipment and taste ingredients.

All of this would not be possible without a belief that good cooking, much like good music, is based on a foundation of objective technique. Some people like spicy foods and others don't, but there is a right way to sauté, there is a best way to cook a pot roast, and there are measurable scientific principles involved in producing perfectly beaten, stable egg whites. Our ultimate goal is to investigate the fundamental principles of cooking to give you the techniques, tools, and ingredients you need to become a better cook. It is as simple as that.

To see what goes on behind the scenes at America's Test Kitchen, check out our social media channels for kitchen snapshots, exclusive content, video tips, and much more. You can watch us work (in our actual test kitchen) by tuning in to *America's Test Kitchen* or *Cook's Country* on public television or on our websites. Listen to *Proof*, *Mystery Recipe*, and *The Walk-In* (AmericasTestKitchen.com/podcasts), to hear engaging, complex stories about people and food. Want to hone your cooking skills or finally learn how to bake—with an America's Test Kitchen test cook? Enroll in one of our online cooking classes. And you can engage the next generation of home cooks with kid-tested recipes from America's Test Kitchen Kids.

Our community of home recipe testers provides valuable feedback on recipes under development by ensuring that they are foolproof. You can help us investigate the how and why behind successful recipes from your home kitchen. (Sign up at AmericasTestKitchen.com/recipe_testing.)

However you choose to visit us, we welcome you into our kitchen, where you can stand by our side as we test our way to the best recipes in America.

Sharing a good home-cooked meal with a loved one is one of the best ways to connect and show you care. That's why, whatever your reasons for wanting to eat plant-based, we made it our goal to help you make this simple ritual a daily reality.

Every recipe in these pages had to satisfy two conditions. First, the food needed to be flavorful, interesting, and truly satisfying. And second, the recipe had to be a practical option for a small plant-based family, taking into account portion sizes, cooking methods, and equipment. We also sought to minimize food waste by using up whole ingredients wherever possible and including handy shopping and food storage guides.

What you won't find: meals that leave you with a week's worth of monotonous leftovers. What you will find: over 200 irresistible recipes for everything from custardy French toast and packable veggie sandwiches to vibrant green fried rice and desserts both easy (like cookies that you can bake up at will) and special occasion–worthy (such as individual-size cakes dripping with a citrusy glaze). Plus, hundreds of Kitchen Improv suggestions guide you in making ingredient substitutions, bulking up your meal, customizing flavors, and more. So turn the page to discover new favorites that make it easy to eat well all day—the vegan way.

2   Cook It Your Way

4   The Plant-Based Pantry

8   A New Look at the Vegan Refrigerator Case

12   Shop Smart

14   Keep It Fresh

18   Use It Up

20   The Right Tools for the Job

21   Building-Block Recipes

Cook It Your Way

Our goal was to create flexible recipes that would fit into your busy life and give you the tools you need to eat the way you want every day. So we didn't just develop foolproof, delicious vegan recipes—we also thought hard about how each could be adapted to suit different personal preferences. That's why nearly every recipe is accompanied by the optional tips and tweaks we call Kitchen Improvs. Here are some of the improvs you'll see most frequently throughout this book.

USE WHAT YOU'VE GOT

Points out opportunities for ingredient substitutions so you can use what you have on hand and adapt recipes to suit your tastes. Here, we swapped zesty cilantro-based Chermoula (page 25) for basil pesto.

LEVEL UP

Gives simple ideas for taking your meal over the top by introducing additional textures, flavors, or unexpected twists—for example, by tossing in a handful of fresh baby greens. See pages 24–27 for easy sauces and garnishes that we use frequently to level up our recipes.

BULK IT UP

Suggests ways to make a light meal more filling, such as by adding a vegan protein or serving with a starch like pita or a cooked grain.

MAKE IT A . . .

Provides ideas for turning your meal into something altogether different. Example: transforming a salad into a hearty wrap.

MIX AND MATCH

We included an entire chapter (pages 266–315) of flexible recipes that can be eaten on their own as snacks, be garnished with additional toppings to become light meals, or be paired with each other as desired to make a customized multi-element meal. See pages 268–269 for more tips on mixing and matching recipes.

DOUBLE DOWN

Most of the recipes in this book can be doubled, so if you're having people over (or if leftovers are your goal), you can easily upsize the recipe to suit your needs.

But first, keep in mind that successful recipe doubling may involve more thought than simply doubling all the ingredients and calling it a day. In some cases you may need to consider using a larger cooking vessel (such as moving a recipe from a 10-inch to a 12-inch skillet, or from a large saucepan to a Dutch oven) to avoid overcrowding. You may also need to adjust cooking times to account for the greater volume of food, so try to rely on the recipe's visual cues for determining doneness more than on the given time ranges.

MAKE IT IN THE TOASTER OVEN

Every recipe in this book that calls for using the oven can also be made in a toaster oven. Follow the recipe directions as written and note that, depending on your toaster oven, cooking times may be on the longer end of the given range. Regardless of the oven rack position suggested for a conventional oven, we recommend sticking to the middle or lower-middle rack when using a toaster oven. Avoid using the convection or air-fryer settings, as these settings can affect cooking times and produce significantly different results when used with recipes that were developed for a conventional oven. Some slight differences, such as less or spottier browning on food, are normal and won't affect the dish's quality.

Our favorite toaster oven (see page 20) can accommodate a standard quarter-sheet pan, but not all toaster ovens can. Measure your cooking vessel and double check that it will fit inside your toaster oven before starting the recipe.

The Plant-Based Pantry

Cooking vegan meals requires rethinking the foods you consider kitchen staples. We recommend keeping at least a few ingredients from each of the following categories on hand for quick and easy meal building.

GRAINS

BARLEY

What it is: A high-fiber, high-protein cereal grain with a nutty flavor similar to that of brown rice

Common types: Hulled barley, sold with the hull removed and its fiber-rich bran intact, is considered a whole grain. Pearl (or pearled) barley has been polished to remove the bran as well and is quicker-cooking than hulled barley.

Use in: Soups and stews, grain salads, risotto

BULGUR

What it is: Parboiled or steamed wheat kernels/berries that are dried, partially stripped of their bran layer, and coarsely ground. Bulgur should be rinsed before use to remove excess starch that can turn it gluey.

Common types: Medium-grind bulgur needs little more than a soak to become tender. Coarse-grind bulgur requires simmering to become tender.

Use in: Pilafs, soups and stews, grain salads, filling for stuffed vegetables

CORNMEAL

What it is: Yellow or white field corn that's been dried and ground

Common types: Conventional cornmeal tends to be finely ground, whereas grits tend to have a thicker grind.

Use in: Cornbread, breading for tofu or vegetables, breakfast grits

DRIED PASTA AND NOODLES

Perhaps the ultimate pantry staple, dried pasta and noodles cook in minutes and can be combined with just about any combination of sauce, vegetable, and topping to make an easy on-the-fly meal.

FARRO

What it is: Hulled whole-wheat kernels with a sweet, nutty flavor and chewy bite

Use in: Soups and stews, grain salads, risotto

FREEKEH

What it is: Durum wheat harvested while green and immature and then fire-roasted to impart a nutty, slightly smoky flavor

Use in: Pilafs, grain salads

OATS

What it is: A fiber-rich cereal grain with a nutty, earthy flavor

Common types: Old-fashioned oats are made by hulling, cleaning, steaming, and rolling whole oats. Steel-cut oats are partially cooked and then cut into pieces with steel blades. Oat groats are the whole hulled oat grain and can be cooked like other whole grains.

Use in: Oatmeal, grain salads, cookies

QUINOA

What it is: The seed (technically not a grain!) of the goosefoot plant, with an almost crunchy texture when cooked and a nutty taste. Unless labeled "prewashed," quinoa should be rinsed before cooking to remove its protective bitter layer (called saponin).

Common types: White, red, and black

Use in: Pilafs, grain salads, soups and stews, chilis

RICE

What it is: The seed of a semi-aquatic grass, ranging from white to black in color and mild and neutral to nutty and earthy in flavor

Common types: So many! Brown, white, red, black, short-grain, long-grain, and more

Use in: Grain bowls, pilafs, simple sides, fried rice, curries, rice pudding

WHEAT BERRIES

What it is: Husked whole wheat kernels containing the bran, germ, and endosperm, with a chewy texture and slightly sweet, nutty flavor

Use in: Grain salads, soups and stews, chilis

PROTEINS

TOFU

What it is: Soymilk that has been coagulated to form curds and then pressed to extract liquid, with a clean, nutty, subtly sweet taste that easily absorbs added flavors

Common types: Tofu commonly comes in silken, soft, firm, and extra-firm varieties, depending on how much of its liquid has been pressed out. Firm and extra-firm tofu are best used in recipes where you want the tofu to hold its shape, and they can easily be substituted for each other in most recipes with some small difference in texture. Soft and silken tofu tend to break down when cooked, as in our Kimchi, Tofu, and Vegetable Soup (page 72).

TEMPEH

What it is: Fermented, cooked soybeans (often with added beans, grains, and flavorings) formed into a dense cake with a strong nutty, slightly funky flavor

Common types: Most tempeh is made from a combination of soybeans and grains, but there are also grain-free and soy-free tempehs.

SEITAN
What it is: A very rich source of plant-based protein made from wheat gluten, with a chewy, sometimes spongy texture

BEANS AND LENTILS
Beans come in dozens of varieties, from chickpeas to soy beans to black-eyed peas, and can be either dried or canned. Lentils come in different sizes and colors, and the variation in texture is considerable, from earthy brown and green lentils that hold their shape when cooked to red lentils that break down into a thick puree as in our Red Lentil Kibbeh (page 251).

THE DYNAMIC DUO
All of the proteins and essential amino acids that a body needs can be found in a well-balanced plant-based diet. You may have heard that to come by "complete" proteins on a plant-based diet you should pair legumes (such as beans, lentils, and soy) with grains. This is indeed a good rule of thumb, as generally legumes and grains each contain a different set of amino acids that add up to a complete profile of essential amino acids. But note that it's not necessary to stress about including both a grain and a legume in every meal; as long as you're eating a variety of each on a regular basis, you should get all the essential amino acids you need. That said, if you have concerns you should speak to a registered dietician about your personal nutritional and dietary needs. (For easy methods for cooked grains and beans that can be added to almost any meal, see pages 270–273.)

LEGUMES   GRAINS

NUTS AND NUT BUTTERS
Nuts can lend richness, substance, and crunch to nearly any recipe. Soaked or cooked until tender and then blended, they can even transform into the base for a rich dairy-free cream sauce or plant-based cheese. Nut butters are great for spreading and dipping, but they can also be used to make sauces or add a toasty, buttery flavor to baked goods.

SEEDS
Seeds, such as sesame seeds, sunflower seeds, chia, flax, and hemp, to name just a few, are excellent additions to many meals. Flaxseeds are sold both whole and ground; ground flaxseeds are sometimes used as a vegan egg substitute, providing a mild binding effect in baked goods. Chia seeds, when combined with liquid as in our chia pudding parfaits (see page 49), swell into tapioca-like beads. Tender hemp hearts are packed with protein and healthful fats, excellent for blending into a smoothie or sprinkling on a salad.

FLAVOR BOOSTERS

CANNED TOMATO PRODUCTS
Tomatoes are full of umami flavor thanks to the glutamates abundantly present in their seeds and pulp. For reliable year-round tomato flavor, we like to keep several types of canned tomatoes (crushed, whole, and diced) on hand. We also stock sun-dried tomatoes and tomato paste; the umami flavor in these products is extraconcentrated thanks to their low moisture content.

CAPERS AND OLIVES
These two refrigerator staples contribute an irresistible piquant brininess wherever they're used. Olives can also bring richness to a meal.

CITRUS ZEST AND JUICE
A splash of acidic citrus juice brightens the flavor of rich dishes. Citrus zest adds concentrated, less sharp, floral citrus flavor. Always juice lemons and limes at the last minute and add the juice toward the end of cooking or just before serving, as the flavor mellows quickly.

HERBS AND SPICES

Spices and dried herbs give meals warmth and identity. Note that the flavor of dried herbs and spices can dull over time. For the freshest flavor, consider buying spices in smaller quantities to ensure that you use them up before they lose their zing.

MISO

Salty, slightly funky, deeply savory miso paste is made by fermenting soybeans and sometimes grains with a mold called koji. Miso will easily keep for up to a year in the refrigerator (and some sources say it keeps indefinitely).

MUSHROOMS

Drying mushrooms concentrates their flavor, so look to pantry-friendly dried mushrooms to boost the savoriness of stocks and soups, as in our Umami Broth (page 22). Earthy shiitake mushrooms are one of the most potent sources of umami flavor, particularly in their dried form, as are morels and porcinis, but even fresh mushrooms of any variety will provide some savory oomph.

NUTRITIONAL YEAST

Affectionately referred to as "nooch" by many, this savory, flaky substance is simply yeast that's grown on a mixture of beet molasses and sugarcane and heated to deactivate its leavening properties. It's often used to mimic the flavor of cheese thanks to its funky, nutty, almost salty depth.

SOY SAUCE

Made from fermented soybeans, salt, water, and sometimes roasted grains, soy sauce is one of the oldest food products in the world. We use it in a wide range of preparations to add both seasoning and deep savory flavor.

VINEGAR

Like citrus juice, sharp-tasting vinegar perks up every food it comes into contact with, but it's particularly beneficial in brightening the flavors of rich, heavy dishes. Red wine, white wine, balsamic, sherry, cider, and even plain old distilled white vinegar each bring a distinct flavor profile to the table, so the type we reach for depends on the recipe.

TAKE ANOTHER LOOK: FOODS THAT MIGHT NOT BE VEGAN

If you're a committed vegan, reading and understanding ingredient labels is your best defense against inadvertently purchasing nonvegan products. Be on the alert for nonvegan ingredients including casein, whey, and lactose (all dairy-derived), albumin (from eggs), and gelatin (from animal bones).

Kimchi, Thai curry paste, and sambal oelek: Many commercial products include fish sauce or shrimp paste among their ingredients, so read ingredient lists carefully to be sure a product is vegan.

Pasta, noodles, and bread: Eggs can hide in dried and fresh pasta and noodles of all shapes and varieties.

Puff pastry: Many commercial varieties of puff pastry are made using vegetable oils and are vegan, but some use butter, so be sure to read the ingredients before buying.

Sugar, chocolate, and sprinkles: Most conventional sugars are filtered through animal bone char as part of the production process. If you're a strict vegan, purchase organic, which does not undergo this process. Chocolate—even dark chocolate—may contain dairy products. And sprinkles often contain shellac (a derivative of insect shells) and/or nonvegan food colorings.

Wine, beer, and spirits: Egg whites or other animal products may be used to remove tiny particles that filtration doesn't capture. If this is a concern, ask the store clerk or refer to an online guide such as barnivore.com.

A New Look at the Vegan Refrigerator Case

These days store shelves abound with processed plant-based foods. From milk to cheese to yogurt to egg substitutes, the list goes on. Recognizing that these store-bought convenience products are not only higher-quality and more widely available than ever before (and a real boon to a time-pressed cook), we embraced them throughout this book. Over the course of our recipe development we tasted dozens of products across multiple categories. Here are our most valuable takeaways.

MILK

There's such a huge range of options when it comes to plant-based milks that it's hard to know where to begin. After experimenting with several, we came up with a few preferences. In all cases, we prefer to buy unsweetened plant-based milk so that we can control the sweetness (or savoriness) of the dish ourselves.

Almond milk is relatively neutral in flavor; we like it best for savory cooking.

Although its flavor is relatively neutral, **soy milk** can give mildly flavored dishes a detectable beany flavor.

Coconut milk is great for adding creamy richness to savory dishes, but baked goods made with it turned out pale and gummy.

We like **oat milk** for sweet dishes. Its high natural sugar content promotes browning, but can make it feel out of place in savory dishes.

Commercial **rice milks** are generally too thin and watery for cooking or baking, so we avoid them.

CREAMER

Just like plant-based milks, plant-based creamers can be made from nuts, oats, peas, and more. What distinguishes these products from regular plant-based milk is their higher fat content as well as their thicker, more viscous consistency. While plant-based creamer works well in most recipes, unlike dairy creamer it doesn't work well for whipping (see page 336 for our coconut-based whipped cream).

CREAMY CHEESES

Plant-based **ricotta** cheeses are soft, spreadable, and creamy, perfect for smearing on toast or dolloping on a plate of pasta. They may not be marketed as ricotta and may instead use descriptive terms such as "soft" or "French-style." Many come with additional flavor add-ins such as cracked black pepper or herbs. (For a home-made alternative to store-bought, see page 22.)

Plant-based **feta** is an ideal crumbling-and-sprinkling cheese. It's generally sold in blocks that look remarkably similar to dairy feta and have an impressive richness and luxurious mouthfeel. We used Violife Just Like Feta during recipe development.

Plant-based **Boursin** is ultrasmooth and melt-on-the-tongue creamy, imbued with garlic and sprinkled liberally with herbs. Unlike dairy Boursin it's almost pure fat (primarily oil that's bound with starch), so it essentially melts back into its liquid oil form when heated. While it may not be the best option for dolloping over something hot, it adds unbeatable richness and flavor when stirred into a dish like our Creamy Orzo with Boursin (page 288). We used Boursin Dairy-Free Cheese Spread Alternative throughout recipe testing.

PARMESAN

High-quality plant-based Parmesan is salty and rich like the real deal. While some brands sell plant-based Parmesan in wedges, you'll most likely find it in grated form, ready for sprinkling over all your favorite foods. (See page 23 for a recipe for homemade Parm that's just as savory and sprinkle-able.)

LET'S TALK MELTY PLANT-BASED CHEESE

When it comes to vegan cheese, meltability may just be the hardest thing to get right. Nevertheless, there are some cheeses that do it, and do it well.

ANATOMY OF MELTY PLANT-BASED CHEESE

Starch: Without casein, a naturally occurring protein found in animal milk that helps dairy cheese melt without splitting, vegan cheeses rely primarily on starch for their meltability and elasticity. Root-based starches such as tapioca and potato starch are the most common, along with cornstarch.

Fat: Fats help cheese melt nicely. Many products use coconut oil, which is a solid when chilled but melts when heated. Some also add liquid oils such as canola or safflower oil to aid in melting.

Flavorings: Added vegan cheese flavors (produced by controlled chemical reactions, heating, or fermentation of plant-based ingredients) give many cheeses a mild flavor similar to Velveeta or boxed mac and cheese.

PUTTING IT TO THE TEST

To find a few melty cheeses that we could rely on while developing our recipes, we first narrowed down the field to cheddar- and mozzarella-style shredded vegan cheese, which are two of the most popular and widely available varieties. We then tasted each cheese raw and melted in simple vegan quesadillas.

TASTING NOTES

Violife Just Like Cheddar Shreds: "Slightly nutty" with a flavor "reminiscent of American cheese"; "gooey" when melted.

Daiya Cheddar Style Shreds: More "assertive" flavor with a touch of "sourness"; "firm" when melted, with "more of a pull than an ooze."

Violife Just Like Mozzarella Shreds: Mild "milky" and subtly funky flavor; "super creamy" melted.

Good Planet Plant-Based Cheese Mozzarella Shreds: Salty but mild, with a "cream-like" flavor; "creamy" and "almost chewy" when melted.

KEY COOKING TAKEAWAYS

1   Use mozzarella- and cheddar-style shreds interchangeably: The generally mild flavor of vegan cheese makes it easy to swap one kind for the other, so use what you have on hand.

2   For the best melt, give it a little help: Pressing down on a grilled cheese or quesadilla during cooking helps the cheese melt completely. Covering the cheese during cooking when possible (say, when baking a lasagna) results in a glossier melt and a more impressive "cheese pull."

3   You can substitute slices for shreds: Unless you're using the cheese as a finishing sprinkle on an already-cooked dish, feel free to use slices. They melt just as well, and we actually preferred their flavor and texture to shreds when eaten raw, as they might be in a sandwich.

BUTTER

Isn't margarine basically the same thing as vegan "butter"? Not necessarily. Though margarine, like plant-based butter, is made primarily of plant oils rather than dairy, it can contain nonvegan ingredients such as buttermilk or whey. Vegan butters, on the other hand, are purely plant-based. These days, you can find vegan butter sold in tubs like margarine as well as in easily measured sticks (also sold as "buttery sticks" or "baking sticks"). We used Earth Balance Vegan Buttery Sticks and Miyoko's Creamery Cultured Vegan Butter throughout recipe development.

YOGURT

Plant-based yogurts can be made with everything from nuts to grains to legumes. They come in a variety of styles, from thicker Greek-style options to thin and drinkable versions. Though flavors and textures can differ radically, we found that even our least favorite products for eating straight out of the container worked well when made into a sauce or incorporated into baked goods such as our Banana-Walnut Muffins (page 54).

MAYONNAISE

Store-bought vegan mayonnaises can vary in quality, but the best of them are creamy, tangy, and supersmooth, easily rivaling traditional mayonnaise. Our go-to during recipe testing was Hampton Creek Just Mayo, Original.

LIQUID EGG SUBSTITUTE

Liquid egg substitutes are meant to mimic the properties of whole chicken eggs. They are not the same thing as the egg replacement powders that are used primarily in egg-free baking. Liquid egg substitute can be used in everything from scrambles to French toast, and we also had success using it in place of whipped aquafaba (the liquid in canned chickpeas) in some baked goods. (Whipping the very small amounts of aquafaba required for the scaled-down recipes in this book proved to be impractical.) While liquid egg substitute doesn't contribute quite the lift of aquafaba or the binding power of chicken eggs, it does provide some binding and emulsification, preventing our baked goods from feeling greasy. (Adding extra leaveners easily fixed the lack of lift.) We used JUST Egg to develop our recipes.

LET'S TALK PLANT-BASED MEAT

Plant-based meat is a huge category that can encompass everything from textured vegetable protein to meatless chicken nuggets. For our purposes, we focused on products intended to realistically mimic ground beef.

WHAT KIND SHOULD YOU BUY?

We prefer buying raw bulk plant-based meat, which generally comes in refrigerated or frozen packages and is cohesive and easy to shape. Beware precooked plant-based meat crumbles (sometimes called soy crumbles), which won't hold their shape in dishes like burgers or meatballs. However, precooked crumbles are fine in applications such as taco fillings and meat sauces where the meat is meant to be broken into small pieces.

KNOW THE DIFFERENCE

Aside from its non-animal origin, plant-based meat differs from animal meat in a few key ways.

Less is more: Because it loses less moisture and volume during cooking than animal meat, 12 ounces of cooked plant-based meat is roughly equivalent to 1 pound of cooked animal meat.

Cooking time: Plant-based meat cooks through very quickly, so begin checking for doneness on the early end of a recipe's time range.

Doneness: Plant-based meat is best cooked to medium doneness (130 to 135 degrees Fahrenheit). Undercooked meat is mushy, while overcooked meat is unpleasantly bouncy and chewy.

OUR TOP 3 TIPS FOR EASY HANDLING

1 Raw plant-based meat is sticky and will readily cling to hands and surfaces. Wear food-handling gloves or moisten your hands with water as needed to prevent sticking during handling.

2 Lacking the myosin proteins that help bind animal meat, plant-based meat is softer and more prone to becoming misshapen. Work with chilled meat straight from the refrigerator and, after any shaping, re-chill the meat for at least 15 minutes to firm it back up before cooking.

3 Use a nonstick skillet as your default pan for cooking plant-based meat (unless a recipe specifically calls for a traditional pan). The nonstick coating helps prevent the meat from sticking to the pan and breaking apart during cooking.

OUR GO-TOS

We gathered four of the top-selling bulk ground products and tasted them cooked plain and in burgers topped with lettuce and ketchup. Two products came out on top.

We enjoyed the relatively neutral savory taste and impressive meatiness of **Impossible Foods' Impossible Burger**. Great at picking up browning and free of off-flavors, this is the product we turned to while developing our recipes.

Beyond Meat's Beyond Beef is another solid option, though we found it to have a more assertive, almost "metallic" flavor.

medium-rare   **medium**   **well-done**

Shop Smart

DITCH THE CART
If you're able, using a shopping basket helps you stay mindful about what (and how much!) you're buying. Unless you're stocking up on pantry items, if it's too much to carry, it's probably too much to buy.

GET CREATIVE IN THE PRODUCE AISLE
If a recipe calls for just a few ounces of a larger vegetable like cauliflower or squash, consider buying precut cubes or florets. This will make it much less likely you'll end up tossing any leftovers, and it'll save you some prep work as a bonus! The same goes for fresh herbs—if you need just a little, you might want to opt for a small container rather than a whole bunch. We also highly recommend weighing your produce before buying to make sure you get only as much as you need. And try shopping your supermarket produce aisle's organic section, where many vegetables are sold loose.

OPT FOR CANNED OR FROZEN
Canning and freezing are both great ways to preserve foods at their peak, and foods preserved in this way will last almost indefinitely, so you can stock up without worrying about looming expiration dates.

Some vegetables, such as peas, corn, spinach, and pearl onions, take particularly well to freezing and may be even higher quality than fresh depending on the time of year. Frozen broccoli, carrots, cauliflower, and green beans work well in dishes like soups and stews, where you're not looking for the crisp texture of fresh vegetables. But beware frozen asparagus, mushrooms, bell peppers, and snow peas: These high-moisture vegetables usually turn mushy once thawed.

SHOP THE SALAD BAR
Your supermarket's salad bar is for more than just salads—it's perfect if you need just half a cup of snap peas or a handful of spinach.

SHOP THE BULK BINS
Whether you want to buy a pound of brown rice for your pantry or a cup of quinoa for a specific recipe, you can buy as much or as little as you need from a bulk bin. If your supermarket doesn't have a bulk section, check out a natural foods store.

LOOK FOR INDIVIDUALLY WRAPPED ITEMS
Many items are available in single-serving packages that make it easy to use just a small amount and keep the rest sealed. Single-serving containers of plant-based yogurt, applesauce, sliced fruit, precooked rice, etc. can help you scale back on food waste.

INGREDIENT HACKS FOR THE FOR-TWO COOK

If you cook for two on a regular basis, you probably know the frustration of being left with a mostly full box of broth or a large bunch of fresh herbs after making a recipe that calls for just half a cup or a few sprigs. Luckily, the following ingredients make it easy to use smaller amounts and avoid waste at the same time.

Bouillon and broth concentrates: These shelf-stable dehydrated and concentrated forms of broth are cost-effective (because you're not paying for the water) and last for up to two years once opened. Our favorite vegetable broth concentrate is Orrington Farms Vegan Chicken Flavored Broth Base & Seasoning.

Boxed wine: Once opened, bottles of wine are rarely usable for more than a week. But boxed wine has an airtight inner bag that prevents exposure to oxygen even after the box is opened, so the wine lasts up to one month.

No-prep aromatics: Store-bought frozen chopped onion, garlic, and ginger can all be used in place of an equal amount of their fresh counterparts. (You can also prep and freeze your own garlic and ginger to have on hand; see page 17.)

Shallots: When a recipe calls for just a small amount of onion, try substituting a shallot. A medium shallot yields just a few tablespoons when minced, perfect for recipes that need just a touch of allium flavor.

Dried herbs: You can substitute dried herbs for fresh in any recipe in which the herbs are cooked; this works especially well with woody herbs such as sage, rosemary, and thyme. Just use one-third the amount called for.

Keep It Fresh

TREAT IT RIGHT

Shopping smart is half the battle against food waste, but what you do with your freshly bought ingredients after getting home is just as important. Following these tips will dramatically extend the time your food is at its best.

ASPARAGUS

Trim ends and set spears upright in 1–2 inches of water. Cover loosely with zipper-lock bag and refrigerate.

AVOCADO

Store cut avocados submerged cut side down in lemon water in refrigerator for up to 2 days. (Avocado may have slightly softer texture and tart flavor.)

THROW OUT THAT AVOCADO PIT

It's a food storage myth that saving the avocado pit will somehow increase the longevity of a cut or mashed avocado. If left in a halved avocado, the pit will block airflow and prevent the center of the avocado, where the pit is attached, from oxidizing, but it won't stop the exposed edges from browning. And likewise, throwing a pit into a bowl of guacamole won't have any effect on the guac's freshness.

BERRIES

Wash berries immediately in bowl with 3 cups water and 1 cup distilled white vinegar. Drain in colander and rinse under running water. Gently dry berries completely and store in loosely covered paper towel–lined container in refrigerator.

Tip: Use paper towel–lined salad spinner to gently and thoroughly dry berries.

CARROTS

Trim leafy tops, place carrots in open zipper-lock bag, and refrigerate.

CELERY

Wrap whole heads loosely in aluminum foil to minimize moisture loss.

CUCUMBERS, ZUCCHINI, AND SUMMER SQUASH

Wrap tightly in plastic wrap to minimize moisture loss.

Tip: Leftover cut pieces can be rewrapped in plastic.

FRESH HERBS

Gently rinse and dry herbs, wrap in damp paper towels, and place in partially open zipper-lock bag in crisper drawer.

Exception: Basil. Wrap basil in clean, dry paper towels, place in partially open zipper-lock bag, and refrigerate; do not rinse.

Tip: Use salad spinner to dry herbs before wrapping them in paper towels.

GRAPES

Leave grapes on stem and refrigerate. Do not rinse until immediately before use.

GREENS

Store bagged or boxed lettuce and other leafy greens in crisper drawer in their original packaging. Wrap intact heads of lettuce or loose bunches of greens in damp paper towels and store in partially open zipper-lock bag.

ONIONS AND OTHER ALLIUMS

Refrigerate chopped or sliced onion in zipper-lock bag. Store delicate scallions, chives, and leeks upright in 1–2 inches of water and cover loosely with zipper-lock bag.

Tip: Rinse onion pieces before using to remove any residual odor.

STORE IT RIGHT

The temperature at which perishable items are stored will also have an impact on their quality and longevity. Some like it chilly, while others are best kept at room temperature. Follow these guidelines for the best results.

ON THE COUNTER

Some produce is especially sensitive to chilling injury, making it subject to dehydration, internal browning, and/or internal and external pitting if stored in the refrigerator.

Avocados*	Pineapple
Bananas*	Tomatoes*
Mangos	Stone fruit (peaches, nectarines, and plums)
Pears	

*Once they've reached their peak ripeness, these can be stored in the refrigerator to prevent overripening. Note that some cosmetic discoloration may occur.

IN THE CUPBOARD

The following produce should be kept at cool room temperature and away from light to prevent sprouting and to prolong shelf life.

Garlic	Onions and shallots
Butternut squash	Potatoes and sweet potatoes

AT THE FRONT OF THE FRIDGE

These items are sensitive to chilling injury and should be placed in the front of the fridge, where the temperatures tend to be higher.

Berries	Corn on the cob
Citrus	Peas

AT THE BACK OF THE FRIDGE

The back is the coldest part of the fridge, which can make it a good place to store highly perishable items. Just try not to shove anything too delicate back there, as the temperatures could cause chilling injury or even freeze them.

IN THE CRISPER DRAWER

These items do best in the humid environment of the crisper drawer.

Asparagus	Eggplant
Beets	Fresh herbs
Broccoli	Green beans
Cabbage	Leafy greens
Carrots	Mushrooms
Cauliflower	Radishes
Celery	Scallions and leeks
Chiles and peppers	Summer squash and zucchini
Cucumbers	

CHILL ANYWHERE

These items are not prone to chilling injury and can be stored anywhere in the fridge, provided the temperature doesn't freeze them.

Apples	Grapes
Cherries	

BEFRIEND YOUR FREEZER

The freezer is a powerful food-preserving ally. Below are our top tips for ensuring that your food emerges from the freezer just as appetizing as it was when it went in.

KEEP IT COLD

The quicker foods freeze, and the fewer fluctuations in temperature they undergo once frozen, the better. Your freezer should register zero degrees Fahrenheit or colder; use a thermometer to check. Make sure your freezer is at the coldest possible setting (unlike your fridge, where the coldest setting is normally too cold).

MINIMIZE HEADROOM

To prevent freezer burn, fill hard-sided containers to ½ inch from the top and place plastic wrap on the food's surface before attaching the lid.

MAXIMIZE AIRFLOW

To help cold air circulate, keep food away from the freezer vents.

DOUBLE WRAP

For solid foods you're wrapping in zipper-lock bags, first wrap in plastic wrap and then put the food in the bag, pressing out as much air as possible before sealing.

FUNKY FRIDGES BEGONE

An overstuffed fridge is a place where leftovers and perishable foods are all too easily shoved to the back and forgotten—at least until it's too late. A good system for organizing and using up your refrigerated foods in a timely fashion is the best defense against spoiled food and a smelly fridge.

Keep it organized: Try not to overcrowd your fridge. This not only promotes better cold air circulation, it also helps you see at a glance what you have on hand, what you're getting low on, and what you need to use up. Pro tip: Try storing some of your most frequently used ingredients on a lazy susan in the fridge; the spinning will provide better visibility and accessibility.

Practice first in, first out: Use up older ingredients first before you break into a new container. As a general rule, the first ingredients to arrive in the kitchen should be the first to leave it!

DID YOU KNOW YOU CAN FREEZE . . .

Beans: Drain, pat beans dry with paper towels, and transfer to zipper-lock bag. Lay bag flat to freeze to save space.

Bread: Slice bread, wrap tightly in aluminum foil, and seal in zipper-lock bag before freezing.

Canned tomato paste: Open both ends of can, push out paste, and freeze in zipper-lock bag. To use, cut off only as much paste as needed from frozen log.

Chipotle chiles in adobo: Freeze spoonfuls of chiles and sauce on parchment paper–lined baking sheet. Transfer frozen chiles to zipper-lock bag.

Citrus zest: Remove zest from entire fruit, mound into ½- or 1-teaspoon piles on plate, and freeze. Transfer frozen zest to zipper-lock bag.

Coconut milk: Transfer to airtight container and freeze. If milk separates after defrosting, blend with immersion blender for about 30 seconds to re-emulsify.

Cooked rice: Spread cooked long-grain white or brown rice in single layer on rimmed baking sheet until completely cooled, then transfer to zipper-lock bag and lay flat to freeze.

Fresh herbs: Place chopped herbs in wells of ice cube tray, cover with water, and freeze. Frozen herb cubes can be added directly to sauces, soups, and more.

Garlic: Place minced garlic in small bowl, cover with enough neutral-tasting oil to coat, then spoon heaping teaspoons onto baking sheet to freeze. Transfer frozen garlic to zipper-lock bag.

Ginger: Cut fresh ginger into 1-inch pieces and freeze in zipper-lock bag. To use, chop or grate ginger directly from freezer.

Wine: Measure 1 tablespoon wine into each well of ice cube tray and freeze. Use paring knife or small spatula to remove frozen wine cubes and add as desired to dishes.

Use It Up

Cooking for two sometimes means ending up with half a head of cabbage or a few ounces of leftover tofu. To help you avoid food waste, we've listed certain key ingredients along with the recipes in the book that call for them. This way, you can easily find ways to use up leftovers before they go bad. Note that our Kitchen Improv suggestions throughout the book also include ideas for using up ingredients.

INGREDIENT	RECIPE	AMOUNT	PAGE
Fresh Produce			
Broccoli	Garlicky Broccoli and Chickpea Salad	½ bunch	153
	Spaghetti with Broccoli and Avocado Pesto	¼ bunch	186
	Grilled Tofu with Charred Broccoli and Peanut Sauce	½ bunch	263
	Skillet Broccoli with Olive Oil and Garlic	½ bunch	298
Broccolini	Panang Curry with Eggplant, Broccolini, and Tofu	¼ bunch	219
	Grilled Potatoes and Vegetables with Pesto	½ bunch	224
Brussels Sprouts	Mushroom, Brussels Sprout, and White Bean Gratin	4 ounces	252
	Pan-Roasted Brussels Sprouts	12 ounces	301
Cabbage	Vegetable and Barley Soup	1 cup	64
	Tofu Katsu Sandwiches	1½ cups	109
	Charred Cabbage Salad with Torn Tofu and Plantain Chips	½ head	156
	Soba Noodle Salad with Edamame, Cabbage, and Peanut-Ginger Sauce	1 cup	174
	Curry Roasted Cabbage Wedges with Tomatoes and Chickpeas	½ head	220
Cauliflower	Vegetable Chowder with Dijon-Panko Topping	1¼ cups florets	80
	Buffalo Cauliflower Wraps	½ head	112
	Spiced Cauliflower Burgers	½ head	125
	Roasted Grape and Cauliflower Salad with Chermoula	¾ head	159
	Creamy Cashew Mac and Cheese	¾ cup florets	189
	Campanelle with Roasted Cauliflower and Garlic Sauce	½ head	193
	Baharat Cauliflower and Eggplant with Peas	1½ cups florets	222
	Cauliflower and Chickpea Paella	1¼ cups florets	235
	Roasted Cauliflower	½ head	304
Green Beans	Soupe au Pistou	3 ounces	66
	Green Bean, Tomato, and Bulgur Stew	8 ounces	95
	Vinadaloo-Spiced Green Beans, Chickpeas, and Potatoes	6 ounces	216
	Cauliflower and Chickpea Paella	4 ounces	235
	Green Fried Rice with Green Beans and Spinach	4 ounces	236
	Lemony Skillet-Charred Green Beans	12 ounces	297
Pantry and Refrigerated Items			
Coconut Milk	Chia Pudding Parfaits with Pineapple and Coconut	¼ cup	49
	Carrot Soup with Thai Curry Paste and Tofu Croutons	½ cup	76
	Moong Dal with Tomatoes, Spinach, and Coconut	⅓ cup	88

INGREDIENT	RECIPE	AMOUNT	PAGE
Coconut Milk (*cont.*)	Okra Pepper Pot	¼ cup	90
	Panang Curry with Eggplant, Broccolini, and Tofu	1 cup	219
	Glazed Tofu with Pigeon Peas and Rice	¾ cup	256
	Grilled Pineapple with Coconut-Rum Sauce	¼ cup	334
Firm or Extra-Firm Tofu	Everything-Crusted Tofu Breakfast Sandwich	½ block	34
	Chickpea and Tofu Shakshuka	½ block	38
	Carrot Soup with Thai Curry Paste and Tofu Croutons	½ block	76
	Tofu Katsu Sandwiches	½ block	109
	Charred Cabbage Salad with Torn Tofu and Plantain Chips	½ block	156
	Panang Curry with Eggplant, Broccolini, and Tofu	½ block	219
	Crispy Baked Tofu Peperonata	½ block	264
	Pan-Seared Tofu	½ block	274
Pizza Dough	Grilled Flatbread with Kale and Apple	8 ounces	132
	Artichoke and Spinach Calzones	8 ounces	135
Plant-Based Creamer	Chocolate Chip–Ginger Scones	¾ cup plus 1 tablespoon	57
	Unstuffed Shells with Butternut Squash and Leeks	⅓ cup	202
	Celery Root Puree	¼ cup	291
Plant-Based Meat	Italian Wedding Soup	4 ounces	70
	Weeknight Meaty Chili	4 ounces	96
	Grilled Kofte Wraps	6 ounces	117
	Not-from-a-Box Weeknight Tacos	6 ounces	120
	Garlic and Herb Burgers with Beet Tzatziki	6 ounces	130
	Meaty Taco Salad with Black Beans	6 ounces	148
	Bún Chả with Cucumbers and Carrot	6 ounces	177
	Linguine with Weeknight Bolognese	6 ounces	197
	Spaghetti with Meatballs and Marinara	6 ounces	198
	Meaty Zoodles with Mango and Garam Masala	6 ounces	205
	Dan Dan Mian	6 ounces	208
Plant-Based Yogurt	Chia Pudding Parfaits with Pineapple and Coconut	1 cup	49
	Banana-Walnut Muffins	½ cup	54
	Spiced Cauliflower Burgers	¼ cup	125
	Garlic and Herb Burgers with Beet Tzatziki	¼ cup	130
	Beet Salad with Watercress and Spiced Yogurt	1 cup	146
	Meaty Zoodles with Mango and Garam Masala	⅓ cup	205
Tempeh	Tempeh Crumbles	½ package	27
	Mangú Breakfast Bowl with Tempeh	½ package	42
	Corn and Poblano Chowder with Tempeh Chorizo	½ package	83
	Loaded Sweet Potato Wedges with Tempeh	½ package	227
Seitan	Kimchi Fried Rice with Seitan	2 ounces	238
	Stir-Fried Seitan with Cashews	12 ounces	260
	Pan-Seared Seitan	12 ounces	274

The Right Tools for the Job

There's no need to load up your kitchen with gimmicky single-use gadgets or minuscule (though admittedly cute) cookware when cooking for two. You can make nearly any recipe in this book with just a good chef's knife, a paring knife, a cutting board, a skillet, and a Dutch oven. But there are a few pieces of equipment that can expand your cooking options even further, streamline prep, and make cleanup a breeze. If you've got the space, consider stocking your kitchen with these versatile tools.

Toaster oven: A good toaster oven can do almost everything a full-size oven can do, without heating up the whole kitchen. (See page 3 for tips for adapting recipes to the toaster oven.) Our favorite is the Breville Smart Oven.

Small rimmed baking sheet: If you plan to do much cooking in the toaster oven, you'll want to have at least one small rimmed baking sheet (also known as a quarter-sheet pan) for maneuvering food in and out. Make sure to measure the interior dimensions of your toaster oven to ensure that the baking sheet will fit; most quarter-sheet pans measure about 8 by 11 inches. We like the Nordic Ware Naturals Quarter Sheet.

8-inch nonstick skillet: If you're only toasting a handful of nuts or a few cloves of garlic, why drag out your full-size skillet? For these occasions, we like the OXO Good Grips Hard Anodized Pro Nonstick 8-Inch Fry Pan.

Small saucepan: A small saucepan is the perfect vessel for cooking just a serving or two of rice or for steaming a handful of vegetables. The All-Clad Stainless 2Qt Saucepan's durability and even cooking makes it a great addition to any cookware collection.

Loaf pan: A loaf pan is useful for a lot more than just bread making. You can use one to make everything from a stellar baked oatmeal (page 46) to herb-dotted brown rice made in the oven (page 284). While we like the sharp edges the USA Pan Loaf Pan, 1 lb Volume produces on baked goods, for easy cleanup we prefer the OXO Good Grips Non-Stick Pro 1 Lb Loaf Pan.

Ramekins: We use ramekins to make individual-size baked goods such as our Individual Lemon–Poppy Seed Cakes (page 328). The straight sides and thick, insulating walls of the Le Creuset Stackable Ramekin make it our favorite.

Small cutting board: A compact board is easier to maneuver and clean, perfect for small cutting jobs. The grippy rubber sides of the OXO Good Grips Utility Cutting Board ensure that it stays put despite its miniature size.

Immersion blender: An immersion blender can save on both cleanup and space, allowing you to puree soups and sauces right in the pot and small enough to fit in a drawer when not in use. We like the Braun Multiquick 5 Hand Blender.

Digital kitchen scale: The smaller the portion you're cooking, the more precise the measurements called for—and there's no more precise way of measuring out ingredients than using a digital kitchen scale. We like the OXO Good Grips 11 lb Food Scale with Pull Out Display.

Mini whisk: When you have just a couple tablespoons of vinaigrette to emulsify, a mini whisk is the tool for the job. The Tovolo Stainless Steel 6" Mini Whisk is sturdy, functional—and cute.

Building-Block Recipes

MAKE IT HOMEMADE

These days, high-quality store-bought vegan ingredients are more widely available than ever (see pages 8–11 for more information about the store-bought products we use throughout this book). But if you, like us, enjoy precisely controlling the ingredients and flavors that go into the foods you eat—or if you're in a DIY kind of mood—we highly recommend you try these simple recipes.

Vegetable Broth Base

**Makes about 1¾ cups base,
enough for 7 quarts broth**

The ultimate in homemade convenience, this broth base is actually a concentrated paste of vegetables and herbs, which is turned into broth by stirring portions of it into boiling water. The concentrate can be stored in the freezer; since it doesn't freeze rock-hard, you can easily scoop out the amount you need directly from the container. For the best balance of flavors, measure the prepped vegetables by weight. The coarseness of the kosher salt aids in grinding the vegetables. To make 1 cup of broth, stir 1 tablespoon of fresh or frozen broth base into 1 cup of boiling water. For particle-free broth, let the broth steep for 5 minutes and then strain it through a fine-mesh strainer.

2 leeks, white and light green parts only, chopped and washed thoroughly (2½ cups or 5 ounces)

2 carrots, peeled and cut into ½-inch pieces (⅔ cup or 3 ounces)

½ small celery root, peeled and cut into ½-inch pieces (¾ cup or 3 ounces)

½ cup (½ ounce) fresh parsley leaves and thin stems

3 tablespoons dried minced onion

2 tablespoons kosher salt

1½ tablespoons tomato paste

3 tablespoons soy sauce

1 Process leeks, carrots, celery root, parsley, minced onion, and salt in food processor, scraping down sides of bowl frequently, until paste is as fine as possible, 3 to 4 minutes. Add tomato paste and process for 1 minute, scraping down sides of bowl every 20 seconds. Add soy sauce and continue to process 1 minute longer.

2 Transfer mixture to airtight container and tap firmly on counter to remove air bubbles. Press small piece of parchment paper flush against surface of mixture and cover. (Broth can be frozen for up to 6 months.)

Umami Broth

Makes 2 quarts

A combination of glutamate-rich nutritional yeast, soy sauce, miso, dried shiitake mushrooms, and fermented black beans yields a vegan broth that rivals the flavor of meat-based stocks. Fermented black beans can be found at Asian markets or online; if you are unable to find them, omit them. Do not substitute black bean paste or canned black beans. Straining the broth through a double layer of cheesecloth yields a clearer broth, though some sediment will remain.

- 2 quarts water
- ¼ cup nutritional yeast
- 2 tablespoons fermented black beans
- 1½ tablespoons soy sauce
- 1 tablespoon white miso
- 1½ teaspoons onion powder
- 1½ teaspoons garlic powder
- ½ ounce dried shiitake mushrooms, rinsed and chopped coarse

1 Combine all ingredients in large pot. Bring to boil, then cover, reduce heat to low, and simmer for 30 minutes.

2 Strain broth through fine-mesh strainer lined with double layer of cheesecloth. (Broth can be refrigerated for up to 4 days or frozen for up to 1 month.)

Aquafaba Mayonnaise

Makes about 1 cup

Aquafaba, the liquid found in canned chickpeas, gives this egg-free mayo volume and emulsified body free of any off flavors.

- ⅓ cup aquafaba (2⅔ ounces)
- 1½ teaspoons lemon juice
- ½ teaspoon table salt
- ½ teaspoon sugar
- ½ teaspoon Dijon mustard
- 1¼ cups vegetable oil
- 3 tablespoons extra-virgin olive oil

1 Process aquafaba, lemon juice, salt, sugar, and mustard in food processor for 10 seconds. With processor running, gradually add vegetable oil in slow, steady stream until mixture is thick and creamy, scraping down sides of bowl as needed, about 3 minutes.

2 Transfer mixture to bowl. Whisking constantly, slowly add olive oil until emulsified. If pools of oil form on surface, stop addition of oil and whisk mixture until well combined, then resume adding oil. Mayonnaise should be thick and glossy with no oil pools on surface. (Mayonnaise can be refrigerated for up to 1 week.)

Cashew Ricotta

Makes about 1 cup

Cashew ricotta is creamy, dreamy, and easy to make. Cashews are high in starch and uniquely low in fiber among nuts, so they readily break down into a smooth-textured, full-bodied ricotta. You will need to soak the raw cashews for at least 8 hours before processing them with the other ingredients.

- 1 cup raw cashews
- 2 tablespoons extra-virgin olive oil
- 2 teaspoons lemon juice, plus extra for seasoning
- ¼ teaspoon table salt

1 Place cashews in bowl and add water to cover by 1 inch. Soak cashews at room temperature for at least 8 hours or up to 24 hours. Drain and rinse well.

2 Process cashews, ¼ cup water, oil, lemon juice, and salt in food processor until smooth, about 2 minutes, scraping down sides of bowl as needed. Adjust consistency with additional water as needed. Season with salt, pepper, and extra lemon juice to taste. (Ricotta can be refrigerated for up to 1 week.)

Lemon-Herb Cashew Ricotta

Increase lemon juice to 4 teaspoons. Stir 3 tablespoons minced fresh parsley, basil, and/or tarragon and 2 teaspoons grated lemon zest into ricotta.

Cashew Parmesan

Makes about 1 cup

We like to keep this dairy-free Parm on hand to satisfy our cravings for the salty, nutty, savory punch that grated Parmesan adds to so many dishes. Cashews contribute toasty sweetness; pine nuts bring savoriness; nutritional yeast brings that desired umami quality and a subtle, irreplicable funkiness; and green olives add a rich brininess. This winning combination even has a texture similar to that of the crystalline bits in high-quality aged dairy Parmesan.

- ¾ cup raw cashews
- 3 tablespoons nutritional yeast
- 2 tablespoons raw pine nuts
- 1 tablespoon chopped green olives, patted dry
- ¾ teaspoon table salt

1 Adjust oven rack to middle position and heat oven to 275 degrees. Process all ingredients in food processor until finely ground, about 1 minute, scraping down sides of bowl as needed.

2 Spread mixture on rimmed baking sheet in even layer. Bake until mixture is light golden and dry to the touch, about 20 minutes, stirring mixture and rotating sheet halfway through baking.

3 Let mixture cool completely, about 15 minutes. Break apart any large clumps before serving. (Parmesan can be refrigerated for up to 1 month.)

SAUCES AND SPRINKLES

Drizzles, dollops, and sprinkles, oh my! Time and time again, we turn to the following recipes to take an already-solid dish to the next level. See pages 268–269 for tips about how to elevate your meal by mixing and matching these fun add-ons with other recipes.

Chimichurri

Makes about ½ cup

Chimichurri is a refreshing herb sauce traditionally used as a condiment for steak. We like to use it to dollop over roasted or grilled vegetables or plant-based proteins such as our Pan-Seared Tempeh Steaks (page 274).

1	cup fresh parsley leaves
¼	cup extra-virgin olive oil
1	tablespoon red wine vinegar
2	garlic cloves, minced
2	teaspoons dried oregano
¼	teaspoon red pepper flakes

Pulse all ingredients in food processor until coarsely chopped, about 10 pulses, scraping down sides of bowl as needed. Season with salt and pepper to taste. (Chimichurri can be refrigerated for up to 3 days.)

Pesto

Makes about ¾ cup

Aromatic basil and sweet toasted garlic live in harmony in this dairy-free green pesto. Basil tends to darken in homemade pesto; the optional parsley provides bright green color that doesn't fade. Two cups of fresh basil leaves weigh about 2 ounces. You can use store-bought plant-based Parmesan or our Cashew Parmesan (page 23) in this recipe.

3	garlic cloves, unpeeled
2	cups fresh basil leaves
2	tablespoons fresh parsley leaves (optional)
¼	cup pine nuts, toasted
3	tablespoons plant-based Parmesan
¼	teaspoon table salt
7	tablespoons extra-virgin olive oil

1 Toast garlic in 8-inch skillet over medium heat, stirring occasionally, until fragrant and skins are just beginning to brown, about 5 minutes. Remove garlic from saucepan and let cool, about 5 minutes. Once cool enough to handle, peel garlic and mince. Place basil and parsley, if using, in heavy-duty quart-size zipper-lock bag; pound with flat side of meat pounder or rolling pin until all leaves are bruised.

2 Process bruised herbs, pine nuts, Parmesan, salt, and garlic in food processor until smooth, scraping down sides of bowl as needed, about 1 minute. With processor running, slowly add oil until incorporated, about 30 seconds. Transfer pesto to bowl and season with salt and pepper to taste. (Pesto can be refrigerated for up to 3 days or frozen for up to 3 months. To prevent browning, press plastic wrap flush to surface, or top with thin layer of olive oil.)

Chermoula

Makes about ¾ cup

Traditionally used as a marinade, chermoula is also excellent as a bright, herby sauce or dressing for plant-based proteins or vegetables.

- ¾ cup minced fresh cilantro
- ¼ cup extra-virgin olive oil
- 2 tablespoons lemon juice
- 4 garlic cloves, minced
- ½ teaspoon ground cumin
- ½ teaspoon paprika
- ⅛ teaspoon cayenne pepper

Whisk all ingredients together in bowl and season with salt and pepper to taste.

Yogurt-Tahini Sauce

Makes about ½ cup

Thick and tangy, this sauce is perfect for adding cooling richness to a variety of vegetable dishes. A rasp-style grater makes quick work of mincing the garlic to a paste.

- ⅓ cup plain plant-based yogurt
- 2 teaspoons lemon juice
- 2 teaspoons tahini
- 1 small garlic clove, minced to paste
- ⅛ teaspoon table salt

Whisk all ingredients together in bowl. Cover and refrigerate until ready to serve. (Sauce can be refrigerated for up to 24 hours.)

Lemon-Herb Yogurt Sauce

Substitute extra-virgin olive oil for tahini. Stir 1 tablespoon minced fresh cilantro, 1 tablespoon minced fresh mint, and ½ teaspoon grated lemon zest into sauce.

Avocado Yogurt Sauce

Substitute ½ avocado, cut into 1-inch pieces, for tahini. Process all ingredients in food processor until smooth, scraping down sides of bowl as needed.

Ranch Dressing

Makes about ½ cup

This vegan ranch dressing is smooth, rich, and tangy. You can use store-bought plant-based mayonnaise or our Aquafaba Mayonnaise (page 22) in this recipe.

- ½ cup plant-based mayonnaise
- 2 tablespoons plain plant-based yogurt
- 1½ teaspoons minced fresh chives
- 1½ teaspoons minced fresh dill
- 1 teaspoon white wine vinegar
- ¼ teaspoon garlic powder
- ⅛ teaspoon table salt
- ⅛ teaspoon pepper

Whisk all ingredients in bowl until smooth. (Dressing can be refrigerated for up to 4 days.)

Quick Lemon-Herb Vinaigrette

Makes about ¼ cup

We like to keep this fresh, bright vinaigrette on hand for tossing with last-minute green salads. You can use store-bought plant-based mayonnaise or our Aquafaba Mayonnaise (page 22) in this recipe.

- 1 tablespoon lemon juice plus ¼ teaspoon zest
- 1 teaspoon minced shallot
- 3 tablespoons extra-virgin olive oil
- 1½ teaspoons fresh thyme, minced
- 1 teaspoon fresh mint, chopped
- 1 teaspoon sugar
- ½ teaspoon plant-based mayonnaise
- ½ teaspoon Dijon mustard
- ⅛ teaspoon table salt
- ⅛ teaspoon pepper

Combine lemon juice and shallot in small jar; let sit for 5 minutes. Add oil, thyme, mint, sugar, mayonnaise, mustard, salt, pepper, and lemon zest to jar, secure lid, and shake vigorously until emulsified, about 30 seconds. (Vinaigrette can be refrigerated for up to 3 days.)

Quick Ginger-Sesame Vinaigrette

Omit thyme, mint, and lemon zest. Substitute unseasoned rice vinegar for lemon juice, 1 tablespoon toasted sesame oil for 1 tablespoon olive oil, and Asian chili-garlic sauce for mustard. Add ½ teaspoon grated fresh ginger before shaking.

Quick Tarragon-Caper Vinaigrette

Omit thyme, mint, and lemon zest. Substitute red wine vinegar for lemon juice. Add 1½ teaspoons minced fresh parsley, 1½ teaspoons minced fresh tarragon, and ½ teaspoon minced rinsed capers before shaking.

Harissa

Makes about ½ cup

A spicy, aromatic paste, harissa is used as both an ingredient and a condiment throughout North Africa. If you can't find Aleppo pepper, you can substitute ¾ teaspoon paprika and ¾ teaspoon finely chopped red pepper flakes.

6	tablespoons extra-virgin olive oil
6	garlic cloves, minced
2	tablespoons paprika
1	tablespoon ground coriander
1	tablespoon ground dried Aleppo pepper
1	teaspoon ground cumin
¾	teaspoon caraway seeds
½	teaspoon table salt

Combine all ingredients in bowl and microwave until bubbling and very fragrant, about 1 minute, stirring halfway through microwaving. Let cool completely. (Harissa can be refrigerated for up to four days.)

Fennel Oil

Makes about ½ cup

This aromatic oil is great for drizzling over soups, stews, and roasted vegetables; strain before using if desired.

½	cup extra-virgin olive oil
1½	tablespoons fennel seeds, cracked

Heat oil and fennel in small saucepan over medium-low heat until fragrant and starting to bubble, 2 to 3 minutes. Off heat, let sit until flavors meld, about 4 hours.

Rosemary Oil

Substitute 1 tablespoon dried rosemary for fennel seeds.

Quick-Pickled Red Onion

Makes about 1 cup

We like to keep quick-pickled onion on hand as a tangy garnish for salads, sandwiches, and more.

1	cup red wine vinegar
⅓	cup sugar
¼	teaspoon table salt
1	red onion, halved and sliced thin through root end

Bring vinegar, sugar, and salt to simmer in small sauce-pan over medium-high heat, stirring occasionally, until sugar is dissolved. Off heat, stir in onion, cover, and let cool completely, about 1 hour. Serve. (Pickled onion can be refrigerated in airtight container for up to 1 week.)

Sumac Onion

Substitute ½ cup lemon juice (3 lemons) for ½ cup vinegar. Reduce sugar to 1 tablespoon. Add ¼ cup sumac and ¼ cup extra-virgin olive oil to brine with onion.

Crispy Shallots

Makes about ½ cup

Microwave-fried shallots add oniony flavor and crunch to recipes with minimal time and cleanup.

- 3 shallots, sliced thin
- ½ cup vegetable oil for frying

Microwave shallots and oil in medium bowl for 5 minutes. Stir shallots, then microwave for 2 more minutes. Repeat stirring and microwaving in 2-minute increments until beginning to brown, then repeat stirring and microwaving in 30-second increments until deep golden brown. Using slotted spoon, transfer shallots to paper towel–lined plate and season with salt to taste. Let drain and crisp for about 5 minutes. (Shallots can be stored in air-tight container at room temperature for up to 1 month.)

Classic Croutons

Makes about 1½ cups

Choose your favorite hearty sandwich bread (either fresh or stale) to make these all-purpose croutons.

- 3 tablespoons extra-virgin olive oil
- 3 slices hearty sandwich bread, crusts removed, cut into ½-inch cubes (1½ cups)
- ⅛ teaspoon table salt
   Pinch pepper

Heat oil in 10- or 12-inch skillet over medium heat until shimmering. Add bread pieces, salt, and pepper and cook, stirring frequently, until golden brown, about 10 minutes. Transfer croutons to paper towel–lined plate and season with salt to taste. (Croutons can be stored in airtight container at room temperature for up to 1 week.)

Umami Croutons

Toss bread pieces with 1 tablespoon nutritional yeast, ½ teaspoon white miso, ½ teaspoon Dijon mustard, and ¼ teaspoon distilled white vinegar before adding to skil-let with salt and pepper.

Garlic Croutons

Add 1 minced garlic clove to skillet during last 1 minute of cooking.

Garlicky Tempeh Crumbles

Makes about ½ cup

Sprinkled atop soups, salads, and more, this crispy spiced tempeh is a great way to add protein, textural interest, and an extra hit of flavor.

- 4 ounces tempeh, crumbled into ¼-inch pieces
- 1 tablespoon extra-virgin olive oil or vegetable oil
- ½ teaspoon garlic powder
- ¼ teaspoon paprika
   Pinch table salt

Toss tempeh with oil, garlic powder, paprika, and salt in medium bowl. Microwave until tempeh is lightly crisped, 2 to 3 minutes, stirring halfway through microwaving.

Chorizo Tempeh Crumbles

Decrease garlic powder to ¼ teaspoon. Substitute 1½ teaspoons chili powder and ½ teaspoon dried oregano for paprika.

Italian Sausage Tempeh Crumbles

Decrease garlic powder to ¼ teaspoon. Substitute ½ teaspoon lightly crushed fennel seeds, ½ teaspoon dried thyme, and pinch red pepper flakes for paprika.

1

BREAKFAST

30 Black Beans on Toast with Tomatoes and Avocado

33 Pa Amb Tomàquet with Lemon-Basil Ricotta

34 Everything-Crusted Tofu Breakfast Sandwich

37 Breakfast Tacos with Scrambled Tofu

with Scrambled Plant-Based Egg

38 Chickpea and Tofu Shakshuka

41 Hash Brown Omelet with Kimchi

42 Mangú Breakfast Bowl with Tempeh

45 Savory Breakfast Grits with Chili and Lime

Sweet Breakfast Grits with Maple and Pecans

46 Baked Oatmeal with Apple and Pecans

with Banana and Chocolate

49 Chia Pudding Parfaits with Pineapple and Coconut

with Matcha and Kiwi

50 Classic Cinnamon French Toast

Crunchy Cinnamon French Toast

53 Whole-Wheat Pancakes

54 Banana-Walnut Muffins

Banana Muffins with Coconut and Macadamia Nuts

57 Chocolate Chip–Ginger Scones

58 Skillet Granola with Apricots and Walnuts

61 No-Bake Cherry and Almond Bars

Black Beans on Toast
WITH TOMATOES AND AVOCADO

SERVES 2

TOTAL TIME 15 minutes

- ¾ cup canned black beans, rinsed
- 2 tablespoons hot water
- 1 teaspoon extra-virgin olive oil, plus extra for drizzling
- ¼ teaspoon grated lime zest plus 1½ teaspoons juice
- ¼ teaspoon table salt
- ⅛ teaspoon pepper
- 2 (½-inch-thick) slices rustic bread, toasted
- ½ avocado, sliced thin
- 2 ounces cherry or grape tomatoes, quartered
- 2 tablespoons Quick Pickled Red Onion (page 26) (optional)
- 2 tablespoons fresh cilantro leaves

  Flake sea salt (optional)

WHY THIS RECIPE WORKS   It's time to break up with the overpriced avocado toast served by trendy brunch places everywhere. In the time it takes to brew your morning cup of coffee, you can step up your home toast game and create a slice to rival even the bougiest brunch spot's. Our version keeps the avocado but adds convenient canned black beans, lime, cherry tomatoes, pickled onions, and cilantro to give the toasts a bold Southwestern flavor profile. And as for equipment, all you need is one bowl in which to mash the beans to a coarse, spreadable consistency with a little hot water, lime zest and juice, and salt and pepper for seasoning. For a splash of color, heat, and acidity, we love the addition of spicy quick-pickled onion, but if you don't have them on hand, a pinch of red pepper flakes will give you some heat. Assembly is simply a matter of smearing the toasts with the hearty bean mixture and then layering on the other fresh toppings. A toast to that!

1   Mash beans, hot water, oil, lime zest and juice, table salt, and pepper with potato masher to coarse puree in bowl, leaving some whole beans intact.

2   Arrange toasts on serving plates. Distribute bean mixture evenly between toasts and spread to edges. Top with avocado; tomatoes; pickled onion, if using; and cilantro. Drizzle with extra oil and sprinkle lightly with sea salt, if using. Serve.

Kitchen Improv

USE WHAT YOU'VE GOT

Substitute other canned beans, such as cannellini, pinto, or navy, for black beans; other pickles for pickled onions; or other fresh leafy herbs for cilantro.

LEVEL UP

Top with jalapeño, lightly dressed greens, crumbled plant-based cheese, and/or Scrambled Plant-Based Egg (page 275).

Pa Amb Tomàquet
WITH LEMON-BASIL RICOTTA

SERVES 2
TOTAL TIME 25 minutes

- ¼ cup plant-based ricotta
- 2 teaspoons shredded fresh basil
- ½ teaspoon lemon zest plus 1 teaspoon juice
- 1 large ripe tomato, halved through equator
- ¼ teaspoon table salt
- 1 (8-inch) piece ciabatta bread, halved horizontally and sliced crosswise into 4 pieces
- 1 garlic clove, peeled and halved crosswise
- 4 teaspoons extra-virgin olive oil
- Flake sea salt (optional)

Kitchen Improv

USE WHAT YOU'VE GOT

Substitute guacamole, hummus, or spreadable plant-based cheese for ricotta. Substitute two ciabatta rolls or 8-inch piece of crusty baguette for ciabatta bread.

LEVEL UP

Top with lightly dressed greens, pickles, and/or Scrambled Plant-Based Egg (page 275).

WHY THIS RECIPE WORKS Pa amb tomàquet ("bread with tomato"), is much more than the sum of its parts: Toasted bread is rubbed with garlic and smeared with the jammy pulp from a ripe tomato, creating a softened (not soggy) layer that contrasts with the crunchy crust. The tomato flavor is then heightened with a simple sprinkle of salt and a drizzle of rich and fruity extra-virgin olive oil. A delightfully homey Catalonian invention, it was created by thrifty cooks as a way to use up leftover ingredients, a challenge that likely sounds all too familiar to anyone who regularly cooks for only one or two. We like to take our pa amb tomàquet over the top with a few dollops of tangy, lemony plant-based ricotta and a sprinkle of shredded basil, but there's almost no end to the flavor possibilities you can play around with. You can use our Cashew Ricotta (page 22) or store-bought plant-based ricotta in this recipe. If possible, use a ripe local tomato. Don't use plum tomatoes here; they're not juicy enough.

1 Adjust oven rack 6 inches from broiler element and heat broiler. Stir ricotta, basil, and lemon zest and juice together in bowl. Season with salt and pepper to taste; set aside.

2 Place box grater in medium bowl. Rub cut sides of tomato against large holes of grater until tomato flesh is reduced to pulp (skins should remain intact). Discard skins. (You should have about ¾ cup pulp.) Stir in table salt.

3 Set wire rack in rimmed baking sheet and arrange bread slices cut side up on rack. Broil until browned, crispy, and starting to char at edges, 2 to 4 minutes. Rub toasts with cut sides of garlic.

4 Arrange toasts on serving plates. Distribute tomato pulp evenly among toasts and spread to edges. Dollop ricotta mixture evenly over tomato mixture. Drizzle with oil and sprinkle lightly with sea salt, if using. Serve.

Everything-Crusted Tofu Breakfast Sandwich

SERVES 2

TOTAL TIME 30 minutes

½   ripe avocado

3   tablespoons finely chopped jarred pepperoncini

2   tablespoons chopped fresh basil

¼   cup salt-free everything bagel seasoning

4   teaspoons cornstarch

7   ounces firm or extra-firm tofu, sliced into 4 even slabs

¼   teaspoon table salt

⅛   teaspoon pepper

1   tablespoon extra-virgin olive oil

2   burger buns, halved and lightly toasted

4   slices tomato

½   cup baby arugula

WHY THIS RECIPE WORKS   Breakfast sandwiches are one of those wonderful foods that are actually much easier to pull off when veganized and scaled for two. No cracking egg after egg or juggling multiple pans: The only element that requires cooking is the tofu, slabs of which get an everything bagel seasoning–cornstarch coating before being pan-seared until crunchy. Tofu is usually pressed to rid it of excess moisture, but here a little moisture helps the coating stick, so skipping this step is a great timesaver. Finally, we slather a couple of burger buns with a creamy spread made from the unexpectedly delicious combo of mashed avocado, tangy pepperoncini, and basil and then layer on slabs of the crusty tofu, sliced tomato, and peppery baby arugula. Since this recipe requires a full ¼ cup of everything bagel seasoning, it's very important to use a salt-free variety or the sandwiches will be overwhelmingly salty. If you can't find salt-free everything bagel seasoning, substitute 1 tablespoon sesame seeds, 1 tablespoon poppy seeds, 1 tablespoon granulated garlic, and 1 tablespoon dried onion flakes. For the 7 ounces of tofu called for here, start by cutting a 14-ounce block of tofu in half crosswise. For ways to use up leftover tofu, see page 19.

1   Mash avocado with fork in small bowl until mostly smooth, then stir in pepperoncini and basil. Season with salt and pepper to taste; set aside.

2   Whisk everything bagel seasoning and cornstarch together in shallow dish. Sprinkle tofu with salt and pepper, then coat on all sides with seasoning mixture, pressing gently to adhere.

3   Heat oil in 10- or 12-inch nonstick skillet over medium heat until shimmering. Add tofu and cook until crust is lightly browned, about 2 minutes per side; transfer to paper towel–lined plate.

4   Spread avocado mixture evenly over bun bottoms. Top each with 2 slabs tofu, tomato, arugula, and bun tops. Serve.

Kitchen Improv

USE WHAT YOU'VE GOT

Substitute other baby greens or sprouts for arugula. Substitute other pickles for pepperoncini. Substitute bagels or sandwich rolls for burger buns. Substitute other fresh leafy herbs for basil.

LEVEL UP

Add spreadable, sliced, or crumbled plant-based cheese.

SWITCH UP THE CRUST

Crust tofu with sesame seeds instead of everything bagel seasoning.

Breakfast Tacos
WITH SCRAMBLED TOFU

SERVES 2
TOTAL TIME 30 minutes

7 ounces soft tofu, drained and patted dry

1 tablespoon vegetable oil

1 green bell pepper, stemmed, seeded, and chopped fine

1 small onion, chopped fine

1 small jalapeño chile, seeded and minced

¼ teaspoon table salt

1½ teaspoons ground cumin

½ teaspoon chili powder

6 (6-inch) corn tortillas, warmed

½ cup jarred or fresh salsa
   Lime wedges

Kitchen Improv

USE WHAT YOU'VE GOT

Substitute silken tofu for soft tofu; increase cooking time in step 2 as needed to cook off any additional moisture.

LEVEL UP

Serve with additional toppings, such as sliced radishes, chopped avocado, shredded greens, fresh or pickled jalapeños, and/or fresh cilantro.

WHY THIS RECIPE WORKS In southern Texas, tacos are fair game at breakfast as well as at lunch and dinner. We think even Texans would love our veganized take on their famous breakfast (or anytime) tacos. Instead of the eggs that are the hallmark of a traditional breakfast taco filling, we turn to soft tofu. Unlike drier firm or extra-firm tofu, soft tofu is creamy and moist straight out of the package, and when broken into irregularly sized pieces it mimics the appearance and texture of scrambled egg curds shockingly well. To up the flavor factor of the filling, we cook the tofu with onion, bell pepper, and jalapeño, plus some cumin and chili powder for layered spice and subtle earthiness. Finishing the tacos with a dollop of salsa (we use store-bought for convenience) gives each bite a hit of bright, balancing acidity. Do not use firm or extra-firm tofu in this recipe. To warm the tortillas, wrap them in a damp dish towel and microwave until warm and pliable, about 30 seconds. Alternatively, heat individual tortillas in a dry skillet or over a gas flame. For the 7 ounces of tofu called for here, start by cutting a 14-ounce block of tofu in half crosswise.

1 Gently crumble tofu into ¼- to ½-inch pieces. Heat oil in 10- or 12-inch nonstick skillet over medium heat until shimmering. Add bell pepper, onion, jalapeño, and salt and cook until softened and lightly browned, 4 to 6 minutes. Stir in cumin and chili powder and cook until fragrant, about 30 seconds.

2 Stir in tofu and cook until warmed through and any excess moisture has evaporated, 2 to 4 minutes. Divide filling evenly among tortillas. Serve with salsa and lime wedges.

VARIATION
Breakfast Tacos with Scrambled Plant-Based Egg

Substitute 8 ounces liquid plant-based egg for tofu and decrease salt to ⅛ teaspoon. Add egg to skillet with bell pepper–onion mixture and cook, constantly and firmly scraping bottom and sides of skillet with rubber spatula, until egg begin to clump and spatula leaves trail on bottom of skillet, 1½ to 2½ minutes. Reduce heat to low and continue to cook, gently but constantly folding egg mixture until clumped and slightly wet, 30 to 60 seconds longer.

Chickpea and Tofu Shakshuka

SERVES 2

TOTAL TIME 30 minutes

7 ounces firm or extra-firm tofu, sliced into 4 even slabs

¾ teaspoon smoked paprika, divided

2 pinches table salt, divided

4 teaspoons extra-virgin olive oil, divided, plus extra for drizzling

½ teaspoon ground cumin

1 (15-ounce) can crushed tomatoes

1 (15-ounce) can chickpeas, rinsed

½ cup jarred roasted red bell peppers, rinsed, patted dry, and chopped coarse

⅛ teaspoon pepper

2 tablespoons chopped fresh parsley

Kitchen Improv

USE WHAT YOU'VE GOT

Substitute other canned beans, such as cannellini, black, or pinto, for chickpeas. Substitute other fresh leafy herbs for parsley.

LEVEL UP

Sprinkle with crumbled plant-based cheese.

WHY THIS RECIPE WORKS   As we've already shown in our recipes for breakfast tacos and breakfast sandwiches (pages 30–37), tofu's ability to take on other flavors is its superpower when it comes to re-creating eggy breakfast foods. To make a vegan shakshuka (a dish enjoyed throughout the Mediterranean, Middle East, and North Africa that traditionally features eggs poached in a spicy tomato sauce), we once again turn to tofu. After a few minutes of simmering in the flavor-packed sauce, the slabs of tofu are infused with smoky, earthy, tomatoey goodness. As for that sauce, we keep things quick and easy by using canned tomatoes and jarred roasted red peppers as the base, with a couple dashes of smoked paprika and cumin for depth. A second nontraditional addition—a can of chickpeas—adds even more heft and textural interest to this saucy dish. We love shakshuka for breakfast, but it's filling and robust enough to be a great dinner option, too. For the 7 ounces of tofu called for here, start by cutting a 14-ounce block of tofu in half crosswise. For ways to use up leftover tofu, see page 19.

1   Pat tofu dry with paper towels and sprinkle with ¼ teaspoon paprika and pinch salt. Heat 1 tablespoon oil in 10- or 12-inch nonstick skillet over medium-high heat until just smoking. Add tofu and cook until golden and crispy on both sides, 5 to 7 minutes; transfer to paper towel–lined plate. Wipe skillet clean with paper towels.

2   Heat remaining 1 teaspoon oil in now-empty skillet over medium heat until shimmering. Add cumin and remaining ½ teaspoon paprika and cook until fragrant, about 30 seconds. Stir in tomatoes, chickpeas, bell peppers, pepper, and remaining pinch salt and bring to simmer. Cover, reduce heat to low, and simmer until bell peppers are softened and beginning to break down, 5 to 10 minutes. Off heat, season with salt and pepper to taste.

3   Using back of spoon, make 4 shallow indentations in sauce (about 2 inches each). Carefully nestle 1 tofu piece into each indentation and spoon some sauce over top. Return tomato mixture to simmer over medium heat. Cover, reduce heat to medium-low, and simmer until tofu is heated through, about 5 minutes. Sprinkle with parsley and drizzle with extra oil before serving.

Hash Brown Omelet
WITH KIMCHI

SERVES 2
TOTAL TIME 35 minutes

SESAME-LIME MAYONNAISE

- 2 tablespoons plant-based mayonnaise
- ¼ teaspoon sesame oil
- ⅛ teaspoon grated lime zest

OMELET

- 1 pound russet potatoes, peeled and shredded
- ¼ teaspoon table salt
- ⅛ teaspoon pepper
- 2 tablespoons vegetable oil, divided
- ⅔ cup vegan cabbage kimchi, patted dry and chopped
- 1 scallion, white and green parts separated and sliced thin
- 1 tablespoon chopped fresh cilantro

Kitchen Improv

USE WHAT YOU'VE GOT

Substitute other styles of kimchi, chopped as needed, for cabbage kimchi.

LEVEL UP

Top with lightly dressed greens, crumbled plant-based cheese, and/or Scrambled Plant-Based Egg (page 275).

WHY THIS RECIPE WORKS A hash brown omelet is exactly what it sounds like: a savory vegetable filling encased between two layers of crispy shredded potatoes—no eggs necessary. High-starch russet potatoes yield hash browns that hold together better than hash browns made with other potato varieties, so we start by shredding a pound of them, squeezing the shreds in a rolled-up dish towel to rid them of excess moisture, and then pressing them firmly into a sizzling-hot skillet. Once the first side is crispy and browned, we use two large plates to gently flip the hash brown before piling on the filling: a combination of tangy-spicy kimchi and oniony scallion whites. To serve, we fold the hash brown over the filling, cut it in two, and give each half a dollop of pungent sesame and lime–spiked mayonnaise. Use the large holes of a box grater or the shredding disk of a food processor to shred the potatoes. To prevent the potatoes from turning brown, shred them just before cooking. You will need a 12-inch nonstick skillet for this recipe; the potato mixture will overcrowd a smaller skillet. You can use store-bought plant-based mayonnaise or our Aquafaba Mayonnaise (page 22) in this recipe.

1 FOR THE SESAME-LIME MAYONNAISE Whisk mayonnaise, sesame oil, and lime zest together in bowl.

2 FOR THE OMELET Place potatoes in center of clean dish towel. Gather ends of towel together, twist tightly, and squeeze over sink to drain as much liquid as possible. Transfer potatoes to large bowl and toss with salt and pepper.

3 Heat 1 tablespoon oil in 12-inch nonstick skillet over medium-high heat until shimmering. Spread potatoes in even layer in skillet and press firmly with spatula to flatten. Reduce heat to medium and cook until bottom is dark golden and crispy, 8 to 10 minutes.

4 Slide hash brown onto large plate. Add remaining 1 tablespoon oil to now-empty skillet. Invert hash brown onto second plate and slide hash brown, browned side up, back into skillet; press firmly with spatula to flatten. Sprinkle kimchi and scallion whites over half of hash brown, then cook over medium heat until bottom is dark golden and crispy, 6 to 8 minutes.

5 Using spatula, fold hash brown in half over filling and slide onto cutting board. Slice in half, then sprinkle with cilantro and scallion greens. Serve with mayonnaise.

Mangú Breakfast Bowl
WITH TEMPEH

SERVES 2

TOTAL TIME 45 minutes

- 1 pound unripe plantains, peeled, and sliced ½ inch thick
- ¼ teaspoon table salt, divided, plus salt for cooking plantains
- 2 tablespoons extra-virgin olive oil, divided
- 1 small red onion, halved and sliced ½ inch thick through root end
- ¼ cup plus ¼ teaspoon red wine vinegar
- 4 ounces tempeh, cut into ½-inch pieces
- 2 teaspoons soy sauce
- 1 teaspoon garlic powder
- ½ teaspoon dried oregano
- ½ teaspoon ground cumin
- ½ avocado, sliced thin
- 2 tablespoons chopped fresh cilantro

WHY THIS RECIPE WORKS   Mangú, a rich Dominican breakfast of mashed plantains, is often served with a trio of accompaniments known as "tres golpes," or "three hits" of flavor—salami, cheese, and eggs. In our vegan version, the subtly sweet, silky plantain mash is pure magic when paired with spiced tempeh, our pleasantly chewy-crispy stand-in for the sausage in traditional tres golpes, and enlivened with a hit of acidity from quick-pickled red onion. You can speed up breakfast prep by cooking and mashing the plantains the night before. Topped with the tempeh, onion, creamy avocado, and citrusy fresh cilantro, it's a plant-based Dominican feast. We like our version as is, but if you're feeling ambitious, you can complete the traditional tres golpes accompaniments vegan-style (see Level Up for suggestions). Look for unripe plantains that are green to yellow green and feel firm and full in their skins. To peel unripe plantains, cut off both ends of each plantain. With the tip of a paring knife, slice the skin lengthwise from end to end, taking care not to cut into the fruit. Pull the skin apart and remove the fruit. For ways to use up leftover tempeh, see page 19.

1   Place plantains and ½ teaspoon salt in large saucepan, add cold water to cover by 2 inches, and bring to boil over high heat. Reduce heat to medium-high and cook until plantains are tender and easily pierced with tip of knife, 15 to 20 minutes. Reserve 1 cup cooking water. Drain plantains and return to now-empty saucepan.

2   Add 2 teaspoons oil, ½ cup of reserved cooking water, and ⅛ teaspoon salt to plantains and mash with potato masher until mostly smooth. Season with salt and pepper to taste. Cover to keep warm. (Plantain mixture will thicken as it cools. Completely cooled mixture can be refrigerated for up to 2 days; reheat in saucepan over medium heat, adjusting consistency with water as desired.)

3   Meanwhile, heat 1 teaspoon oil in 10- or 12-inch nonstick skillet over medium heat until shimmering. Add onion and remaining ⅛ teaspoon salt and cook until softened, 3 to 5 minutes. Stir in ¼ cup vinegar and cook until evaporated, about 1 minute. Transfer onion mixture to small bowl; set aside. Wipe skillet clean with paper towels.

4   Toss tempeh with soy sauce, garlic powder, oregano, cumin, 1 teaspoon oil, and remaining ¼ teaspoon vinegar in medium bowl. Heat remaining 2 teaspoons oil in now-empty skillet over medium heat until shimmering. Add tempeh and cook until browned on all sides, 3 to 5 minutes. Stir plantain mixture to recombine, and adjust consistency with remaining ½ cup reserved cooking water as needed. Top each portion of plantains with tempeh, onion mixture, avocado, and cilantro. Serve.

Kitchen Improv

USE WHAT YOU'VE GOT

Substitute Pan-Seared Tofu (page 274), cooked plant-based sausage, crumbled plant-based cheese, or warmed beans for tempeh. Substitute other fresh leafy herbs for cilantro.

LEVEL UP

Serve with Scrambled Plant-Based Egg (page 275) and crumbled plant-based cheese to complete the tres golpes. Add other thinly sliced vegetables, such as bell pepper, cabbage, carrot, or zucchini, to skillet with onion.

Savory Breakfast Grits
WITH CHILI AND LIME

SERVES 2
TOTAL TIME 30 minutes

2 teaspoons extra-virgin olive oil

1 small red, orange, or yellow bell pepper, chopped fine

1 large shallot, chopped fine

½ cup old-fashioned grits

¼–½ teaspoon chili powder

2 cups plant-based milk

¼ teaspoon grated lime zest, plus lime wedges for serving

¼ teaspoon table salt

2 tablespoons chopped fresh cilantro

Kitchen Improv

USE WHAT YOU'VE GOT

In savory grits, substitute other ground chile powders, such as smoked paprika, ancho, or chipotle, for chili powder. Substitute other fresh leafy herbs for cilantro. In sweet grits, substitute agave for maple syrup; other warm spices, such as allspice, baharat, or pumpkin pie spice, for cinnamon; or other toasted nuts or seeds for pecans.

LEVEL UP

Top savory grits with hot sauce, crumbled or shredded plant-based cheese, nutritional yeast, pickles, olives, and/or capers. Top sweet grits with fresh or dried fruits, granola, and/or chocolate chips.

WHY THIS RECIPE WORKS   A Southern breakfast staple made from little more than water or milk, salt, and ground corn, grits are easy and quick enough to whip up on almost any morning—no question. But when it comes to dressing plain grits up a bit, most of the options that spring to mind are hardly what you'd call vegan-friendly: butter, shrimp, and cheese, oh my! That's where our savory recipe comes in. Its big hits of flavor from the additions of chopped bell pepper and shallot, lime zest, and a pinch of chili powder guarantee that you'll never miss the heavy animal product–laden version. We soften the vegetables in oil before stirring in the grits; adding the grits before the cooking liquid allows them to get lightly toasted in the oil. Boiling the grits in plant-based milk rather than plain water gives them a noticeable boost in rich creaminess. We can't get enough of these savory grits, but if you (or your plus-one) prefer a sweeter start to the day, never fear: These grits can easily be taken over to the sweet side with our variation. For spicier grits, use the greater amount of chili powder.

1   Heat oil in large saucepan over medium heat until shimmering. Add bell pepper and shallot and cook until softened and lightly browned, 4 to 6 minutes. Add grits and chili powder and cook, stirring often, until fragrant, about 1 minute.

2   Whisk in milk, lime zest, and salt and bring to boil. Reduce heat to low, cover, and simmer, whisking often, until thick and creamy, 8 to 12 minutes.

3   Transfer grits to individual bowls and sprinkle with cilantro. Serve with lime wedges.

VARIATION
Sweet Breakfast Grits with Maple and Pecans

Omit oil, bell pepper, shallot, and lime. Decrease salt to ⅛ teaspoon. Substitute 1 teaspoon ground cinnamon for chili powder and add to grits with milk. Whisk in 2 tablespoons maple syrup with plant-based milk. Substitute toasted and chopped pecans for cilantro.

Baked Oatmeal
WITH APPLE AND PECANS

SERVES 2

TOTAL TIME 1 hour

- 1   cup apple cider
- 1   tablespoon vegetable oil
- 1   teaspoon vanilla extract
- 1   teaspoon ground cinnamon
- ¼   teaspoon table salt
- 1   cup old-fashioned rolled oats
- ⅓   cup pecans, toasted and chopped
- 1   apple, shredded (1 cup)

Kitchen Improv

USE WHAT YOU'VE GOT

Substitute apple juice or plant-based milk for apple cider. Substitute other warm spices, such as pumpkin pie spice, for cinnamon. Substitute dried fruit, seeds, or other toasted nuts for pecans. Substitute pear for apple.

LEVEL UP

Serve with a dollop of plant-based yogurt, a drizzle of maple syrup, and/or a spoonful of jam.

WHY THIS RECIPE WORKS   This incredible baked oatmeal will get you into the fall spirit and ready to take on the day before you've so much as changed out of your pajamas. All it takes to create morning magic is to stir old-fashioned rolled oats together with a shredded apple, apple cider, toasted pecans, and cinnamon and bake the mixture in a loaf pan—a favorite for-two-sized vessel. Baking the oatmeal rather than simmering it on the stove is not only more hands-off, but it also suffuses the kitchen with the oatmeal's appetite-whetting aromas: caramelized sugar and baked apples, heady vanilla, toasty nuts, and warm spice. Since waiting for the oats to cook through under these mouthwatering conditions requires all the patience we can muster up, we like to stir the oat mixture together the night before—that way, the baking time is the only wait we'll have to endure come the morning. Do not substitute quick or instant oats in this recipe. The test kitchen's preferred loaf pan measures 8½ by 4½ inches; if you use a 9 by 5-inch loaf pan, start checking the oatmeal for doneness after 25 minutes.

1   Adjust oven rack to middle position and heat oven to 375 degrees. Grease 8½ by 4½-inch loaf pan.

2   Whisk apple cider, oil, vanilla, cinnamon, and salt together in large bowl. Stir in oats and pecans until well combined, then fold in apple until just combined. Transfer oat mixture to prepared pan and spread into even layer. (Oat mixture can be refrigerated in pan for up to 24 hours.)

3   Bake until top of oatmeal is golden brown and edges are deep golden brown, 35 to 40 minutes. Let oatmeal cool in pan on wire rack for 10 minutes before serving.

VARIATION

Baked Oatmeal with Banana and Chocolate

Substitute plant-based milk for apple cider and chocolate chips for pecans. Substitute 1 chopped banana for apple.

Chia Pudding Parfaits
WITH PINEAPPLE AND COCONUT

SERVES 2

TOTAL TIME 30 minutes, plus
8 hours chilling

- 1 cup natural pineapple juice, plus extra as needed
- ⅓ cup chia seeds
- ¼ cup canned coconut milk
- ⅛ teaspoon table salt
- 1 cup plain plant-based yogurt, divided
- 1 cup pineapple chunks, chopped, divided
- 8 teaspoons unsweetened flaked coconut, toasted, divided

Kitchen Improv

USE WHAT YOU'VE GOT

Substitute mango, guava, and/or passion fruit juice for pineapple juice. Substitute other plant-based milks for coconut milk. Substitute chopped mango, kiwi, banana, or papaya for pineapple. Substitute dried fruit or toasted seeds or nuts for coconut.

LEVEL UP

Add layers of store-bought granola or our Skillet Granola with Apricots and Walnuts (page 58).

WHY THIS RECIPE WORKS You're probably at least somewhat familiar with chia pudding, the tapioca-like result of soaking chia seeds in liquid. But if that's as far as your chia adventures have taken you, it's time to explore a new horizon: chia pudding parfaits. To pack as much tropical fruity flavor into these parfaits as possible, we soak the chia seeds in unsweetened pineapple juice, plus a little coconut milk for creaminess, rather than in the more conventional plant-based milk. Once the pudding has thickened (an overnight rest in the fridge will do the trick), we alternate layering the pudding with tangy plant-based yogurt, fresh pineapple, and some toasted flaked coconut to provide a subtle textural contrast. The result is a pair of delicious and impressively striped parfaits that belie the absolute ease with which they come together. Avoid juices with added sugars. Fresh, canned, or thawed frozen pineapple will work here; if using canned, look for pineapple chunks, rings, or tidbits canned in natural pineapple juice and use the fruit and the juice in the recipe. For a portable breakfast, use 2-cup jars with tight-fitting lids to store the parfaits. For ways to use up leftover coconut milk and plant-based yogurt, see pages 18–19.

1 Whisk pineapple juice, chia seeds, coconut milk, and salt together in bowl. Let mixture sit for 15 minutes, then whisk again to break up any clumps. Cover bowl with plastic wrap and refrigerate for at least 8 hours or up to 1 week.

2 Adjust consistency of chia pudding with additional juice as needed. Scoop ¼ cup chia pudding into each of 2 jars or parfait glasses. Top each with ¼ cup yogurt, ¼ cup pineapple, and 2 teaspoons coconut. Repeat layering process with remaining chia pudding, yogurt, pineapple, and coconut. Serve.

VARIATION

Chia Pudding Parfaits with Matcha and Kiwi

Substitute 1¼ cups plant-based milk for pineapple juice and coconut milk. Substitute chopped kiwi for pineapple and cacao nibs for flaked coconut. Whisk 1 tablespoon maple syrup and 1 teaspoon matcha into chia mixture with milk.

Classic Cinnamon French Toast

SERVES 2

TOTAL TIME 40 minutes

- 3 tablespoons cornstarch
- 1 tablespoon sugar
- ½ teaspoon ground cinnamon
- ⅛ teaspoon ground nutmeg
- ⅛ teaspoon table salt
- ½ cup plant-based milk
- 3 tablespoons liquid plant-based egg
- 1 tablespoon vegetable oil
- 1 teaspoon vanilla extract
- 4 slices hearty sandwich bread
   Maple syrup (optional)

Kitchen Improv

USE WHAT YOU'VE GOT

Substitute orange or almond extract for vanilla.

LEVEL UP

Top toasts with nut butter, fresh fruit, fruit preserves, and/or plant-based yogurt.

EXPERIMENT WITH SPICE

Substitute pumpkin pie spice, baharat, five-spice powder, or ras el hanout for cinnamon and nutmeg.

WHY THIS RECIPE WORKS Because the key to the texture of traditional French toast is to soak the bread in an egg-milk mixture, this classic treat can feel out of reach when you're eating plant-based. Our first forays into vegan French toast resulted in toasts with crisp, crunchy exteriors—appealing in their own way, but not quite what we were looking for. Enter the game-changer: liquid plant-based egg. Combined with plant-based milk, cornstarch (for body), and warm spices, plant-based egg gives the mixture a genuinely custardy texture that carries over to the toast itself. Once soaked, four slices of bread fit easily on a single rimmed baking sheet, allowing us to get breakfast for two on the table in a single go, no hovering over a skillet necessary. If you like a crunchier French toast or don't have plant-based egg on hand, we also provide a crunchy variation made without egg substitute. Do not use thin-sliced sandwich bread or rustic artisan loaves here. Different breads will absorb varying amounts of the milk mixture; use the lower end of the time range for soaking softer, more delicate slices. Be sure to use vegetable oil spray, which contains lecithin that keeps the oil well distributed and prevents the toast from sticking. You will need a small rimmed baking sheet (see page 20) for this recipe.

1 Adjust 1 oven rack to lowest position and second rack 6 inches from broiler element. Heat oven to 425 degrees. Generously spray bottom and sides of rimmed baking sheet with vegetable oil spray.

2 Whisk cornstarch, sugar, cinnamon, nutmeg, and salt together in large bowl. Add milk, egg, oil, and vanilla and whisk until combined; transfer to shallow dish. Working with 1 slice of bread at a time, soak bread in milk mixture until just saturated, 15 to 20 seconds per side. Using your hands and spatula for extra support, lift bread out of milk mixture, allowing excess to drip back into dish, then place on prepared sheet. Repeat with remaining bread and milk mixture, arranging bread in single layer on sheet; whisk milk mixture as needed to recombine.

3 Bake until bottoms of slices are golden brown, 12 to 18 minutes, rotating sheet halfway through baking. Heat broiler and broil until tops of slices are golden brown, watching carefully and rotating sheet as needed to prevent burning, 1 to 4 minutes. Transfer toasts, broiled sides down, to serving plates. Serve with maple syrup, if using.

VARIATION

Crunchy Cinnamon French Toast

Omit plant-based egg. Increase plant-based milk to ¾ cup. Decrease soaking time for bread in milk mixture to 3 to 5 minutes per side.

Whole-Wheat Pancakes

SERVES 2 (makes 6 pancakes)
TOTAL TIME 25 minutes

1¼ cups plant-based milk

2 tablespoons plus 2 teaspoons vegetable oil, divided

1 tablespoon lemon juice

1 teaspoon baking powder

¼ teaspoon baking soda

¼ teaspoon table salt

1 cup (5½ ounces) whole-wheat flour

1 tablespoon sugar

Maple syrup (optional)

Kitchen Improv

LEVEL UP

Add aromatic extracts and/or warm spices to pancake batter. Before flipping pancakes, sprinkle with toasted nuts or seeds, chocolate chips, cacao nibs, or chopped fruit.

GO BEYOND MAPLE SYRUP

Top pancakes with nut butter, fresh fruit, fruit preserves, and/or plant-based yogurt.

WHY THIS RECIPE WORKS   Think whole-wheat pancakes that taste fantastic and are superlatively light and fluffy—and that also happen to be completely egg-free—are mere wishful thinking? Think again. Even better, since these nutty-tasting whole-grain vegan pancakes are so good you'll want to enjoy them all the time, you can have two servings prepared, start to finish, in under half an hour. Many whole-wheat pancakes call for a mix of whole-wheat and all-purpose flours, but we found that we got the best results using 100-percent whole-wheat flour. That's because whole-wheat flour contributes to less gluten development (the enemy of tender, fluffy pancakes) than white flour does, so these pancakes cook up light as a cloud. And to our surprise, though we tried making these whole-wheat pancakes with a variety of egg substitutes, we like them best with no egg replacers at all. The protein content of whole-wheat flour makes the pancakes just sturdy enough to support an open, fluffy crumb, and the right combination of baking soda, baking powder, and acidic lemon juice provides all the rising action needed. An electric griddle set at 350 degrees can be used in place of a skillet.

1   Whisk milk, 2 tablespoons oil, and lemon juice in large bowl until well combined. Whisk in baking powder, baking soda, and salt until well combined. Whisk in flour and sugar until smooth.

2   Heat 1 teaspoon oil in 12-inch nonstick skillet over medium heat until shimmering. Using paper towels, carefully wipe out oil, leaving thin film of oil on bottom and sides of pan. Using heaping ¼-cup dry measuring cup, portion batter into pan in 3 places. Cook until edges are set, first side is golden, and bubbles on surface are just beginning to break, 2 to 3 minutes.

3   Flip pancakes and cook until second side is golden, 1 to 2 minutes. Repeat with remaining 1 teaspoon oil and remaining batter. Serve with maple syrup, if using.

Banana-Walnut Muffins

MAKES 6 muffins
TOTAL TIME 1 hour

- 2 very ripe bananas, peeled and mashed (¾ cup)
- ½ cup plain plant-based yogurt
- ⅓ cup plant-based milk
- 3½ tablespoons vegetable oil
- 2 teaspoons vanilla extract
- 1½ teaspoons baking powder
- ¼ teaspoon baking soda
- ¼ teaspoon table salt
- 1⅓ cups (6 ⅔ ounces) all-purpose flour
- ½ cup (3½ ounces) plus ½ teaspoon sugar, divided
- ½ cup walnuts, toasted and chopped fine, divided

Kitchen Improv

USE WHAT YOU'VE GOT

Substitute vanilla-flavored plant-based yogurt for plain plant-based yogurt and vanilla. Substitute other nuts, such as pecans or macadamia nuts, for walnuts.

DON'T LIKE NUTS?

Substitute other mix-ins, such as chocolate chips or dried fruit, for walnuts.

WHY THIS RECIPE WORKS   It can be hard to get your muffin fix as a vegan, especially when you're cooking for only one or two and every recipe under the sun seems to be designed with a crowd in mind. Our recipe slashes the usual 12-muffin yield down to six. Even better, any leftovers can be frozen without compromising their flavor or texture, so you can stash some away to enjoy another day. Ripe bananas flavor and help bind these muffins sans eggs, and the baking powder and baking soda in the batter help the muffins rise tall and develop a fluffy, open crumb. Before baking, we sprinkle sugar and toasted walnuts over the tops to make our muffins as pretty as any found in a bakery case. Use bananas that are very heavily speckled or even black; less-ripe bananas will produce drier, less flavorful muffins. You can substitute thawed frozen bananas for fresh; be sure to add any juice that is released as the bananas thaw. We strongly prefer oat milk in this recipe since it yields the best browning, but any plant-based milk will work. We also prefer almond milk yogurt in this recipe; other yogurts will work, but the batter may be thicker or thinner as a result. For ways to use up leftover plant-based yogurt, see page 19.

1   Adjust oven rack to upper-middle position and heat oven to 375 degrees. Grease 6-cup muffin tin.

2   Whisk bananas, yogurt, milk, oil, and vanilla in large bowl until well combined. Whisk in baking powder, baking soda, and salt until well combined. Stir in flour and ½ cup sugar until just combined. Stir in ¼ cup walnuts.

3   Divide batter evenly among prepared muffin cups (cups will be very full). Sprinkle batter evenly with remaining ½ teaspoon sugar and remaining ¼ cup walnuts. Bake until tops of muffins are golden and toothpick inserted in center comes out clean, 24 to 28 minutes, rotating muffin tin halfway through baking.

4   Let muffins cool in muffin tin on wire rack for 10 minutes, then transfer muffins to wire rack and let cool for at least 5 minutes. Serve warm or at room temperature. (Muffins can be stored at room temperature for up to 24 hours or frozen in zipper-lock bags for up to 1 month. Defrost at room temperature for at least 4 hours or in microwave for about 1 minute; let muffins cool after reheating.)

VARIATION

Banana Muffins with Coconut and Macadamia Nuts

Substitute grated orange zest for vanilla. Substitute ¼ cup finely chopped toasted macadamia nuts for walnuts in step 2 plus ¼ cup toasted sweetened flaked coconut for walnuts in step 3.

Chocolate Chip–Ginger Scones

MAKES 8 scones

TOTAL TIME 50 minutes

2 cups (10 ounces) all-purpose flour

3 tablespoons plus ½ teaspoon sugar, divided

1 tablespoon baking powder

½ teaspoon table salt

5 tablespoons plant-based butter, cut into ¼-inch pieces

1 cup (6 ounces) mini bittersweet chocolate chips

½ cup chopped crystallized ginger

¾ cup plus 1 tablespoon plant-based creamer, divided

Kitchen Improv

USE WHAT YOU'VE GOT

Substitute toasted nuts or seeds or chopped dried fruit for chocolate chips. Substitute shredded coconut for ginger.

WHY THIS RECIPE WORKS   Light, fluffy, and just barely sweet, traditional British cream scones are made by cutting cubes of chilled butter into the dry ingredients so that as the scones bake the butter melts to create the little air pockets that give the scones a flaky texture. In the past our preferred fat for vegan baking has been coconut oil, but these days plant-based butter is more widely available than ever, even coming in convenient, easy-to-measure sticks just like dairy butter. What better recipe to put this product through its paces than these sweet scones? To our delight, plant-based butter works just as well as its dairy counterpart, yielding tender, flaky pastries. To mix the dough, we simply pulse small pieces of the butter into the dry ingredients in a food processor until combined. Adding chocolate chips and spicy candied ginger transforms these scones into a special occasion–worthy breakfast or midday treat. Best of all, since the extras can be frozen for up to a month you can enjoy the sweet rewards of your baking efforts on even the busiest days. For ways to use up leftover plant-based creamer, see page 19.

1   Adjust oven rack to middle position and heat oven to 450 degrees. Line rimmed baking sheet with parchment paper.

2   Pulse flour, 3 tablespoons sugar, baking powder, and salt in food processor until combined, about 3 pulses. Scatter butter over flour mixture and pulse until mixture resembles coarse cornmeal with some pea-size pieces of butter remaining, about 10 pulses. Transfer mixture to large bowl and stir in chocolate chips and ginger. Stir in ¾ cup creamer until dough begins to form, about 30 seconds.

3   Turn dough and any floury bits out onto lightly floured counter and knead with your lightly floured hands until rough, slightly sticky ball forms, 5 to 10 seconds. (Dough will be quite soft and wet.)

4   Pat dough into 8-inch round and cut into 8 wedges. Brush tops of scones with remaining 1 tablespoon creamer and sprinkle with remaining ½ teaspoon sugar. Space desired number of scones at least 1 inch apart on prepared sheet. (Remaining scones can be frozen on large plate, then transferred to zipper-lock bag and stored in freezer for up to 1 month. Bake scones from frozen, increasing baking time to 14 to 18 minutes.)

5   Bake until tops of scones are light golden brown, 12 to 15 minutes, rotating sheet halfway through baking. Transfer scones to wire rack and let cool for at least 10 minutes. Serve warm or at room temperature.

Skillet Granola
WITH APRICOTS AND WALNUTS

MAKES about 3 cups

TOTAL TIME 25 minutes, plus 20 minutes cooling

- ¼ cup maple syrup
- 1 teaspoon vanilla extract
- ½ teaspoon ground cinnamon
- ¼ teaspoon table salt
- 2 tablespoons vegetable oil
- ½ cup walnuts, chopped coarse
- 1½ cups (4½ ounces) old-fashioned rolled oats
- ½ cup dried apricots, chopped

Kitchen Improv

USE WHAT YOU'VE GOT

Substitute other nuts or seeds for almonds. Substitute other dried fruits, such as cherries or raisins, for apricots. Substitute other warm spice blends, such as pumpkin pie spice or baharat, for ground cinnamon.

LEVEL UP

Stir ¼ to ½ cup other chopped dried fruits, chocolate chips, and/or toasted flaked coconut into cooled granola. Serve as a breakfast cereal with plant-based milk and your favorite mix-ins.

MAKE IT A PARFAIT

Layer granola with plant-based yogurt and fresh fruit to make parfaits.

WHY THIS RECIPE WORKS This small-batch granola brims with substantial pieces, simple but high-impact mix-ins, and a balanced sweet-toasty flavor—and we wanted it to involve zero time in the oven. Instead, we use a skillet to toast a handful of walnuts as well as our old-fashioned rolled oats—the base of any good granola—to bring out both ingredients' nutty flavor. We then stir a sticky mixture of maple syrup, vegetable oil, vanilla, and cinnamon right into the hot pan; the maple syrup mixture clings to the dry ingredients and binds them together. To increase the granola's surface area for faster cooling, we transfer it onto a rimmed baking sheet and spread it into an even layer. Once the granola is cooled and broken into crunchy bite-size clusters, a last-minute addition of chewy chopped dried apricots provides textural interest. The granola keeps well, so this recipe makes enough to serve four. On its own this granola makes a great snack or light breakfast; for a more substantial breakfast, see our Kitchen Improv suggestions. Do not substitute quick or instant oats in this recipe. You will need a 12-inch nonstick skillet for this recipe; the granola will overcrowd a smaller skillet.

1 Whisk maple syrup, vanilla, cinnamon, and salt together in bowl; set aside. Line rimmed baking sheet with parchment paper.

2 Heat oil in 12-inch nonstick skillet over medium heat until shimmering. Add walnuts and cook, stirring frequently, until fragrant and just starting to darken, about 4 minutes. Add oats and cook, stirring frequently, until oats are golden and walnuts are toasted, about 6 minutes.

3 Stir in maple syrup mixture and cook, stirring frequently, until liquid is absorbed and mixture darkens slightly, about 3 minutes.

4 Transfer granola to prepared sheet, spread into even layer, and let cool for 20 minutes. Break granola into bite-size pieces and stir in apricots. Serve. (Granola can be stored in an airtight container for up to 2 weeks.)

No-Bake Cherry and Almond Bars

MAKES 6 bars

TOTAL TIME 25 minutes, plus 1 hour chilling

1	cup hot water
¾	cup dried cherries
3	ounces pitted dates, chopped (½ cup)
1	cup raw whole almonds
¼	teaspoon ground cinnamon
¼	teaspoon table salt

Kitchen Improv

USE WHAT YOU'VE GOT

Substitute other dried fruits, such as apricots or raisins, for cherries. Substitute other warm spice blends, such as pumpkin pie spice or baharat, for cinnamon.

LEVEL UP

Drizzle cut bars with melted chocolate; refrigerate bars to set chocolate before serving.

WHY THIS RECIPE WORKS   Quick, portable, and made from just a handful of whole ingredients: There's nothing not to love about these easy fruit-nut bars. One batch makes enough for a few breakfasts, so they're convenient, too. We start with dried fruit—cherries for their tart, assertive flavor, and dates for their natural sweetness—which we rehydrate in hot water. Once the fruit is softened, we pulse it in a food processor with almonds. (Almonds belong to the same plant family as cherries do, so their flavor and aroma are a natural complement to the fruit.) Cinnamon and salt round out the flavor profile. We press the fruit-nut mixture into a smooth layer in a plastic wrap–lined loaf pan (the lining prevents sticking) and give it a quick chill in the fridge to firm it up, making it easy to cut into individual bars. In a hurry? The bars keep in the fridge for a week, so make a batch in advance and then grab one and go. The test kitchen's preferred loaf pan measures 8½ by 4½ inches; you can use a 9 by 5-inch loaf pan, but the bars will be slightly thinner.

1   Line 8½ by 4½-inch loaf pan with plastic wrap, letting excess plastic hang over sides of pan.

2   Combine water, cherries, and dates in bowl. Let sit until fruit has softened, 5 to 10 minutes. Drain well and pat fruit dry with paper towels.

3   Process almonds, cinnamon, and salt in food processor until finely ground, about 20 seconds. Add fruit and pulse until fruit is very finely chopped and mixture starts to clump together, 15 to 20 pulses.

4   Transfer fruit-nut mixture to prepared pan and spread into even layer with rubber spatula. Fold excess plastic wrap over top and, using your hands, press to flatten. Refrigerate until firm, about 1 hour.

5   Transfer mixture to cutting board and discard plastic wrap. Cut mixture crosswise into 6 bars (about 4½ by 1½ inches each). Serve. (Bars can be refrigerated for up to 1 week.)

64 Vegetable and Barley Soup

66 Soupe au Pistou

69 Chilled Watermelon Soup

70 Italian Wedding Soup

72 Kimchi, Tofu, and Vegetable Soup

75 Miso-Ginger Udon Noodle Soup

76 Carrot Soup with Thai Curry Paste and Tofu Croutons

79 Sweet Potato and Peanut Soup

80 Vegetable Chowder with Dijon-Panko Topping

83 Corn and Poblano Chowder with Tempeh Chorizo

84 Sun-Dried Tomato and White Bean Soup

87 Skillet-Roasted Garlic and Chickpea Soup

88 Moong Dal with Tomatoes, Spinach, and Coconut

90 Okra Pepper Pot

92 Summer Vegetable Stew

95 Green Bean, Tomato, and Bulgur Stew

96 Weeknight Meaty Chili

99 Green Jackfruit Chili

Vegetable and Barley Soup

SERVES 2

TOTAL TIME 50 minutes

2 tablespoons extra-virgin olive oil, divided, plus extra for drizzling

1 leek, white and light green parts only, halved lengthwise, sliced ½ inch thick, and washed thoroughly

2 cups vegetable broth

2 cups water

1 Yukon Gold potato (8 ounces), peeled and cut into ½-inch pieces

1 large carrot, peeled and cut into ½-inch pieces

3 tablespoons pearl barley

1 teaspoon soy sauce

2 sprigs fresh thyme

1 dried porcini mushroom, rinsed and minced

1 cup chopped or shredded green cabbage

1 tablespoon minced fresh parsley

1 teaspoon lemon juice

WHY THIS RECIPE WORKS For anyone who regularly eats plant-based, having a well-rounded and hearty vegetable soup in your cooking repertoire should be a point of pride. This soup packs varied vegetable flavor and texture in every bite, and all that vegetable goodness is courtesy of just a single leek, potato, and carrot plus a cup of chopped cabbage. Sautéing the leek builds a base of mild oniony flavor to which we add broth cut with an equal amount of water. Diluting the broth allows the subtle flavors of the sweet and earthy vegetables and woodsy thyme to come through clearly, while the addition of soy sauce and a dried porcini mushroom ups the soup's savoriness. We then add the potato and carrot to the broth to simmer along with some chewy barley, waiting to add the quicker-cooking cabbage until the denser root vegetables are almost tender. After less than an hour of mostly hands-off cooking time, all that's left is to brighten and enrich the soup with a sprinkle of parsley and a drizzle of olive oil. For ways to use up leftover cabbage, see page 18. Serve with crusty bread or crackers.

1 Heat 1 tablespoon oil in large saucepan over medium heat until shimmering. Add leek and cook until softened and lightly browned, 5 to 7 minutes.

2 Stir in broth, water, potato, carrot, barley, soy sauce, thyme sprigs, and porcini mushroom and bring to simmer. Reduce heat to medium-low, partially cover, and simmer for 10 minutes. Stir in cabbage and simmer, stirring occasionally, until barley and vegetables are tender, about 15 minutes.

3 Off heat, stir in parsley, lemon juice, and remaining 1 tablespoon oil and season with salt and pepper to taste. Drizzle individual portions with extra oil before serving. (Soup can be refrigerated for up to 3 days.)

Kitchen Improv

USE WHAT YOU'VE GOT

Substitute 12 ounces other root vegetables, such as parsnips, turnips, rutabaga, or celery root, for carrots and potatoes. Substitute shredded coleslaw mix for green cabbage. Substitute other fresh herbs, such as mint, chives, or basil, for parsley. Substitute wine vinegar for lemon juice.

LEVEL UP

Top with toasted nuts, seeds, croutons, or Umami Croutons (page 27).

BULK IT UP

Add canned cannellini, navy, or small white beans.

Soupe au Pistou

SERVES 2

TOTAL TIME 40 minutes

- 2 tablespoons grated plant-based Parmesan cheese
- 2 tablespoons chopped fresh basil
- 4 teaspoons extra-virgin olive oil, divided
- 3 garlic cloves, minced, divided
- 1 carrot, peeled and cut into ¼-inch pieces
- 1 small leek, white and light green parts only, sliced ½ inch thick and washed thoroughly
- 1½ cups vegetable broth
- 1½ cups water
- ⅛ teaspoon table salt
- 3 ounces green beans, trimmed and cut into ½-inch lengths
- 1 small zucchini (6 ounces), quartered lengthwise and sliced ¼ inch thick
- ¾ cup canned cannellini beans, rinsed
- 1 plum tomato, cored and chopped

WHY THIS RECIPE WORKS Soupe au pistou is a Provençal soup bursting with fresh vegetables, creamy white beans, and fragrant dollops of pistou, France's answer to pesto. Virtually any vegetable can go in the pot, but we like the light and summery flavors and varying shades of green provided by leek, green beans, and zucchini. Using canned white beans rather than dried keeps the timeline manageable enough for a weeknight. Traditional soupe au pistou is made with water, but we like the more rounded flavor of soup made with a combination of water and vegetable broth. We also add the liquid from the canned beans to the broth; this starchy liquid gives the soup a silky, even voluptuous, body. And instead of making a traditional pistou, which involves grinding herbs, oil, aromatics, and cheese into a paste, we simply give the ingredients a quick chop before stirring them together and drizzling over the soup. You can use store-bought plant-based Parmesan or our Cashew Parmesan (page 23) in this recipe. For ways to use up leftover green beans, see page 18. Serve with crusty bread or crackers.

1 Combine Parmesan, basil, 1 teaspoon oil, and one-third of garlic in bowl and season with pepper to taste; set aside.

2 Heat remaining 1 tablespoon oil in large saucepan over medium heat until shimmering. Add carrot and leek and cook until softened, about 5 minutes. Stir in remaining garlic and cook until fragrant, about 30 seconds.

3 Stir in broth, water, and salt, scraping up any browned bits, and bring to simmer. Stir in green beans, return to simmer, and cook until beans are bright green but still crunchy, about 5 minutes. Stir in zucchini, cannellini beans, and tomato and cook until vegetables are tender, about 3 minutes. Off heat, season soup with salt and pepper to taste. Top individual portions with reserved herb mixture before serving. (Soup and herb mixture can be refrigerated separately for up to 3 days.)

Kitchen Improv

USE WHAT YOU'VE GOT

Substitute summer squash and/or asparagus for green beans or zucchini.
Substitute other canned white beans, such as navy or small white beans,
for cannellini. Substitute other fresh herbs, such as mint, chives, or parsley,
for basil.

LEVEL UP

Top with toasted nuts, seeds, croutons, or Umami Croutons (page 27).

Chilled Watermelon Soup

SERVES 2

TOTAL TIME 15 minutes

- ¼ cup fresh basil leaves, plus extra for serving
- ½ cup ice (2 ounces)
- 2 cups 1-inch watermelon pieces
- 1 red, orange, or yellow bell pepper, halved, stemmed, and seeded
- 1 tomato, cored
- ¼ teaspoon pepper
- ⅛ teaspoon table salt
- 1 tablespoon extra-virgin olive oil
- ½ teaspoon red wine vinegar
- ½ avocado, chopped

Kitchen Improv

USE WHAT YOU'VE GOT

Substitute white wine vinegar, balsamic vinegar, or sherry vinegar for red wine vinegar.

LEVEL UP

In addition to avocado and basil, top individual portions with croutons, Umami Croutons (page 27), crumbled plant-based cheese, sliced radishes, diced watermelon, and/or chopped cucumber.

WHY THIS RECIPE WORKS This soup takes heavy inspiration from the flavors of gazpacho, a chilled mixture of chopped vegetables marinated in seasoned vinegar. Cooling, light, and hydrating, it's the perfect refreshing dinner for a hot summer night and is just as appropriate for lunch the next day. Juicy watermelon is the undisputed star; a few sprigs of basil, some bell pepper, and a tomato work together to balance the melon's sweetness, keeping the soup's flavor firmly in savory territory. To meld all the flavors and give the soup its chill in record time, we turn to our trusty blender. Pureeing the ingredients results in a soup with rounded, well integrated flavor that comes together in minutes rather than the hours it would take if we were to simply chop the vegetables and stir them together. Another blending bonus: It allows us to incorporate a few handfuls of ice into the soup, chilling the gazpacho without a lengthy refrigeration. Serve with crusty bread or crackers.

1 In order listed, add basil, ice, watermelon, bell pepper, tomato, pepper, salt, oil, and vinegar to blender and process on low speed until mixture is combined but still coarse in texture, about 10 seconds, scraping down sides of blender jar as needed. Gradually increase speed to high and process until completely smooth, about 1 minute.

2 Adjust consistency with cold water as needed. Top individual portions with avocado and extra basil before serving. (Gazpacho can be refrigerated for up to 24 hours; stir to recombine before serving.)

Italian Wedding Soup

SERVES 2

TOTAL TIME 45 minutes

- 2 tablespoons panko bread crumbs
- 1 tablespoon plus 1 cup water, divided
- ¼ teaspoon garlic powder
- ¼ teaspoon dried oregano

  Pinch ground fennel

  Pinch table salt
- 4 ounces plant-based ground meat
- 1½ cups vegetable broth, plus extra as needed
- 1½ teaspoons vegan Worcestershire sauce
- ½ cup ditalini
- 5 ounces (5 cups) baby kale
- 1 carrot, sliced thin

Kitchen Improv

USE WHAT YOU'VE GOT

Substitute other small pastas, such as tubettini, macaroni, or orzo, for ditalini. Substitute baby power greens, baby spinach, chopped romaine lettuce, or escarole for baby kale.

LEVEL UP

Finish soup with a splash of wine vinegar, a sprinkle of grated plant-based Parmesan, and/or a handful of fresh parsley, basil, or chives.

WHY THIS RECIPE WORKS Italian wedding soup is so named because the meatballs, greens, and pasta live in a harmonious "marriage" bound together by a savory broth. Veganizing this classic dish is simple thanks to plant-based meat, which we season with garlic powder, oregano, and ground fennel and bind with a couple tablespoons of bread crumbs to form tender meatballs with a sausagey flavor profile. While the meatballs chill in the fridge (a necessary step to help them hold their shape when simmered), we turn to the broth. A combination of vegetable broth, water, and vegan Worcestershire sauce results in a broth that's complex and savory but also mild enough to let the flavors of the meatballs and vegetables shine. Assertive yet tender baby kale acts as a counterpoint to the rich meatballs, a single chopped carrot adds sweetness and provides cheerful pops of color, and dainty ditalini adds satisfying wheaty chew to every bite. For ways to use up leftover plant-based meat, see page 19. Serve with crusty bread or crackers.

1 Mash panko, 1 tablespoon water, garlic powder, oregano, fennel, and salt into paste in large bowl. Break ground meat into small pieces and add to bowl with panko mixture. Gently knead with your hands until mixture is well combined. Using your moistened hands, pinch off and roll meat mixture into ¾-inch meatballs. (You should have about 10 meatballs.) Transfer meatballs to plate and refrigerate for at least 15 minutes or up to 24 hours.

2 Bring broth, Worcestershire, and remaining 1 cup water to simmer in large saucepan over medium-high heat. Add ditalini, kale, and carrot, return to simmer, and cook, stirring occasionally, for 5 minutes.

3 Add meatballs to broth, return to simmer, and cook, stirring occasionally, until meatballs are firm and pasta is tender, 3 to 5 minutes. Adjust consistency with extra hot broth as needed. Off heat, season with salt and pepper to taste. Serve. (Soup can be refrigerated for up to 3 days.)

SOUPS, STEWS, AND CHILIS

Kimchi, Tofu, and Vegetable Soup

SERVES 2

TOTAL TIME 45 minutes

1 tablespoon toasted sesame oil, plus extra for serving

4 ounces shiitake mushrooms, stemmed and sliced ¼ inch thick

5 scallions, white and green parts separated and sliced thin

3 garlic cloves, minced

1 tablespoon gochujang

3 cups water

14 ounces soft tofu, cut into 1½-inch pieces

8 ounces daikon radish, trimmed and cut into ½-inch pieces

1 carrot, peeled and cut into ½-inch pieces

1 tablespoon soy sauce, plus extra for seasoning

1 cup vegan cabbage kimchi, chopped, plus extra for serving

WHY THIS RECIPE WORKS Inspired by the kimchi soups that can be found on dinner tables across Korea in an almost limitless number of variations, we devised our own vegan take on warm, tangy, kimchi-centric soup. We start by cooking meaty shiitake mushrooms with sesame oil before stirring in subtly oniony scallion whites, garlic, and spicy gochujang. Kimchi, carrot, and daikon radish make up the rest of the soup's vegetable component. There's so much flavor coming from the other ingredients that we prefer to use plain water rather than broth, scraping up the flavorful browned bits (fond) from the bottom of the pot and adding a splash of soy sauce to bolster the liquid's savoriness. When added to the soup, delicate soft tofu partially breaks down and becomes dispersed throughout; cutting it into 1½-inch pieces before adding to the soup ensures that a few sizeable pieces survive until serving time. Do not drain the kimchi before measuring it; the pickling liquid is quite flavorful. Be sure to cut the tofu into large 1½-inch pieces; they will break down as the soup cooks.

1 Heat oil in large saucepan over medium heat until shimmering. Add mushrooms and cook until softened and lightly browned, 3 to 5 minutes. Stir in scallion whites, garlic, and gochujang and cook until fragrant, about 30 seconds.

2 Stir in water, scraping up any browned bits, then stir in tofu, radish, carrot, and soy sauce. Bring to simmer, partially cover, and cook until radish and carrot are tender and tofu begins to break down, 12 to 15 minutes.

3 Stir in kimchi and return to brief simmer. Off heat, season with extra soy sauce to taste. Top individual portions with scallion greens. Serve with extra oil and extra kimchi. (Soup can be refrigerated for up to 3 days.)

Kitchen Improv

USE WHAT YOU'VE GOT

Substitute other types of radishes for daikon, or omit radish and increase
carrots to 4. Substitute other mushrooms, such as white or cremini,
for shiitake. Substitute other styles of tofu and kimchi for soft tofu and
cabbage kimchi.

LEVEL UP

Substitute Umami Broth (page 22) for water. Serve with rice or noodles.

Miso-Ginger Udon Noodle Soup

SERVES 2

TOTAL TIME 30 minutes

- 6 ounces dried udon noodles
- 4 teaspoons grated fresh ginger
- 2 teaspoons sesame oil, plus extra for drizzling
- 1 carrot, peeled, halved lengthwise, and sliced ¼ inch thick
- ½ cup frozen edamame
- 1 teaspoon soy sauce, plus extra for seasoning
- 2 tablespoons white or red miso
- 2 scallions, sliced thin
- 1 teaspoon sesame seeds, toasted

Kitchen Improv

USE WHAT YOU'VE GOT

Substitute thin spaghetti or somen, soba, vegan ramen, or spiralized vegetable noodles for udon. Alternatively, serve with rice instead of noodles.

LEVEL UP

Substitute Umami Broth (page 22) for water in step 2.

WHY THIS RECIPE WORKS Miso soup is commonly eaten as one part of a larger meal; our version, with assists from noodles, spicy fresh ginger, and a few quick-to-prep vegetables, is ample enough to be a hearty dinner all on its own. We start by boiling thick udon noodles until chewy-tender and then set them aside while we make the soup. Because overheating miso can mute this fermented product's nuanced flavor, we prepare the broth with care. First, we bloom fragrant ginger in nutty sesame oil. We then add water, carrots, and edamame to the pot and cook just until the vegetables are tender. Soy sauce seasons the broth and amps up its umami backbone. Only when the vegetables are cooked do we spoon out a bit of the broth, gently whisk the miso into it off the heat, and then return the broth-miso mixture to the pot with the rest of the soup. (Whisking the miso with a smaller amount of broth before adding it to the pot helps prevent clumps from being left behind.) After we add the udon and portion the soup into individual bowls, scallions, sesame seeds, and a drizzle of sesame oil make fresh and fragrant toppings.

1 Bring 2 quarts water to boil in large pot. Add noodles and cook, stirring often, until tender. Drain noodles, rinse well, and drain again; set aside.

2 Meanwhile, heat ginger and oil in large saucepan over medium-low heat, stirring often, until ginger is fragrant and beginning to brown, about 2 minutes. Stir in 3¾ cups water, scraping up any browned bits, then stir in carrot, edamame, and soy sauce. Increase heat to medium, bring to simmer, and cook until vegetables are tender, 3 to 5 minutes.

3 Transfer ½ cup hot broth to small bowl or measuring cup and whisk in miso. Stir miso mixture and noodles into soup and return to brief simmer. Off heat, season with extra soy sauce to taste. Top individual portions with scallions, drizzle with extra oil, and sprinkle with sesame seeds before serving. (Soup, prepared through step 2, and noodles, tossed with 1 teaspoon oil, can be refrigerated separately for up to 3 days; reheat soup before proceeding with step 3.)

Carrot Soup

WITH THAI CURRY PASTE AND TOFU CROUTONS

SERVES 2
TOTAL TIME 45 minutes

- 5 teaspoons extra-virgin olive oil, divided
- 3 carrots (8 ounces), peeled and cut into ½-inch pieces
- 1 tablespoon Thai red curry paste
- 2 cups vegetable broth, plus extra as needed
- ½ cup canned coconut milk
- 7 ounces firm or extra-firm tofu, patted dry and cut into ½-inch pieces, divided
- 3 tablespoons cornstarch
- 1 teaspoon grated lime zest plus 2 teaspoons juice, plus lime wedges for serving
- ¼ cup chopped fresh cilantro

Kitchen Improv

USE WHAT YOU'VE GOT

Substitute yellow or green Thai curry paste for red. Substitute other fresh herbs, such as mint, chives, or parsley, for cilantro.

LEVEL UP

Top with toasted nuts or seeds. Drizzle soup with sriracha or your favorite hot sauce.

WHY THIS RECIPE WORKS In this richly aromatic carrot soup flavored with Thai red curry paste, lime, coconut, and cilantro, tofu does double duty: Some is blended into the soup to add robustness and smooth body, and the rest is crisped up into "croutons" that we sprinkle on top for contrasting crunch. While this may sound complicated, it's not: Sliced carrots cook quickly when simmered in broth and coconut milk, and once tender, the carrot mixture gets a whiz in the blender with a portion of the tofu. As for making the crispy tofu croutons, there's really nothing to it. An easy way to save 15 minutes: Don't press the tofu! Here, patting the tofu dry with paper towels before dredging the cubes in cornstarch is all that's needed to remove the excess surface moisture that might otherwise hinder crisping. Topped with the crispy tofu, fresh cilantro, and a squeeze of lime juice, this vibrant orange soup is an irresistible sweet-spicy, creamy-crispy master study in contrasts. If you don't have a blender, an immersion blender or food processor will also work. For the 7 ounces of tofu called for here, start by cutting a 14-ounce block of tofu in half crosswise. For ways to use up leftover coconut milk and tofu, see pages 18–19.

1 Heat 2 teaspoons oil in large saucepan over medium-high heat until shimmering. Add carrots and cook until softened and lightly browned, 5 to 7 minutes. Stir in curry paste and cook until fragrant, about 1 minute. Stir in broth and coconut milk, scraping up any browned bits, and bring to simmer. Reduce heat to medium, partially cover, and cook until carrots are tender, 8 to 10 minutes.

2 Transfer carrot mixture and one-third of tofu pieces to blender and process until smooth, about 2 minutes, scraping down sides of blender jar as needed. Return soup to now-empty saucepan and return to brief simmer over medium heat. Adjust consistency with extra hot broth as needed. Off heat, stir in lime zest and juice and season with salt and pepper to taste.

3 Toss remaining two-thirds of tofu pieces gently with cornstarch in bowl until well coated. Transfer to fine-mesh strainer and shake gently to remove excess cornstarch. Heat remaining 1 tablespoon oil in 10- or 12-inch nonstick skillet over medium-high heat until shimmering. Add tofu and cook, turning tofu as needed, until crispy and lightly browned on all sides, 8 to 10 minutes. Transfer tofu to paper towel–lined plate and season with salt and pepper to taste.

4 Top individual portions of soup with tofu and cilantro. Serve with lime wedges. (Soup, prepared through step 2, can be refrigerated for up to 3 days; prepare tofu croutons just before serving.)

SOUPS, STEWS, AND CHILIS

Sweet Potato and Peanut Soup

SERVES 2

TOTAL TIME 40 minutes

- 2 teaspoons vegetable oil
- 1 small onion, chopped fine
- 1 small red bell pepper (4 ounces), chopped fine
- 2 garlic cloves, minced
- ½ teaspoon ground coriander
- ⅛ teaspoon cayenne pepper (optional)
- 2 cups vegetable broth, plus extra as needed
- 1 pound sweet potatoes, peeled and cut into ½-inch pieces
- ½ cup dry-roasted unsalted peanuts, chopped coarse, divided
- ⅛ teaspoon table salt
- 2 tablespoons chopped fresh cilantro

Kitchen Improv

USE WHAT YOU'VE GOT

Substitute other root vegetables, such as carrots or yams, or winter squash, such as butternut or sweet pumpkin, for sweet potatoes. Substitute other fresh herbs, such as tarragon, chives, or parsley, for cilantro.

LEVEL UP

Top with plant-based yogurt or sour cream.

WHY THIS RECIPE WORKS   Move over, grape jelly: This soup, inspired by the peanut and sweet potato soups beloved throughout several West African cuisines, proves that the humble sweet potato is actually a peanut's perfect mate. The combination of the sweet potatoes' satiatingly starchy sweetness and the peanuts' toasty, nutty crunch is hard to beat. To get this soup on the table in a weeknight-appropriate time frame, we pare the ingredient list down to just the essentials—the namesake potatoes and peanuts; onion, bell pepper, and garlic for savory depth; broth for the right soupy consistency; and a few judiciously chosen spices and herbs. We soften the onion and bell pepper over medium heat before adding garlic, warm and citrusy coriander, and a smidge of cayenne to the pot to bloom their flavors. After stirring in the broth, sweet potatoes, and half of the peanuts, we let everything simmer until the vegetables are tender enough to blend into a smooth puree. The remaining peanuts we save until the end to use as a garnish, ensuring that they stay nice and crunchy to offer contrast with the smooth soup. If you don't have a blender, an immersion blender or a food processor will also work. Serve with crusty bread or crackers.

1   Heat oil in large saucepan over medium heat until shimmering. Add onion and bell pepper and cook until softened, 3 to 5 minutes. Stir in garlic; coriander; and cayenne, if using; and cook until fragrant, about 30 seconds.

2   Stir in broth, scraping up any browned bits, then stir in potatoes, ¼ cup peanuts, and salt. Bring to simmer, partially cover, and cook until sweet potatoes are tender, 10 to 15 minutes.

3   Process sweet potato mixture in blender until smooth, about 2 minutes, scraping down sides of blender jar as needed. Return soup to now-empty saucepan and return to brief simmer over medium heat. Adjust consistency with extra hot broth as needed. Off heat, season with salt and pepper to taste. Top individual portions with cilantro and remaining peanuts before serving. (Soup can be refrigerated for up to 3 days.)

Vegetable Chowder
WITH DIJON-PANKO TOPPING

SERVES 2

TOTAL TIME 1 hour

- 3 tablespoons panko bread crumbs
- 4 teaspoons extra-virgin olive oil, divided
- 1½ teaspoons Dijon mustard
- ¼ teaspoon lemon zest plus 1 teaspoon juice, plus lemon wedges for serving
- 1 small fennel bulb (8 ounces), fronds minced, stalks discarded, bulb halved, cored, and sliced thin
- 1 small onion, chopped fine
- 3 garlic cloves, minced
- 1 teaspoon minced fresh thyme or ¼ teaspoon dried
- ¼ cup dry white wine
- 2 cups vegetable broth, plus extra as needed
- 1 cup water
- 12 ounces red potatoes, unpeeled, cut into ½-inch pieces, divided
- 8 ounces cauliflower florets, cut into ½-inch pieces, divided

Kitchen Improv

USE WHAT YOU'VE GOT

Substitute dry vermouth for wine. Substitute Yukon Gold potatoes or celery root for red potatoes. Substitute other fresh herbs, such as tarragon, chives, basil, or parsley, for fennel fronds.

WHY THIS RECIPE WORKS This supercreamy, completely dairy-free vegetable chowder is at once refined and cozy, the perfect centerpiece for a wintry date night in or a casual night spent streaming a show on the couch—your pick. The key to the chowder's creaminess lies not in any store-bought dairy substitute, but in the vegetables themselves, namely cauliflower and potatoes, which are blended into a thick, silky base. The rest of the chowder's intrigue is all in how you dress it up: Here we go for a crispy lemon-mustard bread crumb topping plus a garnish of minced fennel fronds to complement the anise-scented fennel in the chowder. An onion provides aromatic backbone; garlic and woodsy thyme give it grown-up, slightly elevated flair; and a dash of white wine adds the complex hint of acidity that makes this soup taste truly special. Blending only a portion of the vegetables gives the chowder pleasing textural contrast. If you don't have a blender, an immersion blender or a food processor will also work. For ways to use up leftover cauliflower, see page 18.

1 Microwave panko and 1 teaspoon oil in bowl, stirring occasionally, until golden, 2 to 4 minutes; let cool completely. Stir in mustard and lemon zest and season with salt and pepper to taste; set aside.

2 Heat remaining 1 tablespoon oil in large saucepan over medium heat until shimmering. Add sliced fennel and onion and cook until softened and lightly browned, 5 to 7 minutes. Stir in garlic and thyme and cook until fragrant, about 30 seconds. Stir in wine, scraping up any browned bits, and cook until mostly evaporated, about 1 minute.

3 Stir in broth, water, half of potatoes, and half of cauliflower. Bring to simmer, partially cover, and cook until vegetables are tender, 8 to 12 minutes.

4 Process potato-cauliflower mixture in blender until smooth, about 2 minutes, scraping down sides of blender jar as needed. Return mixture to now-empty saucepan and stir in remaining potatoes. Bring to simmer over medium heat, partially cover, and cook, stirring occasionally, until potatoes are tender, 8 to 10 minutes.

5 Stir in remaining cauliflower, return to simmer, and cook, uncovered, until cauliflower is tender, about 5 minutes. Adjust consistency with extra hot broth as needed. Off heat, stir in lemon juice and season with salt and pepper to taste. Top individual portions with panko mixture and fennel fronds. Serve with lemon wedges. (Topping can be stored in airtight container at room temperature for up to 3 days. Chowder can be refrigerated for up to 3 days.)

SOUPS, STEWS, AND CHILIS

Corn and Poblano Chowder

WITH TEMPEH CHORIZO

SERVES 2

TOTAL TIME 40 minutes

- 2 teaspoons vegetable oil
- 3 cups frozen corn, thawed and patted dry
- 2 poblano chiles, stemmed, seeded, and chopped
- 3 garlic cloves, minced
- 1 teaspoon chili powder
- 1½ cups vegetable broth, plus extra as needed
- ⅛ teaspoon table salt
- 2 teaspoons lime juice, plus lime wedges for serving
- 1 recipe Chorizo Tempeh Crumbles (page 27)
- ¼ cup chopped fresh cilantro

Kitchen Improv

USE WHAT YOU'VE GOT

Substitute crumbled tortilla chips, pita chips, or croutons for chorizo tempeh. Substitute fresh corn kernels for frozen. Substitute other fresh herbs, such as parsley or mint, for cilantro.

LEVEL UP

In addition to chorizo tempeh, top soup with plant-based yogurt, crumbled plant-based cheese, diced avocado, sliced radishes, and/or pickled onions, jalapeños, or banana peppers.

WHY THIS RECIPE WORKS Elote is a popular Mexican street food of corn on the cob slathered with crema and sprinkled liberally with spices and cheese. We love elote's entrancing combination of salty, spicy, tangy, rich flavors so much that we used it as the inspiration for this vegan chowder. Opting for frozen corn makes this summery soup a viable year-round option— a good thing, since after tasting it we want to eat it all the time. Sautéing the thawed corn until lightly browned deepens the kernels' sweetness and adds a pleasant light char note. For some heat, an absolute must in this dish, we add a couple of poblanos and a teaspoon of chili powder. And to give it the optimal creamy-yet-rustic texture, we process a portion of the vegetables and broth in a blender, leaving the rest intact. Garnishes of lime juice and cilantro add bright, citrusy freshness, but the chowder's crowning glory is the crumbled tempeh topping that comes together in the microwave; we season it with chile powder and cumin to mimic the flavor of Mexican-style chorizo. If you don't have a blender, an immersion blender or a food processor will also work; if using an immersion blender, pulse corn mixture in saucepan in step 4 until mixture is thickened slightly, about 5 pulses.

1 Heat oil in large saucepan over medium-high heat until shimmering. Add corn and cook until lightly browned, 3 to 5 minutes. Add poblanos, reduce heat to medium, and cook until softened and lightly browned, 5 to 7 minutes.

2 Stir in garlic and chili powder and cook until fragrant, about 30 seconds. Stir in broth and salt, scraping up browned bits, and bring to simmer. Cook until vegetables are tender, about 2 minutes.

3 Process 2 cups corn mixture in blender until smooth, about 2 minutes, scraping down sides of blender jar as needed, then return to saucepan with remaining corn mixture. Return soup to brief simmer over medium heat. Adjust consistency with extra hot broth as needed. Off heat, stir in lime juice and season with salt and pepper to taste. Top individual portions with chorizo tempeh and cilantro. Serve with lime wedges. (Chowder can be refrigerated for up to 3 days.)

Sun-Dried Tomato and White Bean Soup

SERVES 2

TOTAL TIME 25 minutes

1 (15-ounce) can small white beans

1¼ cups vegetable broth, plus extra as needed

3 tablespoons oil-packed sun-dried tomatoes, patted dry and chopped, plus 1 tablespoon tomato oil

1 tablespoon shredded fresh basil, plus extra for serving

2 tablespoons grated plant-based Parmesan cheese

Kitchen Improv

USE WHAT YOU'VE GOT

Substitute other canned white beans, such as cannellini or navy, for small white beans.

LEVEL UP

Top with toasted nuts, seeds, croutons, or Umami Croutons (page 27).

MAKE IT A SOUP-AND-SANDWICH COMBO

Serve with Grilled Cheese Sandwiches with Caramelized Onion and Apple (page 106).

WHY THIS RECIPE WORKS   Cans of tomato soup concentrate may evoke childhood nostalgia, but the happy memories end there. For a more grown-up version that's heartier, tastier, and almost as easy to throw together as the concentrated stuff, we make use of an unexpected ingredient: canned white beans and their liquid. The beans provide the soup with a velvety back-drop, buttery nuttiness, and subtle earthiness, not to mention plenty of protein for long-lasting satisfaction. To keep the grown-up vibe going, instead of canned tomatoes we use sweet, tangy sun-dried tomatoes, which are so potent that a mere 3 tablespoons is plenty to make their tomatoey mark on the soup once simmered and blended in. A couple tablespoons of plant-based Parmesan cheese and fresh basil give the soup an irresistibly salty, rich, and aromatic finish. If you don't have a blender, an immersion blender or food processor will also work. You can use store-bought plant-based Parmesan or our Cashew Parmesan (page 23) in this recipe. Serve with crusty bread or crackers.

1   Bring beans and their liquid, broth, tomatoes, and tomato oil to simmer over medium heat in large saucepan and cook until beans begin to break down, 5 to 7 minutes.

2   Process bean mixture in blender until smooth, about 2 minutes, scraping down sides of blender jar as needed. Return soup to now-empty saucepan and return to brief simmer over medium heat. Adjust consistency with extra hot broth as needed. Off heat, stir in basil and season with salt and pepper to taste. Top individual portions with Parmesan and extra basil before serving. (Soup can be refrigerated for up to 3 days.)

SOUPS, STEWS, AND CHILIS

Skillet-Roasted Garlic and Chickpea Soup

SERVES 2

TOTAL TIME 30 minutes

- 4 garlic cloves, unpeeled
- 1 (15-ounce) can chickpeas
- 1¼ cups vegetable broth, plus extra as needed
- 1 tablespoon extra-virgin olive oil
- 1 tablespoon minced fresh parsley
- 1 tablespoon lemon juice

Kitchen Improv

USE WHAT YOU'VE GOT

Substitute other canned beans, such as cannellini or navy, for chickpeas. Substitute other fresh herbs, such as tarragon or chives, for parsley. Substitute wine vinegar for lemon juice.

LEVEL UP

Top with garlic chips, toasted nuts, seeds, croutons, Umami Croutons (page 27), and/or a drizzle of tahini.

WHY THIS RECIPE WORKS Through the power of garlic and an ordinary blender, a humble can of chickpeas is transformed into a creamy, playful hummus-inspired soup in 30 minutes flat. To coax deep, nuanced flavor from such simple ingredients, we start by toasting skin-on garlic cloves in a clean, dry saucepan until they turn a beautiful golden color and become intensely fragrant. This skillet-toasting technique yields garlic with a mellow, roasty, mildly sweet flavor like that of oven-roasted garlic in a fraction of the time. We then peel the garlic, return it to the saucepan with some broth and a full can of chickpeas and their liquid (the starchy bean liquid adds luscious body to the broth), and then blend the soup until smooth and velvety. A splash of lemon juice and sprinkle of parsley are more than just finishing elements here—their bright freshness cuts through the rich soup and invigorates the soup's taste. If you don't have a blender, an immersion blender or food processor will also work. Serve with crusty bread or crackers.

1 Toast garlic in large saucepan over medium heat, stirring occasionally, until fragrant and skins are just beginning to brown, 3 to 5 minutes. Remove garlic from saucepan and let cool slightly.

2 Once cool enough to handle, peel garlic and return to now-empty saucepan; discard skins. Add chickpeas and their liquid, broth, and oil. Bring to simmer over medium heat and cook until chickpeas begin to break down, 5 to 7 minutes.

3 Process chickpea mixture in blender until smooth, about 2 minutes, scraping down sides of blender jar as needed. Return soup to now-empty saucepan and return to brief simmer over medium heat. Adjust consistency with extra hot broth as needed. Off heat, stir in parsley and lemon juice and season with salt and pepper to taste. Serve. (Soup can be refrigerated for up to 3 days.)

Moong Dal
WITH TOMATOES, SPINACH, AND COCONUT

SERVES 2
TOTAL TIME 40 minutes

- 1 tomato, cored and chopped
- 2 tablespoons chopped fresh cilantro
- 1 tablespoon lime juice, plus lime wedges for serving
- 1 jalapeño chile, stemmed, seeded, and minced, divided
- 2 teaspoons vegetable oil
- 1 small onion, chopped fine
- 1 tablespoon grated fresh ginger
- 2 garlic cloves, minced
- 1 teaspoon ground cumin
- ½ teaspoon ground turmeric
- 2½ cups vegetable broth, plus extra as needed
- 1 cup water
- ¾ cup split mung beans, picked over and rinsed
- ⅓ cup canned coconut milk
- 2 ounces frozen chopped spinach, thawed and squeezed dry

Kitchen Improv

USE WHAT YOU'VE GOT

Substitute plant-based yogurt for coconut milk. Substitute frozen chopped kale for spinach. Substitute other fresh herbs, such as tarragon, chives, or parsley, for cilantro.

LEVEL UP

Drizzle with Fennel Oil (page 26) before serving.

WHY THIS RECIPE WORKS   In India, "dal" is the word both for beans and lentils and for the thick stews made from them. Moong dal is a version made with nutty-tasting split mung beans, which take only 10 or so minutes to cook and give this plant-based dish oodles of staying power thanks to their high protein and fiber content. To create a deeply aromatic flavor base, we first brown an onion in oil to bring out its sweeter side. We then add ginger, garlic, cumin, turmeric, and jalapeño to the oil to bloom the flavors of the spices and aromatics before the broth and mung beans are added. Once cooked, the beans are so tender that just a quick whisk causes them to break down completely, transforming the dish from a brothy bean soup into a thick and hearty stew. Coconut milk stirred in at the end helps marry all the flavors as well as temper the spice slightly with a touch of its cooling richness. Finally, a topping of chopped tomato, cilantro, lime juice, and more jalapeño provides a punch of acidity and spice. If you can't find split mung beans (moong dal), you can substitute split red lentils; do not use yellow lentils or split pigeon peas (toor dal). For ways to use up leftover coconut milk, see page 18.

1   Combine tomato, cilantro, lime juice, and half of jalapeño in small bowl. Season with salt and pepper to taste; set aside.

2   Heat oil in large saucepan over medium heat until shimmering. Add onion and cook until softened and lightly browned, 5 to 7 minutes. Stir in ginger, garlic, cumin, turmeric, and remaining jalapeño and cook until fragrant, about 1 minute.

3   Stir in broth and water, scraping up any browned bits, then stir in beans and bring to simmer. Cook, partially covered, until beans begin to break down, 10 to 12 minutes.

4   Whisk soup vigorously until beans are completely broken down and soup is thickened, about 30 seconds. Stir in coconut milk and spinach, return to simmer, and cook until spinach is heated through, about 2 minutes. Adjust consistency with extra hot broth as needed. Off heat, season with salt and pepper to taste. Top individual portions with tomato mixture before serving. (Soup can be refrigerated for up to 3 days.)

Okra Pepper Pot

SERVES 2

TOTAL TIME 45 minutes

2   teaspoons vegetable oil

1   small red bell pepper
    (4 ounces), stemmed,
    seeded, and chopped fine

2   teaspoons tomato paste

1   teaspoon minced fresh thyme
    or ¼ teaspoon dried

¼   teaspoon allspice

1½ cups vegetable broth

1   small sweet potato
    (8 ounces), peeled and
    cut into 1-inch pieces

1   small Scotch bonnet chile,
    stemmed, seeded, and minced

¼   teaspoon table salt

6   ounces collard greens,
    stemmed and chopped into
    1-inch pieces

12 ounces frozen cut okra

¼   cup canned coconut milk

1   tablespoon minced
    fresh cilantro

    Lime wedges

WHY THIS RECIPE WORKS   Caribbean pepper pot, a stew packed with hot peppers and greens, is usually flavored with beef, mutton, or pork, but is so naturally flavorful that you'll never miss the meat in this vegan version. Okra and cassava (a starchy tuber, also known as yuca, used widely throughout Latin American and Caribbean cuisines) are traditional pepper pot vegetables; here, we keep the okra in a starring role, but because prepping cassava for consumption is a relatively lengthy process, we choose to swap in similarly starchy sweet potatoes. As for the supporting players, we add hearty collard greens, allspice (another Caribbean staple), and earthy thyme, which together produce an incredibly complex aroma. A single Scotch bonnet chile is all it takes to give this dish its traditional heat, which we tamp down ever so slightly with the addition of rich coconut milk. The gelatinous substance released by the cooked okra helps naturally thicken the stew. We recommend wearing gloves while handling the chile. For ways to use up leftover coconut milk, see page 18.

1   Heat oil in large saucepan over medium heat until shimmering. Add bell pepper and cook until softened, about 5 minutes. Stir in tomato paste, thyme, and allspice and cook until fragrant, about 30 seconds. Stir in broth, scraping up any browned bits, then stir in sweet potato, Scotch bonnet, and salt. Bring to simmer, partially cover, and cook until sweet potato is just tender, 4 to 6 minutes.

2   Add collard greens, 1 handful at a time, and cook, stirring occasionally, until wilted, about 2 minutes. Stir in okra, return to simmer, and cook until potato and okra are fully tender, 5 to 10 minutes. Off heat, stir in coconut milk and cilantro and season with salt and pepper to taste. Serve with lime wedges. (Soup can be refrigerated for up to 3 days.)

SOUPS, STEWS, AND CHILIS

Kitchen Improv

USE WHAT YOU'VE GOT

Substitute small habanero or jalapeño chile for Scotch bonnet.
Substitute fresh kale or frozen, thawed kale or collard greens for
fresh collard greens. Substitute fresh okra for frozen: Toss okra
with ½ teaspoon salt and let drain in colander for 1 hour; rinse well
and cut into ½-inch pieces before adding.

BULK IT UP

Add cubed tofu or canned black-eyed peas.

Summer Vegetable Stew

SERVES 2

TOTAL TIME 1¼ hours

- 1 Yukon Gold potato (8 ounces), peeled and cut into ½-inch pieces
- 3 tablespoons extra-virgin olive oil, divided, plus extra for drizzling
- 1 small eggplant (8 ounces), cut into 1-inch pieces
- 1 (14.5-ounce) can whole peeled tomatoes, drained with juice reserved
- 3 garlic cloves, minced
- 1 teaspoon tomato paste
- ½ teaspoon minced fresh oregano or ¼ teaspoon dried
- ¼ teaspoon pepper
- 1½ cups vegetable broth
- 1½ cups water
- 1 small zucchini (8 ounces), halved lengthwise, seeded, and cut into 1-inch pieces
- 2 tablespoons chopped fresh basil
  Grated plant-based Parmesan cheese (optional)

WHY THIS RECIPE WORKS Italy's answer to ratatouille, giambotta is a dish that transforms a bounty of summer vegetables into a fresh, satisfying stew. But given that the stew typically includes zucchini, tomatoes, and eggplant, it's all too easy to wind up eating leftovers all week long if you go a bit too heavy on the vegetables. Our version keeps the quantity in check, calling for just one small eggplant, zucchini, and a single can of tomatoes. Browning the eggplant and sautéing the tomatoes before adding the vegetable broth drives off their excess moisture and amps up their flavor. A little tomato paste adds even more concentrated tomato flavor, and just one buttery Yukon Gold potato provides the dish with plenty of starch and heft; jump-starting the potato's cooking in the microwave ensures that it reaches tenderness at the same time as the other vegetables. Finished with a sprinkle of fresh basil and a drizzle of oil, this is a stew you can, and should, enjoy all summer long. Do not peel the eggplant, as the skin helps hold it together during cooking. You can use store-bought plant-based Parmesan or our Cashew Parmesan (page 23) in this recipe. Serve with crusty bread or crackers.

1 Toss potato with 1 teaspoon oil and microwave in covered bowl until just softened, about 5 minutes. Heat 2 tablespoons oil in large saucepan over medium-high heat until shimmering. Add eggplant and cook until softened and lightly browned, 5 to 7 minutes; transfer to bowl.

2 Heat remaining 2 teaspoons oil in now-empty saucepan over medium heat until shimmering. Stir in tomatoes, garlic, tomato paste, oregano, and pepper and cook until mixture is dry and beginning to brown, 11 to 13 minutes.

3 Stir in broth, water, and reserved tomato juice, scraping up any browned bits, then stir in zucchini, potato, and eggplant. Bring to simmer, partially cover, and cook until vegetables are tender and liquid has thickened, 25 to 35 minutes. Off heat, stir in basil and season with salt and pepper to taste. Top individual portions with Parmesan, if using, and drizzle with extra oil before serving. (Stew can be refrigerated for up to 3 days.)

Kitchen Improv

USE WHAT YOU'VE GOT

Substitute summer squash for zucchini. Substitute other root vegetables, such as parsnips, turnips, rutabaga, or celery root, for potato. Substitute other fresh herbs, such as mint, chives, or parsley, for basil.

LEVEL UP

Top with toasted nuts, seeds, croutons, or Umami Croutons (page 27).

BULK IT UP

Add canned cannellini, navy, lima, or small white beans.

SOUPS, STEWS, AND CHILIS

Green Bean, Tomato, and Bulgur Stew

SERVES 2

TOTAL TIME 1 hour

- 1 tablespoon extra-virgin olive oil
- 1 small onion, chopped fine
- 8 ounces green beans, trimmed and cut into 1-inch lengths
- 2 garlic cloves, minced
- 1½ teaspoons tomato paste
- ¼ cup dry white wine
- 1 (14.5-ounce) can fire-roasted diced tomatoes
- 2 cups water
- ¼ cup medium-grind bulgur, rinsed
- ¼ teaspoon table salt
- 1 tablespoon chopped fresh oregano or 1 teaspoon dried

Kitchen Improv

USE WHAT YOU'VE GOT

Substitute dry vermouth for wine. Substitute traditional diced tomatoes for fire-roasted tomatoes. Substitute coarse-grind bulgur for medium-grind and adjust cooking time as needed; do not substitute fine-grind bulgur. Substitute other fresh herbs, such as parsley, mint, or marjoram, for oregano.

LEVEL UP

Top with plant-based yogurt or plant-based sour cream, or drizzle with harissa or another infused oil before serving.

WHY THIS RECIPE WORKS   Inspired by the many intriguing iterations of tomato and bean stew found throughout Turkey, we came up with a stew that's tangy, smoky, filling, and unbelievably easy. To make the whole thing in one pot, the key is to stagger the cooking so the ingredients that need the most time go in first, followed by those that cook more quickly. We start by cooking onion and green beans until softened and lightly browned and then move on to the other pillars of the stew's flavor: garlic, tomato paste, and white wine. Fire-roasted tomatoes add just a hint of smokiness without requiring extra prep time or cooking vessels. To add some heft to our soup we throw in a couple handfuls of bulgur, a versatile grain made from parboiled cracked wheat. When stirred into a stew, bulgur absorbs the broth's flavors and releases starch into the remaining liquid, thickening it. Since bulgur is so quick-cooking, we stir it in toward the end, giving it just enough time to become tender before serving. When shopping, don't confuse bulgur with cracked wheat, which has a much longer cooking time and will not work in this recipe. For ways to use up leftover green beans, see page 18.

1   Heat oil in large saucepan over medium heat until shimmering. Add onion and green beans and cook until onion is softened and lightly browned, 6 to 8 minutes. Stir in garlic and tomato paste and cook until fragrant, about 30 seconds.

2   Stir in wine, scraping up any browned bits, and cook until reduced by half, about 30 seconds. Stir in tomatoes and their juice and cook until tomatoes begin to break down, about 10 minutes.

3   Stir in water, bulgur, and salt and bring to simmer. Reduce heat to low, cover, and cook until bulgur is tender, about 20 minutes. Off heat, stir in oregano and season with salt and pepper to taste. Serve. (Soup can be refrigerated for up to 3 days.)

Weeknight Meaty Chili

SERVES 2

TOTAL TIME 45 minutes

- 1 tablespoon vegetable oil
- 1 small onion, chopped fine
- 1½ tablespoons chili powder
- 2 garlic cloves, minced
- 1 teaspoon ground cumin
- 4 ounces plant-based ground meat
- ½ cup water
- 1 (15-ounce) can red kidney beans, rinsed
- 1 (14.5-ounce) can diced fire-roasted tomatoes
- 2 tablespoons chopped fresh cilantro leaves

Kitchen Improv

USE WHAT YOU'VE GOT

Substitute other canned beans, such as cannellini, black, or pinto, for red kidney beans.

LEVEL UP

Serve with lime wedges, chopped avocado, plant-based sour cream, plant-based shredded cheese, pickled jalapeños, tortilla chips, hot sauce, and/or salsa.

WHY THIS RECIPE WORKS This speedy, family-friendly chili is a win-win for dedicated vegans and meat-lovers alike, rich and meaty without any animal involvement whatsoever thanks to modern plant-based meat. To create a chili that feels familiar (nostalgic, even), we build an aromatic base from onion and garlic plus chili powder and cumin for heat and sweet earthiness. We then add the plant-based meat and cook just until it begins forming firm crumbles, a sign that it's cooked through, before adding a splash of water and scraping up the flavorful browned bits (fond) from the bottom of the skillet. Convenient canned kidney beans bulk up the chili and, as in our Green Bean, Tomato, and Bulgur Stew (page 95), a can of fire-roasted tomatoes provides the requisite tomatoey smokiness—no need to break out a rimmed baking sheet or turn on the broiler. You will need a 12-inch nonstick skillet with a tight-fitting lid for this recipe; the chili will overfill a smaller skillet. For ways to use up leftover plant-based meat, see page 19.

1   Heat oil in 12-inch nonstick skillet over medium heat until shimmering. Add onion and cook until softened and lightly browned, 5 to 7 minutes. Stir in chili powder, garlic, and cumin and cook until fragrant, about 30 seconds. Stir in ground meat and cook, breaking up meat with wooden spoon, until firm crumbles form, about 3 minutes.

2   Stir in water, scraping up any browned bits, then stir in beans and tomatoes and their juice. Bring to simmer, partially cover, and cook until beans begin to break down and liquid is slightly thickened, 20 to 25 minutes. Off heat, stir in cilantro and season with salt and pepper to taste. Serve. (Chili can be refrigerated for up to 3 days.)

Green Jackfruit Chili

SERVES 2
TOTAL TIME 45 minutes

- 1 (14.5-ounce) can young green jackfruit packed in brine or water, drained (2 cups)
- 4 ounces tomatillos, husks and stems removed, rinsed well
- 2 poblano chiles, stemmed, seeded, and quartered
- 1 small onion, quartered
- 1 jalapeño chile, stemmed, halved, and seeded
- 4 garlic cloves, smashed and peeled
- 2 tablespoons vegetable oil
- ½ cup chopped fresh cilantro, divided
- 3 cups vegetable broth
- 1 (15-ounce) can cannellini beans, rinsed
- 1 teaspoon ground cumin
- ¼ teaspoon table salt

Kitchen Improv

USE WHAT YOU'VE GOT

Substitute canned whole tomatillos for fresh. Substitute other canned beans, such as black, pinto, or kidney, for cannellini beans.

LEVEL UP

Serve with lime wedges, chopped avocado, plant-based sour cream or shredded cheese, sliced fresh or pickled jalapeños, tortilla chips, hot sauce, and/or salsa.

WHY THIS RECIPE WORKS   When ripe, the colossal jackfruit tastes like a combination of papaya, pineapple, and mango. But unripe, green jackfruit is vegetal, dense, and fibrous, tasting more like an artichoke heart with a faintly floral aroma than a fruit. Green jackfruit is generally sold canned in brine, the large fruit cut into smaller segments which soften upon cooking; the fibrous pieces break down to give it the appearance and texture of shredded pork or chicken. Drawing inspiration from traditional chicken chili, we sub jackfruit for the chicken to make our version a vegan-friendly cool-weather feast. The unripe jackfruit is far from the only green element in this green chili; we also incorporate poblano and jalapeño chiles, tomatillos, and cilantro for an herbaceous, tangy, slightly spicy, and undeniably verdant mix. Cannellini beans add protein as well as a welcome creamy texture that contrasts with the texture of the shredded jackfruit. Be sure to use young (unripe) jackfruit packed in brine or water; do not use mature jackfruit packed in syrup. Jackfruit seeds are tender and edible; there's no need to remove them.

1   Adjust oven rack 6 inches from broiler element and heat broiler. Line rimmed baking sheet with aluminum foil; set aside. Place jackfruit in large saucepan, cover with water, and bring to boil over high heat. Reduce heat to medium and simmer for 10 minutes. Drain jackfruit, rinse well, and drain again. Transfer jackfruit to cutting board. Using potato masher or 2 forks, shred jackfruit into bite-size pieces; set aside.

2   Meanwhile, toss tomatillos, poblanos, onion, jalapeño, and garlic with oil, then arrange on prepared sheet with chiles skin side up. Broil until vegetables blacken and start to soften, 5 to 8 minutes, rotating sheet halfway through broiling. Let cool for 10 minutes, then remove skins from poblanos (leave tomatillo and jalapeño skins intact). Transfer vegetables to food processor, add ¼ cup cilantro, and pulse until coarsely chopped, 4 to 6 pulses.

3   Add tomatillo mixture, jackfruit, broth, beans, cumin, and salt to now-empty saucepan. Bring to simmer over medium heat and cook until beans are tender and liquid is slightly thickened, 8 to 12 minutes. Off heat, stir in remaining cilantro and season with salt and pepper to taste. (Chili can be refrigerated for up to 3 days.)

102 Packable Pita Sandwiches with Hummus, Arugula, and Tomato

with Ricotta, Basil, and Roasted Red Peppers

105 Chickpea Salad Sandwiches

Curried Chickpea Salad Sandwiches with Raisins

106 Grilled Cheese Sandwiches with Caramelized Onion and Apple

with Tomato and Pesto

109 Tofu Katsu Sandwiches

111 Philly-Style Broccoli Rabe, Portobello, and Cheese Sandwiches

112 Buffalo Cauliflower Wraps

114 Tempeh Larb Lettuce Wraps

117 Grilled Kofte Wraps

118 Shawarma-Spiced Tofu Wraps with Sumac Onion

120 Not-from-a-Box Weeknight Tacos

123 Citrusy Jackfruit Tacos

125 Spiced Cauliflower Burgers

126 Make-Ahead Lentil and Mushroom Burgers

129 Portobello Mushroom Burgers with Sriracha Slaw

130 Garlic and Herb Burgers with Beet Tzatziki

132 Grilled Flatbread with Kale and Apple

135 Artichoke and Spinach Calzones

Broccoli and Roasted Red Pepper Calzones

Packable Pita Sandwiches
WITH HUMMUS, ARUGULA, AND TOMATO

SERVES 2

TOTAL TIME 15 minutes

- 2 (6-inch) pitas
- ¼ cup hummus
- 2 teaspoons chopped fresh mint
- ¼ teaspoon table salt
- ⅛ teaspoon red pepper flakes
- 1 ounce (1 cup) baby arugula
- 1 small tomato, cored and sliced thin
- ¼ cup dill pickle chips

Kitchen Improv

USE WHAT YOU'VE GOT

Substitute ¼ cup mashed canned white beans for hummus. Substitute baby spinach or baby kale for arugula. Substitute other fresh herbs, such as chives, dill, tarragon, parsley, or basil, for mint. Substitute other pickled vegetables for pickle chips.

BULK IT UP

Add tempeh crumbles (page 27), Pan-Seared Tofu, or Scrambled Plant-Based Egg (pages 274–275) to sandwiches.

WHY THIS RECIPE WORKS Folded up in a soft pita, savory, creamy hummus, crunchy pickles, fresh tomato, and peppery arugula team up to create these bright and lively all-vegan sandwiches. Even better, the sandwiches can be assembled and refrigerated up to a day ahead of time, making them a perfect packable lunch option or light make-ahead dinner. In fact, a rest gives the flavors of the sandwiches time to meld and become even more potent—as long as excess moisture from the pickles and tomato doesn't cause the pita to sog out. The key to preventing soggy sandwiches is all in the construction. Instead of cutting the pita open and stuffing all the ingredients on the inside, we instead layer them on the pitas' surface and simply fold the pitas over. The double wall of pita helps prevent moisture-induced mushiness, and a smear of hummus also provides another moisture barrier when layered between the pita and vegetables.

Lay pitas flat on cutting board. Spread 2 tablespoons hummus on top of each pita, leaving ½-inch border along edge, then sprinkle with mint, salt, and pepper flakes. Arrange ½ cup arugula over 1 half of each pita, then shingle tomato slices and pickle chips over top. Fold pitas in half and serve. (Sandwiches can be refrigerated for up to 24 hours.)

VARIATION
Packable Pita Sandwiches with Ricotta, Basil, and Roasted Red Peppers

You can use store-bought plant-based ricotta or our Cashew Ricotta (page 22) in this recipe.

Substitute plant-based ricotta for hummus, ½ cup fresh basil leaves for baby arugula, and 1 Persian cucumber, sliced thin, for pickle chips. Toss ½ cup chopped roasted red peppers with 2 teaspoons balsamic vinegar; substitute pepper mixture for tomato.

Chickpea Salad Sandwiches

SERVES 2

TOTAL TIME 15 minutes

- 1 (15-ounce) can chickpeas, rinsed, divided
- ¼ cup plant-based mayonnaise
- 2 teaspoons lemon juice
- ¼ teaspoon table salt
- 2 tablespoons minced celery
- 1 scallion, sliced thin
- 1 tablespoon minced fresh parsley
- 4 slices hearty sandwich bread, toasted if desired
- 1 small tomato, cored and sliced thin
- 2 leaves Bibb or Boston lettuce

Kitchen Improv

USE WHAT YOU'VE GOT

Substitute other canned beans, such as cannellini, navy, or small white beans, for chickpeas. Substitute 2 tablespoons minced shallot for scallion.

LEVEL UP

Layer sliced avocado, alfalfa sprouts, and/or pickled vegetables in sandwiches with tomato and lettuce.

MAKE IT A WRAP

Layer chickpea salad and toppings in pitas, lavashes, or flour tortillas to make wraps.

WHY THIS RECIPE WORKS   Is there anything that the humble chickpea can't do? Here, a single can of them is the perfect amount to yield two plant-based renditions of a classic deli egg salad sandwich. We start by mashing a few tablespoons of the tender beans with creamy plant-based mayo and tangy lemon juice until almost completely broken down and smooth before we stir in the rest of the chickpeas, mashing these lightly so that some larger pieces remain to give the chickpea salad its pleasingly coarse and homey texture. Using a potato masher means no dirtying a food processor, another time-saver in this already-quick recipe. Celery, scallion, and parsley also go into the mix to give the salad its familiar, comforting flavor profile before we sandwich it all between a couple slices of hearty bread. For a classic finish, you can't go wrong with juicy tomato and crisp lettuce, but for an even more generous sandwich, see our Level Up suggestions. You can use store-bought plant-based mayonnaise or our Aquafaba Mayonnaise (page 22) in this recipe.

1   Using potato masher or rubber spatula, mash 6 tablespoons chickpeas with mayonnaise, lemon juice, and salt in medium bowl until mostly smooth. Add remaining chickpeas and mash to coarse paste with some larger pieces remaining. Stir in celery, scallion, and parsley and season with salt and pepper to taste. (Chickpea salad can be refrigerated for up to 2 days.)

2   Divide chickpea salad over 2 slices of bread. Top with tomato, lettuce, and remaining bread slices. Serve.

VARIATION

Curried Chickpea Salad Sandwiches with Raisins

Mash 1 teaspoon curry powder with chickpeas. Add ¼ cup raisins with celery.

Grilled Cheese Sandwiches
WITH CARAMELIZED ONION AND APPLE

CARAMELIZED ONION

- 2 teaspoons extra-virgin olive oil
- 1 onion, halved and sliced thin
- 6 tablespoons water, divided
- ¼ teaspoon table salt
- ⅛ teaspoon pepper
- 1 teaspoon Dijon mustard
- ¼ teaspoon minced fresh thyme or pinch dried

SANDWICHES

- 4 (½-inch-thick) slices rustic bread
- 2 teaspoons extra-virgin olive oil, divided
- 1 small apple, cored and sliced thin
- 4 slices (3 ounces) plant-based cheddar cheese

Kitchen Improv

USE WHAT YOU'VE GOT

Substitute shallots for onion, pear for apple, or plant-based mozzarella for cheddar. Substitute 3 ounces plant-based cheddar cheese shreds for slices.

LEVEL UP

Spread 2 tablespoons fig jam or fruit chutney on non-oiled sides of bread slices before layering fillings. Stir up to 2 tablespoons chopped nuts into caramelized onion.

WHY THIS RECIPE WORKS Vegan cheese has come a very long way since its first iterations, and it's time it got some respect. These sandwiches are at once sophisticated and attainable, with sweet quick-caramelized onion, woodsy thyme, tangy mustard, and crisp apple all bound up with the melty plant-based cheese. Weighing the sandwiches down with a heavy Dutch oven helps the cheese melt more thoroughly for mess-free flipping; to save on dishes, we make the sandwiches in the same skillet we use to caramelize the onion. Any variety of sweet apple can be used here. We like to use rustic artisanal bread for this recipe; look for a wide loaf that will yield big slices. Wrap the bottom of your Dutch oven in aluminum foil for easy cleanup. You will need a 12-inch nonstick skillet with a tight-fitting lid for this recipe.

1 FOR THE CARAMELIZED ONION Heat oil in 12-inch nonstick skillet over medium heat until shimmering. Add onion, ¼ cup water, salt, and pepper, cover, and cook until onion has softened and water has evaporated, 5 to 7 minutes. Uncover, reduce heat to medium-low, and continue to cook, stirring occasionally, until onion is golden brown, 13 to 15 minutes longer.

2 Stir in remaining 2 tablespoons water, scraping up any browned bits, and cook until liquid evaporates, about 1 minute. Off heat, stir in mustard and thyme; transfer to small bowl and let cool slightly. (Caramelized onion can be refrigerated for up to 3 days.)

3 FOR THE SANDWICHES Place bread slices on cutting board and brush each slice with ½ teaspoon oil. Flip 2 slices oil-side down and arrange onion, apple, and cheddar in even layers on top. Arrange remaining 2 slices of bread on top oil-side up.

4 Wipe skillet clean with paper towels. Place sandwiches in now-empty skillet and weigh down with large pot or Dutch oven. Cook (keeping pot on sandwiches, but not pressing down) over medium-low heat until first side is golden brown, 5 to 7 minutes. Using 2 spatulas, carefully flip sandwiches, then replace pot and cook until second side is golden brown, 5 to 7 minutes. Serve.

VARIATION
Grilled Cheese Sandwiches with Tomato and Pesto
You can use store-bought fresh pesto or our Pesto (page 24) in this recipe.

Omit caramelized onion. Substitute 4 thin tomato slices for apple and plant-based mozzarella for cheddar. Spread 1 tablespoon pesto on non-oiled sides of bread slices before layering tomatoes and mozzarella.

Tofu Katsu Sandwiches

SERVES 2
TOTAL TIME 35 minutes

- 2 tablespoons ketchup
- 2 teaspoons vegan Worcestershire sauce
- 1 teaspoon soy sauce
- ½ teaspoon garlic powder
- ½ teaspoon sugar, divided
- 3 tablespoons liquid plant-based egg
- 1 tablespoon all-purpose flour
- ⅔ cup panko bread crumbs
- 7 ounces firm or extra-firm tofu
- ¼ teaspoon table salt
- ½ cup vegetable oil, for frying
- 1¼ teaspoons unseasoned rice vinegar
- ¾ teaspoon toasted sesame oil
- 1½ cups shredded red or green cabbage
- 4 slices soft white sandwich bread

Kitchen Improv

USE WHAT YOU'VE GOT

Substitute coleslaw mix or shredded iceberg lettuce for cabbage. Substitute burger buns or rolls for sandwich bread or serve tofu and cabbage mixture with rice.

LEVEL UP

Layer pickled vegetables, cilantro, sliced scallions, and/or sliced avocado in sandwiches with cabbage mixture.

WHY THIS RECIPE WORKS   Japanese katsu involves frying up a thin panko-breaded cutlet and serving it up with a sweet and savory tonkatsu sauce. The sandwiches of the same name take things a step further, layering the cutlets and sauce with shredded cabbage between slices of fluffy Japanese milk bread. Using tofu "cutlets" is the first step to re-creating this mouthwatering sandwich vegan-style. To help the panko crust adhere, we dredge slices of tofu in a mixture of flour and liquid plant-based egg, creating a glue-like paste that locks the panko in place. Ketchup, vegan Worcestershire, soy sauce, garlic powder, and a pinch of sugar make up the tonkatsu sauce. Last but not least is the crunchy cabbage, which needs nothing more than a quick toss with some rice vinegar, toasty sesame oil, and a pinch of sugar for seasoning before it, too, is ready to be piled atop the bread (soft white sandwich bread in lieu of milk bread) and drizzled with sauce. For the 7 ounces of tofu called for here, start by cutting a 14-ounce block of tofu in half crosswise. You will need a 10-inch nonstick skillet for this recipe; the tofu won't crisp as evenly in a larger skillet. For ways to use up leftover cabbage and tofu, see pages 18–19.

1   Whisk ketchup, Worcestershire, soy sauce, garlic powder, and ¼ teaspoon sugar together in small bowl; set aside.

2   Whisk egg and flour together in shallow dish. Place panko in large zipper-lock bag and lightly crush with rolling pin; transfer crumbs to second shallow dish. Slice tofu lengthwise into four ½-inch-thick slabs, pat dry with paper towels, and sprinkle with salt. Working with 1 slab at a time, dip tofu in egg mixture, allowing excess to drip off, then coat all sides with panko, pressing gently to adhere; transfer to large plate.

3   Place wire rack in rimmed baking sheet and line rack with triple layer of paper towels. Heat vegetable oil in 10-inch nonstick skillet over medium-high heat until shimmering. Add tofu and cook until deep golden brown, 2 to 3 minutes per side. Transfer tofu to prepared rack and let drain.

4   Combine vinegar, sesame oil, and remaining ¼ teaspoon sugar in small bowl. Add cabbage, toss to coat, and season with salt and pepper to taste. Arrange cabbage and tofu on 2 slices of bread. Drizzle with reserved sauce and top with remaining bread slices. Serve.

Philly-Style Broccoli Rabe, Portobello, and Cheese Sandwiches

SERVES 2

TOTAL TIME 40 minutes

- 2 tablespoons extra-virgin oil, divided
- 1 pound portobello mushroom caps, sliced ¼-inch thick
- 2 pinches table salt, divided
- ½ teaspoon fennel seeds, cracked
- ½ teaspoon minced fresh rosemary
- 4 slices (3 ounces) plant-based cheddar or mozzarella cheese
- 1 garlic clove, minced
- ⅛ teaspoon red pepper flakes
- 8 ounces broccoli rabe, trimmed, stems cut into 1-inch pieces, leaves and florets left whole
- 2 (8-inch) Italian sub rolls, split lengthwise and toasted
- 1 tablespoon sliced jarred hot cherry peppers (optional)

Kitchen Improv

USE WHAT YOU'VE GOT

Substitute quartered cremini or white mushrooms for portobellos and broccolini for broccoli rabe. Substitute 3 ounces shredded plant-based cheese for sliced cheese. Substitute chopped pepperoncini or giardiniera for cherry peppers.

WHY THIS RECIPE WORKS Stuff a sub roll with spicy, garlicky broccoli rabe, plus meaty portobellos and melty plant-based cheese, and you've got an uber-satisfying hoagie to rival any found in Philly. To cook a full pound of mushrooms (our stand-in for the traditional pork) in a single batch, we start by covering the crowded pan with a lid, trapping in the heat and forcing the portobellos to shed their excess moisture quickly before we uncover the pan to cook off that liquid and allow the mushrooms to brown. Fennel and rosemary add piney, sausagey flavor to the savory mushrooms, and re-covering the pan after layering on the cheese slices helps melt the cheese and keeps everything warm while we turn our attention to the broccoli rabe. It takes just a few minutes to broil the broccoli rabe, which tames its bitterness and turns it nicely crisp-tender. As a finishing touch, hot cherry peppers give the sandwiches a bracing hit of spice and vinegary acidity. To crack the fennel seeds, use a mortar and pestle or place the seeds on a cutting board and rock the bottom edge of a skillet over them until they crack. You will need a 10- or 12-inch nonstick skillet with a tight-fitting lid.

1 Adjust oven rack 6 inches from broiler element and heat broiler. Heat 1½ teaspoons oil in 10- or 12-inch nonstick skillet over medium-high heat until shimmering. Add mushrooms and pinch salt, cover, and cook, stirring occasionally, until mushrooms have released their liquid, 3 to 5 minutes. Uncover and continue to cook, stirring occasionally, until well browned, 5 to 8 minutes longer. Off heat, stir in 1½ teaspoons oil, fennel seeds, and rosemary and season with salt and pepper to taste. Lay cheddar slices over mushrooms and cover to keep warm.

2 Combine garlic, pepper flakes, remaining 1 tablespoon oil, and remaining pinch salt in bowl. Pour oil mixture over broccoli rabe on aluminum foil–lined rimmed baking sheet and toss to coat. Broil until half of leaves are well browned, 2 to 3 minutes. Using tongs, toss to expose unbrowned leaves. Return sheet to oven and continue to broil until most leaves are lightly charred and stems are crisp-tender, 2 to 3 minutes longer.

3 Divide mushrooms, cheese, and broccoli rabe among rolls. Top with cherry peppers, if using, and serve.

Buffalo Cauliflower Wraps

SERVES 2

TOTAL TIME 45 minutes

- 12 ounces cauliflower florets, cut into 1-inch pieces
- 2 teaspoons extra-virgin olive oil
- ¼ teaspoon table salt
- ¼ cup vegan ranch dressing, divided
- 3 tablespoons hot sauce
- 1½ teaspoons packed brown sugar
- 1 teaspoon cider vinegar
- 2 cups chopped romaine or iceberg lettuce
- 1 small tomato, cored and cut into ½-inch pieces
- 1 carrot, peeled and grated
- 2 (12 by 9-inch) lavashes

Kitchen Improv

LEVEL UP

Layer ¼ cup grated radish, chopped cucumber, or thinly sliced bell pepper in wraps with other fillings. Serve with extra ranch dressing for dipping.

MAKE IT A SANDWICH

Substitute burger buns or rolls for lavash to make sandwiches.

WHY THIS RECIPE WORKS Creamy and rich, vinegary and spicy, anything Buffalo-flavored is almost certain to be a hit. We've had previous success in the test kitchen using cauliflower as the base for vegan Buffalo "wings"; when roasted, the cauliflower gets caramelized, nutty, and almost sweet, with a crisp-tender texture and plenty of nooks and crannies for soaking up the spicy sauce. So it was a no-brainer to use these as the jumping-off point for another sure winner: this time, Buffalo cauliflower wraps, which up the ante by adding vegan ranch dressing and a crisp salad of fresh romaine, tomato, and carrot to the mix. To give the Buffalo sauce its richness and clingy consistency without butter, we set aside a portion of our vegan ranch dressing and mix it into the hot sauce before coating the roasted cauliflower florets. The rest of the ranch gets tossed with the salad before everything is wrapped up snugly in lavash (a thin Middle Eastern flatbread) and devoured. You can use store-bought vegan ranch dressing or our Ranch Dressing (page 25) in this recipe. For ways to use up leftover cauliflower, see page 18.

1 Adjust oven rack to middle position and heat oven to 450 degrees. Toss cauliflower with oil and salt and arrange in even layer on rimmed baking sheet. Roast until cauliflower is spotty brown and tender, 20 to 25 minutes, stirring occasionally; let cool slightly.

2 Whisk 1 tablespoon ranch dressing, hot sauce, sugar, and vinegar in large bowl until sugar has dissolved. Add cauliflower and toss gently to combine. Toss lettuce, tomato, and carrot with remaining 3 tablespoons ranch dressing in separate bowl.

3 Working with 1 lavash at a time, place on counter with long side parallel to edge of counter. Spread half of lettuce mixture in rectangle 2 inches from bottom of lavash and about 1 inch from each side. Top lettuce mixture with half of cauliflower mixture. Fold sides of lavash over filling, then fold up bottom of lavash and fold tightly around filling. Cut wraps in half and serve.

Tempeh Larb Lettuce Wraps

SERVES 2

TOTAL TIME 30 minutes

- 3 tablespoons lime juice (2 limes)
- 2 tablespoons soy sauce
- 2 teaspoons packed dark brown sugar
- 2 garlic cloves, minced
- ½–1 Thai chile, stemmed and sliced thin
- ½ cup vegetable broth
- 2 teaspoons vegetable oil
- 8 ounces tempeh, crumbled into ½-inch pieces
- ¼ cup coarsely chopped fresh cilantro
- ¼ cup coarsely chopped fresh mint
- 1 shallot, sliced thin

  Bibb or Boston lettuce leaves

Kitchen Improv

USE WHAT YOU'VE GOT

Substitute ½ teaspoon red pepper flakes for Thai chile. If you only have either mint or cilantro on hand, double the amount. Substitute iceberg or green leaf lettuce for Bibb or Boston lettuce.

WHY THIS RECIPE WORKS This light but satisfying dinner takes its inspiration from larb, a popular street food in Thailand. Essentially a tangy-spicy meat salad, it's usually made with finely chopped meat (though the protein can vary) enhanced with fish sauce, lime juice, chiles, fresh herbs, and nutty toasted rice powder, which helps thicken the sauce. Here, we use crumbled tempeh as the base; when simmered with broth and oil, it plumps up and takes on a yielding texture remarkably similar to that of cooked meat. As the tempeh cooks, some of its starch also mingles with the cooking liquid and thickens it to a clingy, just slightly saucy consistency; intrigued, we found that we could omit the toasted rice powder and rely on the tempeh for both thickening and nuttiness. Though there are vegan fish sauces on the market, we prefer the flavor that similarly salty, umami-rich soy sauce adds here. A thinly sliced shallot adds an allium bite, while a couple pinches of dark brown sugar add a touch of caramelly sweetness. Perked up with fresh lime juice and served in lettuce leaves to give the meal a fun handheld appeal, these easy wraps will have your tastebuds singing in no time. For a spicier dish, use the whole Thai chile.

1 Whisk lime juice, soy sauce, sugar, garlic, and Thai chile in small bowl until sugar has dissolved; set aside.

2 Heat broth and oil in 10- or 12-inch nonstick skillet over medium heat until simmering. Add tempeh, cover, and cook until tempeh is tender and slightly plumped, 3 to 5 minutes. Uncover and continue to cook, stirring occasionally, until liquid has evaporated and tempeh is lightly browned, 3 to 5 minutes longer.

3 Off heat, use potato masher to gently mash tempeh into ¼-inch or smaller pieces. Stir in cilantro, mint, shallot, and reserved lime juice mixture until evenly combined. Season with extra soy sauce to taste. Serve with lettuce leaves. (Tempeh mixture can be refrigerated for up to 2 days.)

SANDWICHES, BURGERS, AND FLATBREADS

Grilled Kofte Wraps

SERVES 2
TOTAL TIME 45 minutes

- ¼ cup panko bread crumbs
- 2 tablespoons pine nuts
- 2 tablespoons chopped fresh parsley or mint
- 1 shallot (½ chopped, ½ sliced thin)
- 1 tablespoon water
- 1 garlic clove, smashed and peeled
- 1 teaspoon baharat
- ½ teaspoon smoked paprika
   Pinch table salt
- 6 ounces plant-based ground meat
- 2 (8-inch) pitas, wrapped in foil
- ¼ cup Yogurt-Tahini Sauce (page 25), plus extra for serving
- 1 tomato, sliced thin
- 1 cup shredded lettuce

Kitchen Improv

USE WHAT YOU'VE GOT

Substitute thinly sliced red onion for shallot. Substitute mix of ¼ teaspoon pepper, ¼ teaspoon ground coriander, ¼ teaspoon ground cumin, and ⅛ teaspoon ground cinnamon for baharat.

LEVEL UP

Add pickled vegetables, additional parsley or mint, and/or additional sauces, such as Harissa (page 26) or zhoug, to wraps.

WHY THIS RECIPE WORKS Throughout the Middle East, kebabs called kofte are made by mixing ground beef with delightfully extravagant quantities of fresh herbs and warm spices. The meat mixture—formed around skewers, rolled into logs, or pressed into patties, depending on region and personal preference—is then grilled over high heat and served with a creamy yogurt sauce. Our vegan kofte can be shaped and refrigerated up to a day ahead of time for maximum convenience; shaping them into logs makes them sturdier and less vulnerable to breaking apart than kofte formed around skewers. The tangy yogurt-tahini sauce cuts through the koftes' richness and spice, and shallot, tomato, and shredded lettuce add a fresh, crisp touch. The intense heat of a charcoal fire mimics that of a kofte grill, but you can use a gas grill instead. Do not substitute meat crumbles, sometimes called soy crumbles, for ground meat; they will not hold their shape when formed into kofte. For ways to use up leftover plant-based meat, see page 19.

1 Process panko, pine nuts, parsley, chopped shallot, water, garlic, baharat, paprika, and salt in food processor until mixture forms cohesive paste, about 30 seconds, scraping down sides of bowl as needed. Add ground meat and pulse to combine, about 10 pulses.

2 Remove processor blade. Using your moistened hands, divide meat mixture into 2 equal portions. Shape each portion into 4½-inch-long cylinder about 1 inch in diameter. Transfer kofte to plate and refrigerate for at least 15 minutes or up to 24 hours.

3A FOR A CHARCOAL GRILL Open bottom vent completely. Light large chimney starter filled with charcoal briquettes (6 quarts). When top coals are partially covered with ash, pour evenly over grill. Set cooking grate in place, cover, and open lid vent completely. Heat grill until hot, about 5 minutes.

3B FOR A GAS GRILL Turn all burners to high, cover, and heat grill until hot, about 15 minutes. Leave all burners on high.

4 Clean and oil cooking grate. Place kofte on grill perpendicular to grill grates. Cook (covered if using gas) until well browned on first side, 2 to 4 minutes. Flip kofte and continue to cook until browned on second side and meat registers 130 to 135 degrees, 2 to 5 minutes longer. Transfer kofte to plate.

5 Meanwhile, place foil-wrapped pitas on grill and cook, flipping foil packet occasionally, until heated through, about 3 minutes. Lay each pita on 12-inch square of foil and spread each with 2 tablespoons sauce. Place 1 kofte in middle of each pita and top with tomato, lettuce, and sliced shallot. Roll into cylindrical shape and serve, passing extra sauce separately.

Shawarma-Spiced Tofu Wraps

WITH SUMAC ONION

SERVES 2

TOTAL TIME 55 minutes

- 14 ounces firm or extra-firm tofu
- ¼ cup extra-virgin olive oil
- 3 garlic cloves, minced
- 2 teaspoons ground sumac
- 1½ teaspoons ground fenugreek
- 1 teaspoon smoked paprika
- ¾ teaspoon ground cumin
- ½ teaspoon table salt
- 2 tablespoons lemon juice
- 1 tablespoon packed brown sugar
- 2 (8-inch) pitas, warmed
- ¼ cup Sumac Onion (page 27)
- ¼ cup Yogurti-Tahini Sauce (page 25)
- ¼ cup chopped fresh parsley and/or mint

Kitchen Improv

USE WHAT YOU'VE GOT

Substitute thinly sliced red onion or other pickled vegetables for Sumac Onion.

LEVEL UP

Add sliced pickled or fresh cucumber, chopped tomato, and/or additional sauces, such as harissa or zhoug, to wraps.

WHY THIS RECIPE WORKS Crispy charred tofu fingers are absolutely loaded with bold spices and garlic in these satisfying and texturally varied vegan wraps. The flavor profile takes its inspiration from street cart Middle Eastern shawarma—we combine the classic shawarma spices sumac, fenugreek, paprika, cumin, and garlic in a marinade that we use to deeply season the tofu. Lemon juice and brown sugar provide well-rounded, complex flavor, and the sugar also aids that impeccable caramelization when the tofu hits the heat. For maximum marinade impact, we apply it twice: first before broiling the tofu so that the intense heat will bloom and deepen the spices' flavors, and a second time after the tofu is cooked so some of the spices' raw bite comes through. We wrap the tofu in warm, fluffy pita and then pile on some shawarma topping treats: tomatoes, sumac onions, and fresh herbs, plus a finishing drizzle of cooling tahini-yogurt sauce. The tofu fingers are delicate and may break while turning; this will not affect the final wraps.

1 Cut tofu crosswise into ½-inch-thick slabs, then slice slabs lengthwise into ½-inch-thick fingers. Spread tofu over paper towel–lined baking sheet, let drain for 20 minutes, then gently press dry with paper towels.

2 Microwave oil, garlic, sumac, fenugreek, paprika, cumin, and salt in medium bowl, stirring occasionally, until fragrant, 30 to 60 seconds. Whisk in lemon juice and sugar until sugar has dissolved. Measure out and reserve ¼ cup marinade.

3 Arrange tofu in a single layer on large plate and spoon remaining marinade evenly over top. Using your hands, gently turn tofu to coat with marinade. (Tofu and reserved marinade can be refrigerated separately for up to 24 hours; let marinade come to room temperature and whisk to recombine before using.)

4 Adjust oven rack 6 inches from broiler element and heat broiler. Line rimmed baking sheet with aluminum foil. Arrange tofu in single layer on prepared sheet, spaced evenly apart. Broil tofu until well browned on first side, 8 to 12 minutes, rotating sheet halfway through broiling. Gently flip tofu and continue to broil until well browned on the second side, 10 to 15 minutes longer, rotating sheet halfway through broiling. Transfer tofu and reserved marinade to large bowl and toss gently to coat.

5 Lay pitas flat on cutting board. Allowing excess marinade to drip from tofu, arrange tofu pieces over center of each pita. Top tofu with sumac onions, tahini sauce, and parsley. Fold pitas in half and serve.

Not-from-a-Box Weeknight Tacos

SERVES 2

TOTAL TIME 30 minutes

- 1½ cups (4 ounces) shredded coleslaw mix
- 2 tablespoons lime juice, plus lime wedges for serving
- ½ teaspoon table salt, divided
- 1½ teaspoons vegetable oil
- 1 small onion, chopped fine
- 1 small green or red bell pepper, stemmed, seeded, and chopped fine
- 1 tablespoon tomato paste
- 2 garlic cloves, minced
- 1½ teaspoons chili powder
- ½ teaspoon ground cumin
- 6 ounces plant-based ground meat
- ¼ cup water
- 6 (6-inch) corn or flour tortillas, warmed

Kitchen Improv

USE WHAT YOU'VE GOT

Substitute shredded green or red cabbage for coleslaw mix.

LEVEL UP

Serve with sliced radishes, cilantro, sliced avocado, fresh or pickled jalapeño, Quick Pickled Red Onion (page 26), shredded plant based cheddar cheese, plant-based sour cream or yogurt, salsa, and/or hot sauce.

WHY THIS RECIPE WORKS   With a few tweaks, an everyday ground beef taco recipe transforms into a plant-based feast for two. The plant-based meat we use as the base of the taco filling cooks quickly, so we hold off on adding it until the last few minutes of cooking to ensure that it browns but also remains supple and moist, not overcooked and pebbly. Before adding the meat, we first cook onion and bell pepper in oil until softened, and then we bloom the spices and tomato paste (which ups the umami) to bring out their flavors. Only then do we add the meat to the pan to cook through. Finishing the filling by simmering it with a splash of water gives it a delightfully saucy consistency, which pairs well with the crunchy cabbage topping made with convenient coleslaw mix. We prefer to use bulk plant-based ground meat here; however, an equal amount of plant-based meat crumbles, sometimes called soy crumbles, can be used as well. To warm the tortillas, wrap them in a damp dish towel and microwave until warm and pliable, about 30 seconds. Alternatively, heat individual tortillas in a dry skillet or over a gas flame. For ways to use up leftover plant-based meat, see page 19.

1   Toss coleslaw mix with lime juice and ¼ teaspoon salt in bowl; set aside for serving.

2   Heat oil in 10- or 12-inch nonstick skillet over medium heat until shimmering. Add onion, bell pepper, and remaining ¼ teaspoon salt and cook until softened and lightly browned, 5 to 7 minutes. Stir in tomato paste, garlic, chili powder, and cumin and cook until fragrant, about 1 minute.

3   Add ground meat and cook, breaking up meat with wooden spoon, until firm crumbles form, about 3 minutes. Stir in water and simmer until sauce is slightly thickened, 2 to 3 minutes. Divide filling evenly among tortillas and top with reserved coleslaw mixture. Serve with lime wedges.

Citrusy Jackfruit Tacos

SERVES 2

TOTAL TIME 55 minutes

- 1 (14.5-ounce) can young green jackfruit packed in brine or water, drained (2 cups)
- 2 tablespoons vegetable oil, divided
- 1 small red onion, grated
- 4 garlic cloves, minced
- ¾ teaspoon dried oregano
- ¾ teaspoon ground cumin
- ¾ teaspoon ground annatto
- ½ teaspoon pepper
- 2 tablespoons orange juice
- 1 tablespoon lime juice, plus lime wedges for serving
- 2 bay leaves
- ½ teaspoon table salt
- 6 (6-inch) corn tortillas, warmed
- ½ cup Quick Pickled Red Onion (page 26)

Kitchen Improv

USE WHAT YOU'VE GOT

Substitute 2 shallots for red onion. Substitute 1 teaspoon paprika for annatto. Substitute other pickled vegetables for pickled onion.

LEVEL UP

Serve with sliced avocado, shredded plant-based cheese, and/or fresh or pickled jalapeños.

WHY THIS RECIPE WORKS   Immature green jackfruit has a superpower: once cooked, it can be shredded into firm but juicy strands just like slow-roasted meat. This makes it the perfect stand-in for shredded meat in plant-based recipes. Drawing flavor inspiration from Yucatecan cochinita pibil, a dish traditionally made with roast suckling pig, we cook the jackfruit with a flavorful sauce that includes red onion, earthy cumin and oregano, annatto, and citrus juice. A combination of orange and lime juice replicates the zip of the sour orange juice typically used in pibil. Annatto (sometimes called achiote) gives this dish its reddish color as well as an irreplicable peppery flavor. Finally, tangy pickled red onion finishes the tacos Yucatecan-style. Be sure to use young (unripe) jackfruit packed in brine or water; do not use mature jackfruit packed in syrup. Jackfruit seeds are tender and edible; there's no need to remove them. You will need a 10- or 12-inch nonstick skillet with a tight-fitting lid for this recipe. Use the large holes of a box grater to grate the onion. Do not use annatto paste, which includes additional spices, here. You can substitute 3 tablespoons sour orange juice for the orange juice and lime juice. To warm the tortillas, wrap them in a damp dish towel and microwave until warm and pliable, about 30 seconds. Alternatively, heat individual tortillas in a dry skillet or over a gas flame.

1   Place jackfruit in large saucepan, cover with water, and bring to boil over high heat. Reduce heat to medium and simmer for 10 minutes. Drain jackfruit, rinse well, and drain again. Transfer jackfruit to cutting board and chop into rough ½-inch pieces; set aside.

2   Heat 1 tablespoon oil in 10- or 12-inch nonstick skillet over medium-high heat until shimmering. Add jackfruit in single layer and cook, stirring occasionally, until spotty brown, 6 to 8 minutes; transfer to plate.

3   Add remaining 1 tablespoon oil and onion to now-empty skillet and cook over medium-low heat until onion is softened and liquid has mostly evaporated, about 2 minutes. Stir in garlic, oregano, cumin, annatto, and pepper and cook until fragrant, about 30 seconds.

4   Stir in 1¼ cups water, orange juice, and lime juice until well combined, then stir in bay leaves, salt, and jackfruit. Bring to simmer over medium heat, cover, and cook until jackfruit is very tender and liquid has thickened, 12 to 15 minutes.

5   Off heat, use potato masher to mash jackfruit until thoroughly shredded and well coated in sauce. Season with salt and pepper to taste. Divide jackfruit mixture evenly among tortillas and top with pickled onion. Serve with lime wedges.

Spiced Cauliflower Burgers

SERVES 2
TOTAL TIME 1 hour

- 12 ounces cauliflower florets, cut into 1-inch pieces
- 4 teaspoons extra-virgin olive oil, divided
- ½ teaspoon ras el hanout
- ¼ teaspoon plus ⅛ teaspoon table salt, divided
- ¼ cup panko bread crumbs
- 1 small carrot, peeled and shredded
- 3 tablespoons golden raisins
- 3 tablespoons liquid plant-based egg
- 2 burger buns, toasted if desired
- ¼ cup plant-based yogurt
- 2 teaspoons sliced almonds, toasted
- ½ cup baby arugula or spinach

Kitchen Improv

USE WHAT YOU'VE GOT

Substitute combination of ¼ teaspoon paprika, ⅛ teaspoon ground coriander, and ⅛ teaspoon ground cumin for ras el hanout. Substitute other chopped dried fruit for raisins.

LEVEL UP

Add extra toppings such as pickled vegetables. Substitute Yogurt-Tahini Sauce (page 25) or Lemon-Herb Yogurt Sauce (page 25) for yogurt.

WHY THIS RECIPE WORKS These burgers burst with exciting contrasts: the earthy-spicy flavor of ras el hanout, the sweetness of carrot and raisins, the peppery bite of baby arugula. There's also the cauliflower patties, with creamy, nutty interiors and crispy, golden-brown exteriors. The trick to achieving fantastic cauliflower flavor is to roast the florets before mashing them to form the base of the patties; the mere 15 to 20 minutes of oven cooking is well worth the wait for the caramelized, nutty sweetness it yields. Before roasting, we toss the florets with oil and ras el hanout, a North African spice blend that contains cumin, coriander, cinnamon, and an array of other warm spices. After allowing the roasted cauliflower to cool slightly, we mash it just until broken into rough ½-inch pieces and then add panko and liquid plant-based egg for binding. Peppery baby arugula and herbed yogurt sauce provide a fresh burst of flavor, and toasted sliced almonds sprinkled over the top add more textural interest. For ways to use up leftover cauliflower and plant-based yogurt, see pages 18–19.

1 Adjust oven rack to middle position and heat oven to 450 degrees. Toss cauliflower with 2 teaspoons oil, ras el hanout, and ¼ teaspoon salt and arrange in even layer on rimmed baking sheet. Roast until cauliflower is well browned and tender, 15 to 20 minutes. Let cool slightly, then transfer to large bowl.

2 Using potato masher, mash cauliflower until broken into rough ½-inch pieces. Stir in panko, carrot, raisins, egg, and remaining ⅛ teaspoon salt until well combined. Divide cauliflower mixture into 2 equal portions. Using your moistened hands, tightly pack each portion into 4-inch-wide patty. Transfer patties to large plate, cover with plastic wrap, and refrigerate until firm, at least 15 minutes or up to 24 hours.

3 Heat remaining 2 teaspoons oil in 10- or 12-inch nonstick skillet over medium heat until shimmering. Gently lay patties in skillet and cook until well browned and crispy on first side, 3 to 5 minutes. Using 2 spatulas, gently flip patties and cook until well browned and crispy on second side, 3 to 5 minutes. Serve burgers on buns, topped with yogurt, almonds, and arugula.

Make-Ahead Lentil and Mushroom Burgers

MAKES 6 patties
TOTAL TIME 40 minutes

- 8 ounces cremini or white mushrooms, trimmed and quartered
- ½ cup raw cashews
- 1 celery rib, cut into 1-inch pieces
- 1 shallot, quartered
- ½ cup medium-grind bulgur
- ¼ cup water
- 3 tablespoons plus 2 teaspoons extra-virgin olive oil, divided
- ½ teaspoon table salt
- 1 (15-ounce) can brown lentils, rinsed
- ½ cup panko bread crumbs
- 3 tablespoons liquid plant-based egg
- 2 slices (1½ ounces) plant-based cheddar or mozzarella cheese (optional)
- 2 burger buns, toasted if desired
- 2 leaves Bibb or Boston lettuce
- 1 small tomato, sliced thin

WHY THIS RECIPE WORKS   Ever wish that serving up made-from-scratch plant-based burgers was as easy as reaching into the freezer and browning up a couple of frozen patties? These supersavory lentil and mushroom burgers make six patties and can be frozen for up to a month, so you can cook up a couple now and save the rest to enjoy later. The patties are made with earthy brown lentils, bulgur (which absorbs excess moisture), and meaty mushrooms, plus a combo of liquid plant-based egg and panko for crumble-proof binding power. Half a cup of buttery cashews add richness and a pleasant chew when ground and mixed into the patties. Don't confuse bulgur with cracked wheat, which has a much longer cooking time and will not work in this recipe. Look for medium-grind bulgur (labeled "#2"), which is roughly the size of mustard seeds. Avoid coarsely ground bulgur; it will not cook through in time. This recipe makes six patties. Two patties are cooked immediately; the remaining four are frozen for later.

1   TO MAKE PATTIES   Pulse mushrooms, cashews, celery, and shallot in food processor until finely chopped, about 10 pulses, scraping down sides of bowl as needed. Transfer vegetable mixture to large bowl and stir in bulgur, water, 3 tablespoons oil, and salt. Microwave, stirring occasionally, until bulgur is softened and most of liquid has been absorbed, about 6 minutes; let cool slightly.

2   Vigorously stir lentils, panko, and egg into vegetable-bulgur mixture until well combined and mixture forms cohesive mass. Using your moistened hands, divide mixture into 6 equal portions (about ½ cup each), then tightly pack each portion into 3½-inch-wide patty. To freeze up to 6 patties, evenly space patties on parchment paper–lined rimmed baking sheet and freeze until firm, about 1 hour. Stack patties between pieces of parchment, wrap in plastic wrap, and place in zipper-lock freezer bag. (Patties can be frozen for up to 1 month. Do not thaw patties before cooking.)

3   TO COOK PATTIES   Heat remaining 2 teaspoons oil in 10- or 12-inch nonstick skillet over medium heat until shimmering. Gently lay 2 patties in skillet and cook until well browned and crispy on first side, 3 to 5 minutes. Using 2 spatulas, gently flip patties; top with cheddar, if using; and cook until well browned and crispy on second side, 3 to 5 minutes. Serve burgers on buns, topped with lettuce and tomato.

Kitchen Improv

USE WHAT YOU'VE GOT

Substitute 3 tablespoons finely chopped onion for shallot.

LEVEL UP

Add extra toppings such as thinly sliced red onion, sliced avocado, alfalfa sprouts, and/or pickled vegetables. Spread a sauce, such as plant-based mayonnaise, plant-based yogurt, ketchup, or barbecue sauce, over bun tops before serving.

Portobello Mushroom Burgers
WITH SRIRACHA SLAW

SERVES 2
TOTAL TIME 45 minutes

- 2 portobello mushroom caps (4 to 5 inches in diameter), gills removed
- 1 tablespoon toasted sesame oil
- 1 tablespoon soy sauce
- 1 garlic clove, minced
- 1 tablespoon plant-based mayonnaise
- 1 teaspoon sriracha
- ½ teaspoon unseasoned rice vinegar
- 1 cup (2¾ ounces) shredded coleslaw mix
- ¼ cup chopped fresh cilantro
- 1 scallion, sliced thin
- 2 burger buns, toasted if desired

Kitchen Improv

USE WHAT YOU'VE GOT

Substitute chili-garlic sauce or gochujang sauce for sriracha. Substitute shredded green or red cabbage for coleslaw mix. Substitute wine vinegar for rice vinegar.

LEVEL UP

Add extra toppings such as sliced avocado or pickled vegetables.

WHY THIS RECIPE WORKS   If you've ever been let down by a lackluster portobello burger—all too often the afterthought "vegan option" at very nonvegan cookouts—we entreat you to give the concept one more chance. These portobello burgers are anything but an afterthought: With just a little love and grilling magic, the mighty portobello undergoes a true transformation, turning dense and downright meaty and full of concentrated savory flavor. But we don't just throw the mushrooms on the grill and call it a day. First, we scrape out the gills (which can have an offputting muddy taste) from each cap and then lightly score each cap in a crosshatch pattern. This scoring provides more avenues of escape for the moisture in the mushrooms, so they cook and become tender in less time. We also toss the caps in a quick marinade of nutty sesame oil, soy sauce, and garlic; the flavors of the marinade soak into the portobellos and are complemented by the topping, a mixture of coleslaw, cilantro, and oniony scallion seasoned with rice vinegar and sriracha and enriched with just a dollop of plant-based mayonnaise. You can use store-bought plant-based mayonnaise or our Aquafaba Mayonnaise (page 22) in this recipe.

1   Cut ¹⁄₁₆-inch-deep slits on top side of mushroom caps, spaced ½ inch apart in crosshatch pattern. Combine oil, soy sauce, and garlic in medium bowl. Add mushrooms and gently turn to coat. Set aside while grill heats, turning occasionally.

2A   FOR A CHARCOAL GRILL   Open bottom vent completely. Light large chimney starter three-quarters filled with charcoal briquettes (4½ quarts). When top coals are partially covered with ash, pour evenly over grill. Set cooking grate in place, cover, and open lid vent completely. Heat grill until hot, about 5 minutes.

2B   FOR A GAS GRILL   Turn all burners to high, cover, and heat grill until hot, about 15 minutes. Leave all burners on high.

3   Clean and oil cooking grate. Place mushrooms gill side up on grill. Cook mushrooms (covered if using gas), flipping them as needed until tender and lightly charred on both sides, 8 to 10 minutes.

4   Combine mayonnaise, sriracha, and vinegar in bowl. Add coleslaw mix, cilantro, and scallion and toss to coat. Serve mushroom caps on buns, topped with coleslaw mixture.

Garlic and Herb Burgers
WITH BEET TZATZIKI

SERVES 2

TOTAL TIME 50 minutes

- 1 small beet, peeled and shredded (⅓ cup)
- 1 Persian cucumber, shredded
- ¼ teaspoon plus ⅛ teaspoon table salt, divided
- ¼ cup plain plant-based yogurt
- 2 teaspoons minced fresh mint
- 1 teaspoon extra-virgin olive oil
- 1 small garlic clove, minced, divided
- 6 ounces plant-based ground meat
- ¾ teaspoon dried oregano or thyme
- 2 burger buns, toasted if desired
- ¾ cup baby arugula or spinach

Kitchen Improv

USE WHAT YOU'VE GOT

Substitute canned beets for fresh. Substitute ¼ English cucumber or ¼ peeled and seeded American cucumber for Persian cucumber. Substitute other fresh herbs, such as chives, parsley, or basil, for mint.

LEVEL UP

Top patties with crumbled plant-based feta after flipping them in step 4.

WHY THIS RECIPE WORKS   Mild plant-based meat is an ideal canvas for creative flavor combos. These burgers are a feast for both the eyes and the taste buds: toothsome patties spiked with potent dried oregano and garlic; topped with a vivid-pink, earthy-sweet beet tzatziki; and piled high with fresh, bright green baby arugula. Plant-based meat makes forming the burgers themselves a snap; we simply knead the garlic and oregano into the meat with our hands, give the patties a brief rest in the fridge (to firm them up for easier handling), and then pop them onto the grill, where they cook through in minutes. A small shredded beet tinges the tzatziki (a garlicky Greek cucumber-and-yogurt sauce) with its standout color. A small Persian cucumber yields the perfect for-two portion without leftover veg. A generous portion of baby arugula lends the burgers a peppery bite. Do not substitute meat crumbles, sometimes called soy crumbles, for ground meat; they will not hold their shape when formed into patties. For ways to use up leftover plant-based meat, see page 19.

1   Toss beet and cucumber with ¼ teaspoon salt in colander set over medium bowl and let sit for 15 minutes. Discard any drained juices and wipe bowl clean with paper towels. Whisk yogurt, mint, oil, and half of garlic together in now-empty bowl, then stir in beet mixture. Season with salt and pepper to taste; set aside. (Tzatziki can be refrigerated for up to 24 hours).

2   Break ground meat into small pieces in medium bowl. Add oregano and remaining garlic and gently knead with your hands until well combined. Using your moistened hands, divide meat mixture into 2 equal portions, then gently shape each portion into 3½-inch-wide patty. Transfer patties to plate and refrigerate for at least 15 minutes or up to 24 hours. Sprinkle patties with remaining ⅛ teaspoon salt.

3A   FOR A CHARCOAL GRILL   Open bottom vent completely. Light large chimney starter three-quarters filled with charcoal briquettes (4½ quarts). When top coals are partially covered with ash, pour evenly over grill. Set cooking grate in place, cover, and open lid vent completely. Heat grill until hot, about 5 minutes.

3B   FOR A GAS GRILL   Turn all burners to high, cover, and heat grill until hot, about 15 minutes. Leave all burners on high.

4   Clean and oil cooking grate. Place patties on grill and cook until well browned on first side, 2 to 3 minutes. Flip patties and continue to cook until browned on second side and meat registers 130 to 135 degrees, 1 to 2 minutes. Serve burgers on buns, topped with tzatziki and arugula.

Grilled Flatbread
WITH KALE AND APPLE

SERVES 2

TOTAL TIME 35 minutes

- ⅓   cup plant-based ricotta
- ½   teaspoon dried oregano
- ¼   teaspoon garlic powder
- ⅛   teaspoon pepper, divided
- 3   ounces kale, stemmed and cut into 1-inch pieces
- 2   tablespoons extra-virgin olive oil, divided
- ⅛   teaspoon table salt
- 1   small apple, cored, halved, and sliced ¼ inch thick
- 3   tablespoons sliced pepperoncini or banana peppers
- 8   ounces pizza dough, room temperature

Kitchen Improv

USE WHAT YOU'VE GOT

Substitute other dried herbs, such as thyme or marjoram, for oregano. Substitute pear for apple.

LEVEL UP

Add roasted winter squash or sweet potato cubes and/or caramelized onion to kale mixture. Sprinkle finished flatbread with Italian Sausage Tempeh Crumbles (page 27), red pepper flakes, and/or toasted nuts or seeds.

WHY THIS RECIPE WORKS   This autumnal flatbread is your excuse to keep the grill out for one (or several) more outdoor cooking sessions as summer winds down. Grilling pizza is actually one of the best uses for your grill—the grill gets hotter than a typical home oven, so the crust picks up unbeatable, flavorful char. We top convenient store-bought pizza dough (most pizza dough is naturally vegan, but check the ingredients to be sure) with earthy kale, crisp apple, and briny, just-spicy-enough pepperoncini. In the intense heat the kale wilts and its edges crisp, adding another pleasant textural element to this early fall dinner. Dollops of plant-based ricotta, added off the heat, offer a rich and creamy counterpoint to the piping-hot flatbread. Be sure to let the dough come to room temperature before rolling it out, which will make rolling it much easier. You can use store-bought plant-based ricotta or our Cashew Ricotta (page 22) in this recipe. For ways to use up leftover pizza dough, see page 19.

1   Combine ricotta, oregano, garlic powder, and pepper in small bowl; set aside. Combine kale, 2 teaspoons oil, and salt in medium bowl. Vigorously squeeze and massage kale mixture with your hands until leaves are uniformly darkened and slightly wilted, about 30 seconds. Add apple and pepperoncini and toss to combine; set aside.

2   Line rimmed baking sheet with parchment paper and dust with flour. On lightly floured counter, press and roll dough to form 12-inch by 8-inch rectangle. Transfer to prepared sheet, reshaping as needed.

3A   **FOR A CHARCOAL GRILL**   Open bottom vent completely. Light large chimney starter ½ filled with charcoal briquettes (3 quarts). When top coals are partially covered with ash, pour evenly over grill. Set cooking grate in place, cover, and open lid vent completely. Heat grill until hot, about 5 minutes.

3B   **FOR A GAS GRILL**   Turn all burners to high, cover, and heat grill until hot, about 15 minutes. Turn all burners to medium.

4   Brush top of dough rectangle with 2 teaspoons oil. Grill oiled side down until underside is spotty brown and top is covered with bubbles, 2 to 3 minutes (pop any large bubbles that form). Working quickly, brush top of dough with remaining 2 teaspoons oil, then flip and scatter kale mixture evenly over browned side of flatbread. Grill until second side is spotty brown, 2 to 3 minutes. Transfer flatbread to cutting board and dollop with reserved ricotta mixture. Cut flatbread into pieces and serve.

Artichoke and Spinach Calzones

SERVES 2

TOTAL TIME 55 minutes

- 4 ounces frozen artichoke hearts, thawed, patted dry, and chopped
- 4 ounces frozen chopped spinach, thawed and squeezed dry
- 2 tablespoons chopped fresh basil
- ⅛ teaspoon pepper
- 8 ounces pizza dough, room temperature, split into 2 pieces
- 4 ounces plant-based mozzarella cheese, shredded (1 cup), divided
- 2 teaspoons extra-virgin olive oil

Kitchen Improv

USE WHAT YOU'VE GOT

Substitute other fresh herbs, such as chives, tarragon, or parsley, for basil.

LEVEL UP

Add 1–2 tablespoons minced pepperoncini, sun-dried tomatoes, olives, and/or roasted garlic to filling. Serve with marinara sauce for dipping.

WHY THIS RECIPE WORKS   Making calzones can easily turn into an all-day affair—fine if you're looking for a project, but a shame if, like us, you wish you could enjoy the glory of a homemade calzone straight from the oven more often. To bring the calzone into the realm of the weeknight (or at the very least, make it a super-attainable weekend option), we use store-bought pizza dough so we can focus most of our effort on creating a flavor-packed filling rather than on waiting around for the dough to rise. We also take a trip to the frozen vegetable aisle for frozen artichoke hearts and spinach, which make for a flavorful and nearly prep-free base for the filling. Chopped basil adds a fresh herbal note, and plant-based mozzarella bubbles up around the other filling elements as the calzones cook, binding them in place. After only about 20 minutes in a hot oven, the calzones bake up without a trace of doughiness. For ways to use up leftover pizza dough, see page 19.

1   Adjust oven rack to middle position and heat oven to 450 degrees. Line rimmed baking sheet with aluminum foil and spray with vegetable oil spray. Combine artichokes, spinach, basil, and pepper in bowl.

2   Press and roll 1 dough piece into 8-inch round on lightly floured counter. Spread half of mozzarella evenly over bottom half of round, leaving 1-inch border at edge. Spread half of vegetable mixture evenly over mozzarella. Fold top half of dough over filling and crimp edges to seal; transfer to prepared sheet. Repeat with remaining dough, cheese, and vegetable filling.

3   Using sharp knife, cut two 1-inch steam vents on top of each calzone, then brush tops evenly with oil. Bake until golden brown, 20 to 25 minutes, rotating sheet halfway through baking. Transfer calzones to wire rack and let cool for 5 minutes before serving.

VARIATION

Broccoli and Roasted Red Pepper Calzones

Substitute frozen broccoli florets for artichoke hearts, ½ cup chopped jarred roasted red peppers for spinach, and plant-based cheddar cheese for mozzarella.

139 Black-Eyed Pea Salad with Peaches and Pecans

140 Caesar Salad with Pan-Roasted Mushrooms

142 Chopped Salad with Kale and Pan-Seared Tofu

145 Hearts of Palm Ceviche with Tomato, Jicama, and Avocado

146 Beet Salad with Watercress and Spiced Yogurt

148 Meaty Taco Salad with Black Beans

150 Carrot Noodle Salad with Harissa, Mint, and Apricots

153 Garlicky Broccoli and Chickpea Salad

155 Warm Escarole and Cannellini Bean Salad

156 Charred Cabbage Salad with Torn Tofu and Plantain Chips

159 Roasted Grape and Cauliflower Salad with Chermoula

160 Roasted Zucchini, Corn, and Tomato Salad with Maple Vinaigrette

163 Grilled Vegetable and Orzo Salad with Lemon and Basil

165 Rainbow Salad with Crispy Tempeh

167 Spinach Salad with White Beans, Corn, and Sumac
with Black Beans, Chili, and Lime

168 Bread and Tomato Salad with Lima Beans, Feta, and Olives
with Cannellini Beans, Mozzarella, and Basil

171 Warm Spiced Couscous Salad

172 Freekeh Salad with Sweet Potato and Walnuts

174 Soba Noodle Salad with Edamame, Cabbage, and Peanut-Ginger Sauce
with Miso-Ginger Sauce

177 Bún Chả

Black-Eyed Pea Salad
WITH PEACHES AND PECANS

SERVES 2
TOTAL TIME 20 minutes

- 2 tablespoons extra-virgin olive oil
- ½ teaspoon grated lime zest plus 1 tablespoon juice
- 1 small garlic clove, minced
- ¼ teaspoon table salt
- 2 (15-ounce) cans black-eyed peas, rinsed
- 2 peaches, halved, pitted, and cut into 1-inch pieces
- 1 small head frisée (4 ounces), trimmed and cut into 2-inch pieces (about 3 cups)
- 1 small shallot, chopped fine
- 2 tablespoons coarsely chopped fresh basil or parsley
- 1 tablespoon chopped toasted pecans
- ½–1 jalapeño chile, stemmed, seeded, and chopped fine

Kitchen Improv

USE WHAT YOU'VE GOT

Substitute escarole, Belgian endive, radicchio, or romaine lettuce for frisée. Substitute nectarines, apricots, or plums for peaches. Substitute other chopped nuts for pecans.

LEVEL UP

Top with Umami Croutons (page 27) or pita chips broken into 1-inch pieces.

WHY THIS RECIPE WORKS When you're in the mood for a truly hearty salad that'll fill you up without weighing you down, this is the one to turn to. Two cans of black-eyed peas and two peaches—one can and one peach per person—are the foundation of this generous salad that's surprisingly light but bursting with satisfying plant-based protein and crisp vegetables. With their delicate skins and creamy interiors, black-eyed peas are excellent when paired with juicy honey-sweet peaches and a tart dressing. To continue the salad's Southern theme, we throw in another beloved Southern ingredient, chopped pecans, which provide an irresistible crunch. Rinsing the beans before adding them to the salad washes away excess sodium. A single small head of lacy frisée fills out the salad with a touch of pleasantly contrasting bitterness to balance the peaches' sweetness. A finely chopped shallot adds subtle bite, and for a little spice we add a chopped jalapeño, its seeds removed to mellow its grassy heat. For a spicier dish, use the whole jalapeño chile.

Whisk oil, lime zest and juice, garlic, and salt together in large bowl. Add black-eyed peas, peaches, frisée, shallot, basil, pecans, and jalapeño and toss to combine. Season with salt and pepper to taste. Serve.

Caesar Salad
WITH PAN-ROASTED MUSHROOMS

SERVES 2

TOTAL TIME 45 minutes

- 3 ounces baguette, cut into ¾-inch cubes (2½ cups)
- 2 tablespoons extra-virgin olive oil, divided
- ¼ teaspoon table salt, divided
- ¼ teaspoon pepper, divided
- 3 tablespoons plant-based mayonnaise
- 1 tablespoon grated plant-based Parmesan, plus extra for serving
- 2 teaspoons lemon juice
- 2 teaspoons capers, rinsed and minced
- 1 teaspoon white wine vinegar
- 1 teaspoon vegan Worcestershire sauce
- 1 small garlic clove, minced
- ½ teaspoon Dijon mustard
- 12 ounces cremini mushrooms, trimmed and halved if small or quartered if large
- 1 romaine lettuce heart (6 ounces), cut into 1-inch pieces

WHY THIS RECIPE WORKS   A few powerhouse ingredients (plant-based Parmesan, capers, mustard, vegan Worcestershire, and white wine vinegar) provide our vegan Caesar dressing with all the intense umami and briny flavors of the Parmesan-, egg-, and anchovy-containing original. With a base of vegan mayo, this dressing whisks up thick and luxurious, perfect for coating crisp romaine lettuce (one romaine heart yields the perfect amount to serve two) and crunchy croutons. But while this is a stellar vegan version of a classic Caesar, lettuce, dressing, and croutons alone aren't quite enough to make this salad stand in for dinner. To solve that problem, we add another element: cremini mushrooms sautéed until golden brown and meaty, which lend their heft and savoriness to the salad to make it definitively worthy of its main-dish status. You will need a 12-inch nonstick skillet with a tight-fitting lid for this recipe; the mushrooms will overcrowd a smaller skillet. You can use store-bought plant-based mayonnaise and plant-based Parmesan in this recipe, or use our Aquafaba Mayonnaise (page 22) and/or Cashew Parmesan (page 23).

1   Adjust oven rack to middle position and heat oven to 350 degrees. Toss baguette with 1 tablespoon oil, ⅛ teaspoon salt, and ⅛ teaspoon pepper and arrange in even layer on rimmed baking sheet. Bake until golden and crispy, 12 to 15 minutes, stirring halfway through baking. Transfer baking sheet to wire rack and let croutons cool, about 10 minutes. (Croutons can be stored in airtight container at room temperature for up to 2 days.)

2   Meanwhile, whisk mayonnaise, Parmesan, lemon juice, capers, vinegar, Worcestershire, garlic, mustard, and remaining ⅛ teaspoon pepper in large bowl until smooth. Adjust consistency with 1 to 2 teaspoons water as needed; set aside.

3   Heat remaining 1 tablespoon oil in 12-inch nonstick skillet over medium heat until shimmering. Add mushrooms and remaining ⅛ teaspoon salt, cover, and cook until mushrooms have released their liquid, 4 to 6 minutes. Uncover, increase heat to medium-high, and cook, stirring occasionally, until mushrooms are lightly browned, 4 to 6 minutes.

4   Add lettuce to bowl with dressing and toss to coat. Add croutons and toss to combine. Transfer salad to serving bowls, top with mushrooms, and sprinkle with extra Parmesan. Serve.

Kitchen Improv

USE WHAT YOU'VE GOT

Substitute any rustic bread for baguette. Substitute 2 teaspoons nutritional yeast for plant-based Parmesan. Substitute portobello, button, shiitake, or oyster mushrooms, cut into 1-inch pieces, for creminis.

BULK IT UP

Toss cannellini beans or chickpeas with lettuce and croutons. Top with tempeh crumbles (page 27) or Pan-Seared Tofu (page 274).

Chopped Salad
WITH KALE AND PAN-SEARED TOFU

SERVES 2

TOTAL TIME 25 minutes

- 2 ounces kale, stemmed and cut into 1-inch pieces
- ⅛ plus ¼ teaspoon table salt, divided
- 2 tablespoons extra-virgin olive oil
- 1 tablespoon lemon juice
- ⅛ teaspoon pepper
- 2 Persian cucumbers, halved lengthwise and sliced ½ inch thick
- 2 ounces plant-based feta cheese, crumbled (⅓ cup)
- 1 small red bell pepper, stemmed, seeded, and cut into ½-inch pieces
- 3 radishes, trimmed and chopped
- ⅓ cup chopped fresh mint, parsley, and/or dill
- 1 shallot, minced
- 1 recipe Pan-Seared Tofu (page 274)

WHY THIS RECIPE WORKS Chopped vegetable salads are a mainstay in many Mediterranean countries—it's common for a fresh and in-season combination of neatly diced vegetables and herbs to appear as a side dish at most every meal. To translate a chopped side salad into a main-dish salad, however, requires adding a few components to bulk it up. To a base of cucumbers, bell pepper, radishes, and a generous amount of fresh mint, we add hearty kale (which becomes tender after just a quick massage with salt), cubes of golden-brown seared tofu, and chunks of briny plant-based feta. Rather than dicing the vegetables as is common in Mediterranean chopped salads, we chop them into slightly larger (roughly ½-inch) pieces to cut down on time-consuming knife work. Tossed with a light lemon and olive oil dressing, this salad is fresh, bright, and easily satisfying enough to warrant its move from side to main. Persian cucumbers (also sold as mini or snacking cucumbers) are similar to seedless cucumbers in flavor and texture; they do not need to be peeled.

1 Toss kale and ⅛ teaspoon salt together in medium bowl, then vigorously squeeze and massage kale with your hands until leaves are uniformly darkened and slightly wilted, about 30 seconds.

2 Whisk oil, lemon juice, pepper, and remaining ¼ teaspoon salt together in large bowl. Add cucumbers, feta, bell pepper, radishes, mint, shallot, and kale and toss to combine. Season with salt and pepper to taste. Transfer salad to serving bowls and top with tofu. Serve.

Kitchen Improv

USE WHAT YOU'VE GOT

Substitute Swiss chard for kale; skip step 1. Substitute ½ English cucumber for Persian cucumbers. Substitute chopped avocado or olives for feta. Substitute jicama for radishes. Substitute tempeh crumbles (page 27) for tofu.

Hearts of Palm Ceviche
WITH TOMATO, JICAMA, AND AVOCADO

SERVES 2

TOTAL TIME 50 minutes

- 6 ounces cherry or grape tomatoes (3 ounces whole, 3 ounces quartered), divided
- 1 jalapeño chile, stemmed and seeded
- 2 tablespoons extra-virgin olive oil, plus extra for drizzling
- 1 garlic clove, smashed and peeled
- ½ teaspoon grated lime zest plus 3 tablespoons juice
- ¼ teaspoon table salt
- 1 (14-ounce) can whole hearts of palm, rinsed, cut into ½-inch rounds
- 6 ounces jicama, peeled and cut into ¼-inch pieces
- 1 mango, peeled, pitted, and cut into ¼-inch pieces
- 1 shallot, minced
- 1 avocado, halved, pitted, and cut into ½-inch pieces
- ½ cup coarsely chopped fresh cilantro
- ½ cup plantain chips, crumbled

WHY THIS RECIPE WORKS Hearts of palm—the inner core and developing bud of certain palm trees—is a common (but many times, forgettable) salad addition. But in this vegan ceviche, its mildly sweet flavor and crisp-tender texture make it the perfect candidate to take center stage as a stand-in for the usual fish. Adding textural contrast are crunchy jicama, rich avocado, and juicy tomatoes. To create the requisite citrus-forward dressing that is the hallmark of ceviche, we use the blender to puree a portion of the tomatoes with lime juice, jalapeño chiles, garlic, and extra-virgin olive oil; the result, after straining out the seeds and skin, is a richly flavored and full-bodied sauce that clings to the vegetables rather than pooling at the bottom of the bowl. Adding chunks of mango takes the salad to new heights of contrasting sweet, sour, spicy flavors, and a sprinkle of plantain chips adds fun crunch. For a spicier dish, add the ribs and seeds from the jalapeño.

1 Process whole tomatoes, jalapeño, oil, garlic, lime zest and juice, and salt in blender until smooth, 30 to 60 seconds, scraping down sides of blender jar as needed. Strain mixture through fine-mesh strainer set over large bowl, pressing on solids to extract as much liquid as possible; discard solids.

2 Add hearts of palm, jicama, mango, shallot, and quartered tomatoes to bowl with dressing and toss to combine. Refrigerate until chilled, about 30 minutes.

3 Add avocado and cilantro to hearts of palm mixture and toss to combine. Season with salt and pepper to taste. Transfer ceviche to serving bowls, drizzle with extra oil, and top with plantain chips. Serve.

Kitchen Improv

USE WHAT YOU'VE GOT

Substitute radishes for jicama. Substitute tortilla chips, corn nuts, or popcorn for plantain chips.

LEVEL UP

Serve over salad greens or tostadas or folded into tortillas.

Beet Salad

WITH WATERCRESS AND SPICED YOGURT

SERVES 2

TOTAL TIME 35 minutes

- 1 pound beets, trimmed, peeled, and cut into ¾-inch pieces
- ½ teaspoon table salt, plus salt for cooking beets
- 1 cup plain plant-based yogurt
- 2 tablespoons chopped fresh cilantro, mint, or dill, divided
- 5 teaspoons extra-virgin olive oil, divided
- 1 teaspoon grated fresh ginger
- ½ teaspoon grated lime zest plus 1 tablespoon juice, divided
- 1 small garlic clove, minced
- ¼ teaspoon ground cumin
- ¼ teaspoon ground coriander
- ⅛ teaspoon pepper
- 2 ounces (2 cups) watercress, torn into bite-size pieces
- 2 tablespoons shelled pistachios or almonds, toasted and chopped, divided

WHY THIS RECIPE WORKS Beets often get short shrift, maybe because cooking them takes time. But vibrant red beets are earthy, sweet, and eye-catching, so we felt it was time to give them their due in this strikingly composed salad. Roasting beets preserves their sweet flavor better than boiling, but it's slow. So instead, we peel the beets, cut them into small pieces, and then microwave them in a covered bowl with a small amount of water—just ½ cup. This small amount of liquid steams the beets quickly, helping them become tender after just 15 minutes in the microwave, without washing away any of their flavor. To maximize the salad's visual appeal, we build it in layers. First we spread serving plates with a layer of lime-spiked spiced plant-based yogurt. Next we toss a couple handfuls of peppery watercress with crunchy pistachios, olive oil, and lime juice until coated. We then top the yogurt mixture with the greens, leaving a border of the yogurt visible. And finally, on goes the crowning glory: the tender, sweet beets. Be sure to wear gloves when peeling and cutting the beets to prevent your hands from becoming stained.

1 Microwave beets, ½ cup water, and ¼ teaspoon salt in covered bowl until beets can be easily pierced with paring knife, about 15 minutes, stirring halfway through microwaving. Drain beets in colander and let cool slightly, about 10 minutes.

2 Whisk yogurt, 1 tablespoon cilantro, 1 tablespoon oil, ginger, lime zest and 2 teaspoons juice, garlic, cumin, coriander, pepper, and ¼ teaspoon salt together in bowl. Spread yogurt mixture over serving plates.

3 Toss watercress with 1 tablespoon pistachios, 1 teaspoon oil, ½ teaspoon lime juice, and remaining ¼ teaspoon salt until well coated. Divide watercress mixture over yogurt mixture on serving plates, leaving 1-inch border of yogurt mixture.

4 Toss beets with remaining 1 teaspoon oil and remaining ½ teaspoon lime juice in now-empty bowl. Season with salt and pepper to taste. Divide beet mixture over watercress mixture. Sprinkle with remaining 1 tablespoon cilantro and remaining 1 tablespoon pistachios. Serve.

Kitchen Improv

USE WHAT YOU'VE GOT

Substitute canned or vacuum-sealed precooked beets for fresh beets;
skip step 1. Substitute baby arugula for watercress.

MAKE IT A WRAP

Spread yogurt sauce over lavashes or pitas, top with watercress and
beets, and fold or roll breads over filling.

Meaty Taco Salad
WITH BLACK BEANS

SERVES 2

TOTAL TIME 40 minutes

TOPPING

- 1 tablespoon vegetable oil
- 1 small onion, chopped fine
- 6 ounces plant-based ground meat
- 2 teaspoons chili powder
- 1 garlic clove, minced
- ¼ cup tomato sauce
- ¼ cup vegetable broth
- 1 teaspoon cider vinegar
- ½ teaspoon light brown sugar

SALAD

- 1 romaine lettuce heart (6 ounces), cut into 1-inch pieces
- 1 (15-ounce) can black beans, rinsed
- 4 ounces cherry or grape tomatoes, quartered
- ¼ cup fresh cilantro leaves, divided
- 1 tablespoon lime juice, plus lime wedges for serving
- 1 cup tortilla chips, broken into 1-inch pieces

WHY THIS RECIPE WORKS   While we love a good old-fashioned taco, there's something to be said for shaking up the formula once in a while. A taco salad bowl is basically just a deconstructed taco—all the usual suspects are present, plus a bonus helping of crisp, refreshing lettuce. And because you're loading up a bowl rather than a tortilla, you can really pile on the toppings if that's your jam. Here we season the plant-based taco meat with chili powder and garlic and simmer it with onion, tomato sauce, and a splash of vegetable broth until the mixture thickens but is still nice and saucy. Brown sugar and cider vinegar add sweet-tangy depth to the mixture. A romaine lettuce heart, can of black beans, and juicy cherry tomatoes make up the salad portion of the dish. There's no need for a separate dressing; in combination with fresh lime juice, the sauce from the meat mixture provides plenty of flavor and ties all the components together. A garnish of crumbled tortilla chips adds welcome crunch. For ways to use up leftover plant-based meat, see page 19.

1   FOR THE TOPPING   Heat oil in 10- or 12-inch nonstick skillet over medium heat until shimmering. Add onion and cook until softened and lightly browned, 4 to 6 minutes. Stir in ground meat and cook, breaking up meat with wooden spoon, until firm crumbles form, about 3 minutes. Stir in chili powder and garlic and cook until fragrant, about 30 seconds.

2   Stir in tomato sauce, broth, vinegar, and sugar and simmer until slightly thickened, about 5 minutes. Off heat, season with salt and pepper to taste.

3   FOR THE SALAD   Toss lettuce, beans, tomatoes, and 2 tablespoons cilantro with lime juice in large bowl. Season with salt and pepper to taste. Transfer salad to serving bowls and top with meat topping, tortilla chips, and remaining 2 tablespoons cilantro. Serve with lime wedges.

Kitchen Improv

USE WHAT YOU'VE GOT

Substitute 1 tablespoon tomato paste for tomato sauce and increase broth to ½ cup. Substitute escarole, iceberg lettuce, or frisée for romaine lettuce. Substitute pinto or cannellini beans or chickpeas for black beans.

LEVEL UP

Top with sliced radishes, chopped avocado, fresh or pickled jalapeño, Quick Pickled Red Onion (page 26), shredded plant-based cheddar cheese, plant-based sour cream or yogurt, and/or hot sauce.

Carrot Noodle Salad
WITH HARISSA, MINT, AND APRICOTS

SERVES 2

TOTAL TIME 15 minutes

3	tablespoons harissa
1	tablespoon lemon juice
1	tablespoon water
1	teaspoon sugar
¼	teaspoon table salt
12	ounces carrot noodles, cut into 6-inch lengths
2	cups (2 ounces) baby arugula
¼	cup chopped fresh mint or parsley, divided
¼	cup dried apricots, sliced thin

Kitchen Improv

USE WHAT YOU'VE GOT

Substitute raisins or dried figs for apricots.

LEVEL UP

Use multicolored carrots to make carrot noodles, or use mixture of beet and carrot noodles. Top with crumbled plant-based cheese and/or toasted nuts or seeds.

BULK IT UP

Top with tempeh crumbles (page 27) or Pan-Seared Tofu (page 274).

WHY THIS RECIPE WORKS   This whimsical salad, composed primarily of naturally sweet curlicue carrot noodles and mildly peppery baby arugula, could hardly be easier. We cut the long noodles into more manageable 6-inch lengths for easier eating before tossing them with the arugula, fresh chopped mint, and a handful of chewy, jammy dried apricots. A harissa–lemon juice dressing brings smoky, tangy heat and earthy spice to the sweet mix of vegetables and fruit. And to gild the jewel-toned lily, everything comes together in record time—a mere 20 minutes—meaning this salad can be enjoyed at practically a moment's notice. We prefer to make our own carrot noodles with a spiralizer, but you can use store-bought carrot noodles. You will need 1 pound of carrots to yield 12 ounces of noodles; look for carrots that are at least ¾ inch wide at the thinnest end and 1½ inches wide at the thickest end. You can use store-bought harissa or our Harissa (page 26) in this recipe.

1   Whisk harissa, lemon juice, water, sugar, and salt together in large bowl. Measure out and reserve 1 tablespoon dressing for serving.

2   Add carrot noodles, arugula, and 3 tablespoons mint to bowl with dressing and toss to coat. Season with salt and pepper to taste. Transfer salad to serving bowls, top with apricots and remaining 1 tablespoon mint, and drizzle with reserved dressing. Serve.

Garlicky Broccoli and Chickpea Salad

SERVES 2

TOTAL TIME 45 minutes

- 3 tablespoons extra-virgin olive oil, divided
- 2 teaspoons lemon juice
- 2 garlic cloves, minced
- 2 teaspoons plant-based mayonnaise
- ¼ teaspoon red pepper flakes
- 1 (15-ounce) can chickpeas, rinsed
- 1 small red onion, halved and sliced ½ inch thick
- ½ teaspoon table salt, divided
- ¼ teaspoon pepper, divided
- 12 ounces broccoli florets, cut into 2-inch pieces

Kitchen Improv

USE WHAT YOU'VE GOT

Substitute cauliflower florets for broccoli. Substitute cannellini or small white beans for chickpeas.

LEVEL UP

Top with grated plant-based Parmesan, crumbled plant-based cheese, and/or toasted nuts or seeds.

WHY THIS RECIPE WORKS   Roasted broccoli is one of the kings of the vegetable kingdom: crisp-tender, sweet, and lightly charred at the edges. Combine the roasted florets with a can of creamy chickpeas and you've got an unbelievably easy salad hearty enough to put at the center of your plate. Instead of heating up the oven, we turn this salad into a one-pan meal by pan-roasting the broccoli in a skillet. After softening a red onion, we transfer it to a bowl with the chickpeas and a creamy lemony-garlicky dressing and then use the same skillet to cook the broccoli. We intentionally slightly overcrowd the pan with broccoli at first; this causes trapped steam to quickly soften the top layer of broccoli, all while the florets on the bottom char and turn crispy through direct contact with the hot pan. Stirring the broccoli at 5-minute intervals redistributes the broccoli so every bit achieves the perfect balance of tenderness and crispy char in no time. If you use a 10-inch skillet, the skillet will look very full when you first add the broccoli, but the broccoli will shrink as it cooks. For ways to use up leftover broccoli, see page 18.

1   Whisk 1 tablespoon oil, lemon juice, garlic, mayonnaise, and pepper flakes together in large bowl. Add chickpeas and toss to combine; set aside.

2   Heat 1 tablespoon oil in 10- or 12-inch nonstick skillet over medium heat until shimmering. Add onion, ¼ teaspoon salt, and ⅛ teaspoon pepper and cook until softened and lightly browned, 4 to 6 minutes. Transfer onion to bowl with chickpea mixture.

3   Heat remaining 1 tablespoon oil in now-empty skillet over medium-low heat until shimmering. Add broccoli, remaining ¼ teaspoon salt, and remaining ⅛ teaspoon pepper. Cook until broccoli is well browned and crispy in spots, about 20 minutes, stirring every 5 minutes. Transfer broccoli to bowl with chickpea mixture and toss to combine. Serve warm or at room temperature.

Warm Escarole and Cannellini Bean Salad

SERVES 2
TOTAL TIME 35 minutes

- 2 tablespoons extra-virgin olive oil, divided
- 1 small shallot, minced
- 1½ teaspoons Dijon mustard
- 1 teaspoon grated lemon zest plus 1 tablespoon juice
- ¾ teaspoon ras el hanout
- ⅛ teaspoon table salt
- 1 (15-ounce) can cannellini beans, rinsed
- 1 carrot, peeled and shredded
- ⅓ cup raisins, chopped
- ¼ cup slivered almonds
- 6 ounces escarole, torn into bite-size pieces (6 cups), divided
- 3 tablespoons chopped fresh mint or parsley

Kitchen Improv

USE WHAT YOU'VE GOT

Substitute combination of ¼ teaspoon cinnamon, ¼ teaspoon coriander, and ¼ teaspoon cumin for ras el hanout. Substitute frisée for escarole. Substitute chickpeas for cannellini beans. Substitute other dried fruits for raisins or other chopped nuts for almonds.

LEVEL UP

Top with Umami Croutons (page 27) and/or crumbled plant-based cheese.

WHY THIS RECIPE WORKS   Ruffled escarole makes a robust, luxuriantly textured canvas for the rest of the bold, flavorful ingredients in this warm salad of creamy cannellini beans and lightly wilted greens. To generate enough heat to just wilt the greens without going overboard and turning them limp and insipid, we turn to a Dutch oven. After using it to sauté the salad's colorful mix-ins of crunchy carrots and almonds and chewy raisins, we remove the pot from the heat and let it cool slightly (the heavy sides of the Dutch oven are very effective at holding on to heat) before we add the escarole. At the same time, we also mix in a lemony, mustardy vinaigrette enhanced with smoky ras el hanout. The Dutch oven's generous surface area and high sides make it a cinch to toss the greens without causing them to spill over onto the stove; a few turns of the tongs later and the greens have just the right slightly softened texture and the vinaigrette is warm and fragrant. As a finishing touch, we top the salad with tender, nutty cannellini beans.

1   Whisk 1 tablespoon oil, shallot, mustard, lemon zest and juice, ras el hanout, and salt together in small bowl. Toss beans with 2 teaspoons dressing in second bowl; set aside.

2   Heat remaining 1 tablespoon oil in Dutch oven over medium heat until shimmering. Add carrot, raisins, and almonds and cook, stirring often, until carrot is softened, 3 to 4 minutes. Off heat, let cool for 5 minutes.

3   Add half of escarole to pot, drizzle with half of remaining dressing, and toss until escarole is slightly wilted, about 1 minute. Add mint, remaining escarole, and remaining dressing and toss until well combined. Season with salt and pepper to taste. Transfer escarole mixture to serving bowls and top with beans. Serve warm or at room temperature.

Charred Cabbage Salad
WITH TORN TOFU AND PLANTAIN CHIPS

SERVES 2
TOTAL TIME 55 minutes

- 7 ounces firm or extra-firm tofu, torn into bite-size pieces
- 2 tablespoons lime juice, divided
- 1 tablespoon soy sauce
- 2 teaspoons grated fresh ginger, divided
- 1 teaspoon sugar
- 2 tablespoons vegetable oil, divided
- 2 teaspoons Thai red curry paste, divided
- 1½ teaspoons ground turmeric, divided
- ⅛ teaspoon table salt
- ½ head red or green cabbage (1 pound), cut into 4 wedges through core
- 2 tablespoons shredded fresh basil
- 1 scallion, sliced thin
- 2 tablespoons plantain chips, crushed

Kitchen Improv

USE WHAT YOU'VE GOT

Substitute dried banana chips, chopped macadamia nuts, or chopped cashews for plantains.

LEVEL UP

Toss bean sprouts or sliced water chestnuts into tofu mixture in step 1.

WHY THIS RECIPE WORKS   This show-stopping salad is a feast for multiple senses, offering up richly colorful bites of red cabbage, emerald-green fresh basil, and golden plantain chips in addition to a wallop of flavor. The flavor inspiration for this salad comes from Southeast Asia. The cabbage gets coated in a mix of Thai red curry paste and turmeric before being roasted in the oven to bring out its natural sweetness, and torn tofu pieces are marinated in a piquant mix of soy sauce, lime juice, ginger, and sugar to transform each piece into a sweet-and-sour flavor bomb. Tearing the tofu produces all sorts of rough nooks and crannies that allow the tofu to hold on to the marinade much more efficiently than tofu with straight-cut sides. A scallion adds pleasant crispness; plantain chips contribute sweet-salty crunch. And to make a warm and impactful dressing to drizzle over everything, we bloom more curry paste, turmeric, and ginger in the microwave before whisking in another dose of tart lime juice. For ways to use up leftover cabbage and tofu, see pages 18–19.

1   Adjust oven rack to lowest position and heat oven to 500 degrees. Line rimmed baking sheet with aluminum foil. Gently press tofu dry with paper towels. Whisk 1 tablespoon lime juice, soy sauce, 1 teaspoon ginger, and sugar together in medium bowl. Add tofu and toss gently to coat; let sit for 20 minutes. (Tofu can be refrigerated for up to 24 hours.)

2   Whisk 1 tablespoon oil, ½ teaspoon curry paste, 1 teaspoon turmeric, and salt together in small bowl. Arrange cabbage wedges in even layer on prepared sheet, then brush cabbage all over with oil mixture. Cover tightly with foil and roast for 10 minutes. Remove foil and drizzle cabbage with 1½ teaspoons oil. Roast, uncovered, until cabbage is tender and bottoms of wedges are well browned, 10 to 15 minutes. Transfer baking sheet to wire rack and let cabbage cool slightly, about 5 minutes.

3   Whisk remaining 1 teaspoon ginger, 1½ teaspoons oil, 1½ teaspoons curry paste, and ½ teaspoon turmeric together in second bowl. Microwave until fragrant, about 10 seconds. Whisk in remaining 1 tablespoon lime juice.

4   Transfer cabbage to cutting board, chop coarse, then transfer to serving plates. Top with basil, scallion, and tofu. Drizzle with dressing and sprinkle with plantain chips. Serve warm or at room temperature.

Roasted Grape and Cauliflower Salad
WITH CHERMOULA

SERVES 2

TOTAL TIME 45 minutes

- 1¼ pounds cauliflower florets, cut into 1-inch pieces
- 1 cup seedless red grapes
- 1 shallot, sliced thin
- ¼ cup extra-virgin olive oil, divided
- ¾ teaspoon table salt, divided
- ¼ cup chopped fresh cilantro, plus whole leaves for serving
- 1 tablespoon lemon juice
- 1 garlic clove, minced
- ¼ teaspoon ground cumin
- ¼ teaspoon paprika
- ¼ teaspoon cayenne pepper
- 1 tablespoon toasted and chopped walnuts or pecans

Kitchen Improv

USE WHAT YOU'VE GOT

Substitute other nuts, such as pecans, almonds, or cashews, for walnuts.

LEVEL UP

Top with Umami Croutons (page 27) or pita chips broken into 1-inch pieces.

BULK IT UP

Top with Pan-Seared Tofu (page 274) or cannellini or small white beans. Serve with crusty bread.

WHY THIS RECIPE WORKS Cauliflower's delicate and versatile flavor makes it an ideal canvas on which to paint other flavors and textures. Here those "paints" come from grapes, cilantro, and shallot, which combine to turn simple roasted cauliflower into a memorable and refined salad. Cauliflower's nutty and sweet flavor shines brightest when roasted, but we don't stop with roasting just the cauliflower. Since we're turning the oven on anyway, we make the most of it by also tossing sweet red grapes and a sliced scallion onto the same sheet as the cauliflower to roast simultaneously, bringing out the caramelized sweetness of all three. At first glance a whole head of cauliflower might sound like a lot to serve two, but it cooks down in the oven's intense heat to yield a serving that's substantial but not at all overwhelming. While the vegetables and grapes roast, we whisk together a quick chermoula, a North African sauce made with hefty amounts of cilantro, lemon, and garlic, to use as a dressing. Fresh cilantro leaves and crunchy walnuts are the finishing touch. For ways to use up leftover cauliflower, see page 18.

1 Adjust oven rack to middle position and heat oven to 450 degrees. Toss cauliflower, grapes, and shallot with 1 tablespoon oil and ½ teaspoon salt and arrange in even layer on rimmed baking sheet. Roast until cauliflower is spotty brown and tender, 20 to 25 minutes, stirring mixture halfway through roasting. Transfer baking sheet to wire rack and let cauliflower mixture cool slightly, about 5 minutes.

2 Whisk chopped cilantro, lemon juice, garlic, cumin, paprika, cayenne, remaining 3 tablespoons oil, and remaining ¼ teaspoon salt together in large bowl. Add cauliflower mixture and toss to coat. Season with salt and pepper to taste. Transfer salad to serving bowls and sprinkle with cilantro leaves and walnuts. Serve warm or at room temperature.

Roasted Zucchini, Corn, and Tomato Salad
WITH MAPLE VINAIGRETTE

SERVES 2
TOTAL TIME 45 minutes

- 3 tablespoons extra-virgin olive oil, divided
- 2½ teaspoons maple syrup, divided
- ¾ teaspoon table salt, divided
- ¼ teaspoon pepper, divided
- 12 ounces zucchini, cut crosswise into 1-inch-thick rounds
- 1½ cups frozen corn, thawed and patted dry
- 2 teaspoons cider vinegar
- 1 small garlic clove, minced
- 1 large tomato (8 ounces), cored, cut into ½-inch-thick wedges, wedges halved crosswise
- 2 ounces (2 cups) baby arugula
- 2 tablespoons roasted unsalted sunflower seeds or pepitas

Kitchen Improv

USE WHAT YOU'VE GOT

Substitute yellow summer squash or pattypan squash, cut into rounds, for zucchini. Substitute fresh corn for frozen corn. Substitute watercress or baby spinach for arugula.

BULK IT UP

Top with chickpeas or cannellini beans, Umami Croutons (page 27), pita chips cut into 1-inch pieces, and/or crumbled plant-based cheese.

WHY THIS RECIPE WORKS   Roasting is a tried and true, hands-off way to coax out sweet, caramelized flavors from fresh vegetables; here, we use this method to add complexity to a hearty zucchini, corn, and tomato salad. We first toss the zucchini and corn in oil and maple syrup. The maple syrup complements the zucchini's sweet, creamy profile, and its sugar promotes browning. Leaving the zucchini in ample 1-inch rounds gives it a real presence in the salad. Preheating the sheet pan before adding the vegetables helps quickly sear them where they make contact with the hot pan, developing a crispy charred exterior, and cooking the squash and corn together shortens the overall cooking time. While the sheet pan heats, we pull together a sweet and tangy dressing made with more maple syrup and cider vinegar. To round out the salad's flavors and textures, we toss the roasted vegetables with peppery arugula and juicy tomatoes, finishing with a sprinkle of roasted sunflower seeds for crunch.

1   Adjust oven rack to lowest position, place rimmed baking sheet on rack, and heat oven to 500 degrees. Whisk 1 tablespoon oil, 1 teaspoon maple syrup, ½ teaspoon salt, and ⅛ teaspoon pepper together in large bowl. Add zucchini and corn and toss to coat.

2   Working quickly, arrange zucchini, cut side down, and corn in even layer on hot sheet. Roast until bottoms of zucchini rounds are browned and zucchini is tender, 12 to 15 minutes. Transfer baking sheet to wire rack and let vegetables cool slightly, about 5 minutes.

3   Whisk vinegar, garlic, and remaining 2 tablespoons oil, 1½ teaspoons maple syrup, ¼ teaspoon salt, and ⅛ teaspoon pepper together in now-empty bowl. Add tomato, arugula, and roasted vegetables and toss to combine. Transfer to serving bowls and sprinkle with sunflower seeds. Serve.

Grilled Vegetable and Orzo Salad
WITH LEMON AND BASIL

SERVES 2
TOTAL TIME 55 minutes

- 2 tablespoons extra-virgin olive oil, divided
- 2 tablespoons chopped fresh basil, plus extra for serving
- 1 teaspoon grated lemon zest plus 1 tablespoon juice, plus lemon wedges for serving
- 1 teaspoon Dijon mustard
- 1 small garlic clove, minced
- ½ teaspoon salt, plus salt for cooking pasta
- ⅛ teaspoon pepper
- 1 small red onion, sliced into ½-inch-thick rounds
- 1 red, orange, yellow, or green bell pepper, stemmed, seeded, and quartered
- 1 zucchini or summer squash, halved lengthwise
- ½ cup orzo
- 2 tablespoons capers, rinsed

Kitchen Improv

USE WHAT YOU'VE GOT

Substitute other vegetables, such as asparagus, whole mushrooms, or broccoli florets, for onion, bell pepper, and/or zucchini. Substitute olives or pepperoncini for capers.

LEVEL UP

Top with crumbled plant-based cheese and/or toasted nuts or seeds. Add baby greens or drained jarred artichoke hearts.

WHY THIS RECIPE WORKS   With fresh produce so abundantly available in the summer, grilled vegetables make for a natural foundation for an al fresco supper. For a hearty vegetable-pasta hybrid salad for two that's tasty enough to be worth firing up the grill, we pair the grilled, char-marked vegetables, cut into substantial 1-inch pieces, with tender orzo, fresh basil, and briny capers. Choosing vegetables with similar cooking times makes grilling a breeze, so here we opt for zucchini, red onion, and bell pepper. Cutting the zucchini lengthwise, the onion into thick rounds, and the bell pepper into quarters creates large pieces that are easy to grill—no fussy fiddling with flipping dozens of tiny pieces. Each piece also takes the same amount of time to cook through as the rest, so there's no need to stagger their cooking and juggle moving pieces on and off the grill. A lemon-and-basil dressing with garlic and Dijon mustard adds richness and brightness that liven up the grilled salad.

1   Whisk 1 tablespoon oil, basil, lemon zest and juice, mustard, garlic, salt, and pepper together in bowl; set aside. Brush onion, bell pepper, and zucchini with remaining 1 tablespoon oil.

2A   FOR A CHARCOAL GRILL   Open bottom vent completely. Light large chimney starter half filled with charcoal briquettes (3 quarts). When top coals are partially covered with ash, pour evenly over grill. Set cooking grate in place, cover, and open lid vent completely. Heat grill until hot, about 5 minutes.

2B   FOR A GAS GRILL   Turn all burners to high; cover; and heat grill until hot, about 15 minutes. Turn all burners to medium.

3   Grill vegetables, covered, until spottily charred, 5 to 8 minutes per side. Transfer vegetables to cutting board.

4   Meanwhile, bring 2 quarts water to boil in large pot. Add orzo and 1½ teaspoons salt and cook, stirring often, until tender. Drain orzo, rinse under cold running water, and drain again thoroughly. Add orzo and capers to bowl with dressing.

5   Cut vegetables into 1-inch pieces, add to bowl with orzo, and toss to combine. Season with salt and pepper to taste. Transfer salad to serving bowls and sprinkle with extra basil. Serve warm or at room temperature with lemon wedges.

Rainbow Salad
WITH CRISPY TEMPEH

SERVES 2

TOTAL TIME 20 minutes

- 1 orange
- 5 ounces (5 cups) baby arugula
- ¼ cup Quick Ginger-Sesame Vinaigrette (page 26), divided
- 1 (15-ounce) can diced beets, rinsed and patted dry
- 6 ounces cherry or grape tomatoes, halved
- 1 recipe Garlicky Tempeh Crumbles (page 27)
- ½ avocado, cut into ½-inch pieces
- 4 radishes, trimmed, halved, and sliced thin
- 2 tablespoons crumbled plant-based feta cheese

Kitchen Improv

USE WHAT YOU'VE GOT

Substitute Pan-Seared Tofu (page 274) for tempeh crumbles.

MAKE IT A BOWL

Serve salad over rice or other grain (see page 270).

WHY THIS RECIPE WORKS Arranging a rainbow of fruits and vegetables on a bed of greens make for a stunning presentation—and luckily, this also happens to be one salad that tastes as good as it looks. Cherry tomatoes and a segmented orange offer bright acidity, which we balance with buttery avocado and crisp radishes for their peppery snap and cheerful pink hue. To contrast with all the crisp raw vegetables, we add a can of tender, purply-red beets. A refreshing ginger-sesame dressing highlights the salad, but to work as a standalone meal it also needs a hit of satiating plant-based protein. Crumbled tempeh to the rescue! This fermented vegan protein is full of complex umami flavor. To give it a crispy texture that would complement the rest of the salad, we microwave it with a little bit of oil and garlic. This microwaving browns and crisps the tempeh as it effectively fries in record time, saving us a pan to clean along the way.

1 Cut away peel and pith from orange. Holding fruit over bowl, use paring knife to slice between membranes to release segments.

2 Toss arugula with 2 tablespoons vinaigrette until well coated. Season with salt and pepper to taste. Transfer arugula to serving bowls and top with beets, tomatoes, tempeh, avocado, radishes, feta, and orange segments. Drizzle with remaining 2 tablespoons vinaigrette. Serve.

Spinach Salad
WITH WHITE BEANS, CORN, AND SUMAC

SERVES 2
TOTAL TIME 40 minutes

- 1 tablespoon extra-virgin olive oil, divided
- 1 cup frozen corn, thawed
- ¼ teaspoon sumac, plus extra for sprinkling
- 1 scallion, sliced thin
- 2 teaspoons red wine vinegar
- ½ teaspoon table salt
- ¼ teaspoon pepper
- 1 tomato, cored and cut into ½-inch pieces
- 2 ounces (2 cups) baby spinach
- 1 (15-ounce) can small white beans, rinsed
- 1 tablespoon chopped fresh basil

Kitchen Improv

USE WHAT YOU'VE GOT

Substitute smoked paprika for sumac. Substitute halved cherry or grape tomatoes for large tomato. Substitute fresh corn for frozen corn.

MAKE IT A BOWL

Serve salad over rice or other grain (see page 270).

WHY THIS RECIPE WORKS Fresh corn salad is a summery addition to a picnic or backyard-barbecue table. To turn this favorite side dish into a full-fledged meal, we add convenient canned cannellini beans. The most typical preparation method for the fresh corn—stripping the kernels off the cob, adding vegetables (usually tomatoes, onions, and/or peppers), and tossing with dressing—produces rather wan salads. Instead, browning thawed frozen kernels lightly in a skillet for a few minutes gives even out-of-season corn a multidimensional nutty flavor and deep sweetness which in turn gives us the option to make this salad a solid year-round option. Looking for even more complexity, we hit upon adding a dash a sumac to the oil with the corn to bloom; the tangy spice adds a unique acidic fruitiness that elevates the whole dish. Tender baby spinach adds bulk to the salad. As for the dressing, equal parts of oil and vinegar create a rich, sharp vinaigrette that balances the creamy beans and sweet corn. Be sure to let the toasted corn cool before adding the tomatoes, as otherwise the heat from the corn will partially cook them.

1 Heat 1 teaspoon oil in 10- or 12-inch nonstick skillet over medium-high heat until shimmering. Add corn and cook, stirring occasionally, until spotty brown, about 5 minutes. Add sumac and cook until fragrant, about 30 seconds. Transfer to large bowl and stir in scallion, vinegar, salt, pepper, and remaining 2 teaspoons oil; let cool completely, about 20 minutes.

2 Add tomato, spinach, beans, and basil to corn mixture and toss to combine. Season with salt, pepper, and extra sumac to taste. Serve.

VARIATION
Spinach Salad with Black Beans, Chili, and Lime
Substitute chili powder for sumac, lime juice for red wine vinegar, black beans for small white beans, and cilantro for basil.

Bread and Tomato Salad
WITH LIMA BEANS, FETA, AND OLIVES

SERVES 2

TOTAL TIME 45 minutes

- 3 tablespoons extra-virgin olive oil, divided
- 2 tablespoons chopped jarred pepperoncini, plus 2 teaspoons pepperoncini brine
- 2 teaspoons red wine vinegar
- ½ teaspoon dried oregano, divided
- ¼ teaspoon Dijon mustard
- ¼ teaspoon table salt
- 6 ounces cherry or grape tomatoes, halved
- 2 Persian cucumbers, halved lengthwise and sliced ½ inch thick
- ¾ cup frozen baby lima beans, thawed
- ¼ cup pitted kalamata olives, halved
- 2 ounces plant-based feta cheese, cut into ½-inch cubes (¾ cup)
- 1 large shallot, halved and sliced thin
- 1 (10-inch) pita, torn into 1-inch pieces
- 1 small garlic clove, minced
- 2 tablespoons chopped fresh dill or basil

WHY THIS RECIPE WORKS   We give a typical bread-and-tomato salad a Greek-inspired flavor twist with this refreshing salad tailor-made for summertime, composed primarily of ripe tomatoes, buttery lima beans, and cucumber. Briny bits of olive and vinegary pepperoncini pop on the taste buds, while torn pita adds substance and soaks up all the flavors of the highly seasoned vinaigrette. For even bigger flavor, we replace some of the vinegar in the vinaigrette with brine from the jarred pepperoncini and add a smidge of spicy Dijon mustard. Tossing the torn pita pieces with olive oil, garlic, and oregano and baking them until crispy infuses them deeply with flavor and heads off any sogginess; for further insurance against soggy pita, we mix the pieces into the moist salad just a few minutes before serving. The variation takes notes from Italian panzanella, with cannellini beans, plant-based mozzarella, and ciabatta. Persian cucumbers (also sold as mini or snacking cucumbers) are similar to seedless cucumbers in flavor and texture; they do not need to be peeled.

1   Adjust oven rack to upper-middle position and heat oven to 400 degrees. Whisk 2 tablespoons oil, pepperoncini brine, vinegar, ¼ teaspoon oregano, mustard, and salt together in medium bowl. Add tomatoes, cucumbers, beans, olives, feta, shallot, and pepperoncini and toss to combine; set aside.

2   Meanwhile, toss pita with garlic, remaining 1 tablespoon oil, and remaining ¼ teaspoon oregano and arrange in even layer on rimmed baking sheet. Bake until golden and crispy, 8 to 10 minutes, stirring pita halfway through baking. Transfer baking sheet to wire rack and let pita chips cool, about 10 minutes. (Pita chips can be stored in airtight container at room temperature for up to 2 days.)

3   Add dill and pita chips to tomato mixture and toss to combine; let sit for 5 minutes. Season with salt and pepper to taste. Serve.

VARIATION

Bread and Tomato Salad with Cannellini Beans, Mozzarella, and Basil

Substitute canned cannellini beans for lima beans, plant-based mozzarella for feta, and green olives for kalamata olives. Substitute ciabatta for pita.

Kitchen Improv

USE WHAT YOU'VE GOT

Substitute cannellini beans, chickpeas, or small white beans for lima
beans. Substitute other fresh leafy herbs, such as parsley or mint, for dill.

Warm Spiced Couscous Salad

SERVES 2

TOTAL TIME 40 minutes

- ½ cup pearl couscous
- 1 carrot, peeled and chopped
- 5 teaspoons extra-virgin olive oil, divided
- ⅛ teaspoon table salt
- ⅔ cup vegetable broth
- ½ teaspoon smoked paprika
- ¼ teaspoon ground cumin
- 1 (15-ounce) can chickpeas, rinsed
- ¼ cup raisins
- ¼ cup chopped fresh parsley or cilantro
- 2 teaspoons lemon juice, plus lemon wedges for serving

Kitchen Improv

USE WHAT YOU'VE GOT

Substitute dried apricots, dates, or dried figs for raisins.

LEVEL UP

Top with pomegranate seeds and/or toasted nuts or seeds. Add baby spinach or baby arugula.

WHY THIS RECIPE WORKS The base of this bright and smoky, sweet-yet-tart salad is made up of couscous, which, despite appearances, is in fact a tiny, quick-cooking pasta and not a whole grain. But whatever its official designation, there's no doubt that couscous makes for a fantastic, hearty salad foundation. Pearl couscous, which comes in bigger pieces than traditional couscous, gives this salad great texture and heft. We toast the couscous in oil while at the same time softening a carrot to bring out its nutty flavor. Next, we stir in vegetable broth, smoked paprika, and earthy cumin and simmer the lot until the couscous is cooked and tender with just a little bit of chew. Raisins add pops of sweetness, and canned chickpeas add satiating protein; a single can of the beans is the perfect amount to serve two when mixed with the rest of the salad's elements. Lemon and parsley brighten everything up. Pearl couscous has grains about the size of capers and is not precooked, unlike traditional couscous; do not substitute traditional couscous here.

1   Combine couscous, carrot, 2 teaspoons oil, and salt in large saucepan and cook over medium heat, stirring often, until half of grains are golden, about 5 minutes. Stir in broth, paprika, and cumin and bring to simmer. Reduce heat to low, cover, and simmer gently, stirring occasionally, until broth is absorbed, 10 to 15 minutes. Off heat, let sit for 3 minutes.

2   Stir chickpeas, raisins, parsley, lemon juice, and remaining 1 tablespoon oil into couscous mixture. Season with salt and pepper to taste. Serve with lemon wedges.

Freekeh Salad
WITH SWEET POTATO AND WALNUTS

SERVES 2
TOTAL TIME 55 minutes

- ¾ cup freekeh
- ½ teaspoon table salt, divided, plus salt for cooking freekeh
- 1 small sweet potato (8 ounces), peeled and cut into 1-inch pieces (about 1 cup)
- 2 tablespoons extra-virgin olive oil, divided
- ¼ teaspoon pepper, divided
- ¼ teaspoon ground fenugreek or curry powder
- 2 tablespoons tahini
- 1 tablespoon lemon juice
- 1 tablespoon water
- ½ cup fresh cilantro leaves
- 2 tablespoons chopped toasted walnuts

Kitchen Improv

USE WHAT YOU'VE GOT

Substitute barley or farro for freekeh; decrease cooking time in step 1 to 20 to 40 minutes for barley or 25 to 35 minutes for farro. Substitute other toasted nuts or seeds for walnuts.

WHY THIS RECIPE WORKS   Grain salads are a heartier alternative to your typical lettuce- or vegetable-based salad, but can often feel out of reach due to the time it takes to cook whole grains. While it's true that whole grains, like the freekeh in this salad, take a little patience, the reward is well worth it: in this case, an ultrasatisfying protein- and fiber-rich grain salad with pleasant chew. The freekeh brings a grassy, slightly smoky flavor unlike that of any other grain. We use the time it takes to cook the freekeh, which is actually a type of wheat, to tenderize a sweet potato in the microwave before briefly sautéing it until golden brown. Walnuts give the salad mild crunch, and the flavor is rounded out with fenugreek, a sweet seed with a unique maple-like flavor, and a rich and nutty tahini-lemon dressing.

1   Bring 2 quarts water to boil in large saucepan. Add freekeh and ½ teaspoon salt, return to boil, and cook until grains are tender with slight chew, 30 to 45 minutes. Drain freekeh, spread onto platter or rimmed baking sheet, and let cool completely, 10 to 15 minutes.

2   Meanwhile, microwave sweet potato in covered bowl until tender, 5 to 8 minutes, stirring halfway through microwaving; drain well. Heat 1 tablespoon oil in 8- or 10-inch nonstick skillet over medium heat until shimmering. Add sweet potato, ¼ teaspoon salt, and ⅛ teaspoon pepper and cook, stirring occasionally, until golden brown, 4 to 6 minutes. Off heat, stir in fenugreek.

3   Whisk tahini, lemon juice, water, and remaining ¼ teaspoon salt, 1 tablespoon oil, and ⅛ teaspoon pepper together in large bowl. Add freekeh, sweet potato, cilantro, and walnuts and toss to combine. Season with salt and pepper to taste. Serve warm or at room temperature.

Soba Noodle Salad

WITH EDAMAME, CABBAGE, AND PEANUT-GINGER SAUCE

SERVES 2

TOTAL TIME 25 minutes

- 6 ounces soba noodles
- 2 tablespoons peanut or almond butter
- 1 tablespoon soy sauce, plus extra for serving
- 2 teaspoons unseasoned rice vinegar
- 1½ teaspoons packed light brown sugar
- 1 teaspoon grated fresh ginger
- 1 small garlic clove, minced
- 1 cup shredded red or green cabbage
- ⅓ cup frozen shelled edamame beans, thawed and patted dry
- ¼ cup fresh cilantro leaves
- 2 tablespoons chopped dry-roasted unsalted peanuts or almonds

   Lime wedges

Kitchen Improv

USE WHAT YOU'VE GOT

Substitute store-bought coleslaw mix for cabbage. Substitute sliced Persian cucumbers, thinly sliced snow peas, thinly sliced radishes, or thinly sliced scallions for edamame, cabbage, cilantro, and/or peanuts.

LEVEL UP

Sprinkle with toasted sesame seeds or crumbled nori or drizzle with hot sauce.

WHY THIS RECIPE WORKS   Soba noodles, made from buckwheat flour or a buckwheat–wheat flour blend, have a chewy texture and nutty flavor and are often enjoyed chilled. For a refreshing cold noodle salad, we cook soba noodles in unsalted boiling water (soba noodles contain salt, so there's no need to add extra) until tender but still resilient before rinsing them under cold running water to quickly halt the cooking process, remove excess starch, and prevent sticking. In keeping with the soba's Japanese origin, we toss the noodles with an umami-loaded dressing of peanut butter, soy sauce, rice vinegar, brown sugar, ginger, and garlic that clings to and flavors the noodles without overpowering their distinct taste. To round out the salad, we then mix in shredded cabbage, edamame, and a hefty dose of fresh cilantro until incorporated throughout the noodles, adding welcome crunch and color. For ways to use up leftover cabbage, see page 18.

1   Bring 2 quarts water to boil in large pot. Add noodles and cook, stirring often, until tender. Drain noodles, rinse well, and drain again; set aside.

2   Whisk peanut butter, soy sauce, vinegar, sugar, ginger, and garlic together in large bowl. Add noodles and toss to combine. Add cabbage, edamame, cilantro, and peanuts and toss to combine. Serve with lime wedges and extra soy sauce.

VARIATION

Soba Noodle Salad with Miso-Ginger Sauce

Persian cucumbers (also sold as mini or snacking cucumbers) are similar to seedless cucumbers in flavor and texture; they do not need to be peeled.

Omit garlic. Substitute 2 tablespoons white miso, 1 tablespoon mirin, 1 tablespoon toasted sesame oil, and 1 tablespoon water for peanut butter, soy sauce, vinegar, and sugar.

Bún Chả

SERVES 2

TOTAL TIME 40 minutes

2 tablespoons lime juice, plus lime wedges for serving

4 teaspoons soy sauce, plus extra for serving

1 tablespoon sugar

½–1 small Thai chile, stemmed, seeded, and minced

1 small garlic clove, minced

1 small shallot, minced

6 ounces plant-based ground meat

4 ounces rice vermicelli

1 tablespoon vegetable oil, divided

2 Persian cucumbers, quartered lengthwise and sliced thin

½ cup fresh cilantro and/or mint leaves, torn if large

Kitchen Improv

USE WHAT YOU'VE GOT

Substitute ½ English cucumber for Persian cucumbers. Thinly sliced bell pepper, radishes, carrot, and/or bean sprouts all work well in place of (or in addition to) cucumbers. Substitute rice or other grain (see page 270) for noodles.

WHY THIS RECIPE WORKS Vietnamese bún chả is a vibrant amalgam of pork, crisp lettuce and cucumber, bright herbs, and rice noodles, all united by a potent sweet-sour-salty sauce known as nước chấm. The traditional version of this meaty salad features grilled pork patties shaped like squished meatballs. Here, we swap the pork for plant-based meat and the grill for a nonstick skillet and press the patties into ½-inch-thick disks to give them even more flat, brownable surface area than the originals. Nước chấm traditionally includes fish sauce; to make up for its absence here, we substitute similarly salty soy sauce. We then use the sauce two ways: A couple tablespoons go into the meat mixture, and the rest goes on the side for drizzling over the salad, meat, and noodles according to individual preference. For a spicier dish, use the whole Thai chile. For the best results, make sure to shake all excess water from the noodles after rinsing them. Persian cucumbers (also sold as mini or snacking cucumbers) are similar to seedless cucumbers in flavor and texture; they do not need to be peeled. For ways to use up leftover plant-based meat, see page 19.

1 Whisk ¼ cup hot water, lime juice, soy sauce, sugar, Thai chile, and garlic in small bowl until sugar has dissolved; set aside. Combine shallot and 1 tablespoon sauce in medium bowl. Break ground meat into small pieces and add to bowl with shallot mixture. Gently knead with your hands until mixture is well combined. Using your moistened hands, divide meat mixture into 6 lightly packed balls, then flatten into ½-inch-thick patties. Transfer patties to plate and refrigerate for 15 minutes or up to 24 hours.

2 Bring 2 quarts water to boil in large saucepan. Off heat, add noodles and let sit, stirring occasionally, until tender, about 5 minutes. Drain noodles, rinse well, and drain again. Toss noodles with ½ teaspoon oil and transfer to serving bowls; set aside.

3 Heat remaining 2½ teaspoons oil in 10- or 12-inch nonstick skillet over medium-high heat until just smoking. Using spatula, transfer patties to skillet and cook until well browned on first side, 2 to 4 minutes. Flip patties and continue to cook until browned on second side and meat registers 130 to 135 degrees, about 2 minutes longer.

4 Top noodles with patties and cucumbers. Drizzle with remaining sauce and top with cilantro. Serve with lime wedges and extra soy sauce.

PASTA AND NOODLES

180 Spaghetti with Garlic, Olive Oil, and Artichokes

182 Skillet Penne with Fresh Tomato Sauce

with Fresh Tomato Sauce and Crispy Caper Crumbs

185 Fettuccine with Summer Squash, Ricotta, and Lemon-Parmesan Crumbs

186 Spaghetti with Broccoli and Avocado Pesto

189 Creamy Cashew Mac and Cheese

with Roasted Cauliflower and Sausage

190 Cashew e Pepe e Funghi

193 Campanelle with Roasted Cauliflower and Garlic Sauce

194 Rigatoni with Quick Mushroom Ragu

197 Linguine with Weeknight Bolognese

198 Spaghetti with Meatballs and Marinara

with Pesto Meatballs

201 Baked Ziti with Creamy Leeks, Kale, and Sun-Dried Tomatoes

202 Unstuffed Shells with Butternut Squash and Leeks

205 Meaty Zoodles with Mango and Garam Masala

206 Stir-Fried Noodles with Mushrooms, Snow Peas, and Bell Peppers

208 Dan Dan Mian

210 Japchae

213 Spicy Basil Rice Noodles with Bok Choy

Spaghetti with Garlic, Olive Oil, and Artichokes

SERVES 2

TOTAL TIME 30 minutes

- 3 tablespoons plus 2 teaspoons extra-virgin olive oil, divided
- 6 garlic cloves (5 minced, 1 minced to paste)
- ½ teaspoon table salt, divided, plus salt for cooking pasta
- ⅛ teaspoon red pepper flakes
- 9 ounces frozen artichoke hearts, thawed and patted dry
- 6 ounces spaghetti
- 2 tablespoons minced fresh parsley
- 1 teaspoon lemon juice, plus lemon wedges for serving

Kitchen Improv

USE WHAT YOU'VE GOT

Substitute linguine or fettuccine for spaghetti. Substitute other fresh herbs, such as basil or chives, for parsley.

LEVEL UP

Add ½ cup thawed frozen peas to pasta with artichokes in step 4. Top with grated plant-based Parmesan and/or chopped nuts.

WHY THIS RECIPE WORKS   Aglio e olio (literally "garlic and oil") is the perfect last-minute supper for two, coming together quickly from a short list of ordinary pantry staples. To make the most of each of the humble components, we start by sautéing a portion of the garlic slowly and gently in some of the oil until it develops a mellow, nutty, rich flavor. Off the heat, we stir in the rest of the garlic still raw to allow its spicy bite to add another layer of flavor. Three table-spoons of fruity, buttery extra-virgin olive oil is just enough to coat the pasta and evenly distribute the garlic without making the dish greasy. A nontraditional ingredient, frozen artichoke hearts, keeps prep supersimple and adds just enough vegetable heft to the dish to make it a solid dinner option. Minced parsley, fresh lemon juice, and a dash of red pepper flakes brighten the flavors. A rasp-style grater makes quick work of turning the garlic into a paste. To thaw the artichokes quickly, microwave them in a covered bowl for about 3 minutes.

1   Cook 2 tablespoons oil, minced garlic, ¼ teaspoon salt, and pepper flakes in 10- or 12-inch nonstick skillet over low heat, stirring often, until garlic foams and is sticky and straw-colored, about 10 minutes. Transfer to bowl and stir in garlic paste and 1 tablespoon oil; set aside.

2   Heat remaining 2 teaspoons oil in now-empty skillet over medium-high heat until shimmering. Add artichokes and remaining ¼ teaspoon salt and cook until artichokes are softened and lightly browned, 4 to 6 minutes. Remove from heat and cover to keep warm.

3   Meanwhile, bring 2 quarts water to boil in large pot. Add pasta and 1½ teaspoons salt and cook, stirring often, until al dente. Reserve ½ cup cooking water, then drain pasta and return it to pot.

4   Add 1 tablespoon reserved cooking water to garlic mixture and stir to loosen. Off heat, add garlic mixture, artichokes, parsley, and lemon juice to pot with pasta and toss to combine. Adjust consistency with remaining reserved cooking water as needed. Season with salt and pepper to taste. Serve with lemon wedges.

Skillet Penne with Fresh Tomato Sauce

SERVES 2

TOTAL TIME 45 minutes

- 1 tablespoon extra-virgin olive oil
- 1 small onion, chopped fine
- 2 garlic cloves, minced
- 2 teaspoons tomato paste
- 1 pound tomatoes, cored and cut into ½-inch pieces
- ¾ teaspoon table salt
- ¼ teaspoon pepper
- ¼ cup dry white wine
- 2 cups water, plus extra as needed
- 6 ounces (2 cups) penne
- 2 tablespoons chopped fresh basil

  Grated plant-based Parmesan cheese (optional)

WHY THIS RECIPE WORKS Most of the year, canned tomatoes, which are picked and preserved at peak ripeness, offer better tomato flavor than their fresh counterparts do. But during that glorious, too-brief window when fresh tomatoes are at their peak, we like to celebrate their ripe juiciness in an effortless summertime pasta dish. To make the fresh tomato sauce, we simmer the tomatoes only briefly, just long enough for them to break down and release their juice without losing their brightness. A little tomato paste adds umami depth, and a small amount of white wine contributes a brightness that rounds out the flavor of the sauce. We then thin the tomato sauce with a couple cups of water and add the pasta right to the pan to cook through, making this a one-pot meal. The starch from the pasta helps thicken the sauce, making it nice and clingy, and in turn the pasta becomes saturated with fresh tomato flavor. You can use store-bought plant-based Parmesan or our Cashew Parmesan (page 23) in this recipe. You will need a 10- or 12-inch nonstick skillet with a tight-fitting lid for this recipe.

1 Heat oil in 10- or 12-inch nonstick skillet over medium heat until shimmering. Add onion and cook until softened, 3 to 5 minutes. Stir in garlic and tomato paste and cook until fragrant, about 1 minute. Stir in tomatoes, salt, and pepper and cook until tomatoes are softened, 5 to 7 minutes. Stir in wine and simmer for 2 minutes.

2 Stir in water and pasta. Cover, increase heat to medium-high, and cook at vigorous simmer, stirring often, until pasta is nearly al dente, 10 to 12 minutes.

3 Uncover and continue to simmer, tossing gently, until pasta is al dente and sauce is thickened, 3 to 5 minutes; if sauce becomes too thick, add extra water as needed. Off heat, stir in basil and season with salt and pepper to taste. Serve, topped with Parmesan, if using.

VARIATION

Skillet Penne with Fresh Tomato Sauce and Crispy Caper Crumbs

Microwave ¼ cup panko bread crumbs, 2 tablespoons rinsed and dried capers, and 1 teaspoon extra-virgin olive oil, stirring occasionally, until golden, 2 to 4 minutes; stir in 2 tablespoons minced fresh parsley and ½ teaspoon grated lemon zest. Sprinkle crumb mixture over finished pasta.

Kitchen Improv

USE WHAT YOU'VE GOT

Substitute dry vermouth for wine. Substitute campanelle, farfalle, medium shells, or rigatoni for penne; cup amounts will vary. Substitute other fresh herbs, such as parsley or oregano, for basil.

BULK IT UP

Top with tempeh crumbles (page 27) or Pan-Seared Tofu (page 274).

Fettuccine with Summer Squash, Ricotta, and Lemon-Parmesan Crumbs

SERVES 2

TOTAL TIME 30 minutes

- 2 tablespoons panko bread crumbs
- 4 teaspoons extra-virgin olive oil, divided
- 2 tablespoons grated plant-based Parmesan cheese, divided
- ½ teaspoon grated lemon zest plus 1 tablespoon juice
- 12 ounces yellow summer squash, halved lengthwise and sliced thin crosswise
- ¼ teaspoon table salt, plus salt for cooking pasta
- 2 garlic cloves, minced
- ¼ teaspoon red pepper flakes
- 6 ounces fettuccine
- ¼ cup torn fresh basil, plus extra for sprinkling
- 2 ounces (¼ cup) plant-based ricotta cheese

Kitchen Improv

USE WHAT YOU'VE GOT

Substitute rinsed and dried capers for plant-based Parmesan. Substitute zucchini for summer squash. Substitute linguine or spaghetti for fettuccine. Substitute other fresh herbs, such as parsley or oregano, for basil.

WHY THIS RECIPE WORKS For such a summery, vegetable-forward pasta dish, it's astonishing how little prep work and time is required for it all to come together. The star ingredient, ripe yellow summer squash, needs only to be sliced into quick-cooking pieces and then sautéed in a bit of oil to become tender and lightly browned. We then stir minced garlic and red pepper flakes into the pan with the softened squash for a spicy kick that plays well against the squash's sweetness. To make efficient use of time, the pasta cooks while the squash sizzles. We then toss the pasta and squash together with some of the reserved pasta water, nutty plant-based Parmesan, and lemon juice and basil for brightness. The starchy pasta water and the partially broken-down squash together create a light, clingy sauce. A few dollops of creamy plant-based ricotta and a sprinkle of lemony toasted panko bread crumbs provide a finishing flourish. You can use store-bought plant-based Parmesan and ricotta or our Cashew Ricotta (page 22) and Cashew Parmesan (page 23) in this recipe.

1 Microwave panko and 1 teaspoon oil in bowl, stirring occasionally, until golden, 2 to 4 minutes. Stir in 1 tablespoon Parmesan and lemon zest; set aside.

2 Heat remaining 1 tablespoon oil in 10- or 12-inch nonstick skillet over medium-high heat until shimmering. Add squash and salt and cook, stirring occasionally, until squash is softened and spotty brown, 5 to 7 minutes. Stir in garlic and pepper flakes and cook until fragrant, about 30 seconds. Remove from heat and cover to keep warm.

3 Meanwhile, bring 2 quarts water to boil in large pot. Add pasta and 1½ teaspoons salt and cook, stirring often, until al dente. Reserve ½ cup cooking water, then drain pasta and return it to pot.

4 Add squash mixture, ¼ cup reserved cooking water, basil, lemon juice, and remaining 1 tablespoon Parmesan to pot with pasta and toss to combine. Adjust consistency with remaining reserved cooking water as needed and season with salt and pepper to taste. Transfer pasta to serving bowls and dollop with ricotta. Sprinkle with panko mixture and extra basil. Serve.

Spaghetti with Broccoli and Avocado Pesto

SERVES 2

TOTAL TIME 30 minutes

6 ounces broccoli, florets cut into 1-inch pieces, stalks peeled and sliced ¼ inch thick

½ teaspoon table salt, plus salt for cooking broccoli and pasta

6 ounces spaghetti

1 avocado, halved and pitted

½ cup coarsely chopped fresh basil

¼ cup shelled pistachios, toasted and chopped, divided

1 tablespoon chopped pitted kalamata olives

1 garlic clove, minced

½ teaspoon fennel seeds, toasted

½ teaspoon grated lemon zest plus 1 tablespoon juice

Kitchen Improv

USE WHAT YOU'VE GOT

Substitute linguine or fettuccine for spaghetti. Substitute other nuts, such as walnuts, pecans, or almonds, or seeds, such as sunflower seeds or pepitas, for pistachios. Substitute other varieties of olives for kalamatas.

WHY THIS RECIPE WORKS This pesto made with broccoli and avocado is just as green and rich as your archetypal basil–pine nut–Parmesan pesto, but our version also brings an unbeatable creaminess and an extra dose of vegetable goodness in every bite. Half a cup of basil and a squeeze of lemon juice contribute lush herbaceousness and brightness. We blanch the broccoli in boiling water until tender and then incorporate it in two ways: We process a small portion right into the pesto and we reserve the rest to stir into the pasta, where it adds a nice contrasting texture to the creamy pesto. Before processing the pesto, we cook the pasta in the same water we used to blanch the broccoli, saving some of the starchy cooking water to thin the thick pesto. Toasted fennel seeds lend the pesto a warm, sweet aroma, while kalamata olives add brininess and toasted pistachios bring crunch. Toast the fennel seeds and pistachios separately in a dry skillet over medium heat until fragrant (about 3 minutes), then remove them from the skillet so they don't scorch. For ways to use up leftover broccoli, see page 18.

1 Bring 2 quarts water to boil in large pot. Add broccoli stalks and 1½ teaspoons salt and cook for 1 minute. Add broccoli florets and cook until stalks and florets are tender, 2 to 3 minutes. Using slotted spoon, transfer broccoli to colander set over bowl (do not discard boiling water). Let broccoli cool slightly, about 5 minutes, then pat dry with paper towels; set aside.

2 Return water to boil, add pasta, and cook, stirring often, until al dente. Reserve ½ cup cooking water, then drain pasta and return it to pot.

3 Process avocado, basil, 2 tablespoons pistachios, olives, garlic, fennel seeds, lemon zest and juice, ½ cup broccoli, and salt in food processor until mostly smooth, about 2 minutes. With processor running, slowly add ¼ cup reserved cooking water until incorporated, about 45 seconds, scraping down sides of bowl as needed.

4 Add pesto to pot with pasta and toss to combine. Adjust consistency with remaining reserved cooking water as needed. Stir in remaining broccoli and season with salt and pepper to taste. Transfer pasta to serving bowls and sprinkle with remaining 2 tablespoons pistachios. Serve.

Creamy Cashew Mac and Cheese

SERVES 2

TOTAL TIME 50 minutes

- 1 tablespoon vegetable oil
- 2 teaspoons dry mustard
- 1½ teaspoons tomato paste
- 1 garlic clove, minced
- ½ teaspoon table salt, plus salt for cooking pasta
- ¼ teaspoon ground turmeric
- 2 cups unsweetened almond milk
- 2 tablespoons nutritional yeast, plus extra for serving
- 1 teaspoon distilled white vinegar, plus extra for seasoning
- 4 ounces cauliflower florets, cut into ½-inch pieces
- ½ cup raw cashews, chopped
- 6 ounces (1½ cups) elbow macaroni

Kitchen Improv

USE WHAT YOU'VE GOT

Substitute small shells for elbow macaroni.

LEVEL UP

Sprinkle with store-bought plant-based Parmesan or our Cashew Parmesan (page 23).

WHY THIS RECIPE WORKS For a creamy vegan mac that lives up to its name, we turn to an unexpected duo: cauliflower and cashews. Simmered with almond milk until the cauliflower is tender and then blended until smooth, the rich cashews and the silken texture of the cauliflower make for a decadent, pasta-coating sauce. Funky nutritional yeast, umami-rich tomato paste, sharp mustard powder, and tangy vinegar give the dish a remarkable cheesy flavor. We prefer the mild, nutty flavor of almond milk here. Do not substitute other nuts for the cashews in this recipe. The sauce will be loose as you add the macaroni, but it will thicken. For ways to use up leftover cauliflower, see page 18.

1 Heat oil in large saucepan over medium heat until shimmering. Add mustard, tomato paste, garlic, salt, and turmeric and cook until fragrant, about 30 seconds. Stir in almond milk, nutritional yeast, and vinegar, scraping up any browned bits, and bring to simmer.

2 Stir in cauliflower and cashews; reduce heat to medium-low; and cook, partially covered, until cauliflower is very tender and beginning to break down, about 20 minutes. Process cauliflower mixture in blender until smooth, about 2 minutes, scraping down sides of blender jar as needed. Return cauliflower mixture to now-empty saucepan and bring to gentle simmer over medium-low heat.

3 Meanwhile, bring 2 quarts water to boil in large pot. Add macaroni and 1½ teaspoons salt and cook, stirring often, until al dente. Reserve ½ cup cooking water, then drain macaroni and return it to pot.

4 Add macaroni to saucepan with cauliflower mixture and cook over medium heat, stirring constantly, until macaroni is fully tender and sauce is slightly thickened, about 2 minutes. Adjust consistency with reserved cooking water as needed and season with salt, pepper, and extra vinegar to taste. Serve with extra nutritional yeast.

VARIATION

Creamy Cashew Mac and Cheese with Roasted Cauliflower and Sausage

Increase cauliflower to 9 ounces. Adjust oven rack to lowest position and heat oven to 500 degrees. Line rimmed baking sheet with aluminum foil. Toss 5 ounces cauliflower florets with 1 teaspoon vegetable oil and pinch salt. Arrange cauliflower on half of baking sheet and place one 4-ounce plant-based sausage on other half. Roast until cauliflower is tender, 8 to 10 minutes. Transfer sausage to cutting board and cut into ½-inch pieces. Proceed with recipe, stirring roasted cauliflower and sausage into macaroni before serving.

Cashew e Pepe e Funghi

SERVES 2
TOTAL TIME 45 minutes

¼ cup roasted cashews

2 tablespoons nutritional yeast

1 tablespoon white miso

½ teaspoon table salt, plus salt for cooking pasta

2 tablespoons extra-virgin olive oil

4 ounces oyster mushrooms, trimmed and chopped

2 garlic cloves, sliced thin

½ teaspoon coarsely ground pepper

6 ounces spaghetti

1 tablespoon chopped fresh parsley

1 teaspoon lemon juice

Kitchen Improv

USE WHAT YOU'VE GOT

Substitute red or yellow miso for white miso. Substitute white, cremini, or portobello mushrooms for oyster mushrooms; cooked mushrooms will not be as crispy. Substitute fettuccine or linguine for spaghetti.

WHY THIS RECIPE WORKS   This oh-so-creamy dish includes the best hallmarks of two Italian favorites: pasta carbonara and pasta cacio e pepe. Cashews provide a thick and creamy (but not heavy) sauce base because of their uniquely low fiber and high starch content. Breaking the cashews up in a blender (to increase their surface area) before soaking them means that they require only 15 minutes of soaking with the other flavorful sauce ingredients before we can give them a whiz and break them down completely into a silky-smooth sauce. Using roasted cashews here rather than more neutral tasting raw cashews adds nuanced, toasty warmth. Miso and nutritional yeast each contribute different aspects of umami flavor to the sauce. But the most delectable part may just be the mushrooms. Oyster mushrooms, which contain very little moisture (relative to other mushrooms), quickly cook into crispy-chewy, golden, almost bacon-y nuggets that set off the creamy pasta to perfection. Do not substitute other nuts for the cashews in this recipe.

1   Process cashews in blender on low speed until mixture has consistency of fine gravel mixed with sand, 10 to 15 seconds. Add ½ cup water, nutritional yeast, miso, and salt and process on low speed until combined, about 5 seconds. Scrape down sides of blender jar and let sit for 15 minutes.

2   Process cashew mixture on low speed until well blended, about 1 minute. Scrape down sides of blender jar, then process on high speed until sauce is completely smooth, 3 to 4 minutes.

3   Heat oil in 10- or 12-inch skillet over medium-high heat until shimmering. Add mushrooms and cook until well browned and crispy, 7 to 10 minutes. Off heat, stir in garlic and pepper and cook, using residual heat of skillet, until fragrant, about 1 minute. Cover to keep warm.

4   Meanwhile, bring 2 quarts water to boil in large pot. Add pasta and 1½ teaspoons salt and cook, stirring often, until al dente. Reserve ½ cup cooking water, then drain pasta and return it to pot.

5   Add sauce, mushroom mixture, parsley, and lemon juice to pot with pasta and toss until sauce is slightly thickened and pasta is well coated, about 1 minute. Adjust consistency with reserved cooking water as needed and season with salt and pepper to taste. Serve.

Campanelle with Roasted Cauliflower and Garlic Sauce

SERVES 2

TOTAL TIME 45 minutes

- 10 whole garlic cloves, smashed and peeled
- 3 tablespoons extra-virgin olive oil, divided
- 1 pound cauliflower florets, cut into 1-inch pieces
- ½ teaspoon table salt, plus salt for cooking pasta
- ¼ teaspoon pepper
- ⅛ teaspoon sugar
- 6 ounces (2 cups) campanelle
- ¼ cup grated plant-based Parmesan cheese
- 2 tablespoons chopped fresh parsley
- 1 tablespoon lemon juice, plus extra for seasoning
- ⅛ teaspoon red pepper flakes

Kitchen Improv

USE WHAT YOU'VE GOT

Substitute farfalle, medium shells, penne, or rigatoni for campanelle; cup amounts will vary.

WHY THIS RECIPE WORKS Sweet and nutty roasted garlic can give the simplest dishes complex flavor in an instant. The only barrier to using it everywhere, especially when cooking in smaller portions or on busy weeknights, is the fact that making it requires turning on the oven and waiting for the garlic to caramelize, which can take some time. Here, though, since we were already roasting the cauliflower (the other main component of this pasta dish), it was easy to throw in a few cloves of garlic to roast simultaneously, no extra time or cooking vessels needed. A very hot 500-degree oven creates excellent browning on the cauliflower, leaving us with tender florets and sweet, roasty garlic in a mere 10 minutes—less time than it takes to bring the water to a boil and cook the pasta. After roasting, we mash the garlic into a creamy sauce with olive oil, lemon juice, plant-based Parmesan, and some of the pasta cooking water before tossing it with the pasta and cauliflower. You can use store-bought plant-based Parmesan or our Cashew Parmesan (page 23) in this recipe. For ways to use up leftover cauliflower, see page 18.

1 Adjust oven rack to lower-middle position and heat oven to 500 degrees. Place garlic cloves in center of 12-inch square of aluminum foil and drizzle with 1 tablespoon oil. Pull sides of foil up around garlic, keeping cloves in single layer, and crimp tightly to seal. Place packet on rimmed baking sheet.

2 Toss cauliflower with 1 tablespoon oil, salt, pepper, and sugar and arrange in even layer on empty side of baking sheet. Roast until cauliflower is well browned and tender and garlic is very soft, 10 to 15 minutes. Carefully open foil packet, allowing steam to escape away from you, and let garlic cool slightly, about 2 minutes.

3 Meanwhile, bring 2 quarts water to boil in large pot. Add pasta and 1½ teaspoons salt and cook, stirring frequently, until al dente. Reserve ¾ cup cooking water, then drain pasta and return it to pot.

4 Transfer garlic to medium bowl and mash with fork or whisk until mostly smooth. Whisk in ⅓ cup reserved cooking water, Parmesan, parsley, lemon juice, pepper flakes, and remaining 1 tablespoon oil.

5 Add cauliflower mixture and garlic sauce to pot with pasta and toss to combine. Adjust consistency with remaining reserved cooking water as needed. Season with salt, pepper, and extra lemon juice to taste. Serve.

Rigatoni with Quick Mushroom Ragu

SERVES 2

TOTAL TIME 40 minutes

- 8 ounces cremini or white mushrooms, trimmed and quartered
- 1 small carrot, peeled and chopped
- 1 shallot, chopped
- 1 tablespoon extra-virgin olive oil
- ½ teaspoon table salt, plus salt for cooking pasta
- 2 tablespoons tomato paste
- 2 garlic cloves, minced
- ¼ teaspoon red pepper flakes
- ¼ cup dry white wine
- 6 ounces (2⅓ cups) rigatoni
- 2 tablespoons grated plant-based Parmesan cheese, plus extra for serving

Kitchen Improv

USE WHAT YOU'VE GOT

Substitute dry vermouth for wine. Substitute campanelle, farfalle, medium shells, or penne for rigatoni; cup amounts will vary.

WHY THIS RECIPE WORKS Cooking a ragu doesn't have to be an all-day affair. This 40-minute ragu is hearty, comforting, and nuanced thanks to umami-rich tomato paste, mushrooms, and a glug of white wine. We blitz the mushrooms, carrot, and shallot for the base of the ragu in a food processor to get the prep work done in a flash, no fancy knife skills necessary. We cook the vegetables until softened and a layer of fond (browned bits) forms on the bottom of the pan and then scrape up that flavorful browning and incorporate it back into the sauce to capture all its deep, savory flavor. Tomato paste, garlic, and dry white wine give the sauce its undeniable ragu essence; a splash of pasta cooking water gives the sauce its pasta-coating consistency. Letting the rigatoni sit in the sauce for a few minutes helps it soak up its flavor and excess liquid. You will need a large saucepan with a tight-fitting lid for this recipe. You can use store-bought plant-based Parmesan or our Cashew Parmesan (page 23) in this recipe.

1 Pulse mushrooms, carrot, and shallot in food processor until finely chopped, about 8 pulses, scraping down sides of bowl as needed. Heat oil in large saucepan over medium heat until shimmering. Add mushroom mixture and salt; cover; and cook, stirring occasionally, until vegetables have released their liquid, about 5 minutes. Uncover, increase heat to medium-high, and cook until vegetables begin to brown, 3 to 5 minutes.

2 Stir in tomato paste, garlic, and pepper flakes and cook until fragrant, about 1 minute. Stir in wine, scraping up any browned bits, and cook until nearly evaporated, about 30 seconds. Remove from heat and cover to keep warm.

3 Meanwhile, bring 2 quarts water to boil in large pot. Add pasta and 1½ teaspoons salt and cook, stirring often, until nearly al dente. Reserve 1 cup cooking water, then drain pasta.

4 Add pasta and ½ cup reserved cooking water to saucepan with vegetable mixture and cook over medium heat, stirring occasionally, until pasta is al dente, about 3 minutes. Off heat, let sit for 5 minutes. Stir pasta to recombine and adjust consistency with remaining reserved cooking water as needed. Stir in Parmesan and season with salt and pepper to taste. Serve with extra Parmesan.

Linguine with Weeknight Bolognese

SERVES 2

TOTAL TIME 55 minutes

- 1 small onion, chopped coarse
- 1 carrot, peeled and chopped coarse
- ½ celery rib, chopped coarse
- 1 tablespoon extra-virgin olive oil
- ⅛ teaspoon table salt, plus salt for cooking pasta
- ⅛ teaspoon pepper
- 2 tablespoons tomato paste
- ¼ cup dry red wine
- 6 ounces plant-based ground meat
- 1 cup vegetable broth
- 6 ounces linguine

Kitchen Improv

USE WHAT YOU'VE GOT

Substitute fettuccine or spaghetti for linguine.

WHY THIS RECIPE WORKS An Italian Bolognese is the meatiest of pasta sauces: thick, rich, homey sustenance. There are many ways to make it, from long-cooked Sunday-supper versions featuring several different cuts of meat to streamlined ground beef–based versions. This fast version made with savory ground plant-based meat is every bit as comforting as a hug from an Italian grandmother, with rich, savory flavor. The only tomato presence in this dish comes from a few tablespoons of tomato paste, which boosts the sauce's umami flavor and deepens its color. Rather than sear the plant-based meat to build fond, which could cause it to overcook and become tough, we build plenty of fond by simply sautéing the mirepoix of onion, carrot, and celery plus tomato paste. We then mix in the meat and cook it gently for just a few minutes before adding the liquid. The sauce looks loose at first, but it thickens as the pasta soaks up the extra moisture. You will need a large saucepan with a tight-fitting lid for this recipe. For ways to use up leftover plant-based meat, see page 19.

1 Pulse onion, carrot, and celery in food processor until mixture has paste-like consistency, 12 to 15 pulses, scraping down sides of bowl as needed. Heat oil in large saucepan over medium heat until shimmering. Add vegetable mixture, salt, and pepper and cook, stirring occasionally, until excess liquid has evaporated, 3 to 5 minutes. Stir in tomato paste and continue to cook until mixture is rust colored and bottom of saucepan is dark brown, 1 to 2 minutes.

2 Stir in wine, scraping up any browned bits, and cook until nearly evaporated, about 1 minute. Add ground meat and cook, breaking up meat with wooden spoon, until firm bite-size crumbles form, about 3 minutes. Stir in broth and bring to simmer. Cover, reduce heat to low, and simmer for 15 minutes (sauce will look thin). Remove from heat and cover to keep warm.

3 Meanwhile, bring 2 quarts water to boil in large pot. Add pasta and 1½ teaspoons salt and cook, stirring often, until al dente. Reserve ½ cup cooking water, then drain pasta and return it to pot.

4 Add sauce to pot with pasta and toss to combine. Adjust consistency with reserved cooking water as needed. Season with salt and pepper to taste. Serve.

Spaghetti with Meatballs and Marinara

SERVES 2

TOTAL TIME 1¼ hours

1 tablespoon extra-virgin olive oil

1 small onion, chopped fine

¼ teaspoon table salt, divided, plus salt for cooking pasta

¾ teaspoon garlic powder, divided

¾ teaspoon dried oregano, divided

   Pinch red pepper flakes

¼ cup dry red wine

1 (14.5-ounce) can crushed tomatoes

¼ cup panko bread crumbs

6 ounces plant-based ground meat

6 ounces spaghetti

1 tablespoon chopped fresh basil

Kitchen Improv

USE WHAT YOU'VE GOT

Substitute fettuccine or linguine for spaghetti.

WHY THIS RECIPE WORKS Spaghetti with meatballs and marinara sauce is an iconic dish with three equally important parts: the slurpable pasta; the bright-red, fresh-tasting sauce; and the tender meatballs. Recipes for plant-based meatballs made with grains, beans, and other ingredients abound, but for the quickest moist, truly meaty meatballs, we opt for ground plant-based meat. This allows us to skip the bulk of the labor-intensive prep work; we simply season and gently shape the meat before plopping the meatballs directly into the simmering marinara sauce to cook through. These meatballs are so good we couldn't stop at one version, so we also crafted a variation with pesto mixed right into the meatballs to give them a fresh, herbal flavor shake-up. You will need a large saucepan with a tight-fitting lid for this recipe. For ways to use up leftover plant-based meat, see page 19.

1 Heat oil in large saucepan over medium heat until shimmering. Add onion and ⅛ teaspoon salt and cook until softened, 3 to 5 minutes. Stir in ½ teaspoon garlic powder, ½ teaspoon oregano, and pepper flakes and cook until fragrant, about 30 seconds.

2 Stir in wine and cook until nearly evaporated, about 1 minute. Stir in tomatoes and 2 tablespoons water. Bring to simmer and cook until sauce is thickened, about 30 minutes. Remove from heat and cover to keep warm.

3 Meanwhile, combine panko, 1 tablespoon water, remaining ⅛ teaspoon salt, remaining ¼ teaspoon garlic powder, and remaining ¼ teaspoon oregano in medium bowl. Break ground meat into small pieces and add to bowl with panko mixture. Gently knead with your hands until mixture is evenly combined. Using your moistened hands, pinch off and roll meat mixture into 1½-inch meatballs. (You should have 6 meatballs.) Transfer meatballs to plate and refrigerate for at least 15 minutes or up to 24 hours.

4 Nestle meatballs into sauce in saucepan and bring to simmer over medium-high heat. Cover, reduce heat to medium-low, and simmer until meatballs are firm and warmed through, about 15 minutes. Season with salt and pepper to taste.

5 Meanwhile, bring 2 quarts water to boil in large pot. Add pasta and 1½ teaspoons salt and cook, stirring often, until tender. Reserve ½ cup cooking water, then drain pasta and return it to pot.

6 Add basil and several spoonfuls of sauce (without meatballs) to pot with pasta and toss to combine. Adjust consistency with reserved cooking water as needed. Season with salt and pepper to taste. Serve pasta with meatballs and remaining sauce.

VARIATION

Spaghetti with Pesto Meatballs

You can use store-bought fresh pesto or our Pesto (page 24) in this recipe.

Omit water, oregano, garlic powder, and salt from meatballs. Stir 2 tablespoons pesto into meat mixture with panko.

Baked Ziti with Creamy Leeks, Kale, and Sun-Dried Tomatoes

SERVES 2

TOTAL TIME 1 hour

- ¼ cup panko bread crumbs
- 2 tablespoons extra-virgin olive oil, divided
- ½ teaspoon grated lemon zest, plus lemon wedges for serving
- 1 pound leeks, white and light green parts only, halved lengthwise, sliced thin, and washed thoroughly
- ½ teaspoon table salt, divided, plus salt for cooking pasta
- 1 teaspoon minced fresh thyme or ½ teaspoon dried
- ¼ cup dry white wine
- 3 garlic cloves, minced
- ⅛ teaspoon red pepper flakes
- 3 cups (3 ounces) baby kale
- 2 tablespoons oil-packed sun-dried tomatoes, chopped coarse
- 6 ounces (2 cups) ziti
- 1 tablespoon chopped fresh parsley

Kitchen Improv

USE WHAT YOU'VE GOT

Substitute dry vermouth for wine. Substitute penne or rigatoni for ziti; cup amounts will vary. Substitute baby spinach or 8 ounces mature kale, stemmed and chopped, for baby kale.

WHY THIS RECIPE WORKS   The often-underestimated leek is the backbone of the aromatic sauce in this fresh and vegetable-forward baked ziti. We sauté 1 pound of sliced leeks until they begin to caramelize, add some thyme, deglaze the pan with a splash of white wine, and then simmer the mixture in water until the leeks are meltingly soft and ready to be blended into a smooth, velvety sauce. Sun-dried tomatoes and a generous dose of garlic and red pepper flakes deliver robust flavor, while baby kale provides another hearty vegetable element. Baking the relatively small portion of pasta in an 8-inch square baking dish creates tons of surface area for crisping the lemony panko topping, adding crunch that contrasts with the creamy interior. You will need a large saucepan with a tight-fitting lid for this recipe. You can bake the pasta in an 8½ by 4½-inch loaf pan, but the topping will be slightly less crunchy.

1   Adjust oven rack to upper-middle position and heat oven to 450 degrees. Combine panko, 1½ teaspoons oil, and lemon zest in small bowl; set aside.

2   Heat 1 tablespoon oil in large saucepan over medium heat until shimmering. Add leeks and ¼ teaspoon salt and cook until softened and lightly browned, 8 to 10 minutes. Stir in thyme and cook until fragrant, about 30 seconds. Stir in wine, scraping up any browned bits, and cook until nearly evaporated, about 1 minute. Stir in 1 cup water and bring to boil. Reduce heat to low, cover, and simmer until leeks are very tender, 6 to 8 minutes. Process leek mixture in blender until smooth, about 2 minutes; set aside.

3   Cook remaining 1½ teaspoons oil, garlic, and pepper flakes in now-empty saucepan over medium heat until fragrant, about 1 minute. Add kale, sun-dried tomatoes, and remaining ¼ teaspoon salt and cook, stirring occasionally, until kale is wilted and tomatoes are softened, about 2 minutes.

4   Meanwhile, bring 2 quarts water to boil in large pot. Add pasta and 1½ teaspoons salt and cook, stirring often, until al dente. Reserve ¾ cup cooking water, then drain pasta. Add pasta, leek mixture, and ½ cup reserved cooking water to saucepan with kale mixture. Adjust consistency with remaining reserved cooking water as needed (sauce should be thick but still creamy) and season with salt and pepper to taste.

5   Transfer pasta mixture to broiler-safe 8-inch square baking dish, smoothing top with rubber spatula. Cover tightly with aluminum foil and bake until sauce is bubbling, 10 to 12 minutes. Remove dish from oven and heat broiler. Remove aluminum foil and sprinkle panko mixture evenly over pasta. Broil until panko mixture is golden brown, about 2 minutes. Sprinkle with parsley and serve with lemon wedges.

Unstuffed Shells with Butternut Squash and Leeks

SERVES 2

TOTAL TIME 45 minutes

¼ cup plant-based ricotta cheese

3 tablespoons shredded fresh mint, divided

½ teaspoon grated lemon zest

⅛ teaspoon pepper

1 tablespoon extra-virgin olive oil, plus extra for drizzling

12 ounces (2 cups) butternut squash, cut into ½-inch pieces

1 leek, white and light green parts only, halved lengthwise, sliced thin, and washed thoroughly

¾ teaspoon table salt

2 garlic cloves, minced

¼ cup dry white wine

2¼ cups vegetable broth

⅓ cup plant-based creamer

6 ounces jumbo pasta shells

Kitchen Improv

USE WHAT YOU'VE GOT

Substitute other fresh herbs, such as basil or parsley, for mint. Substitute dry vermouth for wine. Substitute large or medium shells, penne, rigatoni, or ziti for jumbo shells.

WHY THIS RECIPE WORKS   Jumbo stuffed shells are undeniably fun to eat, but all the prep work required can be an ordeal, especially when you only want enough to serve you plus one. Enter our clever unstuffed version, which skips the laborious preboiling and stuffing steps but keeps all the pasta-y, cheesy appeal. Here, the pasta is cooked directly in the sauce made with sweet butternut squash, oniony leeks, and plant-based creamer. Sautéing the vegetables briefly before adding the pasta and cooking liquid deepens their flavor and ensures that the pasta and squash finish cooking at the same time. Instead of stuffing the shells with cheese, we dollop a rich, bright, nutty plant-based lemon-ricotta mixture over everything before serving. You will need a 10- or 12-inch nonstick skillet with a tight-fitting lid for this recipe. The skillet may appear very full when you add the shells in step 3 (stir gently to start) but will become more manageable as the liquid evaporates and the shells soften. You can use store-bought plant-based ricotta or our Cashew Ricotta (page 22) in this recipe. For ways to use up leftover plant-based creamer, see page 19.

1   Combine ricotta, 2 tablespoons mint, lemon zest, and pepper in small bowl; set aside.

2   Heat oil in 10- or 12-inch nonstick skillet over medium heat until shimmering. Add squash, leek, and salt and cook until leeks are softened, 5 to 7 minutes. Stir in garlic and cook until fragrant, about 30 seconds. Stir in wine and cook until nearly evaporated, about 1 minute.

3   Stir in broth, creamer, and pasta. Bring to simmer, cover, and cook, stirring often, until pasta is tender and sauce is thickened, 15 to 17 minutes. Off heat, season with salt and pepper to taste. Dollop evenly with ricotta mixture, sprinkle with remaining 1 tablespoon mint, and drizzle with extra oil. Serve.

Meaty Zoodles with Mango and Garam Masala

SERVES 2

TOTAL TIME 30 minutes

- 1 small mango, peeled, pitted, and cut into ¼-inch pieces
- 2 tablespoons chopped fresh cilantro, divided
- ½ teaspoon grated lemon zest plus 5 teaspoons juice, divided
- ⅓ cup plain plant-based yogurt
- 2 garlic cloves, minced, divided
- 1 tablespoon vegetable oil, divided
- 6 ounces plant-based ground meat
- 1 teaspoon grated fresh ginger
- 2 teaspoons garam masala, divided
- ½ teaspoon table salt
- ¼ teaspoon pepper
- 1 pound zucchini noodles, cut into 6-inch lengths, divided

Kitchen Improv

USE WHAT YOU'VE GOT

Substitute 1 cup peeled, diced peaches or pineapple for mango. Substitute summer squash for zucchini. Substitute 8 ounces tempeh for plant-based meat; cook until well browned, about 8 minutes.

NO SPIRALIZER, NO PROBLEM

Use vegetable peeler to create thin zucchini ribbons from 1½ pounds zucchini.

WHY THIS RECIPE WORKS   Zucchini noodles are a lighter, fresher alternative to wheat-based or rice-based noodles, and when paired with warmly spiced plant-based meat and a cooling yogurt sauce, they're cause for real mealtime excitement. For big impact with little effort, we season plant-based meat with garam masala, an Indian spice blend containing an array of spices including cumin, coriander, cinnamon, and pepper. Fresh ginger and garlic bring their distinct bite to the mix; we give the meat a few minutes' head start before adding them and the garam masala to the skillet to prevent the spices from burning or mellowing too much in the heat. Chopped mango adds brilliant color and nectary sweetness. We prefer to make our own zucchini noodles with a spiralizer, but you can use store-bought zucchini noodles. You will need 1½ pounds of zucchini to yield 1 pound of noodles. For ways to use up leftover plant-based meat and yogurt, see page 19.

1   Combine mango, 1 tablespoon cilantro, and 2 teaspoons lemon juice in bowl; season with salt and pepper to taste and set aside. Whisk yogurt, half of garlic, remaining 1 tablespoon cilantro, and lemon zest and remaining 1 tablespoon juice together in bowl; season with salt and pepper to taste and set aside.

2   Heat 2 teaspoons oil in 10- or 12-inch nonstick skillet over medium heat until shimmering. Add ground meat and cook, breaking up meat with wooden spoon, until firm bite-size crumbles form, about 3 minutes. Stir in ginger, 1 teaspoon garam masala, salt, pepper, and remaining garlic and cook until fragrant, about 30 seconds. Transfer to bowl and cover to keep warm.

3   Heat remaining 1 teaspoon oil in now-empty skillet over medium-high heat until shimmering. Add zucchini noodles and remaining 1 teaspoon garam masala and cook, tossing gently, until crisp-tender, about 1 minute. Season with salt and pepper to taste. Transfer noodles to serving bowls. Top noodles with meat mixture, mango mixture, and yogurt sauce. Serve.

Stir-Fried Noodles with Mushrooms, Snow Peas, and Bell Peppers

SERVES 2

TOTAL TIME 35 minutes

5 scallions, white and green parts separated and sliced thin

3½ teaspoons toasted sesame oil, divided, plus extra for drizzling

1 teaspoon grated fresh ginger

¼ cup vegetable broth

1 tablespoon soy sauce

1 tablespoon Shaoxing wine

1 tablespoon unseasoned rice vinegar, plus extra for drizzling

1 tablespoon mushroom oyster sauce

1 tablespoon hoisin sauce

½ teaspoon cornstarch

8 ounces fresh Chinese wheat noodles

4 ounces shiitake mushrooms, stemmed and halved if small or quartered if large

4 ounces snow peas, strings removed

1 small red bell pepper, stemmed, seeded, and sliced thin

Kitchen Improv

USE WHAT YOU'VE GOT

Substitute dry sherry or white wine for Shaoxing wine. Substitute fresh ramen noodles or 6 ounces dried Chinese wheat noodles, udon noodles, or spaghetti for fresh Chinese wheat noodles.

WHY THIS RECIPE WORKS   Hearty, chewy noodles are traditionally the star of lo mein, which may get its name from the Cantonese "lou minh," meaning "stirred noodles." The boiled noodles are indeed stir-fried with a sauce and tossed with stir-fried meat, vegetables, or both. This basic formula can be varied using different proteins and vegetables. For our vegan version, we sub the traditional lo mein noodles, which are usually made with egg, for similar eggless fresh Chinese wheat noodles, into which we mix a hearty medley of bell pepper, scallions, snow peas, and shiitake mushrooms. Once the vegetables are cooked, we push them to the side of the pan and cook a pungent mixture of scallion whites, ginger, and sesame oil in the center. Combined with an umami-rich mixture including broth, soy sauce, mushroom-based "oyster" sauce, and cornstarch, the aromatics become the base of the noodle-coating sauce. A sprinkle of scallion greens brings a fresh finish to this savory meal.

1   Combine scallion whites, 1 teaspoon oil, and ginger in small bowl; set aside. Whisk broth, soy sauce, wine, vinegar, oyster sauce, hoisin, and cornstarch in second small bowl until cornstarch has dissolved; set aside.

2   Bring 2 quarts water to boil in large pot. Add noodles and cook, stirring often, until just tender (center should still be firm with slightly opaque dot). Drain noodles, rinse well, and drain again. Toss noodles with 1 teaspoon oil; set aside.

3   Meanwhile, heat remaining 1½ teaspoons oil in 14-inch flat-bottomed wok or 10- or 12-inch nonstick skillet over medium-high heat until just smoking. Add mushrooms, snow peas, and bell pepper, increase heat to high, and cook, stirring often, until vegetables are crisp-tender, 3 to 6 minutes.

4   Push vegetables to 1 side of wok. Add scallion white mixture to clearing and cook, mashing mixture into wok, until fragrant, about 30 seconds. Stir scallion white mixture into vegetables. Add noodles and broth mixture and cook, tossing gently, until noodles are well coated and tender, 2 to 4 minutes. Transfer noodles to serving bowls and sprinkle with scallion greens. Serve.

Dan Dan Mian

SERVES 2

TOTAL TIME 35 minutes

2 tablespoons Chinese sesame paste or tahini

1 tablespoon unseasoned rice vinegar, plus extra for serving

1 tablespoon soy sauce, divided

1 tablespoon hoisin sauce, divided

2 teaspoons Asian chili-garlic sauce

1 teaspoon sugar

8 ounces fresh Chinese wheat noodles

1 tablespoon toasted sesame oil

4 teaspoons vegetable oil, divided

6 ounces plant-based ground meat

1 tablespoon Shaoxing wine

3 scallions, white parts sliced thin, green parts sliced thin on bias

2 garlic cloves, minced

½ teaspoon red pepper flakes

¼ teaspoon coarsely ground Sichuan peppercorns, plus extra for serving (optional)

WHY THIS RECIPE WORKS   Dan dan mian—Sichuan noodles awash in a moderately spicy chili sauce and heaped with savory bits of pork—gets a supersatisfying plant-based twist. Substantial and filling thanks to the plant-based meat and chewy wheat noodles, rich and spicy from toasted sesame oil and a red pepper flake–spiked garlic oil, and with a bit of crunch from thinly sliced scallions, each bite contains a world of intense flavor. Plant-based meat, broken into small pieces and seared until lightly browned, stands in for the traditional pork. We whisk up a sauce of hoisin and chili-garlic sauce for sweet heat, glutamate-rich soy to underscore the meatiness, and a splash of rice vinegar for zing. Chinese sesame paste, like a more deeply roasted, nuttier version of tahini, helps thicken the sauce and bolster the dish's nutty sesame flavor. For ways to use up leftover plant-based meat, see page 19.

1   Whisk ½ cup hot water, sesame paste, vinegar, 2 teaspoons soy sauce, 1 teaspoon hoisin, chili-garlic sauce, and sugar in small bowl until sugar has dissolved; set aside.

2   Bring 2 quarts water to boil in large pot. Add noodles and cook, stirring often, until just tender (center should still be firm with slightly opaque dot). Drain noodles and rinse under hot running water, tossing gently, for 1 minute. Drain noodles again, return to pot, and toss with sesame oil; cover to keep warm.

3   Meanwhile, heat 2 teaspoons vegetable oil in 14-inch flat-bottomed wok or 10- or 12-inch nonstick skillet over medium-high heat until shimmering. Add ground meat and cook, breaking up meat with wooden spoon, until firm bite-size crumbles form, about 3 minutes. Stir in wine, remaining 1 teaspoon soy sauce, and remaining 2 teaspoons hoisin and cook until liquid is evaporated, 2 to 3 minutes. Transfer to pot with noodles.

4   Add remaining 2 teaspoons vegetable oil; scallion whites; garlic; pepper flakes; and Sichuan pepper, if using, to now-empty wok and cook over medium heat, mashing mixture into pan, until fragrant, about 30 seconds. Transfer to pot with noodles, add reserved sesame paste mixture, and toss to coat. Sprinkle with scallion greens and extra Sichuan pepper, if using. Adjust consistency with hot water as needed. Serve with extra vinegar and extra Sichuan pepper, if using.

Kitchen Improv

USE WHAT YOU'VE GOT

Substitute dry sherry or white wine for Shaoxing wine. Substitute fresh
ramen noodles or 6 ounces dried Chinese wheat noodles, udon noodles,
or spaghetti for fresh Chinese wheat noodles.

Japchae

SERVES 2

TOTAL TIME 40 minutes

6 ounces (⅛-inch-wide) dried sweet potato noodles, broken into 12-inch lengths

1 tablespoon toasted sesame oil, divided

2 tablespoons vegetable oil, divided

2 scallions, white and green parts separated and sliced thin

2 garlic cloves, minced, divided

2 tablespoons soy sauce

1½ teaspoons sugar

1½ teaspoons sesame seeds, toasted

4 ounces shiitake mushrooms, stemmed and sliced thin

1 carrot, peeled and cut into 2-inch-long matchsticks

1 small onion, sliced thin

4 ounces (4 cups) baby spinach

Kitchen Improv

USE WHAT YOU'VE GOT

Substitute dried bean thread (also sold as cellophane) or vermicelli rice noodles for sweet potato noodles; adjust cooking time as needed. Substitute portobello mushrooms for shiitakes.

WHY THIS RECIPE WORKS One of Korea's most beloved celebratory dishes, japchae is made using semi-transparent sweet potato starch noodles and a riot of colorful vegetables for a result that is both stunning and delicious. The flavorful, balanced sauce made from sesame oil, soy sauce, sugar, sesame seeds, and garlic makes it clear why throughout much of history this dish was reserved for Korean royalty. After cooking the noodles, we stir-fry earthy shiitake mushrooms with carrot and onion until just crisp-tender before stirring in a generous portion of baby spinach, which takes just a minute or two to wilt. You will need a 12-inch nonstick skillet or a 14-inch wok with a tight-fitting lid for this recipe. Sweet potato noodles are sometimes sold as sweet potato starch noodles or sweet potato glass noodles. Toast the sesame seeds in a dry skillet over medium heat until fragrant (about 3 minutes), and then remove the skillet from the heat so the seeds don't scorch.

1 Bring 2 quarts water to boil in large pot. Off heat, add noodles and let sit, stirring occasionally, until softened and pliable but not fully tender, about 10 minutes. Drain noodles, rinse well, and drain again. Toss noodles with 1 teaspoon sesame oil; set aside.

2 Meanwhile, combine 1 tablespoon vegetable oil, scallion whites, and half of garlic in small bowl; set aside. Whisk soy sauce, sugar, sesame seeds, remaining 2 teaspoons sesame oil, and remaining garlic in second small bowl until sugar has dissolved; set aside.

3 Heat remaining 1 tablespoon vegetable oil in 14-inch flat-bottomed wok or 10- or 12-inch nonstick skillet or over medium-high heat until just smoking. Add mushrooms, carrot, and onion; increase heat to high; and cook, stirring often, until vegetables are crisp-tender and lightly browned, 5 to 7 minutes. Stir in spinach and cook until wilted, about 2 minutes.

4 Push vegetables to 1 side of wok. Add scallion white mixture to clearing and cook, mashing mixture into wok, until fragrant, about 30 seconds. Stir scallion white mixture into vegetables. Add noodles and soy sauce mixture and cook, tossing gently, until noodles are well coated and tender, 2 to 4 minutes. Transfer noodles to serving bowls and sprinkle with scallion greens. Serve.

Spicy Basil Rice Noodles with Bok Choy

SERVES 2

TOTAL TIME 50 minutes

- 4 ounces (⅜-inch-wide) flat rice noodles
- 1 teaspoon plus 2 tablespoons vegetable oil, divided
- 1 cup vegetable broth
- 1½ tablespoons lime juice
- 1 tablespoon packed brown sugar
- 1 tablespoon soy sauce, plus extra as needed
- 1–3 Thai chiles, stemmed, seeded, and chopped coarse
- 2 shallots, chopped coarse
- 3 garlic cloves, chopped coarse
- 8 ounces bok choy, sliced ¼ inch thick and washed thoroughly
- 1 small red bell pepper, stemmed, seeded, and sliced thin
- 1 ounce sugar snap peas, strings removed, sliced thin on bias
- 1 cup fresh Thai basil leaves, torn into 1-inch pieces

Kitchen Improv

USE WHAT YOU'VE GOT

Substitute dried bean thread (also sold as cellophane) or sweet potato noodles for rice noodles; adjust cooking time as needed.

BULK IT UP

Top with Garlicky Tempeh Crumbles (page 27) or Pan-Seared Tofu (page 274).

WHY THIS RECIPE WORKS Inspired by the flavors of Thai cuisine, we combine chewy rice noodles with pungent Thai basil, crisp-tender vegetables, and a feisty sauce in this tastebud-awakening dish. We use a blender to make a quick paste of Thai chiles, garlic, and shallots, cooking the mixture to deepen and mellow the flavor of the aromatics. A couple teaspoons of soy sauce (our salty stand-in for the fish sauce that's ubiquitous in Thai cuisine), brown sugar, lime juice, and vegetable broth add a nuanced sweet-and-savory punch. At first glance the whopping 1 cup of Thai basil may seem like a lot for a dish meant to serve just two people, but it's essential for giving this dish its trademark spicy freshness; we stir it in off the heat to keep its flavor bright and prominent. Snap peas, red bell pepper, and bok choy add vegetable heft and crunch that contrasts with the noodles. For a spicier dish, use the greater amount of chiles.

1 Bring 2 quarts water to boil in large pot. Off heat, add noodles and let sit, stirring occasionally, until softened and pliable but not fully tender, about 15 minutes. Drain noodles, rinse well, and drain again. Toss noodles with 1 teaspoon oil; set aside.

2 Meanwhile, whisk broth, lime juice, sugar, and soy sauce in small bowl until sugar has dissolved; set aside. Process chiles, shallots, and garlic in blender until mixture has paste-like consistency, 15 to 20 seconds, adding up to 3 tablespoons water and scraping down sides of blender jar as needed.

3 Heat 1 tablespoon oil in 14-inch flat-bottomed wok or 10- or 12-inch nonstick skillet over medium-high heat until shimmering. Add bok choy, bell pepper, and snap peas. Increase heat to high and cook, tossing slowly but constantly, until crisp-tender, about 4 minutes; transfer to bowl.

4 Heat remaining 1 tablespoon oil in now-empty wok over medium-high heat until shimmering. Add chile mixture and cook until color deepens slightly, 3 to 5 minutes. Add noodles and broth mixture and cook, tossing gently, until noodles are well coated and tender, 2 to 4 minutes. Add vegetable mixture and toss to combine. Off heat, stir in basil and season with extra soy sauce to taste. Serve.

VEGETABLE, GRAIN, AND BEAN MAINS

216 Vindaloo-Spiced Green Beans, Chickpeas, and Potatoes

219 Panang Curry with Eggplant, Broccolini, and Tofu

220 Curry Roasted Cabbage Wedges with Tomatoes and Chickpeas

222 Baharat Cauliflower and Eggplant with Peas

224 Grilled Potatoes and Vegetables with Pesto

Grilled Squash and Vegetables with Chimichurri

227 Loaded Sweet Potato Wedges with Tempeh

228 Roasted Acorn Squash with Bulgur and Chickpeas

230 Stuffed Eggplant with Lentils, Pomegranate, and Cashew Ricotta

232 Sweet Potato and Black Bean Enchiladas

235 Cauliflower and Chickpea Paella

236 Green Fried Rice with Green Beans and Spinach

239 Kimchi Fried Rice with Seitan

240 Beet-Barley Risotto with Kale

243 Risotto Primavera with Mushrooms, Asparagus, and Peas

244 Pearl Couscous with White Beans, Tomatoes, and Fennel

247 Espinacas con Garbanzos

248 Red Beans and Rice

251 Red Lentil Kibbeh

252 Mushroom, Brussels Sprout, and White Bean Gratin

254 Tofu Mole with Zucchini Ribbon Salad

256 Glazed Tofu with Pigeon Peas and Rice

259 Crispy Tempeh with Sambal

260 Stir-Fried Seitan with Cashews

263 Grilled Tofu with Charred Broccoli and Peanut Sauce

264 Crispy Baked Tofu Peperonata

Vindaloo-Spiced Green Beans, Chickpeas, and Potatoes

SERVES 2

TOTAL TIME 1 hour

SPICE PASTE

¾ cup water

1 (2-inch) piece ginger, peeled and sliced into ⅛-inch thick rounds

6 garlic cloves, peeled

2 teaspoons Kashmiri chile powder

2 teaspoons paprika

2 teaspoons ground cumin

1 teaspoon pepper

¾ teaspoon table salt

½ teaspoon ground cinnamon

½ teaspoon ground cardamom

¼ teaspoon ground cloves

¼ teaspoon ground nutmeg

VEGETABLES

2 tablespoons vegetable oil

1 small onion, chopped fine

1 cup vegetable broth

1 (15-ounce) can chickpeas, rinsed

6 ounces green beans, trimmed and cut into 1-inch lengths

6 ounces Yukon Gold potatoes, unpeeled, cut into ¾-inch pieces

1 tablespoon cider vinegar, plus extra for seasoning

WHY THIS RECIPE WORKS The word "vindaloo" has evolved to indicate a searingly hot curry because of its adoption into British cuisine, but the original dish from the Goan region is a brightly flavored but relatively mild braise made with dried Kashmiri chiles and plenty of spices such as cinnamon, cardamom, and cloves. While vindaloo is traditionally made with pork, we build this hearty vegan version on a foundation of vegetables and protein-rich chickpeas. The Kashmiri chile powder provides the dish with bright color, heat, earthy flavor, and a hint of astringency. After softening an onion, we add our spice paste to the pan to allow all its complex flavors to bloom in the oil before stirring in the broth, chickpeas, and vegetables. Vindaloo should have a pronounced vinegary tang; we hold off on adding a glug of cider vinegar until the last few minutes of cooking to ensure that its characteristic acidity isn't dulled by long exposure to heat. For ways to use up leftover green beans, see page 18.

1 FOR THE SPICE PASTE Process all ingredients in blender on low speed until rough paste forms, about 1 minute. Scrape down sides of blender jar and blend on high speed until paste is smooth, about 1 minute. (Spice paste can be refrigerated for up to 3 days.)

2 FOR THE VEGETABLES Heat oil in large saucepan over medium heat until shimmering. Add onion and cook until softened and lightly browned, 5 to 7 minutes. Add spice paste and cook until fragrant, about 1 minute.

3 Stir in broth, scraping up any browned bits. Add chickpeas, green beans, and potatoes and bring to boil. Reduce heat to medium-low, partially cover, and simmer until potatoes are just tender, 15 to 18 minutes.

4 Uncover and stir in vinegar. Increase heat to medium-high and cook until potatoes are fully tender and sauce is slightly thickened, 2 to 3 minutes. Season with salt, pepper, and extra vinegar to taste. Serve.

Kitchen Improv

USE WHAT YOU'VE GOT

Substitute frozen cut green beans for fresh. Substitute red potatoes for Yukon Gold.

BULK IT UP

Serve over rice or other grain (see page 270).

DON'T HAVE KASHMIRI CHILE POWDER?

Toast and grind 1 large guajillo chile and substitute 2 teaspoons guajillo chile powder for Kashmiri chile powder.

VEGETABLE, GRAIN, AND BEAN MAINS

Panang Curry

WITH EGGPLANT, BROCCOLINI, AND TOFU

SERVES 2

TOTAL TIME 50 minutes

- 2 tablespoons vegetable oil, divided
- 1 small onion, chopped fine
- ¼ teaspoon table salt
- 8 ounces eggplant, cut into 1-inch pieces
- 3 tablespoons vegan panang curry paste
- 1 cup canned coconut milk
- ¼ cup water, plus extra as needed
- 5 ounces broccolini, florets cut into 1-inch pieces, stalks cut on bias into ½-inch pieces
- 1 small red, orange, or yellow bell pepper, stemmed, seeded, and cut into 1-inch pieces
- 7 ounces firm or extra-firm tofu, cut into 1-inch pieces
- 8 fresh Thai basil leaves, torn
- ⅓ cup dry-roasted peanuts, chopped

  Lime wedges

Kitchen Improv

USE WHAT YOU'VE GOT

Substitute Thai red or green curry paste for panang curry paste. Substitute broccoli florets for broccolini.

BULK IT UP

Serve over rice or other grain (see page 270).

WHY THIS RECIPE WORKS   Savory-sweet, fragrant, and deeply rich, panang curry is a full-bodied, velvety, coconut milk–spiked curry often made with beef or shrimp. Our vegan for-two version puts the vegetables at the forefront, using eggplant, bell pepper, and broccolini to provide a variety of flavors and textures, plus tofu to imbue the dish with plenty of satisfying protein. We start by sautéing the onion and eggplant to soften them and begin to cook off their excess water. We then fry the panang curry paste in oil to enhance its flavor. To complete the sweet, rich, and nutty flavor profile of this panang curry we use a combination of coconut milk and water to create a full-bodied sauce for the vegetables and we throw in a handful of roasted peanuts, another traditional panang element. A handful of Thai basil and a quick squeeze of lime juice finish the dish on a fresh note. You will need a 10- or 12-inch nonstick skillet with a tight-fitting lid for this recipe. Note that not all panang curry pastes are vegan; check the ingredient list carefully to make sure. For ways to use up leftover broccolini, coconut milk, and tofu, see pages 18–19.

1   Heat 1 tablespoon oil in 10- or 12-inch nonstick skillet over medium-high heat until shimmering. Add onion and salt and cook until softened and lightly browned, 5 to 7 minutes. Stir in eggplant and cook until beginning to soften, 2 to 4 minutes. Transfer to bowl. Heat remaining 1 tablespoon oil in now-empty skillet over medium-high heat until shimmering. Add curry paste and cook, stirring frequently, until paste is fragrant and darkens in color to brick red, 5 to 8 minutes.

2   Stir in coconut milk and water, scraping up any browned bits, then stir in broccolini, bell pepper, tofu, and eggplant mixture and bring to boil. Reduce heat to low, cover, and simmer, stirring occasionally, until vegetables are fully tender, 14 to 16 minutes.

3   Adjust consistency with extra hot water as needed. Off heat, stir in basil and season with salt and pepper to taste. Sprinkle with peanuts and serve with lime wedges.

Curry Roasted Cabbage Wedges
WITH TOMATOES AND CHICKPEAS

SERVES 2
TOTAL TIME 1 hour

- 3 tablespoons vegetable oil, divided
- 1½ teaspoons curry powder, divided
- ½ teaspoon sugar
- ¼ teaspoon table salt
- ⅛ teaspoon pepper
- ½ small head green cabbage (1 pound)
- 2 garlic cloves, minced
- 1 teaspoon grated fresh ginger
- 1 (15-ounce) can chickpeas
- 5 ounces grape or cherry tomatoes, halved
- 2 tablespoons chopped fresh cilantro

Kitchen Improv

USE WHAT YOU'VE GOT

Substitute combination of 1 teaspoon ground coriander and ½ teaspoon ground cumin for curry powder. Substitute canned white beans for chickpeas. Substitute other fresh herbs, such as basil or mint, for cilantro.

LEVEL UP

Top with slivered almonds. Serve with Lemon-Herb Yogurt Sauce (page 25).

WHY THIS RECIPE WORKS   Cabbage may lack the dramatic appearance of other cruciferous vegetables—the bumpy reptilian leaves of Lacinato kale or striking hue of purple cauliflower—but cut it into wedges and roast it, creating charred, crispy edges with tender, sweet layers underneath, and this humble vegetable absolutely deserves to be at the center of your plate. We first brush the wedges with oil spiked with curry powder and a little sugar to help with browning. We then cover the cabbage with aluminum foil before putting the baking sheet on the lower rack of a hot oven to steam the wedges and jump-start browning on the undersides. Uncovering the wedges for the last part of cooking crisps and browns their upper sides while maximizing browning underneath. To complete the meal, we simmer chickpeas, tomatoes, and more curry powder on the stovetop while the cabbage roasts. When slicing the cabbage into wedges, be sure to slice through the core, leaving it intact so the wedges don't fall apart. For ways to use up leftover cabbage, see page 18.

1   Adjust oven rack to lowest position and heat oven to 450 degrees. Combine 2 tablespoons oil, 1 teaspoon curry powder, sugar, salt, and pepper in small bowl. Cut cabbage into four roughly 2-inch-wide wedges, leaving core intact.

2   Arrange cabbage wedges evenly on rimmed baking sheet, then brush all over with oil mixture. Cover tightly with aluminum foil and roast for 10 minutes. Remove foil and continue to roast until cabbage is tender and sides touching sheet are well browned, about 15 minutes longer.

3   Combine remaining 1 tablespoon oil, garlic, ginger, and remaining ½ teaspoon curry powder in large saucepan and cook over medium-high heat until fragrant, about 30 seconds. Stir in chickpeas and their liquid and tomatoes and bring to simmer. Cook, stirring frequently, until tomatoes begin to break down and mixture has thickened slightly, 6 to 8 minutes. Divide cabbage among serving plates and top with chickpea mixture and cilantro. Serve.

Baharat Cauliflower and Eggplant
WITH PEAS

SERVES 2

TOTAL TIME 1 hour

- 1 (1-pound) eggplant, trimmed, halved lengthwise, and sliced ½ inch thick
- ½ teaspoon table salt, divided
- 8 ounces cauliflower florets, cut into 1-inch pieces
- 2 tablespoons extra-virgin olive oil
- 1½ teaspoons baharat
- ½ cup frozen peas, thawed
- 3 tablespoons tahini
- 3 tablespoons lemon juice, divided, plus lemon wedges for serving
- 4 teaspoons water, plus extra as needed
- 1 small garlic clove, minced to paste
- ¼ teaspoon sugar
- ⅛ teaspoon cayenne pepper (optional)
- ¼ cup chopped fresh cilantro
- ½ cup Quick-Pickled Red Onion (page 26)
- 2 pitas, warmed

WHY THIS RECIPE WORKS Warm spice and cauliflower always make for a great pairing. In this vegetable-forward sheet-pan meal, baharat (a popular Middle Eastern spice blend that typically includes black pepper, coriander, cumin, and cinnamon) brings out the nuttiness and subtle sweetness of the cauliflower. Eggplant is the other star ingredient; after salting it, we toss it with the baharat and cauliflower and roast everything until tender and browned. Since peas take only a couple minutes to warm through, we add them at the end of the roasting period for a burst of color and sweet contrast. We then toss the roasted vegetables with lemon juice and cilantro for brightness and serve them with a lemony tahini sauce for drizzling (or dousing) as desired, plus tangy pickled onion and warm pitas. A rasp-style grater makes quick work of turning the garlic into a paste. For ways to use up leftover cauliflower, see page 18.

1 Adjust oven rack to lower-middle position and heat oven to 450 degrees. Arrange eggplant in even layer on paper towel–lined plate, sprinkle all over with ¼ teaspoon salt, and let sit for 10 minutes. Pat eggplant dry with paper towels.

2 Line rimmed baking sheet with aluminum foil and spray with vegetable oil spray. Toss eggplant, cauliflower, oil, baharat, and remaining ¼ teaspoon salt together in large bowl, then arrange in even layer on prepared sheet. Roast until eggplant begins to soften, 15 to 20 minutes. Flip vegetables and continue roasting until vegetables are very tender and spotty brown, 15 to 20 minutes longer. Remove sheet from oven, add peas, toss gently to combine, and continue to roast until peas are heated through, about 2 minutes longer.

3 Whisk tahini; 2 tablespoons lemon juice; water; garlic; sugar; and cayenne, if using, in small bowl until smooth. Add extra water, 1 teaspoon at a time, as needed until sauce is thick but pourable. Season with salt and pepper to taste.

4 Gently toss vegetables with cilantro and remaining 1 tablespoon lemon juice and season with salt and pepper to taste. Serve with tahini sauce, pickled onion, pitas, and lemon wedges.

Kitchen Improv

USE WHAT YOU'VE GOT

Substitute broccoli or broccolini for cauliflower. Substitute combination of ½ teaspoon pepper, ½ teaspoon ground coriander, ¼ teaspoon ground cumin, and ⅛ teaspoon ground cinnamon for baharat. Substitute other fresh herbs, such as parsley or mint, for cilantro. Substitute Lemon-Herb Yogurt Sauce (page 25) for tahini sauce.

BULK IT UP

Toss canned chickpeas with vegetables and baharat before roasting. Serve with rice or other grain (see page 270).

Grilled Potatoes and Vegetables
WITH PESTO

SERVES 2

TOTAL TIME 40 minutes

- 12 ounces small red or yellow potatoes, unpeeled, halved
- 4 teaspoons extra-virgin olive oil, divided
- ¾ teaspoon table salt, divided
- ¼ teaspoon pepper, divided
- 12 ounces broccolini, trimmed, stems halved lengthwise if greater than ½ inch thick
- 2 red, orange, or yellow bell peppers, stemmed, seeded, and quartered
- 1 lemon, halved
- ¼ cup basil pesto

Kitchen Improv

USE WHAT YOU'VE GOT

Substitute broccoli rabe for broccolini. Substitute Chermoula (page 25) or Quick Lemon-Herb Vinaigrette (page 25) for pesto.

LEVEL UP

Sprinkle with toasted nuts or seeds, dollop with plant-based ricotta, or sprinkle with plant-based feta or Parmesan cheese. Roughly chop vegetables and toss with salad greens, such as arugula or baby spinach.

BULK IT UP

Serve with rice or other grain (see page 270).

WHY THIS RECIPE WORKS   The prospect of deeply browned, caramelized vegetables with gorgeous char marks, crispy edges, and creamy-tender interiors is, in our opinion, one of the most compelling reasons to fire up the grill. We give grilled vegetables the spotlight they deserve by building a dinner platter around crispy grilled potatoes, sweet bell peppers, and just-charred-enough broccolini dolloped with flavorful pesto. Along with the pesto, the potatoes add richness and satiating volume to the plate. Giving the potatoes a jump-start in the microwave ensures that they finish cooking on the grill at the same time as the other vegetables. Use small red or yellow potatoes measuring 1 to 2 inches in diameter. You can use store-bought vegan pesto or our Pesto (page 24) in this recipe. For ways to use up leftover broccolini, see page 18.

1   Toss potatoes in bowl with 1 teaspoon oil, ½ teaspoon salt, and ⅛ teaspoon pepper. Cover and microwave until potatoes offer slight resistance when pierced with tip of paring knife, 4 to 6 minutes, stirring halfway through microwaving. Drain, if necessary, and set aside.

2   Toss broccolini with 2 teaspoons oil, ⅛ teaspoon salt, and remaining ⅛ teaspoon pepper. Rub bell peppers evenly with remaining 1 teaspoon oil and sprinkle with remaining ⅛ teaspoon salt.

3A   FOR A CHARCOAL GRILL   Open bottom vent completely. Light large chimney starter ½ filled with charcoal briquettes (3 quarts). When top coals are partially covered with ash, pour evenly over grill. Set cooking grate in place, cover, and open lid vent completely. Heat grill until hot, about 5 minutes.

3B   FOR A GAS GRILL   Turn all burners to high, cover, and heat grill until hot, about 15 minutes. Turn all burners to medium.

4   Clean and oil cooking grate. Grill vegetables and lemon halves until well browned and tender, 8 to 12 minutes, flipping them as needed. Transfer vegetables and lemon halves to serving platter as they finish cooking. Dollop vegetables with pesto and serve.

VARIATION
Grilled Squash and Vegetables with Chimichurri

Using chef's knife, separate bulb and neck of one 1½- to 2-pound butternut squash; set bulb aside for another use. Peel butternut squash neck, halve lengthwise, then slice crosswise ½ inch thick. Substitute squash for potatoes and increase squash grilling time to 14 to 16 minutes. Substitute Chimichurri Sauce (page 24) for pesto.

Loaded Sweet Potato Wedges
WITH TEMPEH

SERVES 2

TOTAL TIME 55 minutes

- 1 pound sweet potatoes, unpeeled, cut lengthwise into 2-inch-wide wedges
- 2 tablespoons extra-virgin olive oil, divided
- ½ teaspoon table salt, divided
- 4 ounces tempeh, crumbled into ½-inch pieces
- ½ teaspoon ground cumin
- ½ teaspoon ground coriander
- ½ teaspoon smoked paprika
- ⅛ teaspoon ground cinnamon
- 2 ounces cherry or grape tomatoes, halved
- 2 radishes, trimmed, halved, and sliced thin
- 1 jalapeño chile, stemmed and sliced into thin rings
- ¼ cup chopped fresh cilantro
- 2 scallions, sliced thin
  Lime wedges

Kitchen Improv

USE WHAT YOU'VE GOT

Substitute 1½ teaspoons chili powder for cumin, coriander, paprika, and cinnamon.

LEVEL UP

Top with diced avocado and/or Quick-Pickled Red Onion (page 26). Serve with Avocado Yogurt Sauce (page 25).

WHY THIS RECIPE WORKS Sturdy caramelized wedges of sweet potatoes are an incredible base for a layered (and fun!) plant-based meal when combined with nutty, crispy spiced tempeh and a bevy of vibrant fresh toppings. While the sweet potato wedges roast hands-off in the oven, we brown crumbled tempeh with a generous dose of spices—cumin, coriander, paprika, and cinnamon—to give this excellent source of protein an earthy, warm flavor that complements the sweet tubers. But the toppings don't end there: Sweet cherry tomatoes, crisp radishes, spicy jalapeño, and citrusy fresh cilantro add even more vegetable goodness, loads of flavor and textural contrast, and a veritable explosion of color. A drizzle of lime juice and a sprinkle of scallions provide an ultrafresh finish. You can plate this dish however you like, but we think it's a great opportunity to eat dinner with your hands.

1 Adjust oven rack to middle position and heat oven to 450 degrees. Line rimmed baking sheet with aluminum foil and spray with vegetable oil spray. Toss potatoes in bowl with 1 tablespoon oil and ¼ teaspoon salt. Arrange potato wedges cut sides down in single layer on prepared sheet. Roast until tender and bottoms of potatoes are well browned, about 30 minutes.

2 Meanwhile, heat remaining 1 tablespoon oil in 10- or 12-inch skillet over medium heat until shimmering. Add tempeh, cumin, coriander, paprika, cinnamon, and remaining ¼ teaspoon salt and cook until tempeh is well browned, 8 to 12 minutes, stirring often. Off heat, season with salt and pepper to taste. Cover to keep warm.

3 Transfer potatoes to serving plates and top with tempeh, tomatoes, radishes, jalapeño, cilantro, and scallions. Serve with lime wedges.

Roasted Acorn Squash
WITH BULGUR AND CHICKPEAS

SERVES 2

TOTAL TIME 45 minutes

- 1 (1-pound) acorn squash, quartered pole to pole, seeds removed
- 1 (15-ounce) can chickpeas, rinsed
- ¼ cup extra-virgin olive oil, divided, plus extra for drizzling
- 1 teaspoon ground coriander
- ½ teaspoon table salt, divided, plus salt for cooking bulgur
- Pinch ground cinnamon
- 2 tablespoons cider vinegar
- ½ cup medium-grind bulgur
- ¼ cup chopped fresh parsley
- 2 tablespoons chopped toasted walnuts
- 2 tablespoons chopped dried figs
- 2 tablespoons crumbled plant-based feta cheese

Kitchen Improv
USE WHAT YOU'VE GOT

Substitute wine vinegar or sherry vinegar for cider vinegar. Substitute other nuts or dried fruits for walnuts and/or figs.

WHY THIS RECIPE WORKS There's a reason for the perennial popularity of stuffed vegetables: They're a great way to get a vegetable-forward dinner on the table in a tidy package. Here, acorn squash quarters overflow with a hearty bulgur filling, while roasted spiced chickpeas, toasted walnuts, dried figs, and plant-based cheese contribute to the meal's array of flavors and textures. To save time we roast the squash and chickpeas simultaneously on the same rimmed baking sheet after tossing both elements with a fragrant mixture of coriander and cinnamon. While they roast, we whisk together a quick vinaigrette and simmer the bulgur until tender. Assembly couldn't be easier: We toss the bulgur and chickpeas with the vinaigrette, layer this mixture atop the squash quarters, and then sprinkle with the crunchy nuts, sweet figs, and creamy plant-based feta. When shopping, don't confuse bulgur with cracked wheat, which has a much longer cooking time and will not work in this recipe.

1 Adjust oven rack to middle position and heat oven to 450 degrees. Line rimmed baking sheet with parchment paper. Toss squash, chickpeas, 1 table-spoon oil, coriander, ¼ teaspoon salt, and cinnamon together in large bowl.

2 Arrange squash quarters in single layer on half of prepared sheet and roast until bottoms are lightly browned, 10 to 15 minutes. Add chickpeas to empty side of sheet and roast until squash is tender and well browned and chickpeas are lightly browned, 15 to 20 minutes. Whisk vinegar, remaining 3 tablespoons oil, and remaining ¼ teaspoon salt together in now-empty bowl; set aside.

3 Meanwhile, bring 2 quarts water to boil in large saucepan. Add bulgur and ½ teaspoon salt and return to boil. Reduce heat to medium-low and simmer until tender, 5 to 8 minutes. Drain.

4 Add bulgur, parsley, and chickpeas to bowl with dressing and toss to combine. Transfer two squash quarters to each serving plate, top with bulgur mixture, walnuts, figs, and feta, and drizzle with extra oil. Serve.

Stuffed Eggplant
WITH LENTILS, POMEGRANATE, AND CASHEW RICOTTA

SERVES 2

TOTAL TIME 1 hour

- 3 tablespoons boiling water
- 3 tablespoons couscous
- 1 (1-pound) eggplant, halved lengthwise
- 2 tablespoons extra-virgin olive oil, divided
- ½ teaspoon baharat, divided
- ½ teaspoon table salt, divided
- 2 teaspoons pomegranate molasses, plus extra for serving
- 2 teaspoons lemon juice
- 1 (15-ounce) can lentils, rinsed
- ¼ cup fresh parsley leaves
- 2 tablespoons chopped toasted pistachios, plus extra for serving
- ¼ cup Lemon-Herb Cashew Ricotta (page 22)

WHY THIS RECIPE WORKS For a showstopping vegan main that puts a vegetable squarely (and beautifully) in the spotlight, we stuff tender roasted eggplant halves with a flavorful lentil and couscous filling full of spices, herbs, and textural contrast. A 1-pound eggplant is the perfect size to serve two people, so we first score its flesh (to help it release its moisture and cook more quickly) and then roast it until tender but still sturdy enough not to collapse when filled. While the eggplant roasts, we make a simple but flavorful filling of canned lentils, which require no additional time or prep, and quick-cooking couscous flavored with lemon, baharat, fresh parsley, and sweet-tart pomegranate molasses. Green pistachios add crunch and contrasting color and dollops of plant-based ricotta add creamy richness. For an accurate measurement of boiling water, bring a kettle of water to a boil and then measure out the desired amount.

1   Adjust oven rack to lower-middle position, place parchment paper–lined rimmed baking sheet on rack, and heat oven to 400 degrees. Combine boiling water and couscous in small bowl. Cover and let sit for 10 minutes. Fluff couscous with fork and season with salt and pepper to taste; set aside.

2   Score flesh of each eggplant half in 1-inch diamond pattern, about 1 inch deep. Brush scored sides of eggplant with 1 tablespoon oil and sprinkle with ¼ teaspoon baharat and ¼ teaspoon salt. Arrange eggplant cut sides down on hot sheet and roast until flesh is tender, 40 to 50 minutes. Transfer eggplant cut sides down to paper towel–lined baking sheet and let drain.

3   Meanwhile, whisk pomegranate molasses, lemon juice, remaining 1 tablespoon oil, remaining ¼ teaspoon baharat, and remaining ¼ teaspoon salt together in large bowl. Add lentils, parsley, pistachios, and couscous and toss to combine. Season with salt and pepper to taste.

4   Transfer eggplant cut sides up to serving plates. Using 2 forks, gently push eggplant flesh to sides to make room for filling. Gently mound lentil mixture into eggplant halves and pack lightly with back of spoon. Dollop ricotta mixture evenly over lentils. Sprinkle with extra pistachios and drizzle with extra pomegranate molasses before serving.

Kitchen Improv

USE WHAT YOU'VE GOT

Substitute combination of ⅛ teaspoon pepper, ⅛ teaspoon ground coriander, ⅛ teaspoon ground cumin, and pinch ground cinnamon for baharat. Substitute other chopped nuts, such as pecans, hazelnuts, or walnuts, for pistachios.

LEVEL UP

Sprinkle with pomegranate seeds and/or Crispy Shallots (page 27).

Sweet Potato and Black Bean Enchiladas

SERVES 2

TOTAL TIME 45 minutes

- 5 teaspoons vegetable oil, divided
- ½ small onion, chopped fine
- 2 tablespoons chili powder
- 2 tablespoons all-purpose flour
- 2 tablespoons tomato paste
- 1 garlic clove, minced
- 1 cup vegetable broth
- 1 cup water
- 1 small sweet potato (8 ounces), peeled and cut into ½-inch pieces
- 1 (15-ounce) can black beans, rinsed
- 6 (6-inch) corn tortillas

  Lime wedges

Kitchen Improv

USE WHAT YOU'VE GOT

Substitute flour tortillas for corn. Substitute pinto beans for black beans.

LEVEL UP

Sprinkle with chopped fresh cilantro, sliced scallions, sliced olives, chopped tomatoes, pickled jalapeños, and/or diced avocado. Dollop with plant-based yogurt.

WHY THIS RECIPE WORKS From cooking the sauce to preparing the filling, making enchiladas can be a labor-intensive endeavor. This one-pan version is a triumph of streamlining, coming together on the stovetop in well under an hour. To make the filling vegan, we turn to sweet potato and black beans, two ingredients that pair beautifully with the bold flavors in the sauce and give our enchiladas the heartiness we expect. One can of beans and a single small potato, softened in the microwave to save time, yield an ample amount of filling for two servings. While the sweet potato cooks, we make the sauce: a combination of chili powder, tomato paste, garlic, onion, vegetable broth, and flour (for thickening). We incorporate a portion of this sauce into the filling before rolling it up in tortillas, which we place side by side right in the skillet with the remaining sauce and simmer to warm through and meld all the flavors. You will need a 10- or 12-inch nonstick skillet with a tight-fitting lid for this recipe.

1 Heat 1 tablespoon oil in 10- or 12-inch nonstick skillet over medium heat until shimmering. Add onion and cook until softened, about 3 minutes. Stir in chili powder, flour, tomato paste, and garlic and cook until fragrant, about 1 minute. Gradually whisk in broth and water, bring to simmer, and cook until slightly thickened, about 4 minutes. Off heat, measure out and reserve 1½ cups sauce; leave remaining sauce in skillet.

2 Meanwhile, toss sweet potato in bowl with remaining 2 teaspoons oil, cover, and microwave until very tender, 6 to 8 minutes, stirring halfway through microwaving. Add beans and ¼ cup reserved sauce and toss gently to combine.

3 Stack tortillas and wrap in damp dish towel. Microwave until pliable, 30 to 60 seconds. Spread rounded 2 tablespoons sweet potato mixture across center of 1 tortilla. Roll tortilla tightly around filling and place seam side down in sauce in skillet. Repeat with remaining tortillas and remaining filling, arranging enchiladas side by side in single row. Pour remaining reserved sauce over enchiladas and top with any remaining filling.

4 Heat sauce and enchiladas over medium heat until sauce is simmering. Reduce heat to medium-low, cover, and simmer until enchiladas are heated through, about 10 minutes. Serve with lime wedges.

Cauliflower and Chickpea Paella

SERVES 2
TOTAL TIME 1 hour

- 2 tablespoons extra-virgin olive oil, divided
- 6 ounces cauliflower florets, cut into 1-inch pieces (1¼ cups)
- 4 ounces green beans, trimmed and cut into 2-inch lengths
- 1 small red bell pepper, stemmed, seeded, and cut into ½-inch-wide strips
- 3 garlic cloves, minced
- 2 teaspoons tomato paste
- 1 teaspoon smoked paprika
- ⅛ teaspoon table salt
- ⅛ teaspoon saffron threads, crumbled (optional)
- ¼ cup dry sherry
- ½ cup Calasparra or Bomba rice
- 1 (15-ounce) can chickpeas, rinsed
- 1½ cups vegetable broth
  Lemon wedges

Kitchen Improv

USE WHAT YOU'VE GOT

Substitute arborio rice for Calasparra or Bomba rice. Substitute butter beans or cannellini beans for chickpeas. Substitute dry vermouth or white wine for sherry.

LEVEL UP

Dollop with plant-based yogurt.

WHY THIS RECIPE WORKS Paella de verduras is a vibrant approach to the beloved Spanish rice dish that puts vegetables front and center. Our version features crisp-tender green beans, chunky cauliflower florets, eye-catching red bell pepper, and nutty chickpeas. We build this vegan paella's flavor base layer by layer, first browning the bell pepper to deepen its flavor, stirring in umami-packed tomato paste, loading up on garlic, and mixing in smoked paprika, saffron, and nutty-tasting dry sherry for brightness and depth. We cover the rice for part of its cooking time to trap moisture and ensure well-hydrated grains. We then continue to cook the mixture uncovered until all the liquid evaporates and leaves behind a layer of caramelized rice known as socarrat; this step is optional, but we think it's well worth the few extra minutes to create that irresistible crispy-chewy-tender contrast that paella is known for. Letting the paella rest for a few minutes before serving helps the socarrat layer firm up so it releases easily from the pan. You will need a 10-inch skillet with a tight-fitting lid for this recipe. For ways to use up leftover cauliflower and green beans, see page 18.

1 Heat 1 tablespoon oil in 10-inch skillet over medium heat until shimmering. Add cauliflower and green beans and cook until vegetables are spotty brown, 5 to 7 minutes; transfer to bowl.

2 Add remaining 1 tablespoon oil and bell pepper to now-empty skillet and cook over medium heat until softened, about 3 minutes. Stir in garlic; tomato paste; paprika; salt; and saffron, if using, and cook until fragrant, about 30 seconds. Stir in sherry and cook, stirring constantly, until excess moisture has evaporated and mixture forms large clumps, 1 to 2 minutes.

3 Add rice and stir until very well combined. Off heat, smooth rice mixture into even layer. Scatter chickpeas evenly over rice. Scatter cauliflower and green beans evenly over chickpeas. Gently pour broth all over, making sure rice is fully submerged (it's OK if parts of vegetables aren't submerged).

4 Bring to simmer over medium heat and simmer until broth is just below top of rice, 10 to 12 minutes. Cover and continue to cook until rice is cooked through, 3 to 5 minutes longer. Uncover and continue to cook until rice pops and sizzles and all excess moisture has evaporated (to test, use butter knife to gently push aside some rice and vegetables), about 3 minutes longer. (If socarrat is desired, continue to cook, rotating skillet quarter turn every 20 seconds, until rice on bottom of skillet is well browned and slightly crusty, 2 to 3 minutes longer.) Off heat, let rest for 5 minutes. Season with salt and pepper to taste. Serve with lemon wedges.

Green Fried Rice

WITH GREEN BEANS AND SPINACH

SERVES 2
TOTAL TIME 40 minutes

- 2 garlic cloves (1 whole unpeeled, 1 minced)
- ¼ cup fresh cilantro leaves
- ¼ cup fresh Thai basil leaves
- 5 ounces (5 cups) baby spinach, divided
- 1 jalapeño chile, stemmed, seeded, and chopped coarse
- ½ teaspoon table salt, divided
- 2 teaspoons plus 2 tablespoons vegetable oil, divided
- 4 ounces green beans, trimmed and halved
- 1 teaspoon grated fresh ginger
- 2 cups cooked long-grain white rice (see page 270), room temperature
- ½ cup frozen peas
  Lime wedges

Kitchen Improv

USE WHAT YOU'VE GOT

Substitute Italian basil for Thai basil. Substitute baby kale for baby spinach. Substitute asparagus for green beans.

BULK IT UP

Top with Pan-Seared Tofu (page 274) or Scrambled Plant-Based Egg (page 275).

WHY THIS RECIPE WORKS   Fried rice has a ton going for it: It's comforting, comes together in one pan, and can be customized with just about any stir-ins you like. Here we give the basic concept a vibrant, bright-green spin, combining fistfuls of fragrant herbs (made into a paste to cling to each and every grain of rice) with baby spinach, green beans, peas, and, of course, the requisite deliciously crisped rice. We stir-fry in stages to avoid overloading our wok (a nonstick skillet will also work), first browning the vegetables and aromatics and then frying the rice and herb paste. A food processor makes quick work of creating the herb paste, but in a pinch you can mince the toasted garlic, cilantro, basil, spinach, and jalapeño by hand. We prefer jasmine rice, but you can use any long-grain white rice in this recipe. Day-old rice works best; alternatively, cook your rice 2 hours ahead, spread it on a rimmed baking sheet, and let it cool completely before chilling it for 30 minutes. Rice should be roughly room temperature when you stir-fry. For ways to use up leftover green beans, see page 18.

1   Toast unpeeled garlic clove in 14-inch flat-bottomed wok or 10- or 12-inch nonstick skillet over medium heat, shaking pan occasionally, until softened and spotty brown, about 8 minutes. When garlic is cool enough to handle, remove skin and discard, then chop coarse. Process chopped garlic, cilantro, basil, 1 cup spinach, jalapeño, and ⅛ teaspoon salt in food processor until finely chopped, about 15 seconds, scraping down sides of bowl as needed; set aside.

2   Heat 2 teaspoons oil in now-empty wok over medium-high heat until shimmering. Add green beans and ⅛ teaspoon salt and cook, tossing slowly but constantly, until spotty brown, 1 to 2 minutes. Add remaining 4 cups spinach and cook until wilted, 1 to 2 minutes. Add ginger and minced garlic and cook until fragrant, about 30 seconds. Transfer vegetables to bowl and cover to keep warm.

3   Heat remaining 2 tablespoons oil in again-empty wok over medium-high heat until shimmering. Add rice and herb mixture (it's OK if rice has some clumps) and cook, tossing slowly but constantly, until grains are separate and heated through, 2 to 4 minutes. Add peas and cook until warmed through, about 2 minutes. Season with salt and pepper to taste. Transfer rice mixture to serving bowls and top with green bean mixture. Serve with lime wedges.

Kimchi Fried Rice
WITH SEITAN

SERVES 2
TOTAL TIME 40 minutes

- 1 (8-inch square) sheet gim
- 2 ounces seitan, cut into ½-inch pieces
- 2 teaspoons vegetable oil, divided
- 1 small onion, chopped
- 3 scallions, white and green parts separated and sliced thin
- 1 cup vegan cabbage kimchi, drained with 2 tablespoons juice reserved, cut into ¼-inch strips
- 2 tablespoons water
- 2 teaspoons soy sauce
- 2 teaspoons gochujang paste
- ¼ teaspoon pepper
- 2 cups cooked short-grain white rice (page 270), room temperature
- 2 teaspoons toasted sesame oil
- 1½ teaspoons sesame seeds, toasted

Kitchen Improv

USE WHAT YOU'VE GOT

Substitute plain pretoasted seaweed snacks for gim; skip toasting in step 1.

BULK IT UP

Top with Pan-Seared Tofu (page 274) or Scrambled Plant-Based Egg (page 275).

WHY THIS RECIPE WORKS   Quick-cooking Korean comfort food, kimchi bokkeumbap is typically made with leftover short-grain rice and well-fermented kimchi, but from there seasonings and additions to bulk it up vary widely. We start by stir-frying some aromatics (chopped onion and sliced scallions) with chopped seitan, which provides protein and a pleasantly springy texture. Next we add lots of chopped cabbage kimchi along with some of its punchy juice, savory soy sauce, spicy gochujang paste, and nutty toasted sesame oil. After stirring in the rice, we top everything off with thin strips of gim (dried seaweed), scallion greens, and sesame seeds. Day-old rice works best; alternatively, cook your rice 2 hours ahead, spread it on a rimmed baking sheet, and let it cool completely before chilling it for 30 minutes. Rice should be roughly room temperature when you stir-fry. If your kimchi doesn't yield 2 tablespoons of juice, make up the difference with water. Seitan is sold in blocks, chunks, or strips; any of those options will work in this recipe. For ways to use up leftover seitan, see page 19.

1   Grip gim with tongs and hold 2 inches above low flame on gas burner. Toast gim, turning every 3 to 5 seconds, until it is aromatic and shrinks slightly, about 20 seconds. (If you do not have a gas stove, toast gim on rimmed baking sheet in 275-degree oven until it is aromatic and shrinks slightly, 20 to 25 minutes, flipping gim halfway through toasting.) Using kitchen shears, cut gim into four 2-inch-wide strips. Stack strips and cut crosswise into thin strips.

2   Pat seitan dry with paper towels. Heat 1 teaspoon vegetable oil in 14-inch flat-bottomed wok or 10- or 12-inch nonstick skillet over medium-high heat until shimmering. Add seitan and cook, tossing slowly but constantly, until beginning to brown at edges, about 3 minutes; transfer to plate.

3   Heat remaining 1 teaspoon vegetable oil in now-empty wok over medium-high until shimmering. Add onion and scallion whites and cook, tossing slowly but constantly, until softened and lightly browned, 3 to 5 minutes. Stir in kimchi and reserved juice, water, soy sauce, gochujang paste, and pepper and cook until kimchi is soft and translucent, 3 to 5 minutes.

4   Add rice (it's OK if rice has some clumps) and seitan and cook, tossing slowly but constantly, until mixture is evenly combined, about 3 minutes. Stir in sesame oil, increase heat to medium-high, and cook, tossing occasionally, until mixture begins to stick to pan, about 4 minutes. Off heat, sprinkle with sesame seeds, scallion greens, and gim. Serve.

Beet-Barley Risotto
WITH KALE

SERVES 2

TOTAL TIME 1 hour

- 1½ cups water, plus extra as needed
- 1 cup vegetable broth
- 1 tablespoon extra-virgin olive oil, plus extra for drizzling
- 1 small onion, chopped fine
- ½ cup pearl barley
- 2 garlic cloves, minced
- ½ teaspoon minced fresh thyme or ¼ teaspoon dried
- ¼ cup dry white wine
- 1 (15-ounce) can whole beets, rinsed, patted dry, and shredded
- 1 ounce (1 cup) baby kale
- ¼ cup grated plant-based Parmesan cheese, plus extra for serving
- 2 tablespoons chopped fresh parsley

Kitchen Improv

BULK IT UP

Top with Pan-Seared Tofu (page 274).

WHY THIS RECIPE WORKS A good risotto might seem to depend upon refined white rice for its texture, since the release of starch is what produces the dish's hallmark creaminess (usually aided by butter and cheese). However, other grains, such as the pearl barley in this recipe, can be cooked to create a similarly supple, velvety sauce. To complement the hearty grain and give the risotto a vibrant hue, we add sweet, earthy, and convenient canned beets. We help the beets incorporate evenly by shredding them before stirring them into the barley. Salty plant-based Parmesan cheese, woodsy thyme, and a splash of wine bring depth to the saucy risotto, while a couple handfuls of baby kale add pretty pops of green. Do not substitute hulled, hull-less, quick-cooking, or presteamed barley for the pearl barley. Use the shredding disk of a food processor or the large holes of a box grater to shred the beets. You can use store-bought plant-based Parmesan cheese or our Cashew Parmesan (page 23) in this recipe.

1 Combine water and broth in 4-cup liquid measuring cup or medium bowl and microwave until simmering, about 5 minutes. Cover to keep warm.

2 Heat oil in large saucepan over medium heat until shimmering. Add onion and cook until softened and lightly browned, 4 to 6 minutes. Add barley and cook, stirring often, until grains are lightly toasted, about 3 minutes. Stir in garlic and thyme and cook until fragrant, about 30 seconds. Stir in wine and cook until fully absorbed, about 2 minutes.

3 Stir in beets and 1 cup warm broth and bring to simmer. Cook, stirring often, until liquid is absorbed and bottom of saucepan is dry, 10 to 15 minutes. Repeat with 1 cup warm broth.

4 Add kale and remaining ½ cup broth and continue to cook, stirring often, until kale is wilted and barley is cooked through but still somewhat firm in center, 5 to 10 minutes. Off heat, stir in Parmesan and adjust consistency with extra warm water as needed. Season with salt and pepper to taste. Divide risotto between serving bowls, top with parsley, and drizzle with extra oil. Serve with extra Parmesan.

Risotto Primavera
WITH MUSHROOMS, ASPARAGUS, AND PEAS

SERVES 2
TOTAL TIME 1 hour

1¾ cups vegetable broth

½ cup water, plus extra
as needed

2 tablespoons extra-virgin
olive oil, divided

3 ounces cremini mushrooms,
trimmed and sliced thin

½ teaspoon table salt, divided

1 small onion, chopped fine

½ cup arborio rice

3 ounces asparagus, trimmed
and cut into ½-inch pieces

¼ cup frozen peas

¼ cup grated plant-based
Parmesan cheese, plus
extra for serving

2 tablespoons chopped fresh
basil or parsley

2 teaspoons lemon juice

Kitchen Improv

USE WHAT YOU'VE GOT

Substitute white or portobello
mushrooms for cremini mushrooms.

LEVEL UP

Dollop with store-bought vegan
pesto or our Pesto (page 24).

WHY THIS RECIPE WORKS Most risotto recipes require constant stirring while adding hot broth by the ladleful from a nearby saucepan—a labor of love to be sure, but one that can be hard to justify when you only want two servings. Our recipe eliminates both the extra saucepan and the never-ending stirring to bring risotto into the realm of the everyday. Instead of simmering the broth on the stovetop, we warm it in the microwave. And by keeping the temperature fairly low and the pot covered while the rice cooks, we make the process mostly hands-off; just a few minutes of stirring at the very end is enough to release the rice's starch and result in a remarkably creamy risotto. Springtime vegetables and meaty mushrooms add heft, and lemon juice and fresh herbs bring brightness. You can use store-bought plant-based Parmesan cheese or our Cashew Parmesan (page 23) in this recipe.

1   Combine broth and water in 4-cup liquid measuring cup or medium bowl and microwave until simmering, about 5 minutes. Cover to keep warm.

2   Heat 2 teaspoons oil in large saucepan over medium heat until shimmering. Add mushrooms and ¼ teaspoon salt, cover, and cook until mushrooms begin to release their liquid, about 3 minutes. Uncover and continue to cook until liquid has evaporated and mushrooms begin to brown, about 3 minutes; transfer to bowl.

3   Heat 2 teaspoons oil in now-empty saucepan over medium heat until shimmering. Add onion and remaining ¼ teaspoon salt and cook until softened, about 3 minutes. Add rice and cook, stirring constantly, until grains are translucent around edges, about 1 minute.

4   Stir in 1½ cups warm broth and bring to simmer. Reduce heat to medium-low, cover, and simmer until almost all liquid is absorbed, 10 to 12 minutes. Stir in asparagus, cover, and cook for 2 minutes. Add ½ cup warm broth and cook, stirring constantly, until liquid is absorbed, about 3 minutes. Add peas and remaining broth and cook, stirring constantly, until rice is creamy and tender, about 3 minutes.

5   Off heat, stir in mushrooms, cover, and let sit until warmed through, about 2 minutes. Stir in Parmesan, basil, lemon juice, and remaining 2 teaspoons oil. Adjust consistency with extra warm water as needed. Season with salt and pepper to taste. Serve with extra Parmesan.

Pearl Couscous

WITH WHITE BEANS, TOMATOES, AND FENNEL

SERVES 2

TOTAL TIME 40 minutes

- 2 tablespoons extra-virgin olive oil, plus extra for drizzling
- 1 small fennel bulb, 2 tablespoons fronds minced, stalks discarded, bulb halved, cored, and sliced thin
- 1 small onion, chopped fine
- 2 garlic cloves, minced
- 1 teaspoon minced fresh rosemary or ½ teaspoon dried
- ½ teaspoon fennel seeds, cracked
- ½ teaspoon table salt
- ⅛ teaspoon red pepper flakes
- 1⅓ cups water
- 1 (15-ounce) can cannellini beans, rinsed
- 5 ounces cherry or grape tomatoes
- ½ cup pearl couscous
- 1½ teaspoons lemon juice, plus lemon wedges for serving

WHY THIS RECIPE WORKS   Couscous is a popular foundation for meals throughout the Mediterranean because it cooks quickly and its satisfying wheaty chew pairs well with just about anything. For all the same reasons, it also makes a perfect base for a simple but impactful plant-based meal for two. Here, we combine pearl couscous, which has more robust grains than smaller Moroccan couscous, with flavors inspired by Sardinian cuisine: licorice-scented fennel and piney rosemary. We cook a fresh fennel bulb with onion for its sweet, aromatic quality, and later add fennel seeds for their more intense flavor and fennel fronds for freshness. Cannellini beans and cherry tomatoes provide heartiness and bursts of sweet acidity; the liquid from the burst tomatoes gets incorporated into the dish to create a risotto-like texture. A final splash of lemon juice heightens all the flavors. Use a rolling pin or the bottom of a small saucepan or skillet to crack the fennel seeds.

1   Heat oil in large saucepan over medium heat until shimmering. Add fennel and onion and cook until vegetables are softened and lightly browned, 5 to 7 minutes. Stir in garlic, rosemary, fennel seeds, salt, and pepper flakes and cook until fragrant, about 30 seconds.

2   Stir in water, beans, tomatoes, and couscous and bring to boil. Reduce heat to medium-low and simmer, stirring occasionally, until couscous is tender and tomatoes have burst, 8 to 10 minutes. Stir in lemon juice and fennel fronds and season with salt and pepper to taste. Transfer to serving bowls and drizzle with extra oil. Serve with lemon wedges.

Kitchen Improv

USE WHAT YOU'VE GOT

Substitute other canned white beans for cannellini beans.

LEVEL UP

Dollop with store-bought vegan pesto or our Pesto (page 24).

VEGETABLE, GRAIN, AND BEAN MAINS

Espinacas con Garbanzos

SERVES 2
TOTAL TIME 45 minutes

- 1 plum tomato, halved lengthwise
- 1 (15-ounce) can chickpeas, rinsed
- ¾ cup vegetable broth
- 1 (7-inch) piece baguette (4 ounces), cut on bias into 3 slices
- 2 tablespoons extra-virgin olive oil, divided, plus extra for drizzling
- 3 garlic cloves, minced
- 1 teaspoon smoked paprika
- ½ teaspoon ground cumin
- Pinch ground cinnamon
- Pinch cayenne pepper
- Pinch saffron (optional)
- 2 teaspoons sherry vinegar, plus extra for seasoning
- 5 ounces frozen chopped spinach, thawed and squeezed dry
- ½ cup water

Kitchen Improv

USE WHAT YOU'VE GOT

Substitute wine vinegar or cider vinegar for sherry vinegar. Substitute frozen chopped kale for spinach. Substitute 1 small vine-ripened tomato for plum tomato.

WHY THIS RECIPE WORKS At first glance, espinacas con garbanzos, or spinach with chickpeas, sounds like the kind of food you might eat dutifully but without much enthusiasm when trying to get in your daily servings of greens. Think again. This stewy mixture of spinach and, yes, chickpeas, is a popular cold-weather tapa in southern Spain, but it can also serve on its own as a light meal. The two eponymous ingredients are bolstered by savory tomato, aromatic garlic, and bright sherry vinegar, and the dish's Arab influence is made clear with the additions of warm cumin and cinnamon in addition to paprika and saffron. Briefly simmering canned chickpeas in vegetable broth tenderizes them and ensures that the flavor of the main ingredient is extra savory. A picada—a paste of garlic and bread cooked in plenty of olive oil—thickens the sauce so it clings to every delectable bite. Using frozen spinach keeps prep easy. A little patience at the very end pays dividends, as allowing the dish to sit for just a few minutes gives time for all the flavors to meld into a cohesive whole that's anything but boring.

1 Using box grater, shred flesh of tomato into small bowl and set aside; discard skin. Bring chickpeas and broth to boil in large saucepan over high heat. Adjust heat to maintain simmer and cook until level of liquid is just below top layer of chickpeas, 8 to 10 minutes.

2 Meanwhile, tear one bread slice into 1-inch pieces and process in food processor until finely ground (you should have about ½ cup crumbs). Heat 1 tablespoon oil in 8- or 10-inch nonstick skillet over medium heat until just shimmering. Add bread crumbs and cook, stirring often, until deep golden brown, 3 to 4 minutes. Stir in garlic; paprika; cumin; cinnamon; cayenne; and saffron, if using, and cook until fragrant, about 30 seconds. Off heat, stir in vinegar and reserved tomato.

3 Stir bread mixture, spinach, and water into chickpeas and bring to simmer over medium heat. Cook, stirring occasionally, until mixture is thick and stew-like, 5 to 10 minutes. Off heat, stir in remaining 1 tablespoon oil. Cover and let sit for 5 minutes. Season with salt and extra vinegar to taste. Divide chickpea mixture between serving bowls and drizzle with extra oil. Serve with remaining bread.

Red Beans and Rice

SERVES 2

TOTAL TIME 50 minutes

1 tablespoon vegetable oil

3 scallions, white parts minced, green parts sliced thin

1 small green bell pepper, stemmed, seeded, and chopped fine

1 celery rib, minced

1 teaspoon minced fresh thyme or ¼ teaspoon dried

½ teaspoon smoked paprika

⅛ teaspoon cayenne pepper

1 (15-ounce) can small red beans, rinsed

1 (14.5-ounce) can diced tomatoes, drained

¾ cup vegetable broth

¾ cup water

1 teaspoon red wine vinegar, plus extra for seasoning

2 cups cooked long-grain white rice (page 270)

Hot sauce

WHY THIS RECIPE WORKS Rice and beans are the hard-working foundation of many a vegan dish, but often fade into the background as supporting players. New Orleans–style red beans and rice allows this dependable duo to take the limelight. This Cajun dish traditionally calls for Camellia-brand dried red beans and tasso ham. Our version builds balanced, nuanced flavor without meat by carefully fine-tuning the proportions of the sautéed bell pepper, scallions, and celery that make up the dish's vegetable backbone. To save time, we also switch to canned red beans, skipping the lengthy brining and cooking process required for dried beans. Smoked paprika adds savory depth as well as a hint of the smokiness that the ham provides in traditional versions. Finally, we finish the beans with a splash of tangy red wine vinegar before spooning them over a bowlful of fluffy white rice. This dish is beautiful in its simplicity, but it's also easy to bolster with extra protein or vegetables if desired; see the Kitchen Improv section for ideas.

1 Heat oil in large saucepan oven over medium heat until shimmering. Add scallion whites, bell pepper, and celery and cook until vegetables are softened, 5 to 7 minutes. Stir in thyme, paprika, and cayenne and cook until fragrant, about 30 seconds.

2 Stir in beans, tomatoes, broth, and water. Bring to boil, reduce heat to medium-low, and simmer until beans are softened and liquid is thickened, 25 to 30 minutes.

3 Off heat, stir in vinegar and season with salt, pepper, and extra vinegar to taste. Divide rice between serving bowls and top with bean mixture and scallion greens. Serve with hot sauce.

Kitchen Improv

USE WHAT YOU'VE GOT

Substitute canned black beans, black-eyed peas, or pigeon peas for small red beans.

LEVEL UP

Add 4 ounces frozen okra, thawed and patted dry, to pan with tomatoes.

BULK IT UP

Add 4 ounces plant-based sausage, halved lengthwise and cut into ¼-inch half-moons, to pan with vegetables in step 1.

Red Lentil Kibbeh

SERVES 2
TOTAL TIME 1 hour

- 4 teaspoons extra-virgin olive oil, divided
- 1 small onion, chopped fine
- 1 small red bell pepper, stemmed, seeded, and chopped fine
- ¾ teaspoon table salt
- 1 tablespoon harissa
- 1 tablespoon tomato paste
- ½ cup medium-grind bulgur
- 2 cups water
- ⅓ cup dried red lentils, picked over and rinsed
- ¼ cup chopped fresh parsley
- 1 tablespoon lemon juice, plus lemon wedges for serving

    Bibb or Boston lettuce leaves

    Plain plant-based yogurt

Kitchen Improv

MAKE IT A MEZZE PLATTER

Serve kibbeh with prepared foods such as Cashew Ricotta (page 22), baba ghanoush, or hummus; pickled vegetables; olives; and/or pita.

WHY THIS RECIPE WORKS   Kibbeh is a popular Middle Eastern dish made from bulgur, onions, varying spices, and, traditionally, ground meat. During Lent, however, kibbeh is often prepared with lentils in lieu of meat, making this a flavor-packed, naturally vegan meal. Our version uses red lentils for their vibrant hue and enhances both their color and flavor with two red pastes: Tomato paste brings sweetness and umami, and harissa (a paste of red peppers, garlic, olive oil, and warm spices) adds spicy, smoky complexity. To balance the aromatics, we stir in fresh-tasting lemon juice and parsley at the end. Once the lentils are cooked, we whisk the mixture vigorously until the lentils partially break down. The cohesive mash that's formed is perfect for spooning into lettuce leaves and drizzling with plant-based yogurt for a dinner you can eat with your hands. You can use store-bought harissa or our Harissa (page 26) in this recipe. Do not substitute brown or green lentils for the red lentils.

1   Heat 2 teaspoons oil in large saucepan over medium heat until shimmering. Add onion, bell pepper, and salt and cook until vegetables are softened, about 5 minutes. Stir in harissa and tomato paste and cook until fragrant, about 1 minute.

2   Stir in bulgur and water and bring to boil. Reduce heat to low, cover, and simmer until bulgur is just tender, about 8 minutes. Stir in lentils, cover, and cook, stirring occasionally, until lentils and bulgur are fully tender, 8 to 10 minutes.

3   Off heat, lay clean folded dish towel underneath lid and let sit for 10 minutes. Sprinkle parsley, lemon juice, and remaining 2 teaspoons oil over lentil mixture and stir vigorously until mixture is cohesive. Season with salt and pepper to taste. Serve kibbeh with lettuce leaves, passing yogurt and lemon wedges separately.

Mushroom, Brussels Sprout, and White Bean Gratin

SERVES 2

TOTAL TIME 1 hour

- 3 tablespoons extra-virgin olive oil
- 3 garlic cloves, minced
- 1 teaspoon minced fresh thyme or ¼ teaspoon dried
- ½ teaspoon grated lemon zest plus 2 teaspoons juice
- 4 ounces brussels sprouts, trimmed and quartered
- 4 ounces cremini mushrooms, trimmed and sliced ½ inch thick
- 1 small onion, sliced thin
- ½ teaspoon table salt
- ¼ teaspoon pepper
- 2 teaspoons tomato paste
- 1 teaspoon all-purpose flour
- ¼ cup dry white wine or dry vermouth
- 1 (15-ounce) can great northern beans, rinsed
- 1 cup vegetable broth
- 2–3 slices country-style bread, cut into ½-inch cubes (2 cups)
- 1 tablespoon chopped fresh parsley

WHY THIS RECIPE WORKS Gratins don't need cheese or dairy to qualify as elevated comfort food. This rendition features creamy white beans, meaty cremini mushrooms, tender brussels sprouts, and a crisp, toasty bread layer. For a complex savoriness, we start by sautéing the mushrooms and aromatics until a flavorful browned fond develops on the bottom of the skillet and then deglaze the skillet with wine, scraping up all that concentrated umami flavor and stirring it back into the dish. A small amount of flour—just 1 teaspoon—adds sauce-thickening starch. We bake the gratin in a low oven after topping it with bread cubes doused in olive oil seasoned with garlic, thyme, and lemon zest. As the gratin bakes, the lower portion of the bread soaks up moisture from the beans below, almost melting into the sauce, while the tops of the cubes dry out and crisp. A last-minute drizzle of the remaining seasoned oil gives the gratin a rich and fragrant finish. You will need a 10- or 12-inch ovensafe skillet for this recipe.

1 Adjust oven rack to middle position and heat oven to 350 degrees. Microwave oil, garlic, thyme, and lemon zest in small bowl until fragrant, 10 to 20 seconds.

2 Toss brussels sprouts, mushrooms, and onion with salt, pepper, and 1 tablespoon oil mixture in large bowl. Transfer vegetables to 10- or 12-inch ovensafe skillet and cook over medium-high heat, stirring occasionally, until well browned, 8 to 12 minutes.

3 Stir in tomato paste and flour and cook until fragrant, about 1 minute. Stir in wine, scraping up any browned bits. Stir in beans and broth and bring to brief simmer; remove from heat.

4 Toss bread with half of remaining oil mixture in now-empty bowl. Arrange bread mixture evenly over top of vegetable-bean mixture. Transfer skillet to oven and bake until bread is golden brown, 18 to 24 minutes.

5 Using potholder, carefully remove skillet from oven and let rest for 5 minutes. Stir parsley and lemon juice into remaining oil mixture and drizzle over gratin. Serve.

Kitchen Improv

USE WHAT YOU'VE GOT

Substitute canned cannellini or navy beans for great northern beans.
Substitute other hearty fresh herbs, such as rosemary or sage, for thyme.

BULK IT UP

Add 4 ounces plant-based sausage, halved lengthwise and cut into
¼-inch half-moons, to skillet with beans.

Tofu Mole
WITH ZUCCHINI RIBBON SALAD

SERVES 2
TOTAL TIME 45 minutes

- 2 tablespoons extra-virgin olive oil, divided
- 1 small onion, chopped
- 1 tomato, cored and chopped
- 2 tablespoons ancho chile powder
- ½ ounce bittersweet or semisweet chocolate, chopped coarse
- ½ teaspoon ground cinnamon
- 1½ cups vegetable broth
- 2 tablespoons raisins
- 1 tablespoon almond butter
- 2 tablespoons toasted sesame seeds, divided
- 14 ounces firm or extra-firm tofu
- ½ teaspoon table salt, divided
- ¼ teaspoon pepper, divided
- ¼ teaspoon lime zest plus 1 tablespoon juice, plus lime wedges for serving
- 1 zucchini, shaved lengthwise into ribbons
- ¼ cup fresh cilantro leaves

WHY THIS RECIPE WORKS Preparing mole poblano—a rich, velvety sauce made with chiles, chocolate, and nuts, among other ingredients—is a task often reserved for special occasions due to its complexity. We wanted to be able to enjoy mole more often, so we came up with this quicker but still nuanced and flavorful version. The pared-down ingredient list focuses on the heavy hitters. Using ancho chile powder (anchos are the dried form of poblano chiles) saves us the trouble of toasting and grinding the chiles ourselves and yields an earthy, smoky, and subtly spicy base. Almond butter adds richness, nuttiness, and body; onion and cinnamon contribute sweetness and warmth; and a sprinkle of chopped bittersweet chocolate adds a hint of fruity bitterness. We simmer the mole ingredients together to meld their flavors before blending everything into a smooth sauce and then giving it a final simmer with some tofu to coat and flavor the tofu all the way through.

1 Heat 1 tablespoon oil in 12-inch nonstick skillet over medium heat until shimmering. Add onion and tomato and cook until softened, 6 to 8 minutes. Stir in chile powder, chocolate, and cinnamon and cook until chocolate is melted and bubbly, about 1 minute.

2 Stir in broth, scraping up any browned bits, then stir in raisins, almond butter, and 1 tablespoon sesame seeds. Bring mixture to simmer and cook, stirring occasionally, until sauce is thickened and measures about 2 cups, about 5 minutes. Transfer mixture to blender and process until smooth, about 1 minute. Season with salt and pepper to taste. (Sauce can be refrigerated for up to 3 days; loosen with water as needed before continuing.)

3 Cut tofu in half crosswise, then cut each half crosswise into 4 even slices (you should have 8 pieces). Sprinkle tofu with ¼ teaspoon salt and ⅛ teaspoon pepper. Return mole to skillet, nestle tofu into sauce, and spoon portion of sauce over top. Bring to simmer over medium heat, then cover, reduce heat to medium-low, and cook until tofu is heated through, about 5 minutes.

4 Whisk lime zest and juice, remaining 1 tablespoon oil, remaining ¼ teaspoon salt, and remaining ⅛ teaspoon pepper together in medium bowl. Add zucchini and cilantro and toss to combine. Sprinkle tofu with remaining 1 tablespoon sesame seeds and serve with zucchini salad and lime wedges.

Kitchen Improv

USE WHAT YOU'VE GOT

Substitute peanut butter for almond butter. Substitute 1 tablespoon cocoa powder for chocolate. Substitute summer squash for zucchini.

LEVEL UP

Top with finely chopped onion, sliced radishes, and/or diced avocado.

BULK IT UP

Serve with warmed tortillas and/or rice (see page 270).

Glazed Tofu
WITH PIGEON PEAS AND RICE

SERVES 2

TOTAL TIME 45 minutes

14   ounces firm or extra-firm tofu

4   teaspoons vegetable oil

1   small onion, chopped fine

1   jalapeño chile, stemmed, seeded, and minced

½   cup long-grain white rice

1   (15-ounce) can pigeon peas, rinsed

¾   cup canned coconut milk

⅓   cup plus 1½ tablespoons water, divided

½   teaspoon table salt, divided

¼   cup pineapple preserves

1   tablespoon lime juice, plus lime wedges for serving

1½   teaspoons curry powder

⅛   teaspoon red pepper flakes

Kitchen Improv

USE WHAT YOU'VE GOT

Substitute canned black-eyed peas, small red beans, or black beans for pigeon peas. Substitute canned apricot or peach preserves for pineapple preserves.

WHY THIS RECIPE WORKS   Seared until golden and crispy and coated in a sweet and spicy glaze of curry powder and pineapple preserves, this tofu is anything but mild-mannered. The curry powder adds a nuanced heat that sets off the sweetness of the preserves, and a splash of lime juice brightens the flavor of the glaze. A base of rice and pigeon peas (a popular ingredient in West Indian cooking) lends complementary flavor, texture, and heartiness; a full can of pigeon peas and a 14-ounce block of tofu make for a protein-packed dish that will keep you satisfied for hours. To make the most efficient use of time, we start cooking the rice while the tofu drains, enriching the cooking liquid with creamy coconut milk and stirring in the canned peas to allow them to heat through. After giving the tofu a quick pan-sear and brushing the pieces with the glaze, we layer the glossy pieces on top and dig in. Canned pigeon peas can be found in most supermarkets. For more heat, include the jalapeño seeds and ribs. For ways to use up leftover coconut milk, see pages 18–19.

1   Cut tofu in half crosswise. Cut each half crosswise into 4 even slices (you should have 8 pieces). Arrange tofu in even layer on paper towel–lined plate; set aside.

2   Heat 1 teaspoon oil in large saucepan over medium-high heat until shimmering. Add onion and jalapeño and cook until softened, about 5 minutes. Stir in rice and cook until opaque, about 1 minute. Stir in peas, coconut milk, ⅓ cup water, and ¼ teaspoon salt and bring to boil. Reduce heat to low, cover, and simmer until rice is tender, 20 to 25 minutes. Off heat, season with salt and pepper to taste; cover to keep warm.

3   Place preserves in small bowl and microwave until bubbling, about 30 seconds. Whisk in lime juice and remaining 1½ tablespoons water.

4   Pat tofu dry with paper towels and sprinkle with curry powder, pepper flakes, and remaining ¼ teaspoon salt. Heat remaining 1 tablespoon oil in 12-inch nonstick skillet over medium-high heat until just smoking. Add tofu and cook until golden and crispy on both sides, 5 to 7 minutes. Add pineapple mixture and simmer, turning tofu to coat, until glaze thickens, about 1 minute. Divide rice-pea mixture between serving bowls and top with glazed tofu. Serve with lime wedges.

Crispy Tempeh
WITH SAMBAL

SERVES 2
TOTAL TIME 30 minutes

- ½   cup vegetable oil for frying
- 8   ounces tempeh, cut into ½-inch pieces
- ¾   cup vegan sambal oelek
- ¼   cup water
- 1   tablespoon kecap manis
- ¾   cup fresh Thai lemon basil leaves

Kitchen Improv

USE WHAT YOU'VE GOT

Substitute ½ cup chili-garlic sauce or sriracha for sambal oelek. Substitute combination of 2¼ teaspoons dark brown sugar and ½ teaspoon soy sauce for kecap manis. Substitute Thai basil or Italian basil for Thai lemon basil.

LEVEL UP

Before frying tempeh, stir-fry vegetables such as green beans, thinly sliced carrots, or broccolini pieces over high heat until tender; transfer to bowl. Return vegetables to wok with tempeh in step 2.

BULK IT UP

Serve with rice (see page 270).

WHY THIS RECIPE WORKS   Tempeh, a traditional Javanese food made from fermented, nutty-tasting cooked soybeans, is hugely popular across Indonesia. "Sambal" refers to a whole class of condiments made primarily of red chile peppers, salt, and vinegar; there are hundreds of versions in Indonesia, but our go-to is sambal oelek, in which the chiles and spices are ground to form a thick paste. Fried in oil to deepen its flavor and then combined with tempeh (which has also been fried!) it makes up the foundation of the spicy, savory, utterly satisfying dish known as tempeh sambal goreng. Shallow frying cubes of tempeh in just ½ cup of oil delivers irresistibly crispy edges without the hassle of deep-frying. We then use a small portion of the remaining oil to fry the sambal oelek, partially taming its heat while deepening the flavors of the chiles and other spices. Last-minute additions of kecap manis (an Indonesian soy sauce with a viscous consistency and sweet, molasses-like flavor) and aromatic Thai lemon basil add dimension. Note that some sambal oeleks may contain shrimp paste or other nonvegan ingredients, so check the ingredient list carefully.

1   Heat oil in 14-inch flat-bottomed wok or 10- or 12-inch nonstick skillet over medium-high heat to 375 degrees. Carefully add tempeh to hot oil and increase heat to high. Cook, turning tempeh as needed, until golden brown, 3 to 5 minutes, adjusting burner if necessary to maintain oil temperature between 350 and 375 degrees. Transfer tempeh to paper towel–lined plate.

2   Carefully pour off all but 2 tablespoons oil from wok. Add sambal oelek to oil left in wok and cook over medium-high heat, tossing slowly but constantly, until darkened in color and dry paste forms, 7 to 10 minutes. Off heat, stir in water and kecap manis until well combined. Add tempeh and basil and toss until well coated. Serve.

Stir-Fried Seitan

WITH CASHEWS

SERVES 2

TOTAL TIME 35 minutes

12 ounces seitan, cut into 1-inch pieces

1 tablespoon cornstarch

2 teaspoons Shaoxing wine

2 teaspoons soy sauce, divided, plus extra for seasoning

½ teaspoon toasted sesame oil

2 tablespoons water

1 tablespoon hoisin sauce

1½ teaspoons Chinese black vinegar

1½ tablespoons vegetable oil

½ cup raw cashews

1 celery rib, sliced thin

3 scallions, white parts sliced thin, green parts cut into 1-inch pieces

1 garlic clove, minced

1 teaspoon grated fresh ginger

¼ teaspoon red pepper flakes

Kitchen Improv

USE WHAT YOU'VE GOT

Substitute dry sherry or white wine for Shaoxing wine. Substitute peanuts for cashews. Substitute balsamic vinegar for Chinese black vinegar.

BULK IT UP

Serve with rice (see page 270).

WHY THIS RECIPE WORKS Cashew chicken has a lot going for it: This crunchy, savory-sweet stir-fry comes together with just a little simple prep work and a few minutes of cooking, making it an excellent dinner option for busy cooks. To make it vegan, we turn to seitan, a plant-based protein made from wheat gluten which mimics chicken's texture and mild flavor. Our version of cashew seitan features crunchy, golden-brown, buttery cashews and tender morsels of stir-fried seitan in a salty-sweet sauce. To ensure that the seitan is seasoned through and through and remains tender and juicy after cooking, we give it a quick soak in a mixture of soy sauce, Shaoxing wine, toasted sesame oil, and cornstarch. The cornstarch not only protects the seitan's exterior from becoming dry and tough and also thickens the stir-fry sauce, giving it an attractive glossy sheen. Deeply toasting the cashews in the same oil we later use for the stir-fry allows their toasty flavor to permeate the whole dish. Seitan is sold in blocks, chunks, or strips; any of those options will work in this recipe. For ways to use up leftover seitan, see page 19.

1 Pat seitan dry with paper towels. Whisk cornstarch, wine, 1 teaspoon soy sauce, and sesame oil together in bowl. Add seitan and toss to coat. Combine water, hoisin, vinegar, and remaining 1 teaspoon soy sauce in small bowl.

2 Heat vegetable oil in 14-inch flat-bottomed wok or 10- or 12-inch nonstick skillet over medium heat until shimmering. Add cashews and cook, stirring constantly, until golden brown, 4 to 6 minutes, reducing heat if cashews begin to darken too quickly. Using slotted spoon, transfer cashews to plate.

3 Heat oil remaining in wok over medium-high heat until just smoking. Add seitan mixture and cook, tossing slowly but constantly, until seitan begins to brown, 3 to 5 minutes. Stir in celery, scallion whites, garlic, ginger, and pepper flakes and cook until celery is just softened, about 2 minutes.

4 Add hoisin mixture, bring to simmer, and cook until sauce is thickened, 1 to 3 minutes. Off heat, stir in scallion greens and cashews. Serve, passing extra soy sauce separately.

Grilled Tofu
WITH CHARRED BROCCOLI AND PEANUT SAUCE

SERVES 2
TOTAL TIME 30 minutes

- 14 ounces firm or extra-firm tofu
- 2 tablespoons hot water, plus extra as needed
- 2 tablespoons creamy peanut butter
- 1 tablespoon vegan Thai red curry paste, divided
- ¼ teaspoon grated lime zest plus ½ teaspoon juice, plus lime wedges for serving
- 12 ounces broccoli crowns, cut into 4 wedges if 3 to 4 inches in diameter, or 6 wedges if 4 to 5 inches in diameter
- 2 tablespoons vegetable oil, divided
- ½ teaspoon table salt, divided
- ⅛ teaspoon pepper, divided
- 2 tablespoons chopped fresh cilantro
- 1 tablespoon chopped dry-roasted peanuts

Kitchen Improv

USE WHAT YOU'VE GOT

Substitute Thai green curry paste for red curry paste.

LEVEL UP

Top with Quick-Pickled Red Onion (page 26) or Crispy Shallots (page 27).

BULK IT UP

Serve with rice or other grain (see page 270).

WHY THIS RECIPE WORKS To create a vibrant vegan dinner from the grill we pair firm slabs of tofu with hearty broccoli wedges, both of which do well after exposure to the high heat and char of the grill. For an easy way to add complex flavors we turn to Thai red curry paste; a single spoonful contains an assortment of aromatic ingredients including chiles, lemongrass, galangal, and makrut lime leaves. We use the curry paste two ways to contribute spicy, tangy, and subtly sweet notes: brushed over the tofu as a makeshift marinade, and stirred into a quick peanut sauce that we use as a last-minute drizzle to unite the tofu and broccoli. Grilling broccoli is by far one of the best ways to cook this cruciferous vegetable, adding char while the stalks tenderize. A sprinkle of chopped cilantro and roasted peanuts add crunch and freshness. Note that not all Thai red curry pastes are vegan; check the ingredient list carefully to make sure. For ways to use up leftover broccoli, see page 18.

1 Slice tofu lengthwise into 4 even slabs. Arrange tofu in even layer on paper towel–lined plate; set aside.

2 Whisk hot water, peanut butter, 1 teaspoon curry paste, and lime zest and juice in bowl until smooth. Add extra hot water, 1 teaspoon at a time, as needed until sauce is thick but pourable. Season with salt and pepper to taste; set aside.

3 Toss broccoli with 1 tablespoon oil, ¼ teaspoon salt, and pinch pepper in bowl; set aside. Whisk remaining 2 teaspoons curry paste, 1 tablespoon oil, ¼ teaspoon salt, and pinch pepper together in bowl. Pat tofu dry with paper towels and brush tofu all over with curry mixture.

4A **FOR A CHARCOAL GRILL** Open bottom vent completely. Light large chimney starter filled with charcoal briquettes (6 quarts). When top coals are partially covered with ash, pour evenly over grill. Set cooking grate in place, cover, and open lid vent completely. Heat grill until hot, about 5 minutes.

4B **FOR A GAS GRILL** Turn all burners to high, cover, and heat grill until hot, about 15 minutes. Leave all burners on high.

5 Clean and oil cooking grate. Grill broccoli and tofu until broccoli is charred in spots and tofu is well browned, 6 to 10 minutes, turning broccoli as needed and gently flipping tofu halfway through grilling. Transfer tofu and broccoli to serving platter. Drizzle with peanut sauce and sprinkle with cilantro and peanuts. Serve with lime wedges.

Crispy Baked Tofu Peperonata

SERVES 2
TOTAL TIME 1 hour

7	ounces firm or extra-firm tofu, cut into 1-inch pieces
¼	cup extra-virgin olive oil, divided
¼	cup cornstarch
½	teaspoon salt, divided
¼	teaspoon pepper, divided
2	red, orange, or yellow bell peppers, stemmed, seeded, and cut into ½-inch-wide strips
1	small red onion, cut through root end into 1-inch wedges
6	ounces cherry or grape tomatoes
3	garlic cloves, peeled
3	tablespoons capers, rinsed, divided (2 tablespoons left whole, 1 tablespoon minced)
2	teaspoons red wine vinegar
2	teaspoons minced fresh thyme
½	teaspoon red pepper flakes

Kitchen Improv

USE WHAT YOU'VE GOT

Substitute coarsely chopped brine-cured olives for capers. Substitute fresh rosemary for thyme. Substitute white wine vinegar or sherry vinegar for red wine vinegar.

BULK IT UP

Serve with rice or other grain (see page 270).

WHY THIS RECIPE WORKS   Peperonata is a quiet hero of Italian cuisine, a roasted vegetable mélange that can be made with a single pan. While the dish is usually stewed, here we give the classic recipe a twist by roasting everything together on a rimmed baking sheet for hands-off cooking and easy cleanup and by adding crispy tofu to the mix. Coating the tofu pieces in a seasoned cornstarch mixture helps them pick up a nice golden color and crispy bite during roasting. Vibrant bell peppers, onion, and tomatoes make up the base of the bright and colorful dish, and capers add pops of briny flavor. After about 30 minutes in the oven, the tomatoes are blistered and juicy, the tofu is golden, and the onion and peppers are tender and sweet. To add a little extra love to this recipe, we also create a sauce of sharp red wine vinegar, red pepper flakes, olive oil, savory fresh thyme, and minced capers, plus some mashed roasted garlic and a few of the roasted tomatoes, for drizzling all over. The tomato skins won't fully break down into the sauce, but this is OK; you won't notice their texture when combined with the rest of the dish. For ways to use up leftover tofu, see page 19.

1   Adjust oven rack to lowest position and heat oven to 450 degrees. Arrange tofu in even layer on paper towel–lined plate and let sit for 15 minutes. Brush rimmed baking sheet with 1 tablespoon oil.

2   Whisk cornstarch, ¼ teaspoon salt, and ⅛ teaspoon pepper together in medium bowl. Pat tofu dry with paper towels, add to cornstarch mixture, and toss until well coated.

3   Brush off any excess cornstarch from tofu and arrange in even layer on one half of prepared sheet. Arrange bell peppers, onion, tomatoes, and garlic on empty side of sheet and sprinkle vegetables with remaining ¼ teaspoon salt and remaining ⅛ teaspoon pepper. Drizzle vegetables and tofu evenly with 2 tablespoons oil.

4   Bake until bottoms of tofu pieces are golden and crispy, 12 to 15 minutes. Using thin metal spatula, flip tofu pieces and gently stir vegetables. Sprinkle vegetables with whole capers. Continue to bake until tofu is golden and crispy on second side, vegetables are softened and spotty brown, and tomatoes are softened, 12 to 15 minutes longer.

5   Whisk vinegar, thyme, pepper flakes, minced capers, and remaining 1 tablespoon oil together in medium bowl. Add garlic and 4 roasted tomatoes and mash garlic and tomatoes with whisk to coarse paste, then whisk vigorously until mixture is evenly combined. Transfer tofu peperonata to serving bowls and drizzle with dressing. Serve.

Basic Proteins

274 Pan-Seared Tofu

274 Pan-Seared Seitan

274 Pan-Seared Tempeh Steaks

275 Scrambled Plant-Based Egg

Beans and Starches

277 Easy Black Beans
with Chipotle and Lime
with Bell Pepper and Cumin

279 Garlicky Braised Chickpeas
Braised Chickpeas with Bell Pepper and Basil
Braised Chickpeas with Smoked Paprika and Cilantro

281 Curried Lentils
Lentils with Ras el Hanout and Lemon
Lentils with Carrots and Mint

282 Herbed Couscous
Couscous with Tomato, Scallion, and Lemon
Couscous with Saffron, Raisins, and Almonds

284 Hands-Off Baked Brown Rice
with Peas and Mint
with Pine Nuts and Basil

287 Bulgur Pilaf with Dried Apricots and Almonds
with Tomatoes and Kalamata Olives
with Shiitake Mushrooms and Edamame

288 Creamy Orzo with Boursin
Orzo with Pesto and Sun-Dried Tomatoes
Orzo with Shallot, Capers, and Dill

291 Celery Root Puree
Extracreamy Celery Root Puree
with Horseradish and Scallions

292 Roasted Red Potatoes with Rosemary
with Fennel Seeds and Olives
with Curry Powder and Ginger

Vegetables

294 Roasted Artichoke Hearts with Fennel and Tarragon
with Bell Pepper and Olives

297 Lemony Skillet-Charred Green Beans
Skillet-Charred Green Beans with Crispy Bread Crumb Topping

298 Skillet Broccoli with Olive Oil and Garlic
with Rosemary Oil and Orange

301 Pan-Roasted Brussels Sprouts
with Gochujang and Sesame Seeds

302 Roasted Carrots with Yogurt-Tahini Sauce
with Chimichurri

304 Roasted Cauliflower
with Smoked Paprika and Shallots

306 Cauliflower Steaks with Chimichurri

309 Grilled Eggplant with Ginger-Sesame Vinaigrette
with Lemon-Herb Yogurt Sauce

311 Sautéed Baby Spinach with Almonds and Raisins
with Leeks and Hazelnuts

312 Chile-Rubbed Butternut Squash Steaks

315 Grilled Zucchini with Lemon-Basil Vinaigrette
with Curried Vinaigrette

Mix and Match Like a Pro

Whether you're throwing together a quick snack, preparing a light meal, or going all out to make a multi-dish dinner, cooking should be all about satisfying your individual preferences. In this chapter we strove to go beyond basic side dishes and provide you with easy, versatile small plates that you can enjoy on their own, level up with a garnish or sauce, or combine with other small plates to create meals that are as light or hearty, simple or intricate as you like.

When it comes to mixing and matching the elements on your plate, we have a few guidelines we like to follow for consistently delicious results. But don't feel limited by our suggestions here; whether it's pairing two vegan proteins or playing with unexpected flavor combos, the perfect plate is the one you create to satisfy your cravings.

Add a vegetable: Vegetables boost a plate's flavor, nutrition, visual appeal, and textural contrast. Try adding one of our vegetable-based small plates (pages 294–315) to your meal, or add a raw vegetable of your choice. To add interest to just about any vegetable option, you can try shredding, chopping, slicing into half-moons, cutting matchsticks, cutting on the bias, or even peeling it into ribbons to change up the appearance and texture of your meal.

Pick a solid foundation: This is the part of the meal meant to fill you up and sustain you. It can be anything from a grain to a protein to a starchy vegetable (see pages 270–294), or even a combination of two grains, a starchy vegetable and a protein, etc. For an extra-hearty meal packed with complete plant-based protein (see page "The Dynamic Duo" on page 6 for more information), consider pairing a grain-based dish with a legume-based one.

If you want, finish with flair: A saucy drizzle, crunchy garnish, creamy dollop, or sprinkle of fresh herbs is often just the thing to tie a mixed-and-matched meal together. Try drizzling with one of our homemade sauces on pages 24–26 (store-bought is fine, too!), adding a handful of toasted nuts or seeds, or topping with our easy Crispy Shallots (page 27). See our Level Up suggestions for even more inspiration.

Grain Cooking Chart

With just two simple cooking methods—boiling and cooking pilaf-style—you can confidently prepare any whole grain you like. For ease, we break things down for you by grain and cooking method in the chart below.

Pilaf-style directions: Rinse and then dry grain on clean dish towel. Heat 1 tablespoon oil in medium saucepan (preferably nonstick) over medium-high heat until shimmering. Stir in grain and toast until lightly golden and fragrant, 2 to 3 minutes. Stir in water and salt. Bring mixture to simmer, then reduce heat to low, cover, and continue to simmer until grain is tender and has absorbed all of water. Off heat, let grain stand for 10 minutes, then fluff with fork.

Boiling directions: Bring water to boil in large saucepan. Stir in grain and salt. Return to boil, then reduce to simmer and cook until grain is tender. Drain.

Storing and reheating: Each cup of raw grain yields about 2 cups once cooked. Cooked grains can be cooled and then stored in airtight container for up to 3 days. To reheat, microwave in covered bowl until hot, fluffing with fork halfway through microwaving, then season to taste. (Reheating time will vary depending on quantity and type of grain.) Alternatively, enjoy cooked grains cold or at room temperature, tossed with a vinaigrette or drizzled with a fresh sauce.

Type of Grain	Cooking Method	Amount of Grain	Amount of Water	Amount of Salt	Cooking Time
Pearled Barley	Pilaf-style	1 cup	1⅔ cups	¼ teaspoon	20 to 40 minutes
	Boiled	1 cup	4 quarts	1 tablespoon	20 to 40 minutes
Bulgur (medium- to coarse-grind)	Pilaf-style*	1 cup	1½ cups	¼ teaspoon	16 to 18 minutes
	Boiled	1 cup	4 quarts	1¼ teaspoons	5 minutes
Farro	Boiled	1 cup	4 quarts	1 tablespoon	15 to 30 minutes
Wheat Berries	Boiled	1 cup	4 quarts	1½ teaspoons	1 hour to 1 hour 10 minutes
Freekeh	Boiled	1 cup	4 quarts	1 tablespoon	30 to 45 minutes
Long-Grain White Rice	Pilaf-style	1 cup	1½ cups	½ teaspoon	16 to 18 minutes
	Boiled	1 cup	2 quarts	½ teaspoon	10 to 15 minutes
Short-Grain White Rice	Boiled**	1 cup	1 cup	¼ teaspoon	10 minutes
Long-Grain Brown Rice	Pilaf-style	1 cup	1¾ cups	¼ teaspoon	40 to 50 minutes
	Boiled	1 cup	4 quarts	1 tablespoon	25 to 30 minutes
Quinoa	Pilaf-style	1 cup	1¼ cups	¼ teaspoon	18 to 20 minutes
Wild Rice	Boiled	1 cup	2 quarts	½ teaspoon	35 to 40 minutes
Oat Berries	Boiled	1 cup	2 quarts	½ teaspoon	30 to 40 minutes

* For bulgur pilaf, do not rinse, and skip toasting step, adding bulgur to pot with water.

** For short-grain white rice, add rice, water, and salt to pot at same time. Do not drain; at end of cooking time, remove from heat, lay clean folded dish towel under lid, and let sit for 15 minutes.

Bean Cooking Chart

Cooking dried beans or lentils takes a little more time up front than opening up a can, but once cooked, a big batch of beans can be stored in the fridge for several days and used as desired as an easy meal base or a hearty last-minute addition. One pound of dried beans yields approximately 6 cups cooked, just right for keeping on hand to use up throughout the week. Two cups of home-cooked beans can be used in place of every 1 can of beans called for in a recipe.

First, brine the beans: Brining dried beans before cooking helps minimize blowouts. (Brining is unnecessary for lentils.) Brine 1 pound beans for at least 8 hours or up to 24 hours in 2 quarts cold water plus 1½ tablespoons table salt. Alternatively, quick-brine beans by combining beans, salt, and water in pot, bringing to boil, and then removing from heat and letting beans sit for 1 hour. Drain and rinse beans after brining.

Stovetop cooking instructions: Bring 1 pound brined beans or 2 cups lentils, water, and salt to boil. Reduce to gentle simmer and cook until beans are tender, following time given in chart. Stir beans occasionally to prevent them from sticking to bottom of pan, adjusting heat as needed to maintain gentle simmer. Drain.

Pressure cooking instructions: Combine 1 pound brined beans or 2 cups lentils in pressure cooker with water, 1 tablespoon extra-virgin olive oil (to prevent foaming), and salt. Lock lid into place and close pressure-release valve. Select low pressure-cook function and set cooking time according to chart. (If using stovetop pressure cooker, place cooker on medium heat and start timer once pressure is reached.) Turn off pressure cooker or remove from heat once done. Let pressure release naturally for 15 minutes and then quickly release any remaining pressure, or quickly release pressure as directed in chart. Carefully remove lid, allowing steam to escape away from you. Remove any floating beans or lentils. Drain.

Type of Bean	Cooking Method	Water for Cooking	Salt for Cooking	Cooking Time	Release Type
Black Beans	Stovetop	4 quarts	2½ teaspoons	½ to 2 hours	-
	Pressure Cooker	8 cups	½ teaspoon	1 minute*	Natural
Black-Eyed Peas	Stovetop	4 quarts	2½ teaspoons	1 to 1¼ hours	-
	Pressure Cooker	8 cups	½ teaspoon	1 minute*	Natural
Cannellini Beans	Stovetop	4 quarts	2½ teaspoons	1 to 1¼ hours	-
	Pressure Cooker	8 cups	½ teaspoon	4 minutes	Natural
Chickpeas	Stovetop	4 quarts	2½ teaspoons	1½ to 2 hours	-
	Pressure Cooker	8 cups	½ teaspoon	1 minute	Natural
Great Northern Beans	Stovetop	4 quarts	2½ teaspoons	1 to 1¼ hours	-
	Pressure Cooker	8 cups	½ teaspoon	1 minute	Natural
Kidney Beans	Stovetop	4 quarts	2½ teaspoons	1 to 1¼ hours	-
	Pressure Cooker	8 cups	½ teaspoon	3 minutes	Natural
Navy Beans	Stovetop	4 quarts	2½ teaspoons	1 to 1¼ hours	-
	Pressure Cooker	8 cups	½ teaspoon	1 minute	Natural
Pinto Beans	Stovetop	4 quarts	2½ teaspoons	1 to 1¼ hours	-
	Pressure Cooker	8 cups	½ teaspoon	3 minutes	Natural
Small Red Beans	Stovetop	4 quarts	2½ teaspoons	1 to 1¼ hours	-
	Pressure Cooker	8 cups	½ teaspoon	3 minutes	Natural
French Green Lentils (Lentilles du Puy)	Stovetop	4 quarts	2½ teaspoons	20 to 30 minutes	-
	Pressure Cooker	8 cups	½ teaspoon	1 minute*	Natural
Brown or Green Lentils	Stovetop	4 quarts	2½ teaspoons	20 to 30 minutes	-
	Pressure Cooker	8 cups	½ teaspoon	3 minutes	Quick

* As soon as pressure is reached, turn off pressure cooker or remove from heat.

Basic Proteins

Pan-Seared Tofu

Serves 2

Simply seasoned tofu is an incredibly versatile protein option that can be paired with just about any vegetable and sauce combo you can imagine. This recipe can be easily doubled using a 12-inch nonstick skillet.

- 7 ounces soft, firm, or extra-firm tofu, cut into ¾-inch pieces
- ¼ teaspoon table salt
- ⅛ teaspoon pepper
- 1 teaspoon extra-virgin olive oil

1 Spread tofu over paper towel–lined baking sheet and let drain for 20 minutes. Gently press tofu dry with paper towels and sprinkle with salt and pepper.

2 Heat oil in 8- or 10-inch nonstick skillet over medium-high heat until shimmering. Add tofu and cook until lightly browned on all sides, 6 to 8 minutes. Serve.

Pan-Seared Seitan

Serves 2

Seitan is a chewy plant-based protein made from wheat gluten. Like tofu, it pairs well with a huge range of flavors. Seitan is sold in blocks, chunks, or strips; any of those options will work in this recipe.

- 12 ounces seitan, drained, patted dry, and cut into 1-inch pieces
- ⅛ teaspoon table salt
- ⅛ teaspoon pepper
- 1½ tablespoons vegetable oil

Sprinkle seitan with salt and pepper. Heat oil in 12-inch nonstick skillet over medium heat until just smoking. Add seitan and cook, stirring frequently, until lightly browned on all sides, 4 to 6 minutes. Serve.

Pan-Seared Tempeh Steaks

Serves 2

Tempeh is a nutty, savory protein made from fermented soybeans and oftentimes grains. Cut into steak-like slabs and seared, it develops irresistibly crispy edges and has a substantial and satisfying meaty chew.

- 1 (8-ounce) slab tempeh, halved crosswise
- ¼ teaspoon table salt
- 2 tablespoons vegetable oil

1 Using chef's knife, cut each piece of tempeh horizontally into 2 slabs, being careful to cut pieces of even thickness.

2 Pat tempeh dry and sprinkle with salt. Heat oil in 10- or 12-inch nonstick skillet over medium heat until shimmering. Add tempeh and cook until golden brown on first side, 2 to 4 minutes. Flip tempeh, reduce heat to medium-low, and continue to cook until golden brown on second side, 2 to 4 minutes. Serve.

Scrambled Plant-Based Egg

Serves 2

Liquid plant-based egg can be scrambled just like chicken eggs, resulting in tender curds perfect for eating on their own for breakfast or using as a protein-boosting topping for savory dishes. Be sure to shake the liquid egg well before using. For more information about liquid plant-based egg, see page 10.

- 1 cup liquid plant-based egg
- ⅛ teaspoon table salt
- Pinch pepper
- 1 teaspoon vegetable oil
- 1 tablespoon chopped fresh chives (optional)

1 Whisk egg, salt, and pepper together in small bowl. Heat oil in 10- or 12-inch nonstick skillet over medium-high heat until shimmering. Add egg mixture and cook, constantly and firmly scraping bottom and sides of skillet with rubber spatula, until egg begins to clump and spatula leaves trail on bottom of skillet, 1½ to 2½ minutes.

2 Reduce heat to low and continue to cook, gently but constantly folding egg mixture until clumped and just slightly wet, 30 to 60 seconds longer. Season with salt and pepper to taste and sprinkle with chives, if using. Serve immediately.

Easy Black Beans

SERVES 2

TOTAL TIME 15 minutes

- 1 tablespoon extra-virgin olive oil
- 1 large shallot, minced
- 2 garlic cloves, minced
- 1 teaspoon minced fresh oregano or ¼ teaspoon dried
- ⅛ teaspoon pepper
- 1 (15-ounce) can black beans, drained with liquid reserved, divided

Kitchen Improv

LEVEL UP

Sprinkle with chopped cilantro, thinly sliced scallions, shredded plant-based cheese, chopped tomatoes, hot sauce, and/or fresh or pickled jalapeno.

MAKE IT A MEAL

Serve with rice or other grain (see page 270), Quick Pickled Red Onion (page 26), plant-based yogurt, plantain chips, and/or sliced avocado.

WHY THIS RECIPE WORKS   This supersimple bean dish should be the official poster child for recipes that are actually improved by using a supposed shortcut method. In this case, that shortcut is opting for canned beans, which we love for many reasons but are especially helpful here because they come with lots of starchy, body-building bean liquid built in. Our basic recipe requires little more than opening a can and heating the beans up with fragrant shallot, garlic, and a sprinkle of minced oregano. We leave some of the beans whole to give this dish its rustic texture, mashing the rest of the beans along with the bean liquid to create a creamy, thickened sauce that luxuriously coats the whole beans. This couldn't-be-easier baseline paves the way for additional variations: a spicy-smoky version with chipotle chile powder as well as a Cuban-inspired take with earthy cumin and chopped bell pepper.

1   Heat oil in medium saucepan over medium heat until shimmering. Add shallot and cook until softened, about 2 minutes. Stir in garlic, oregano, and pepper and cook until fragrant, about 30 seconds.

2   Off heat, add ½ cup beans and reserved bean liquid and mash with potato masher until mostly smooth. Stir in remaining beans and cook over medium heat until warmed through, 2 to 3 minutes. Season with salt and pepper to taste. Serve.

VARIATIONS

Easy Black Beans with Chipotle and Lime

Substitute ½ teaspoon chipotle chile powder for pepper. Stir ¼ teaspoon grated lime zest into bean mixture before serving and serve with lime wedges.

Easy Black Beans with Bell Pepper and Cumin

Add ½ green bell pepper, finely chopped, to saucepan with shallot. Add ¼ teaspoon ground cumin to saucepan with garlic.

Garlicky Braised Chickpeas

SERVES 2

TOTAL TIME 15 minutes

2 tablespoons extra-virgin olive oil

2 garlic cloves, sliced thin

1 large shallot, minced

1 (15-ounce) can chickpeas

1 tablespoon minced fresh parsley, cilantro, or chives

1 teaspoon lemon juice, plus lemon wedges for serving

Kitchen Improv

LEVEL UP

Drizzle with Fennel Oil (page 26). Serve with plant-based yogurt and/or sprinkle with extra chopped fresh herbs.

MAKE IT A MEAL

Add cooked pasta and/or wilted greens such as spinach, kale, or Swiss chard, or serve over a swoosh of Lemon-Herb Yogurt Sauce (page 25) with a side of pita.

WHY THIS RECIPE WORKS   Chickpeas are a vegan's best friend. In addition to their starring role in heavy-hitters like hummus and falafel, these superhero legumes are perfect for sprinkling on top of grain bowls, salads, and plant-based side dishes alike for an extra dose of protein and satiating fiber. Looking for another recipe where we could let this pantry staple shine all on its own, we hit upon this dish, which tastes like it takes hours but can actually be on your table in less than 20 minutes. Consisting of little more than chickpeas and sticky-sweet toasted garlic, it has the toasty, lemony flavor of hummus with the hearty savor of whole beans. As in our Easy Black Beans (page 277), we rely on the bean liquid already present in a can of chickpeas to help thicken the rich sauce that clings to and glazes the chickpeas as it reduces. And, also like our black bean recipe, it's a natural fit for creative flavor variations and, with a few quick additions, can easily become a meal in its own right. You will need an 8- or 10-inch skillet with a tight-fitting lid for this recipe.

1   Cook oil and garlic in 8- or 10-inch skillet over medium-low heat, stirring occasionally, until garlic turns pale gold, about 2 minutes. Stir in shallot and cook until softened, about 2 minutes. Stir in chickpeas and their liquid, cover, and cook until chickpeas have warmed through, about 2 minutes.

2   Uncover, increase heat to medium, and simmer until liquid has reduced slightly, about 3 minutes. Off heat, stir in parsley and lemon juice and season with salt and pepper to taste. Serve with lemon wedges.

VARIATIONS

Braised Chickpeas with Bell Pepper and Basil

Add ½ red bell pepper, cut into ½-inch pieces, to skillet with shallot; cook until softened, about 5 minutes, before adding chickpeas. Substitute chopped fresh basil for parsley.

Braised Chickpeas with Smoked Paprika and Cilantro

Omit garlic. Add ¼ teaspoon smoked paprika to skillet once shallot has softened. Substitute minced fresh cilantro for parsley and ½ teaspoon sherry vinegar for lemon juice.

Curried Lentils

SERVES 2
TOTAL TIME 25 minutes

- 1 tablespoon extra-virgin olive oil
- 1 shallot, minced
- 2 garlic cloves, minced
- 2 teaspoons curry powder
- 1 (15-ounce) can brown lentils, rinsed
- ½ cup vegetable broth

Kitchen Improv

USE WHAT YOU'VE GOT

Substitute other warm spice blend, such as garam masala, baharat, or berbere, for curry powder.

LEVEL UP

Serve with plant-based yogurt and/ or crumbled plant-based cheese.

MAKE IT A MEAL

Serve with rice, naan, and/or plant-based yogurt. Pair with Herbed Couscous (page 282), Hands-Off Baked Brown Rice (page 284), or Sautéed Baby Spinach with Almonds and Raisins (page 311).

WHY THIS RECIPE WORKS   Creamy and tender, aromatic and nurturing—this curried lentil side is easy to pull together on a weeknight; makes a complete and filling meal when paired with cooked grain, quinoa, or roasted vegetables (succulent squash or sweet potato are particular favorites here); and reheats beautifully for lunch the next day. Hearty, earthy lentils don't take long to cook from dried, but for an even quicker route to dinner we cut out the 15 or so minutes of simmering time and instead turn to canned lentils. (You can use dried lentils if you like—see page 272 for cooking instructions.) We pair the lentils with just a few low-prep, high-impact staples you likely already have on hand—curry powder, garlic, and shallot—and simmer everything with a splash of vegetable broth. The superquick simmer is meant not to cook the already tender lentils, but merely to warm them up and give them a chance to soak up all the savory flavor from the spiced broth.

1   Heat oil in small saucepan over medium heat until shimmering. Add shallot and cook until softened and lightly browned, 3 to 5 minutes. Stir in garlic and curry powder and cook until fragrant, about 30 seconds.

2   Stir in lentils and broth and bring to simmer. Reduce heat to medium and cook, stirring occasionally, until flavors meld and lentils just begin to break down about 5 minutes. Season with salt and pepper to taste. Serve.

VARIATIONS

Lentils with Ras el Hanout and Lemon

Substitute 1 teaspoon ras el hanout and 1 teaspoon grated lemon zest for curry powder. Serve with lemon wedges.

Lentils with Carrots and Mint

Add 1 small carrot, peeled and chopped fine, to saucepan with shallot. Substitute 1 teaspoon cumin for curry powder. Stir 1 tablespoon minced fresh mint into lentils before serving.

Herbed Couscous

SERVES 2

TOTAL TIME 35 minutes

⅓ cup couscous

1 tablespoon extra-virgin olive oil, divided

1 shallot, minced

1 garlic clove, minced

Pinch cayenne pepper

½ cup vegetable broth

¼ cup minced fresh parsley

Kitchen Improv

USE WHAT YOU'VE GOT

Substitute other fresh leafy herbs, such as basil, mint, chives, or cilantro, for parsley.

MAKE IT A MEAL

Double amounts of all ingredients, cooking couscous in medium or large saucepan; sprinkle with cooked beans such as chickpeas or cannellini beans; and serve with plant-based yogurt and/or a green salad.

WHY THIS RECIPE WORKS Couscous, the tiny round pasta popular throughout the Mediterranean, cooks quickly and has a neutral flavor profile that makes it a versatile base for mix-ins and creatively seasoned side dishes. For these reasons, it's one of our go-tos when we want a fast, easy side or light dinner. For a basic version that we could easily translate into additional flavor variations, we start by considering the spice. A single pinch of cayenne pepper bloomed in oil gives the couscous a friendly warmth, and aromatic shallot and garlic add depth. We also quickly toast the couscous to coax out more of its natural nuttiness before adding a splash of flavorful hot vegetable broth. We simply let the couscous and broth sit until the grains are tender and hydrated before giving the mixture a quick fluff with a fork and a final enriching addition of oil.

1 Toast couscous in small saucepan over medium-high heat, stirring often, until some grains begin to brown, about 3 minutes. Transfer couscous to medium bowl.

2 Heat 1½ teaspoons oil in now-empty saucepan over medium heat until shimmering. Add shallot and cook until softened, about 2 minutes. Stir in garlic and cayenne and cook until fragrant, about 30 seconds. Stir in broth and bring to boil.

3 Pour boiling broth mixture over couscous in bowl, cover bowl tightly with plastic wrap, and let sit until couscous is tender, about 12 minutes. Uncover and fluff couscous with fork. Stir in parsley and remaining 1½ teaspoons oil. Season with salt and pepper to taste. Serve.

VARIATIONS

Couscous with Tomato, Scallion, and Lemon

Substitute 2 thinly sliced scallions for parsley. Add 1 cored and chopped tomato, 1 teaspoon lemon juice, and ¼ teaspoon grated lemon zest to couscous with oil in step 3.

Couscous with Saffron, Raisins, and Almonds

Substitute pinch crumbled saffron threads and pinch ground cinnamon for garlic. Add ¼ cup raisins and 2 tablespoons toasted sliced almonds to couscous with oil in step 3.

Hands-Off Baked Brown Rice

SERVES 2
TOTAL TIME 1¼ hours

1¼ cups boiling water or
vegetable broth

¾ cup long-grain brown rice,
rinsed

2 teaspoons extra-virgin
olive oil

¼ teaspoon table salt

Kitchen Improv

USE WHAT YOU'VE GOT

Substitute medium-grain or
short-grain brown rice for
long-grain brown rice.

LEVEL UP

Substitute Fennel Oil or Rosemary
Oil (page 26) for olive oil.

WHY THIS RECIPE WORKS   Brown rice has a distinctly nutty flavor
and great chew, but the bran (the grain's tough outer layer) that gives it these
qualities also makes it more difficult for liquid to permeate the rice, which can
lead to uneven cooking and extended cooking times. To avoid the pitfalls of
burnt and undercooked rice, we turn to the oven. Baking the rice allows us
more precise temperature control than cooking on the stovetop, and the steady,
even heat eliminates the risk of scorching. A loaf pan handily contains two
servings of rice and creates the ideal amount of surface area for evaporation.
Bringing the water to a boil before adding it to the pan also speeds up the
cooking time. We use this light and fluffy rice to bulk up other dishes or as an
interesting side in its own right with the addition of herbs and select mix-ins.
For an accurate measurement of boiling water, bring a full kettle of water to a
boil, then measure out the desired amount. Our preferred loaf pan measures
8½ by 4½ inches; if you use a 9 by 5-inch loaf pan, start checking for doneness
5 minutes early.

1   Adjust oven rack to middle position and heat oven to 375 degrees. Combine
boiling water, rice, oil, and salt in 8½ by 4½-inch loaf pan. Cover pan tightly
with double layer of aluminum foil. Bake until rice is tender and no water
remains, 45 to 55 minutes.

2   Remove pan from oven and fluff rice with fork, scraping up any rice that
has stuck to bottom. Cover pan with clean dish towel, then re-cover loosely
with foil. Let rice sit for 10 minutes. Season with salt and pepper to taste. Serve.

VARIATIONS

Hands-Off Baked Brown Rice with Peas and Mint

Add ½ cup thawed frozen peas, 2 tablespoons chopped fresh mint, and
¼ teaspoon grated lemon zest to pan when fluffing rice.

Hands-Off Baked Brown Rice with Pine Nuts and Basil

Add ¼ cup toasted pine nuts and 2 tablespoons shredded fresh basil to
pan when fluffing rice.

Bulgur Pilaf
WITH DRIED APRICOTS AND ALMONDS

SERVES 2
TOTAL TIME 45 minutes

- 1 tablespoon extra-virgin olive oil
- 1 shallot, minced
- ¼ teaspoon table salt
- ¼ teaspoon ground cinnamon
- 1 bay leaf
- ½ cup medium-grind bulgur, rinsed
- ⅔ cup vegetable broth
- 2 tablespoons finely chopped dried apricots
- 2 tablespoons minced fresh mint
- 2 tablespoons toasted sliced almonds
- 2 teaspoons lemon juice

Kitchen Improv

LEVEL UP

Drizzle pilaf with plant-based yogurt or tahini.

MAKE IT A MEAL

Pair with Pan-Seared Tofu (page 274), Garlicky Braised Chickpeas (page 279), Roasted Carrots with Yogurt-Tahini Sauce (page 302), or Grilled Zucchini with Lemon-Basil Vinaigrette (page 315).

WHY THIS RECIPE WORKS   Bulgur, a form of wheat that's been parboiled and dried, is quick-cooking and versatile. Like rice, it takes well to the pilaf cooking method in which the grain is toasted, simmered, and then allowed to rest briefly to yield intact, distinct grains. Here we skip the toasting and instead use our time to soften a shallot and bloom a dash of cinnamon to create an aromatic flavor base for the bulgur. We then cook the bulgur in vegetable broth along with a handful of chopped dried apricots, infusing the grain with savory vegetable flavor and hydrating the chewy dried fruit at the same time. A sprinkle of crunchy almonds and bright mint and lemon juice round out the flavors. Don't confuse bulgur with cracked wheat, which has a much longer cooking time and will not work in this recipe.

1   Heat oil in large saucepan over medium heat until shimmering. Add shallot and salt and cook until softened and lightly browned, 3 to 5 minutes. Stir in cinnamon and bay leaf and cook until fragrant, about 30 seconds.

2   Stir in bulgur, broth, and apricots, and bring to simmer. Cover, reduce heat to low, and simmer until bulgur is tender, 12 to 14 minutes.

3   Off heat, lay clean folded dish towel underneath lid, and let bulgur sit, covered, for 5 minutes. Remove bay leaf. Add mint, almonds, and lemon juice and fluff bulgur with fork to combine. Season with salt and pepper to taste. Serve.

VARIATIONS

Bulgur Pilaf with Tomatoes and Kalamata Olives

Omit salt and lemon juice. Substitute ground coriander for cinnamon, parsley for mint, ½ cup halved cherry tomatoes for apricots, and chopped pitted kalamata olives for almonds.

Bulgur Pilaf with Shiitake Mushrooms and Edamame

Omit bay leaf and almonds. Substitute 4 minced scallion whites plus 2 ounces stemmed and chopped shiitake mushrooms for shallot, 1 tablespoon grated fresh ginger for cinnamon, thinly sliced scallion greens for mint, ¼ cup thawed frozen shelled edamame beans for apricots, and 2 teaspoons rice vinegar for lemon juice.

Creamy Orzo
WITH BOURSIN

SERVES 2
TOTAL TIME 30 minutes

- 1 tablespoon extra-virgin olive oil
- ½ cup orzo
- 1 garlic clove, minced
- 1¾ cups vegetable broth, plus extra as needed
- 3 tablespoons plant-based Boursin

Kitchen Improv

LEVEL UP

Stir in canned beans, such as chickpeas or cannellini beans, or vegetables, such as chopped carrots, green beans, or thawed frozen peas, before serving.

MAKE IT A MEAL

Pair with roasted artichoke hearts (see page 294), Lemony Skillet-Charred Green Beans (page 297), or skillet broccoli (see page 298).

WHY THIS RECIPE WORKS This ultracreamy pasta side is just the thing to cozy up to after a long day. Inspired by the thick and saucy texture of risotto but looking for a quicker option, we hit upon orzo, a small pasta similar in size and shape to rice. Cooking the orzo on the stovetop with a little garlic, oil, and broth yields a dish that's all the more comforting thanks to its ease. Using a relatively small amount of broth means that we don't have to wait long to achieve the creamy, saucy consistency we prefer; as we stir the orzo to encourage it to release its starch into the cooking liquid, it thickens up almost as if by magic. A last-minute addition of rich and herby plant-based Boursin cheese takes the dish's richness and flavor over the top. Enamored with our results, we used this basic formula to create a couple intriguing flavor variations: one with pesto and umami-rich sun-dried tomatoes, and a second with shallot, briny capers, and dill.

1 Cook oil, orzo, and garlic in small saucepan over medium heat until fragrant, about 1 minute. Stir in broth, bring to simmer, and cook, stirring often, until orzo is tender, 17 to 20 minutes.

2 Off heat, vigorously stir in Boursin until creamy. Adjust consistency with extra hot broth as needed and season with salt and pepper to taste. Serve.

VARIATIONS

Orzo with Pesto and Sun-Dried Tomatoes

Substitute 1 tablespoon vegan pesto for Boursin. Stir in ¼ cup thinly sliced oil-packed sun-dried tomatoes before serving.

Orzo with Shallot, Capers, and Dill

Omit garlic and Boursin. Cook 1 small minced shallot in oil until softened, about 2 minutes, before adding orzo. Stir 1 tablespoon rinsed capers and 1 tablespoon chopped fresh dill into orzo before serving.

Celery Root Puree

SERVES 2

TOTAL TIME 30 minutes

1½   pounds celery root, peeled and cut into 2-inch pieces

1   tablespoon extra-virgin olive oil

½   cup vegetable broth

⅛   teaspoon baking soda

¼   cup unsweetened plant-based creamer

Kitchen Improv

USE WHAT YOU'VE GOT

Substitute plant-based yogurt or extra vegetable broth for plant-based creamer.

MAKE IT A MEAL

Pair with Pan-Seared Tempeh Steaks (page 274) or Chile-Rubbed Butternut Squash Steaks (page 312).

WHY THIS RECIPE WORKS   We love a good old-fashioned mashed potato, but now and then we like to mix up our mashed root vegetable game. Gnarled celery root may not be the most visually appealing vegetable at first glance, but with a little love and attention it can transform into a mildly sweet puree that's every bit as comforting as the potato standard. We first process chunks of the peeled root in the food processor, drastically increasing the vegetable's surface area to speed up its cooking. We also add a small amount of baking soda to the vegetable broth in which we simmer the celery root, creating an alkaline environment that further encourages the root to soften and break down. Once the root is softened, we return it to the food processor and whiz it with a splash of vegan creamer to form a smooth, mellow puree. When buying celery root, look for those with few roots for easy peeling and minimal waste. Use a chef's knife to peel the celery root: Trim the top and bottom of the root first, and then cut the skin away from the sides. Once it's prepped, you should have about 1 pound of celery root. For ways to use up leftover plant-based creamer, see page 19.

1   Pulse celery root in food processor until finely chopped, about 20 pulses.

2   Heat oil in large saucepan over medium heat. Stir in celery root, broth, and baking soda. Reduce heat to low, cover, and cook, stirring often (some sticking to bottom of pot is OK), until celery root is very soft and translucent and mixture resembles applesauce, 15 to 18 minutes.

3   Uncover and cook, stirring vigorously to further break down celery root and thicken remaining cooking liquid, about 1 minute. Transfer celery root mixture to clean, dry food processor along with creamer and process until smooth, about 40 seconds. Season with salt to taste. Serve.

VARIATIONS

Extracreamy Celery Root Puree

Add 3 tablespoons plant-based Boursin to food processor with cooked celery root.

Celery Root Puree with Horseradish and Scallions

For a spicier dish, use the greater amount of horseradish.

Stir 1 to 2 tablespoons prepared horseradish, drained, and 2 thinly sliced scallions into puree before serving.

Roasted Red Potatoes
WITH ROSEMARY

SERVES 2
TOTAL TIME 50 minutes

1 pound red potatoes, unpeeled, cut into ½-inch wedges

1½ tablespoons extra-virgin olive oil

¼ teaspoon table salt

¼ teaspoon pepper

1 tablespoon minced fresh rosemary

2 garlic cloves, minced

Kitchen Improv
USE WHAT YOU'VE GOT

Substitute small Yukon Gold potatoes for red potatoes. Substitute other fresh woody herbs, such as oregano or thyme, for rosemary.

WHY THIS RECIPE WORKS   Roasted potatoes don't need much of an introduction; their perfect combination of golden, crispy exterior and creamy-soft inside speaks for itself. Nor do they need a lot of fancying up—a simple side of roasted potatoes is a welcome addition to nearly any meal. We make our easy roasted potatoes with red potatoes; the high moisture content of these spuds means that, when cut into wedges and covered with foil on a rimmed baking sheet before going into the oven, they steam in their own moisture and turn flawlessly tender. Finishing the potatoes uncovered crisps the outsides. Contact with the baking sheet is important for browning, so we flip the potatoes partway through for crispiness on every side. A sprinkle of rosemary and garlic is all the adornment these potatoes need—though we couldn't resist creating a couple extra flavor variations for these versatile potatoes.

1   Adjust oven rack to middle position and heat oven to 425 degrees. Toss potatoes with oil, salt, and pepper and arrange cut side down in single layer on rimmed baking sheet. Cover sheet tightly with aluminum foil and roast potatoes for 20 minutes.

2   Remove foil and continue to roast, uncovered, until bottoms of potatoes are golden and crusty, 8 to 10 minutes longer. Remove sheet from oven and, using spatula, flip potatoes and sprinkle with rosemary. Return sheet to oven and continue to roast potatoes until crusty and golden on second side, about 5 minutes longer. Remove sheet from oven and toss potatoes with garlic. Season with salt and pepper to taste. Serve.

VARIATIONS
Roasted Red Potatoes with Fennel Seeds and Olives
Substitute 1½ teaspoons cracked fennel seeds for rosemary. Toss potatoes with ¼ cup pitted and halved green olives in addition to garlic before serving.

Roasted Red Potatoes with Curry Powder and Ginger
Omit garlic. Substitute 2 tablespoons coarsely chopped peanuts for rosemary. While potatoes roast, whisk 2 teaspoons lime juice, 1 teaspoon grated lime zest, 1 teaspoon curry powder, and 1 teaspoon grated fresh ginger together in large bowl. Toss potatoes in dressing and sprinkle with ¼ cup chopped fresh cilantro before serving.

Roasted Artichoke Hearts

WITH FENNEL AND TARRAGON

SERVES 2

TOTAL TIME 35 minutes

- 9 ounces frozen artichoke hearts, thawed and patted dry
- 1 small fennel bulb, stalks discarded, bulb halved, cored, and sliced thin
- 1 garlic clove, peeled
- 5 teaspoons extra-virgin olive oil, divided

  Pinch pepper
- 2 teaspoons lemon juice
- 1 teaspoon whole-grain mustard
- 2 teaspoons chopped fresh tarragon

Kitchen Improv

USE WHAT YOU'VE GOT

Substitute jarred artichoke hearts for frozen. Substitute other fresh leafy herbs, such as parsley or basil, for tarragon.

MAKE IT A MEAL

Serve with Garlicky Braised Chickpeas (page 279), Lentils with Ras el Hanout and Lemon (page 281), or Roasted Red Potatoes with Rosemary (page 292).

WHY THIS RECIPE WORKS   For this quick side dish, we wanted to bring out the delicate, vegetal flavor of tender artichoke hearts without extensive hands-on time. Frozen artichoke hearts eliminate the tedious prep work that fresh artichokes require, but the frozen hearts contain a considerable amount of water, which can prevent browning and dilute the flavor of the dish. To encourage deep caramelization, we preheat a rimmed baking sheet in a hot 450-degree oven. The excess water in the thawed artichoke hearts quickly evaporates when they make contact with the sizzling-hot pan, allowing the artichokes to develop crispy, caramelized edges and deep, roasty flavor. Lining the baking sheet with foil makes cleanup a snap. After roasting, we toss together a simple dressing of lemon juice, olive oil, mustard, tarragon, and garlic (which we roast alongside the artichokes) to highlight the vegetable's flavor without overpowering it.

1   Adjust oven rack to middle position, place aluminum foil–lined rimmed baking sheet on rack, and heat oven to 450 degrees. Toss artichokes and fennel with garlic, 1 tablespoon oil, and pepper and carefully arrange in single layer on hot sheet. Roast vegetables until browned around edges, 15 to 20 minutes.

2   Mince roasted garlic. Whisk garlic, lemon juice, mustard, tarragon, and remaining 2 teaspoons oil together in large bowl. Add vegetables and toss to coat. Season with salt and pepper to taste, and serve.

VARIATION

Roasted Artichoke Hearts with Bell Pepper and Olives

Omit fennel. Toss artichokes with 1 thinly sliced red bell pepper and ¼ cup pitted and halved kalamata olives before spreading on baking sheet. Substitute parsley for tarragon.

Lemony Skillet-Charred Green Beans

SERVES 2
TOTAL TIME 15 minutes

12	ounces green beans, trimmed
2	tablespoons water
1	tablespoon extra-virgin olive oil
⅛	teaspoon table salt
⅛	teaspoon pepper
½	teaspoon grated lemon zest plus 1 teaspoon juice

Kitchen Improv

USE WHAT YOU'VE GOT

Substitute thawed frozen whole green beans for fresh.

LEVEL UP

Sprinkle with chopped or slivered almonds. Drizzle with chili oil, Harissa (page 26), or Lemon-Herb Yogurt Sauce (page 25).

WHY THIS RECIPE WORKS   Green beans are often sold by weight, so it's easy to buy the precise amount you need, making them a great option when cooking for two—but how can you turn an average green bean side into something special? Answer: Burn them (partially, that is). These blistered, browned beans have a light chew and concentrated flavor. Many skillet-charred green bean recipes require precooking the green beans before charring them in the skillet; our hybrid skillet method allows us to first steam and then char the beans without changing the cooking vessel. First we cook the beans covered with a small amount of water, steaming them until crisp-tender. After we uncover the beans, the oil chars their outsides, giving them a deep, almost smoky flavor. Once the beans finish cooking, we toss them in lemon zest and juice for a bright hit of citrus flavor. You will need a 10- or 12-inch nonstick skillet with a tight-fitting lid for this recipe.

1   Combine green beans, water, oil, salt, and pepper in 10- or 12-inch nonstick skillet. Cover and cook over medium-high heat, shaking skillet occasionally, until water has evaporated, 6 to 8 minutes.

2   Uncover and continue to cook until green beans are blistered and browned, about 2 minutes. Off heat, stir in lemon zest and juice and season with salt and pepper to taste. Serve.

VARIATION

Skillet-Charred Green Beans with Crispy Bread Crumb Topping

Combine 3 tablespoons panko bread crumbs and 1 tablespoon extra-virgin olive oil in skillet. Cook over medium-low heat, stirring frequently, until light golden brown, 5 to 7 minutes; transfer to bowl and let cool slightly. Stir 2 tablespoons minced fresh parsley, dill, cilantro and/or basil, and pinch salt into cooled crumbs. Wipe skillet clean with paper towels before proceeding with recipe. Sprinkle bread crumbs over green beans before serving.

Skillet Broccoli
WITH OLIVE OIL AND GARLIC

SERVES 2
TOTAL TIME 20 minutes

- 2 tablespoons extra-virgin olive oil, divided
- 1 garlic clove, minced
- ¼ teaspoon minced fresh thyme
- 12 ounces broccoli florets, cut into 1-inch pieces
- ¼ teaspoon table salt
- 2 tablespoons water

WHY THIS RECIPE WORKS   Bright-green with deeply browned spots, a sweet-nutty flavor, and a crisp-tender texture—what's not to adore about perfectly cooked broccoli? Maybe the fact that the delicate outer buds all too often overcook and begin to fall apart before the hardier core is tender. Luckily, this problem is easy to remedy. First, we cut the broccoli into small florets, which increases its surface area and creates lots of flat surfaces for better picking up flavorful browning. Once the broccoli is starting to brown, we add a couple tablespoons of water to the skillet to steam the florets to cook them through, and finally we add pungent garlic and a small sprinkle of fresh thyme to the pan for a boost in flavor. Using precut broccoli florets rather than a bunch of broccoli can cut down on prep time and leftovers. If buying broccoli in a bunch instead, you will need about 1¼ pounds of broccoli in order to yield 12 ounces of florets. For ways to use up leftover broccoli, see page 18.

1   Combine 1 tablespoon oil, garlic, and thyme in bowl. Heat remaining 1 tablespoon oil in 10-inch skillet over medium-high heat until just smoking. Add broccoli and salt and cook, without stirring, until beginning to brown, about 2 minutes.

2   Add water, cover, and cook until broccoli is bright green but still crisp, about 2 minutes. Uncover and continue to cook until water has evaporated and broccoli is crisp-tender, about 2 minutes.

3   Push broccoli to sides of skillet. Add garlic mixture and cook, mashing mixture into skillet, until fragrant, about 30 seconds. Stir garlic mixture into broccoli. Season with salt and pepper to taste, and serve.

VARIATION
Skillet Broccoli with Rosemary Oil and Orange

Substitute strained Rosemary Oil (page 26) for olive oil. Add 1 teaspoon grated orange zest to garlic mixture. Drizzle broccoli with 1 teaspoon champagne vinegar or white wine vinegar before serving.

Pan-Roasted Brussels Sprouts

SERVES 2

TOTAL TIME 15 minutes

12 ounces brussels sprouts, trimmed and halved

1 tablespoon extra-virgin olive oil

¼ teaspoon table salt

Lemon wedges

Kitchen Improv

LEVEL UP

Sprinkle with chopped toasted nuts, store-bought plant-based Parmesan or our Cashew Parmesan (page 23), and/or fresh leafy herbs such as parsley, basil, or mint.

WHY THIS RECIPE WORKS   Cooked in hot oil until deeply browned, crispy, and sweet, brussels sprouts transform into an irresistible treat. But no one loves undercooked or overly greasy brussels sprouts, so we set out to create flavorful sprouts that were deeply browned on the cut sides while still bright green on the uncut sides and crisp-tender within. We start the tiny cabbages in a single layer in a cold skillet with olive oil. Starting them cold helps avoid the messy splattering that happens when adding sprouts to hot oil, as well as the hectic rush to get all of them situated before the first that went in start to burn. Cooking them covered at first gently heats the sprouts in the steamy environment created by the evaporation of their own moisture. We then remove the lid and continue to cook the sprouts cut sides down so they have time to develop a substantial, caramelized crust. You will need a 12-inch nonstick skillet with a tight-fitting lid for this recipe.

1   Arrange brussels sprouts in single layer, cut sides down, in 12-inch nonstick skillet. Drizzle with oil and sprinkle with salt. Cover skillet, place over medium-high heat, and cook until sprouts are bright green and cut sides have started to brown, about 4 minutes.

2   Uncover and continue to cook until cut sides of sprouts are deeply and evenly browned and paring knife slides in with little to no resistance, 3 to 4 minutes longer, adjusting heat and moving sprouts as necessary to prevent them from overbrowning. Season with salt and pepper to taste. Serve with lemon wedges.

VARIATION

Pan-Roasted Brussels Sprouts with Gochujang and Sesame Seeds

Omit lemon wedges. Combine 1 tablespoon sesame oil, 1 tablespoon gochujang paste, and 1 tablespoon unseasoned rice vinegar in bowl. Toss cooked brussels sprouts with oil mixture and sprinkle with 1 teaspoon toasted sesame seeds before serving.

Roasted Carrots
WITH YOGURT-TAHINI SAUCE

SERVES 2
TOTAL TIME 40 minutes

- 6   carrots (1 pound), peeled and halved lengthwise
- 1   tablespoon vegetable oil
- ¼   teaspoon table salt
- ¼   teaspoon pepper
- ¼   cup Yogurt-Tahini Sauce (page 25)
- ¼   cup minced fresh cilantro or parsley
- 2   tablespoons coarsely chopped pistachios

Kitchen Improv

USE WHAT YOU'VE GOT

Substitute other nuts, such as almonds, pecans, peanuts, or walnuts, for pistachios.

LEVEL UP

Top with Sumac Onion (page 27).

WHY THIS RECIPE WORKS   You don't need 20-20 vision to see why carrots are one of the most popular vegetables around. Though they're delicious crunchy and raw, roasting them intensifies their flavors, bringing out their natural sweetness as their exteriors caramelize and their interiors turn supple and fork-tender. A full pound of carrots will feed two as a substantial side dish, and we start by drizzling them with olive oil and sprinkling with salt and pepper to season them all over. We then roast them in a hot 450-degree oven until tender, well-browned, and oh-so-sweet. But we don't stop there: For a bit of flair, we drizzle the steamy roasted carrots with a creamy sauce of tangy plant-based yogurt and nutty tahini. A handful of chopped pistachios adds a pop of contrasting color and crunch. An equally delicious variation relies on herby, olive oil–rich chimichurri sauce and almonds for its brightness and crunch.

Adjust oven rack to lowest position and heat oven to 450 degrees. Toss carrots with oil, salt, and pepper and spread in even layer cut sides down on aluminum foil–lined rimmed baking sheet. Roast until tender and cut sides are well browned, 20 to 30 minutes. Season with salt and pepper to taste. Transfer carrots to serving platter, drizzle with yogurt sauce, and sprinkle with cilantro and pistachios. Serve.

VARIATION

Roasted Carrots with Chimichurri

Omit cilantro. Toss carrots with 1 teaspoon paprika before arranging on baking sheet. Substitute Chimichurri (page 24) for Yogurt-Tahini Sauce and almonds for pistachios.

Roasted Cauliflower

SERVES 2
TOTAL TIME 35 minutes

½   head cauliflower (1 pound)

2   tablespoons extra-virgin olive oil, divided

⅛   teaspoon table salt, divided

⅛   teaspoon pepper, divided

Kitchen Improv

LEVEL UP

Substitute Fennel Oil or Rosemary Oil (page 26) for olive oil. Sprinkle with toasted chopped nuts or seeds such as pine nuts, almonds, or pistachios, and/or fresh herbs such as parsley, cilantro, chives, or mint.

MAKE IT A MEAL

Stir into cooked pasta with Pesto (page 24). Pair with Pan-Seared Tofu (page 274) or Herbed Couscous (page 282) and sauce such as Chermoula (page 25) or yogurt sauce (page 25).

WHY THIS RECIPE WORKS   We wanted a recipe for roasted cauliflower that allowed its nutty, delicately sweet flavor, well-browned edges, and tender texture to shine unimpeded. Since browning takes place only where the cauliflower makes direct contact with the hot baking sheet, we slice half a head of cauliflower into four wedges, creating tons of flat surface area for picking up browning. To keep the cauliflower from drying out, we start it covered in a hot oven, which allows it to steam until just barely softened. We then remove the foil to allow the oven's dry heat to caramelize and brown the wedges. Flipping each slice halfway through roasting ensures even cooking and color. Thanks to its natural sweetness and flavor, our roasted cauliflower needs little enhancement—just a drizzle of olive oil and a sprinkle of salt and pepper—although it's easy to customize any way you like with the addition of extra spices, herbs, or aromatics. For ways to use up leftover cauliflower, see page 18.

1   Adjust oven rack to lowest position and heat oven to 475 degrees. Line rimmed baking sheet with aluminum foil.

2   Trim outer leaves off cauliflower and cut stem flush with bottom. Cut cauliflower into 4 equal wedges. Arrange wedges cut side down on prepared sheet, drizzle with 1 tablespoon oil, and sprinkle with pinch salt and pinch pepper. Gently rub seasonings and oil into cauliflower, then flip cauliflower and season other cut side with remaining 1 tablespoon oil, pinch salt, and pinch pepper.

3   Cover sheet tightly with foil and roast cauliflower for 10 minutes. Carefully remove top piece of foil and continue to roast, uncovered, until bottoms of cauliflower pieces are golden, about 4 minutes longer. Remove sheet from oven and, using spatula, carefully flip cauliflower. Return sheet to oven and continue to roast cauliflower until golden all over, about 4 minutes longer. Season with salt and pepper to taste. Serve.

VARIATION

Roasted Cauliflower with Smoked Paprika and Shallots

Add 1 teaspoon smoked paprika to oil before rubbing on cauliflower. Spread 2 quartered shallots on baking sheet with cauliflower before roasting. In medium bowl, whisk 1 tablespoon minced fresh parsley, additional 1 teaspoon olive oil, and 1 teaspoon sherry vinegar together. Gently toss roasted cauliflower in oil mixture before serving.

Cauliflower Steaks
WITH CHIMICHURRI

SERVES 2
TOTAL TIME 45 minutes

- 1 (2-pound) head cauliflower
- 2 tablespoons extra-virgin olive oil, divided
- ¼ teaspoon table salt, divided
- ⅛ teaspoon pepper, divided
- ½ cup Chimichurri (page 24)
   Lemon wedges

Kitchen Improv

USE WHAT YOU'VE GOT

Substitute store-bought pesto or our Pesto, Chermoula, or Harissa (pages 24–26) for Chimichurri.

MAKE IT A MEAL

Serve with Garlicky Braised Chickpeas (page 279), Curried Lentils (page 281), and/or sliced rustic bread.

WHY THIS RECIPE WORKS   Vegetable steaks may sound like an oxymoron, but once you get a taste of these thick and hearty cauliflower steaks you'll understand that there's no contradiction. When you roast thick planks of cauliflower, they develop a meaty texture and become nutty, sweet, and caramelized. Many recipes, however, are fussy, involving transitions between stovetop and oven. Wanting a simpler method that produces two perfectly cooked cauliflower steaks simultaneously, we opt for a rimmed baking sheet and a scorching-hot oven. Steaming the cauliflower briefly under aluminum foil followed by high-heat uncovered roasting produces well-caramelized steaks with tender interiors. We then pair the steaks with a vibrant chimichurri sauce, brushing the hot steaks with the sauce right out of the oven so they soak up its bright, herby flavor. Look for fresh, firm, bright-white heads of cauliflower that feel heavy for their size and are free of blemishes or soft spots; florets are more likely to separate from older heads of cauliflower.

1   Adjust oven rack to lowest position and heat oven to 500 degrees. Discard outer leaves of cauliflower and trim stem flush with bottom florets. Halve cauliflower lengthwise through core. Cut 1½-inch-thick slab lengthwise from each half, trimming any florets not connected to core. (You should have 2 steaks; reserve remaining cauliflower for another use.)

2   Place cauliflower steaks on rimmed baking sheet and drizzle with 1 tablespoon oil. Sprinkle with ⅛ teaspoon salt and pinch pepper and rub to distribute. Flip steaks and repeat with remaining 1 tablespoon oil, ⅛ teaspoon salt, and pinch pepper.

3   Cover baking sheet tightly with aluminum foil and roast for 5 minutes. Remove foil and roast until bottoms of steaks are well browned, 8 to 10 minutes. Gently flip steaks and continue to roast until tender and second sides are well browned, 6 to 8 minutes longer.

4   Transfer steaks to platter and brush evenly with 2 tablespoons chimichurri. Serve with lemon wedges, passing remaining chimichurri separately.

Grilled Eggplant
WITH GINGER-SESAME VINAIGRETTE

SERVES 2
TOTAL TIME 25 minutes

- 1 pound eggplant, sliced into ¼-inch-thick rounds
- 3 tablespoons extra-virgin olive oil
- ¼ teaspoon table salt
- ⅛ teaspoon pepper
- ¼ cup Quick Ginger-Sesame Vinaigrette (page 26)
- 2 tablespoons chopped roasted peanuts
- 1 scallion, sliced thin

Kitchen Improv

USE WHAT YOU'VE GOT

Substitute other chopped toasted nuts, such as almonds, walnuts, or pecans, for peanuts.

WHY THIS RECIPE WORKS Eggplant is a natural fit for the grill: the mildly flavored flesh turns soft and silken over the intense heat of the open fire and picks up complex charred flavors that complement and intensify the eggplant's earthy taste. To achieve grilled eggplant that isn't leathery or spongy, the size of the slice is crucial; grilled over high heat, ¼ inch is just the right thickness to produce a charred exterior and tender flesh without either over- or undercooking the vegetable. Instead of marinating the eggplant slices before grilling, we save time and effort by simply oiling and salting them before popping them on the grill and then drizzling the rounds with a flavorful ginger and sesame vinaigrette off the heat. Roasted peanuts and a sliced scallion play well with the flavors in the vinaigrette and give the dish a fresh, crunchy finish.

1 Brush eggplant all over with oil and sprinkle with salt and pepper.

2A FOR A CHARCOAL GRILL Open bottom vent completely. Light large chimney starter filled with charcoal briquettes (6 quarts). When top coals are partially covered with ash, pour evenly over grill. Set cooking grate in place, cover, and open lid vent completely. Heat grill until hot, about 5 minutes.

2B FOR A GAS GRILL Turn all burners to high, cover, and heat grill until hot, about 15 minutes. Turn all burners to medium-high.

3 Clean and oil cooking grate. Arrange eggplant on grill and cook (covered if using gas) until tender and grill marks appear, about 4 minutes per side. Transfer to serving platter, drizzle with vinaigrette, and sprinkle with peanuts and scallion. Serve.

VARIATION

Grilled Eggplant with Lemon-Herb Yogurt Sauce

Substitute Lemon-Herb Yogurt Sauce (page 25) for vinaigrette, pomegranate seeds for peanuts, and ¼ cup fresh cilantro leaves for scallion.

Sautéed Baby Spinach
WITH ALMONDS AND RAISINS

SERVES 2
TOTAL TIME 20 minutes

- 9   ounces (9 cups) baby spinach
- 4   teaspoons extra-virgin olive oil, divided
- ¼   cup golden raisins
- 2   garlic cloves, sliced thin crosswise
- ⅛   teaspoon red pepper flakes
- ⅛   teaspoon table salt
- 2   tablespoons toasted slivered almonds
- 1   teaspoon sherry vinegar

Kitchen Improv

USE WHAT YOU'VE GOT

Substitute other dried fruit, such as chopped dried cherries, figs, or apricots, for raisins. Substitute other wine vinegar for sherry vinegar. Substitute other nuts, such as chopped walnuts or pecans, for almonds.

WHY THIS RECIPE WORKS   Baby spinach is undeniably convenient—no tough stems to remove or sandy grit to rinse out—but cooking often turns these tender greens into a watery, mushy mess. We were determined to find a method for cooking baby spinach that would give us a side dish worthy of standing on its own. To this end, we parcook the spinach in the microwave to help the vegetable release plenty of liquid. We then press the microwaved spinach against a colander to extract more of its water, coarsely chop it, and press it again. After that, a quick sauté warms it through and cooks off any remaining flavor-dulling liquid. Raisins, slivered almonds, and a splash of sherry vinegar add complementary flavors and appealing textures to finish the dish. If you don't have a bowl large enough to accommodate the entire amount of spinach, cook it in a smaller bowl in two batches. Reduce the water to 1 tablespoon per batch and cook the spinach for about 1½ minutes.

1   Microwave spinach and 2 tablespoons water in covered bowl until spinach is wilted and decreased in volume by half, 3 to 4 minutes. Remove bowl from microwave and keep covered for 1 minute. Carefully transfer spinach to colander and, using back of rubber spatula, gently press spinach against colander to release excess liquid. Transfer spinach to cutting board and chop coarse. Return spinach to colander and press again.

2   Cook 1 tablespoon oil, raisins, garlic, and pepper flakes in 10- or 12-inch skillet over medium-high heat, stirring constantly, until garlic is light golden brown and beginning to sizzle, 3 to 6 minutes. Stir in spinach and salt and cook until uniformly wilted and glossy green, about 2 minutes. Stir in almonds and vinegar. Drizzle with remaining 1 teaspoon oil and season with salt to taste. Serve immediately.

VARIATION
Sautéed Baby Spinach with Leeks and Hazelnuts

Substitute 1 leek, white and light green part only, halved lengthwise, sliced thin, and washed thoroughly, for raisins, garlic, and pepper flakes and cook until softened, 10 to 15 minutes, adding 1 teaspoon water to skillet if leek begins to brown. Add ¼ teaspoon grated lemon zest and pinch ground nutmeg to skillet with spinach. Substitute 1½ teaspoons lemon juice for vinegar and chopped skinned hazelnuts for almonds.

Chile-Rubbed Butternut Squash Steaks

SERVES 2

TOTAL TIME 45 minutes

- 2 tablespoons extra-virgin olive oil, divided
- 1 teaspoon sugar
- 1 teaspoon smoked paprika
- ¾ teaspoon table salt
- ½ teaspoon garlic powder
- ¼ teaspoon pepper
- ¼ teaspoon chipotle chile powder
- 1 (3-pound) butternut squash

  Lime wedges (optional)

Kitchen Improv

USE WHAT YOU'VE GOT

Substitute 2 teaspoons other warm spice blend, such as curry powder, garam masala, or ras el hanout, for paprika, chile powder, garlic powder, and pepper.

LEVEL UP

Serve with plant-based yogurt sauce (page 25) or Ranch Dressing (page 25). Top with fresh leafy herbs, toasted nuts or seeds, and/or pickled vegetables.

WHY THIS RECIPE WORKS   Butternut squash's dense texture gives it a meaty bite and its mild flavor makes it a great canvas for bold seasonings, so it's no surprise that it, like cauliflower (see page 306) is another great candidate for the steak treatment. To create the steaks, we use the neck of a large butternut squash, peeling and slicing it lengthwise into thick slabs. Roasting the steaks before searing them in a hot skillet ensures that the interior is tender. This method also dries out the exterior so that it can develop a crispy charred crust in the skillet. We score the surface in a crosshatch pattern to create more surface area for absorbing our smoky-spicy rub (a bold Southwestern combination of smoked paprika, chipotle chile powder, garlic powder, salt, pepper, and a little sugar for balance), as well as to speed up the process of drying out the exterior and give our steaks the appearance of grill marks. Look for a butternut squash with a neck at least 5 inches long and 2½ to 3½ inches in diameter.

1   Combine 1 tablespoon oil, sugar, paprika, salt, garlic powder, pepper, and chile powder in small bowl.

2   Adjust oven rack to middle position and heat oven to 450 degrees. Cut squash crosswise into 2 pieces at base of neck; reserve bulb for another use. Peel away skin and fibrous threads just below skin (squash should be completely orange, with no white flesh), then carefully cut neck of squash in half lengthwise. Cut one ¾-inch-thick slab lengthwise from each half. (You should have 2 squash steaks; reserve remaining squash for another use.)

3   Place steaks on wire rack set in rimmed baking sheet. Cut 1⁄16-inch-deep slits on both sides of steaks, spaced ½ inch apart, in crosshatch pattern, and brush evenly with half of spice mixture. Flip steaks and brush second side with remaining spice mixture. Roast until nearly tender and knife inserted into steaks meets with some resistance, 15 to 17 minutes; remove from oven.

4   Heat remaining 1 tablespoon oil in 12-inch nonstick skillet over medium-high heat until just smoking. Carefully place steaks in skillet and cook, without moving them, until well browned and crispy on first side, about 3 minutes. Flip steaks and continue to cook until well browned and crispy on second side, about 3 minutes longer. Serve with lime wedges, if using.

Grilled Zucchini
WITH LEMON-BASIL VINAIGRETTE

SERVES 2
TOTAL TIME 30 minutes

- 1 pound zucchini, trimmed, sliced lengthwise into ¾-inch-thick planks
- 2 teaspoons plus 2 tablespoons extra virgin olive oil, divided
- ⅛ teaspoon plus ¼ teaspoon table salt, divided
- ⅛ teaspoon pepper
- 1 teaspoon grated lemon zest, plus 1 tablespoon juice
- 1 small garlic clove, minced
- ¼ teaspoon Dijon mustard
- 2 tablespoons chopped fresh basil or parsley

Kitchen Improv

USE WHAT YOU'VE GOT

Substitute yellow summer squash for zucchini.

WHY THIS RECIPE WORKS   For a simple side from the grill, we turn to two quintessential summertime ingredients: zucchini and basil. Grilling the zucchini in thick planks just until grill marks appear keeps the vegetable's moisture-filled flesh from turning mushy. We keep the zucchini prep simple by sticking to a straightforward brush of olive oil, salt, and pepper. Off the heat, we drizzle the zucchini with a zingy lemony-garlicky vinaigrette to add brightness to the mildly sweet charred squash. As a finishing touch, a generous sprinkle of fresh basil makes this side feel fresh and composed. An easy variation features the warmth of curry powder, which is both rubbed onto the zucchini itself and incorporated into the vinaigrette for a double wallop of complexity and subtle heat.

1   Brush zucchini all over with 2 teaspoons oil and sprinkle with ⅛ teaspoon salt and pepper. Whisk lemon zest and juice, garlic, mustard, remaining 2 tablespoons oil, and remaining ¼ teaspoon salt together in small bowl; set aside.

2A   FOR A CHARCOAL GRILL   Open bottom vent completely. Light large chimney starter half filled with charcoal briquettes (3 quarts). When top coals are partially covered with ash, pour evenly over grill. Set cooking grate in place, cover, and open lid vent completely. Heat grill until hot, about 5 minutes.

2B   FOR A GAS GRILL   Turn all burners to high, cover, and heat grill until hot, about 15 minutes. Turn all burners to medium.

3   Clean and oil cooking grate. Grill zucchini until tender and grill marks appear, 10 to 12 minutes, turning zucchini halfway through grilling. Transfer to serving platter. Add basil to vinaigrette and whisk to recombine. Drizzle vinaigrette over zucchini and serve.

VARIATION
Grilled Zucchini with Curried Vinaigrette

Rub oiled zucchini with ¼ teaspoon curry powder before grilling. Add ¼ teaspoon curry powder to vinaigrette. Substitute chopped fresh cilantro for basil.

DESSERTS

318 Chocolate–Peanut Butter Truffles

321 Thin and Crispy Chocolate Chip Cookies

322 Chewy Peanut Butter Cookies

325 Fudgy Brownies

326 Fig Streusel Bars

328 Individual Lemon–Poppy Seed Cakes

Orange-Almond Cakes

Funfetti Cakes

330 Melon, Plums, and Cherries with Mint and Vanilla

Plums, Blackberries, and Strawberries with Basil and Pepper

333 Roasted Pears with Dried Apricots and Pistachios

334 Grilled Pineapple with Coconut-Rum Sauce

Grilled Mango with Coconut–Five Spice Sauce

336 Strawberry Shortcakes

Peach Shortcakes

338 Blueberry Hand Pies

340 Free-Form Summer Fruit Tartlets

343 Easy Apple Galette

344 Garam Masala–Spiced Mango Crisp

Peach Crisp

347 Rice Pudding

Coconut-Cardamom Rice Pudding

Lemon–Bay Leaf Rice Pudding

348 Dark Chocolate–Avocado Pudding

351 Berry Granitas

Chocolate–Peanut Butter Truffles

- ½ cup (2 ounces) confectioners' sugar
- ¼ cup creamy or chunky peanut butter
- 2 tablespoons plant-based butter, cut into 2 pieces and softened

 Pinch table salt

- 3 ounces bittersweet or semisweet chocolate, chopped fine, divided

Kitchen Improv

USE WHAT YOU'VE GOT

Substitute other nut or seed butters, such as almond or sunflower, for peanut butter.

LEVEL UP

Sprinkle truffles with chopped toasted nuts, vegan sprinkles, cocoa powder, and/or flake sea salt before refrigerating.

WHY THIS RECIPE WORKS There are few things that go together better than peanut butter and chocolate, and even fewer that are easier to whip up than these irresistible confections of sweetened peanut butter coated in a glossy chocolate shell. To create a light but not sticky filling that we can roll into balls by hand, we mix peanut butter with plant-based butter and confectioners' sugar, shaping the peanut butter filling into balls before we pop them into the freezer to harden. While they firm up, we temper the chocolate by melting a portion of it in the microwave and then stirring in the remaining chocolate until the entire mixture is smooth and glossy, ensuring that the finished truffles will have a beautiful sheen. We then dunk the firmed-up peanut butter balls into the chocolate and give them one last quick rest in the fridge to allow the coating to harden. Note that not all chocolate is vegan; read the ingredient list carefully to be sure.

1 Using rubber spatula, mash sugar, peanut butter, butter, and salt in bowl until well combined and lightened in color. Divide into 8 portions, roll into balls, and place on parchment paper–lined plate. Freeze for 15 minutes.

2 Microwave two-thirds of chocolate in 1-cup liquid measuring cup at 50 percent power, stirring often, until nearly melted, 2 to 3 minutes. Stir in remaining chocolate until melted and smooth. (Return chocolate to microwave if not fully melted and microwave in 5-second intervals, stirring in between, until smooth.)

3 Drop 1 peanut butter ball in melted chocolate and, using 2 forks, gently flip it to coat all over. Lift truffle from chocolate with fork, allowing excess chocolate to drip back into measuring cup, then return truffle to plate. Repeat with remaining peanut butter balls. Refrigerate truffles, uncovered, until chocolate has hardened, about 10 minutes. Serve. (Truffles can be refrigerated for up to 1 week.)

Thin and Crispy Chocolate Chip Cookies

MAKES 16 cookies

TOTAL TIME 45 minutes, plus 20 minutes cooling

- 1 cup (5 ounces) all-purpose flour
- ¾ teaspoon table salt
- ¼ teaspoon baking soda
- 8 tablespoons plant-based butter, melted and cooled
- ⅓ cup (2⅓ ounces) granulated sugar
- ⅓ cup packed (2⅓ ounces) brown sugar
- 3 tablespoons liquid plant-based egg
- 2 teaspoons vanilla extract
- ¾ cup (4½ ounces) mini bittersweet or semisweet chocolate chips

Kitchen Improv

USE WHAT YOU'VE GOT

Substitute finely chopped bar chocolate or nuts, such as walnuts, pecans, or almonds, for mini chocolate chips.

WHY THIS RECIPE WORKS These slim, crunchy rounds get their notable butterscotch flavor and crispy texture from a combination of granulated and brown sugar, which interact in different ways with the moisture in the dough. Plenty of plant-based butter adds nuanced richness and makes a thin batter that spreads in the oven; rather than creaming it with the sugar, as we would if we wanted chewier cookies, we melt it before stirring it together with the sugar. This works much less air into the batter, ensuring that the cookies stay nice and flat. A small amount of baking soda promotes browning and caramelization without causing the cookies to puff up too much, and a few tablespoons of liquid plant-based egg help emulsify the batter so the fat doesn't split when the dough is chilled and baked, preventing the cookies from having an undesirable greasy mouthfeel. Note that this recipe calls for mini (not full-size) chocolate chips, and that not all chocolate chips are vegan; check the ingredient list carefully to be sure.

1 Adjust oven rack to middle position and heat oven to 350 degrees. Line 2 baking sheets with parchment paper. Whisk flour, salt, and baking soda together in bowl.

2 Using stand mixer fitted with paddle, mix melted butter, granulated sugar, and brown sugar on low speed until fully combined. Increase speed to medium-high and beat until mixture is lightened in color, about 1 minute. Reduce speed to low, add egg and vanilla, and mix until combined. Slowly add flour mixture and mix until just combined, scraping down bowl as needed. Using rubber spatula, stir in chocolate chips.

3 TO BAKE COOKIES Using greased 1-tablespoon measure, evenly space up to 8 heaping-tablespoon portions of dough on 1 prepared sheet. Bake cookies until deep golden brown, 16 to 18 minutes, rotating sheet halfway through baking. Let cookies cool on sheet for 20 minutes. Serve. (Cookies can be stored at room temperature for up to 3 days.)

4 TO FREEZE REMAINING DOUGH Evenly space heaping-tablespoon portions of remaining dough on second prepared sheet. Freeze sheet of cookies until firm, about 1 hour. Transfer cookies to 1-gallon zipper-lock bag and freeze for up to 1 month. Bake frozen cookies as directed; do not thaw.

Chewy Peanut Butter Cookies

MAKES 12 cookies
TOTAL TIME 45 minutes

- ¾   cup (3¾ ounces) all-purpose flour
- ½   teaspoon baking soda
- ¼   teaspoon table salt
- ¾   cup packed (5¼ ounces) brown sugar
- ½   cup (4½ ounces) creamy peanut butter
- 3   tablespoons liquid plant-based egg
- 2   tablespoons plant-based butter, melted and cooled
- 1   tablespoon agave syrup
- ½   teaspoon vanilla extract
- ¼   cup dry-roasted peanuts, chopped fine

Kitchen Improv

MAKE IT AN ICE CREAM SANDWICH

Place 1 scoop slightly softened plant-based ice cream between two cookies, gently pressing and twisting sandwich between your hands until ice cream spreads to edges of cookies. Freeze sandwiches to firm up ice cream.

WHY THIS RECIPE WORKS   The chewy texture and robust peanutty flavor of these cookies are achieved by counterintuitively using a relatively modest amount of peanut butter. The starch in peanut butter can lead to dry and stunted cookies if added in too great an amount, so we stick to just ½ cup, stirring in finely chopped dry-roasted peanuts to bolster the cookies' peanut flavor and give them a faint crunch. Melted and cooled plant-based butter gives the dough a soft, scoopable consistency that's easy to stir together by hand. Brown sugar deepens the color of the dough and adds notes of caramel, sweet agave syrup aids in browning, and a few tablespoons of liquid plant-based egg help emulsify the fat so the cookies bake up rich and chewy but not greasy. To ensure that the cookies have the proper texture, use a traditional creamy peanut butter in this recipe; do not substitute crunchy or natural peanut butter. It's important to let the melted butter cool completely before whisking it together with the other ingredients; otherwise, the cookies may spread too much in the oven.

1   Adjust oven rack to middle position and heat oven to 350 degrees. Line 2 rimmed baking sheets with parchment paper. Whisk flour, baking soda, and salt together in medium bowl.

2   In large bowl, whisk sugar, peanut butter, egg, melted butter, agave, and vanilla until smooth. Add flour mixture and stir with rubber spatula until soft, homogeneous dough forms. Stir in peanuts until evenly distributed.

3   TO BAKE COOKIES   Working with 2 tablespoons dough at a time (or using #30 portion scoop), roll up to 6 portions of dough into balls and evenly space on 1 prepared sheet. Using your fingers, gently flatten dough balls to 2 inches in diameter. Bake cookies until edges are just set, 10 to 13 minutes, rotating sheet after 6 minutes. Let cookies cool on sheet for 5 minutes. Using wide metal spatula, transfer cookies to wire rack and let cool completely before serving.

4   TO FREEZE REMAINING DOUGH   Evenly space 2-tablespoon portions of remaining dough on second prepared sheet and gently flatten using your fingers. Freeze sheet of cookies until firm, about 1 hour. Transfer cookies to 1-gallon zipper-lock bag and freeze for up to 1 month. Bake frozen cookies as directed; do not thaw.

Fudgy Brownies

MAKES 12 brownies

TOTAL TIME 50 minutes plus 1½ hours cooling

- 1 cup (5 ounces) all-purpose flour
- ½ teaspoon baking powder
- ½ teaspoon table salt
- ½ cup boiling water
- 1½ ounces unsweetened chocolate, chopped fine
- ⅓ cup (1⅛ ounces) Dutch-processed cocoa powder
- ¾ teaspoon instant espresso powder (optional)
- 1¼ cups (8¾ ounces) sugar
- ¼ cup vegetable oil
- 1½ teaspoons vanilla extract
- ¼ cup (1½ ounces) bittersweet or semisweet chocolate chips

Kitchen Improv

LEVEL UP

Add up to ½ cup finely chopped toasted nuts, such as walnuts, pecans, or hazelnuts, to batter with chocolate chips. Serve with plant-based ice cream.

WHY THIS RECIPE WORKS   Chewy, fudgy, ultrachocolaty brownies take very little work for an immensely satisfying reward. And without dairy, which can mute chocolate flavor, these vegan brownies taste even more intensely chocolaty—and they last longer before going stale, too. The rich chocolate flavor comes from three forms of chocolate—unsweetened chocolate, cocoa powder, and chocolate chips—and instant espresso powder, which further amplifies the chocolate flavor. These brownies freeze so well that you can make a whole panful at once, enjoy a couple right away, and save the rest to enjoy later on. If you use a glass baking dish, let the brownies cool for 10 minutes before removing them from the dish. (The superior heat retention of glass can lead to overbaking.) For an accurate measurement of boiling water, bring a full kettle of water to a boil and then measure out the desired amount. Do not omit the chocolate chips; they add cohesiveness to the brownies' texture. Note that not all chocolate chips are vegan; read the ingredient list carefully to be sure.

1   Adjust oven rack to lowest position and heat oven to 350 degrees. Make foil sling for 8-inch square baking pan by folding 2 long sheets of aluminum foil so each is 8 inches wide. Lay sheets of foil in pan perpendicular to each other, with extra foil hanging over edges of pan. Push foil into corners and up sides of pan, smoothing foil flush to pan. Grease foil.

2   Whisk flour, baking powder, and salt together in bowl. Whisk boiling water; unsweetened chocolate; cocoa; and espresso powder, if using, in large bowl until well combined and chocolate is melted. Whisk in sugar, oil, and vanilla. Using rubber spatula, stir flour mixture into chocolate mixture until combined; fold in chocolate chips.

3   Scrape batter into prepared pan and smooth top. Bake until toothpick inserted halfway between edge and center comes out with few moist crumbs attached, 25 to 30 minutes. Let brownies cool in pan on wire rack for 1 hour.

4   Using foil overhang, lift brownies from pan. Return brownies to wire rack and let cool completely, about 30 minutes. Cut into squares and serve. (Brownies can be stored at room temperature for up to 4 days or wrapped tightly in plastic wrap and frozen for up to 1 month; thaw at room temperature for 1 hour before serving.)

Fig Streusel Bars

MAKES 12 bars

TOTAL TIME 1 hour, plus 1 hour cooling

- 1¼ cups (6¼ ounces) all-purpose flour
- ⅓ cup (2⅓ ounces) granulated sugar
- ¼ teaspoon table salt
- 8 tablespoons plant-based butter, cut into 8 pieces
- 1½ tablespoons water
- ¼ cup old-fashioned rolled oats
- ¼ cup pecans, toasted and chopped fine
- 2 tablespoons packed brown sugar
- ½ cup fig jam
- 1½ teaspoons lemon juice

Kitchen Improv

USE WHAT YOU'VE GOT

Substitute other fruit jam, such as strawberry, raspberry, or apricot, for fig jam. Substitute other nuts, such as walnuts or almonds, for pecans.

LEVEL UP

Add up to ⅛ teaspoon cinnamon, nutmeg, or ground ginger, ½ teaspoon lemon or orange zest, and/or ¼ teaspoon vanilla or almond extract to jam filling.

WHY THIS RECIPE WORKS   For the very best vegan fig streusel bars, we wanted a flavorful but low-effort fig filling, a tender shortbread crust, and a crumbly topping. First we mix together a rich dough that does duty as both the shortbread crust and the base of the nutty streusel topping, using just flour, plant-based butter, and a little sugar and salt. We press a portion of this mixture into the pan for the crust and then add oats, brown sugar, and pecans to the remaining mixture and pinch it into clumps to create the topping. A thin layer of fig jam (plus a squeeze of lemon to balance the jam's sweetness) spread across the still-warm parbaked crust adds serious fig flavor. Finally, we sprinkle on the streusel and pop the pan back into the oven until the figgy filling is bubbling up around the toasty golden-brown topping. Do not use quick or instant oats in this recipe.

1   Adjust oven rack to middle position and heat oven to 375 degrees. Make foil sling for 8-inch square baking pan by folding 2 long sheets of aluminum foil so each is 8 inches wide. Lay sheets of foil in pan perpendicular to each other, with extra foil hanging over edges of pan. Push foil into corners and up sides of pan, smoothing foil flush to pan. Grease foil.

2   Pulse flour, granulated sugar, and salt in food processor until combined, about 3 pulses. Scatter butter over flour mixture, then sprinkle with water. Pulse until mixture resembles damp sand, about 20 pulses; set aside ½ cup of flour mixture in medium bowl for topping. Sprinkle remaining flour mixture into prepared pan and press into even layer using bottom of dry measuring cup. Bake until edges of crust begin to brown, 14 to 18 minutes, rotating pan halfway through baking.

3   Meanwhile, stir oats, pecans, and brown sugar into reserved flour mixture and pinch into clumps of streusel. Combine jam and lemon juice in small bowl.

4   Spread jam mixture evenly over hot crust, then sprinkle evenly with streusel. Bake until filling is bubbling and topping is golden brown, 20 to 24 minutes, rotating pan halfway through baking. Let bars cool completely in pan on wire rack, about 1 hour. Using foil overhang, lift bars from pan. Cut into squares and serve. (Bars can be stored at room temperature for up to 4 days or wrapped tightly in plastic wrap and frozen for up to 1 month; thaw at room temperature for 1 hour before serving.)

Individual Lemon–Poppy Seed Cakes

SERVES 2

TOTAL TIME 1¼ hours, plus 1 hour cooling

CAKE

- ½ cup (2½ ounces) all-purpose flour
- 1 tablespoon poppy seeds, plus extra for sprinkling
- ½ teaspoon baking powder
- ⅛ teaspoon table salt
- ⅓ cup (2⅓ ounces) sugar
- 3 tablespoons plant-based butter, melted and cooled
- ¼ cup liquid plant-based egg
- 1½ teaspoons grated lemon zest plus ½ teaspoon juice
- ¼ teaspoon vanilla extract

LEMON GLAZE

- ¼ cup confectioners' sugar
- 1½–2 teaspoons lemon juice

Kitchen Improv

LEVEL UP

Garnish cakes with chopped candied citrus peel and/or candied violets after glazing.

WHY THIS RECIPE WORKS   When you're in need of an elevated homemade dessert (for impressing a special someone, perhaps?), look no further than these cute individual-size cakes. We use 6-ounce ramekins instead of a cake pan to bake these classic lemon–poppy seed cakes that feature a tender crumb and tons of floral, tart lemon flavor. Liquid plant-based egg helps emulsify the batter and provide some binding, but it doesn't provide the same lift as chicken eggs, so we add ½ teaspoon of baking powder—a lot considering the relatively small amount of flour—to the batter to ensure good rise. Vegan butter gives the cakes richness and a buttery flavor. For bold lemon flavor throughout, we use both lemon zest and fresh lemon juice, and we drizzle the cakes with a simple lemon glaze while they cool. You will need two 6-ounce ramekins for this recipe. Alternatively, the batter can be doubled, spread evenly into a greased 6-inch round cake pan, and baked as directed. Placing a sheet of parchment paper beneath the cooling rack helps catch errant crumbs and glaze for easy cleanup.

1   FOR THE CAKE   Adjust oven rack to middle position and heat oven to 325 degrees. Grease and flour two 6-ounce ramekins.

2   Whisk flour, poppy seeds, baking powder, and salt together in bowl. Whisk sugar, melted butter, egg, lemon zest and juice, and vanilla in medium bowl until smooth. Whisk in flour mixture in 2 additions until few streaks of flour remain.

3   Scrape batter into prepared ramekins, smooth tops with rubber spatula, and wipe sides clean with paper towels. Gently tap ramekins on counter to release air bubbles. Bake until toothpick inserted in center comes out clean, 35 to 40 minutes, rotating ramekins halfway through baking.

4   Let cakes cool on wire rack set over parchment paper for 10 minutes, then run thin knife between cakes and sides of ramekins and turn cakes onto rack.

5   FOR THE LEMON GLAZE   Whisk sugar and 1½ teaspoons lemon juice together in bowl, thinning glaze with remaining ½ teaspoon lemon juice as needed. Drizzle glaze over cakes, sprinkle with extra poppy seeds, and let cool completely, about 1 hour. Serve.

VARIATIONS

Individual Orange-Almond Cakes

Omit poppy seeds. Substitute orange zest and juice for lemon zest and juice. Substitute almond extract for vanilla extract. Sprinkle tops of cakes with 2 tablespoons toasted sliced almonds after glazing.

Individual Funfetti Cakes

Omit lemon zest and juice in cake and increase vanilla to ½ teaspoon. Substitute vegan sprinkles for poppy seeds and plant-based milk for lemon juice in glaze. Sprinkle tops of cakes with additional sprinkles after glazing.

Melon, Plums, and Cherries
WITH MINT AND VANILLA

SERVES 2

TOTAL TIME 25 minutes

- 2 teaspoons sugar
- 1½ teaspoons shredded fresh mint
- 1½ cups ½-inch cantaloupe pieces
- 6 ounces plums, halved, pitted, and cut into ½-inch pieces
- 4 ounces fresh sweet cherries, pitted and halved
- ⅛ teaspoon vanilla extract
- 1½ teaspoons lime juice, plus extra for seasoning

Kitchen Improv

USE WHAT YOU'VE GOT

Substitute other stone fruit, such as peaches, nectarines, and/or apricots, for plums. Substitute fresh berries, such as raspberries, or blueberries, for cherries.

LEVEL UP

Drizzle fruit with up to 1 tablespoon orange or elderflower liqueur. Serve with plant-based yogurt, ice cream, or sorbet.

WHY THIS RECIPE WORKS A perfectly ripe piece of fruit needs little adornment to make it a worthy finish to a meal. This fresh fruit salad is as satisfying to eat as it is to look at. A combination of cantaloupe, plums, and cherries offers a range not only of complementary flavors but also of colors and textures that work together to create an eye-catching and palate-pleasing dish. To boost the salad's flavor, we macerate the fruit with a small amount of sugar, which encourages it to release its juices. Mashing the sugar with fresh mint before stirring it into the fruit ensures that the fragrant herb is evenly distributed. A squeeze of fresh lime juice balances the sweetness. Perhaps best of all, this easy recipe is so versatile that you can change it up to suit your whims (and your current fruit bounty), as in our variation with berries, basil, and balsamic vinegar.

Combine sugar and mint in medium bowl. Using rubber spatula, press mixture into side of bowl until sugar becomes damp, about 30 seconds. Add cantaloupe, plums, cherries, and vanilla and toss gently to combine. Let sit at room temperature, stirring occasionally, until fruit releases its juices, 15 to 30 minutes. Stir in lime juice and season with extra lime juice to taste. Serve.

VARIATION

Plums, Blackberries, and Strawberries with Basil and Pepper

Omit vanilla extract. Substitute 1 tablespoon shredded fresh basil for mint and add ¼ teaspoon pepper to sugar-basil mixture. Substitute 5 ounces blackberries for cantaloupe; 5 ounces hulled, quartered strawberries for cherries; and balsamic vinegar for lime juice. Increase plums to 12 ounces.

Roasted Pears
WITH DRIED APRICOTS AND PISTACHIOS

SERVES 2
TOTAL TIME 1 hour

- 1   tablespoon vegetable oil
- 2   ripe but firm Bosc pears (7 to 8 ounces each), peeled, halved, and cored
- 1   cup dry white wine
- ¼   cup dried apricots, quartered
- ¼   cup sugar
- ⅛   teaspoon ground cardamom
     Pinch table salt
- ¼   cup shelled pistachios, toasted and chopped

Kitchen Improv

USE WHAT YOU'VE GOT

Substitute dry red wine for white wine. Substitute other dried fruits, such as dates, figs, or cherries, for apricots. Substitute other nuts, such as walnuts, hazelnuts, or almonds, for pistachios.

LEVEL UP

Serve with plant-based yogurt, store-bought plant-based whipped cream, or our Whipped Coconut Cream (page 336).

WHY THIS RECIPE WORKS   Pears are often poached, but when they're roasted until bronzed and adorned with a few simple embellishments, they make an even lovelier after-dinner treat. Getting good browning on the pears requires first driving off their extra moisture, so we start by cooking the pears on the stovetop before transferring them, skillet and all, to the oven. The gentle, even heat of the oven then works its magic to yield all-over browning and fork-tender fruit. To take advantage of the flavorful browned fruit bits left in the pan, we also stir together a quick dessert pan sauce with white wine, lemon juice, and cardamom for a sweet and aromatic flavor profile. A small amount of sugar and some dried apricots bring balanced sweetness. For textural contrast, we sprinkle on a handful of toasted pistachios just before serving. We prefer Bosc pears in this recipe, but Comice and Bartlett pears also work. Use a medium-bodied dry white wine such as Sauvignon Blanc or Pinot Grigio. You will need an ovensafe 10- or 12-inch skillet for this recipe.

1   Adjust oven rack to middle position and heat oven to 450 degrees. Heat oil in 10- or 12-inch ovensafe skillet over medium-high heat until shimmering. Place pears cut sides down in skillet and cook, without moving them, until browned, 6 to 8 minutes.

2   Transfer skillet to oven and roast pears for 15 minutes. Being careful of hot skillet handle, flip pears and continue to roast until toothpick slips easily in and out of pears, 10 to 15 minutes longer.

3   Being careful of hot skillet handle, remove skillet from oven and carefully transfer pears to serving platter. Add wine, apricots, sugar, cardamom, and salt to now-empty skillet and bring to simmer over medium-high heat. Cook, whisking to scrape up any browned bits, until sauce is reduced and has consistency of maple syrup, 10 to 12 minutes. Pour sauce over pears and sprinkle with pistachios. Serve.

Grilled Pineapple
WITH COCONUT-RUM SAUCE

SERVES 2

TOTAL TIME 30 minutes

- ¼ cup packed brown sugar
- ¼ cup canned coconut milk
- ¼ teaspoon grated lime zest plus 1 teaspoon juice
- 1 teaspoon white or aged rum (optional)
- ½ small pineapple, peeled, cored and cut lengthwise into 4 wedges
- 1 teaspoon vegetable oil
- 1 tablespoon unsweetened shredded coconut, toasted

Kitchen Improv

USE WHAT YOU'VE GOT

Substitute tequila, brandy, orange liqueur, or coffee liqueur for rum.

LEVEL UP

Sprinkle with toasted, chopped nuts, such as walnuts, pistachios, or macadamia nuts. Serve with plant-based yogurt, ice cream, store-bought plant-based whipped cream, or our Whipped Coconut Cream (page 336).

WHY THIS RECIPE WORKS Grilled fruit makes a simple, elegant, and delicious dessert, particularly when paired with a sweet sauce—like in this recipe—or a scoop of ice cream. Pineapple's firm texture makes it a perfect candidate for throwing on the grill. Cutting it lengthwise into relatively large wedges allows for easy handling on the grill and helps the interior stay sweet and juicy even as the exterior picks up charred grill marks. To accompany the grilled pineapple, we simmer a mixture of coconut milk and brown sugar in the microwave, which saves us a pot and the effort of turning on the stove. Once it's reduced to the thickness of heavy cream, we add lime juice and rum to offset the coconut's sweetness and intensify the dish's tropical vibe. Sprinkles of lime zest and toasted coconut complete our fast and delicious grilled dessert. For ways to use up leftover coconut milk, see pages 18–19.

1 Combine sugar and coconut milk in small bowl and microwave until thickened to consistency of heavy cream, 3 to 4 minutes, stirring twice during microwaving. Stir in lime juice and rum, if using; set aside until ready to serve.

2A FOR A CHARCOAL GRILL Open bottom vent completely. Light large chimney starter three-quarters filled with charcoal briquettes (4½ quarts). When top coals are partially covered with ash, pour evenly over grill. Set cooking grate in place, cover, and open lid vent completely. Heat grill until hot, about 5 minutes.

2B FOR A GAS GRILL Turn all burners to high, cover, and heat grill until hot, about 15 minutes. Turn all burners to medium-high.

3 Clean and oil cooking grate. Brush pineapple with oil and grill until lightly charred and beginning to soften, about 8 minutes, turning pineapple as needed. Transfer pineapple to individual plates, drizzle with sauce, and sprinkle with coconut and lime zest. Serve.

VARIATION

Grilled Mango with Coconut–Five Spice Sauce

Omit rum. Add ⅛ teaspoon five spice powder to coconut milk mixture before microwaving. Substitute 2 mangoes for pineapple. Peel 1 mango and cut thin slice from 1 end so that it sits flat on counter. Rest mango on flat side and cut down along each side of flat pit to remove 2 large pieces of flesh. Trim around pit to remove any remaining flesh and reserve for another use; repeat with second mango. Grill 4 large pieces of mango in step 3; reduce grilling time to about 5 minutes.

Strawberry Shortcakes

SERVES 2

TOTAL TIME 40 minutes, plus 30 minutes cooling

WHIPPED COCONUT CREAM

- 1 (14-ounce) can coconut milk
- 1½ teaspoons sugar
- ½ teaspoon vanilla extract

STRAWBERRIES

- 8 ounces strawberries, hulled and quartered, divided
- 1½ tablespoons sugar

SHORTCAKES

- ½ cup (2½ ounces) all-purpose flour
- 2¼ teaspoons sugar, divided
- ½ teaspoon baking powder
- ⅛ teaspoon baking soda
- ⅛ teaspoon table salt
- 3 tablespoons plant-based milk, chilled
- 2 tablespoons plant-based butter, melted and cooled
- ¾ teaspoon lemon juice

Kitchen Improv

USE WHAT YOU'VE GOT

Substitute other fresh berries, such as raspberries, blueberries, or blackberries, for some or all of strawberries.

WHY THIS RECIPE WORKS Strawberry shortcakes are a classic and whimsical summertime treat, but their three-part construction of strawberries, cake, and whipped cream can take a while to make. To make them a realistic option for two, we use rustic drop biscuits instead of cake as the base. Vegan butter, milk, and lemon juice give the biscuits richness and buttermilk-style tang. To top things off, we whip coconut cream (scooped from the top of a can of chilled coconut milk) into velvety billows. We prefer to make our own whipped coconut cream, but you can substitute ½ cup of your favorite store-bought plant-based whipped cream. To ensure that the cream whips properly, be sure to use full-fat coconut milk. For ways to use up leftover coconut milk, see pages 18–19. We strongly prefer oat milk in the biscuits since it yields the best browning, but any plant-based milk will work.

1 FOR THE WHIPPED COCONUT CREAM Refrigerate unopened can of coconut milk for at least 24 hours; 2 distinct layers should form. Skim top layer of coconut cream from can and measure out ½ cup cream (save milky liquid and any extra cream for another use). Using hand mixer fitted with whisk attachment, whip coconut cream, sugar, and vanilla in bowl on low speed until well combined, about 30 seconds. Increase speed to high and whip until mixture thickens and soft peaks form, about 2 minutes. Cover and refrigerate until ready to use. (Whipped coconut cream can be refrigerated for up to 4 days.)

2 FOR THE STRAWBERRIES Using potato masher, mash one-third of strawberries with sugar in separate bowl to coarse pulp. Stir in remaining strawberries, cover, and let sit while making shortcakes, at least 30 minutes or up to 2 hours.

3 FOR THE SHORTCAKES Adjust oven rack to middle position and heat oven to 475 degrees. Line rimmed baking sheet with parchment paper. Whisk flour, 1½ teaspoons sugar, baking powder, baking soda, and salt together in large bowl. Whisk milk, melted butter, and lemon juice together in second bowl. Stir milk mixture into flour mixture until just incorporated. (Dough will be quite sticky.)

4 Using greased ¼-cup dry measuring cup, gently scoop dough into 2 even mounds on prepared sheet, about 1½ inches apart. Sprinkle evenly with remaining ¾ teaspoon sugar. Bake until tops are golden, 12 to 14 minutes, rotating sheet halfway through baking. Transfer biscuits to wire rack and let cool completely, about 30 minutes. (Cooled biscuits can be stored in airtight container for up to 1 day.)

5 Split each biscuit in half and place bottoms on individual plates. Using slotted spoon, portion strawberries over biscuit bottoms, then dollop with whipped coconut cream. Top with biscuit tops and serve.

VARIATION

Peach Shortcakes

Peel, pit, and cut 2 ripe peaches into ¼-inch-thick wedges; substitute peaches for strawberries. Toss one-third of peaches with sugar and microwave, stirring occasionally, until bubbling, 1 to 2 minutes. Using potato masher, mash hot peaches to coarse pulp before stirring in remaining peaches.

Blueberry Hand Pies

MAKES 8 hand pies

TOTAL TIME 1½ hours, plus 15 minutes cooling

- 1 pound (3¼ cups) fresh or frozen blueberries
- ½ cup (3½ ounces) plus 1 tablespoon sugar, divided
- 1 teaspoon grated lemon zest
- ¼ teaspoon table salt
- ¼ teaspoon ground cinnamon
- 1 tablespoon cornstarch
- 1 tablespoon water
- 2 (9½ by 9-inch) sheets puff pastry, thawed
- 3 tablespoons liquid plant-based egg

Kitchen Improv

LEVEL UP

Add pinch of cinnamon to sugar for sprinkling on top of hand pies. Serve with plant-based ice cream.

WHY THIS RECIPE WORKS What's not to love about hand pies? They're portable, perfect for parties, picnics, or on the go, and can easily cross over from dessert to sweet snack—or even breakfast. To make them as easy as they are versatile, we start with store-bought puff pastry and a simple precooked filling of blueberries flavored with cinnamon and lemon zest. Cutting sufficient steam vents—three 1-inch-long slits in the tops are ideal—is key to preventing the turnovers from bursting open and leaking filling as they bake. Brushed with a few tablespoons of plant-based egg and sprinkled with sugar, these turnovers are crispy, flaky, and full of luscious, gooey blueberry filling. Note that not all puff pastry is vegan; check the ingredient list carefully to be sure. Let the puff pastry thaw completely before using; otherwise, it can crack and break apart. To thaw frozen puff pastry, let it sit either in the refrigerator for 24 hours or on the counter for 30 minutes to 1 hour.

1 Cook blueberries, ½ cup sugar, lemon zest, salt, and cinnamon in medium saucepan over medium heat, stirring occasionally, until blueberries begin to break down and release their juices, about 8 minutes. Reduce heat to medium-low and continue to cook until mixture thickens and spatula starts to leave trail when pulled through, 8 to 10 minutes.

2 Whisk cornstarch and water together in bowl, then stir into blueberry mixture. Cook until mixture has thickened to jam-like consistency, about 1 minute (you should have about 1¼ cups filling). Let cool completely, about 30 minutes.

3 Adjust oven rack to middle position and heat oven to 400 degrees. Line 2 rimmed baking sheets with parchment paper. Working with 1 sheet of pastry at a time, roll into 10-inch square on floured counter. Cut pastry into four 5-inch squares. Place 2 tablespoons blueberry filling in center of each square.

4 Brush edges of squares with egg, then fold dough over filling to form rectangle. Using fork, crimp edges of dough to seal. Cut three 1-inch slits on top (do not cut through filling). Brush tops of pies with remaining egg and sprinkle with remaining 1 tablespoon sugar.

5 Transfer desired number of pies to 1 prepared sheet and bake until well browned, about 25 minutes, rotating sheet halfway through baking. Transfer pies to wire rack and let cool slightly, about 15 minutes. Serve warm or at room temperature.

6 Transfer remaining unbaked pies to second prepared sheet and freeze until firm, about 15 minutes. (Once frozen, pies can be transferred to airtight container and stored in freezer for up to 1 month; do not thaw before baking.)

Free-Form Summer Fruit Tartlets

SERVES 2

TOTAL TIME 1½ hours, plus 1½ hours chilling and cooling

DOUGH

- ¾ cup (3¾ ounces) all-purpose flour
- ¼ teaspoon table salt
- 5 tablespoons plant-based butter, cut into ½-inch pieces and chilled
- 2–3 tablespoons ice water

TARTLETS

- 8 ounces peaches, peeled, pitted, and cut into ½-inch wedges
- 2½ ounces (¼ cup) raspberries or blackberries
- 3–5 tablespoons sugar, divided

Kitchen Improv

USE WHAT YOU'VE GOT

Substitute other stone fruit, such as nectarines, plums, apricots, and/or cherries, for peaches.

LEVEL UP

Serve with plant-based ice cream, store-bought plant-based whipped cream, or our Whipped Coconut Cream (page 336).

WHY THIS RECIPE WORKS A free-form tart delivers all the goodness of a fruit pie with half the work, requiring just a single layer of dough that's folded up around the juicy fresh fruit. To make the crust for these individual-size tartlets, we press vegan butter into the flour with the heel of our hands (a French method known as fraisage) to create long, thin sheets full of flaky, leak-proof layers. Juicy peaches and sweet-tart raspberries need only a sprinkling of sugar to bring out their sweetness. We prefer to use our homemade tartlet dough here, but you can substitute two 9-inch store-bought vegan pie dough rounds if you prefer; trim rounds to 7 inches and refrigerate as directed in step 3.

1 FOR THE DOUGH Process flour and salt in food processor until combined, about 5 seconds. Scatter butter over top and pulse until mixture resembles coarse crumbs and butter pieces are about size of small peas, 6 to 8 pulses. Continue to pulse, adding 1 tablespoon ice water at a time, until dough begins to form small curds and holds together when pinched with your fingers (dough will be crumbly), about 10 pulses.

2 Turn dough crumbs onto lightly floured counter and gather into rectangular-shaped pile about 8 inches long and 3 inches wide, with short side facing you. Starting at farthest end, use heel of your hand to smear small amount of dough against counter. Continue to smear dough until all crumbs have been worked. Gather smeared crumbs together into another rectangular-shaped pile and repeat process. Divide dough in half and form each half into 3-inch disk. Wrap disks tightly in plastic wrap and refrigerate for 1 hour. Let chilled dough sit on counter to soften slightly, about 10 minutes, before rolling. (Wrapped dough can be refrigerated for up to 2 days or frozen for up to 2 months. If frozen, let dough thaw completely on counter before rolling.)

3 Roll each disk of dough into 7-inch circle between 2 small sheets of floured parchment paper. (If dough sticks to parchment, gently loosen and lift sticky area with bench scraper and dust parchment with additional flour.) Slide dough circles, still between parchment sheets, onto rimmed baking sheet and refrigerate until firm, 15 to 30 minutes. (If refrigerated longer and dough is hard and brittle, let sit at room temperature until pliant.)

4 FOR THE TARTLETS Adjust oven rack to lower-middle position and heat oven to 400 degrees. Gently toss peaches and raspberries with 2 tablespoons sugar in bowl. (If fruit tastes tart, add up to 2 tablespoons more sugar.) Remove top sheet of parchment from each dough circle. Mound half of fruit in center of 1 circle, leaving 1½-inch border around edge of fruit. Being careful to leave ½-inch border of dough around edge of fruit, fold outermost 1 inch of dough over fruit, pleating it every 1 to 2 inches as needed; gently pinch pleated dough to secure, but do not press dough into fruit. Repeat with remaining fruit and dough circle.

5   Working quickly, brush top and sides of dough with water and sprinkle tartlets evenly with remaining 1 tablespoon sugar. Bake until crust is deep golden brown and fruit is bubbling, 40 to 45 minutes, rotating sheet halfway through baking.

6   Transfer tartlets with sheet to wire rack and let cool for 10 minutes, then use parchment to gently transfer tartlets to wire rack. Use metal spatula to loosen tartlets from parchment and remove parchment. Let tartlets cool on rack until juices have thickened, about 20 minutes; serve slightly warm or at room temperature.

Easy Apple Galette

SERVES 2

TOTAL TIME 1½ hours

- ½ (9½ by 9-inch) sheet puff pastry, thawed
- 1 large Granny Smith apple (8 ounces), peeled, halved, cored, and sliced ⅛ inch thick
- ½ tablespoon plant-based butter, cut into ¼-inch pieces
- 2 teaspoons sugar
- 1 tablespoon apple jelly
- 1 teaspoon water

Kitchen Improv

LEVEL UP

Serve with plant-based ice cream, store-bought plant-based whipped cream, or our Whipped Coconut Cream (page 336).

WHY THIS RECIPE WORKS   An apple galette marries buttery, flaky pastry with sweet, tender slices or chunks of apple. For ease, we use commercial puff pastry for our base; half a sheet provides just enough for a for-two-size dessert. Tart Granny Smith apples taste great and have the best texture here. To prevent the slices from drying out during baking, we sprinkle them with sugar, which draws out their moisture and caramelizes under the oven's heat. Finally, we brush the apple slices with apple jelly straight out of the oven to give them an attractive sheen and enhance the apple's fruity tartness. Note that not all commercial puff pastry is vegan; check the ingredient list carefully to be sure. Let the puff pastry thaw completely before using; otherwise, it can crack and break apart. To thaw frozen puff pastry, let it sit either in the refrigerator for 24 hours or on the counter for 30 minutes to 1 hour. Leftover puff pastry can be wrapped tightly in plastic wrap and refrozen.

1   Adjust oven rack to middle position and heat oven to 400 degrees. Line rimmed baking sheet with parchment paper. Transfer puff pastry to prepared sheet and fold edges over by ¼ inch; crimp to create ¼-inch-thick border.

2   Starting in 1 corner of tart, shingle apple slices into crust in tidy diagonal rows, overlapping them by about half, until surface is completely covered. Dot apple with butter and sprinkle evenly with sugar. Bake until bottom of tart is deep golden brown and apple has caramelized, 40 to 45 minutes, rotating sheet halfway through baking.

3   Combine apple jelly and water in bowl and microwave until mixture begins to bubble, about 30 seconds. Brush glaze over apple and let tart cool slightly on sheet for 15 minutes. Serve warm or at room temperature.

Garam Masala–Spiced Mango Crisp

SERVES 2

TOTAL TIME 1¼ hours

- 3 cups frozen mango chunks
- ¼ cup packed brown sugar, divided
- 1½ teaspoons cornstarch
- ¼ teaspoon plus ⅛ teaspoon garam masala, divided
- Pinch table salt
- ¼ cup (1¼ ounces) all-purpose flour
- 2 tablespoons old-fashioned rolled oats
- 2 tablespoons plant-based butter, cut into 4 pieces and chilled

Kitchen Improv

USE WHAT YOU'VE GOT

Substitute other frozen fruit (cut into 1-inch pieces, if necessary) for mangos. Substitute other warm spice blend, such as five spice powder or baharat, for garam masala.

LEVEL UP

Serve with plant-based ice cream.

WHY THIS RECIPE WORKS Like many fruit desserts, a successful fruit crisp starts with juicy, ripe fruit. But depending on the time of year, perfectly ripe, in-season fruit can be hard to find. Our secret weapon for a stellar crisp that we can enjoy any time of year? Frozen fruit. Frozen fruit is convenient and consistently high-quality; here, we opt to use frozen mangos and garam masala for a warmly spiced, nectary-sweet, any-season dessert. We microwave and drain the fruit to thaw it and eliminate excess liquid. We then add sugar, garam masala, and a bit of cornstarch for thickening. To make the topping, we mix chilled plant-based butter with flour and oats until slightly clumpy crumbs form. Baking the crisp in a hot oven ensures that the topping becomes golden brown and crunchy and the mango filling bubbly and thickened; a loaf pan is just the right size cooking vessel for containing two servings. The test kitchen's preferred loaf pan measures 8½ by 4½ inches; if you use a 9 by 5-inch loaf pan, start checking for doneness 5 minutes early.

1 Adjust oven rack to lower-middle position and heat oven to 425 degrees. Microwave mangos in bowl until steaming and juices start to bubble, about 3 minutes, stirring occasionally. Drain off any liquid, then toss mangos with 2 tablespoons sugar, cornstarch, ¼ teaspoon garam masala, and salt. Spread mango filling in 8½-by 4½-inch loaf pan.

2 Whisk flour, oats, remaining 2 tablespoons sugar, and remaining ⅛ teaspoon garam masala together in medium bowl. Add butter and, using your fingers, blend into dry ingredients until dime-size clumps form. Pinch together any powdery parts, then sprinkle topping evenly over filling.

3 Bake until filling is bubbling around edges and topping is golden brown, about 30 minutes, rotating pan halfway through baking. Let cool on wire rack for 15 minutes before serving.

VARIATION

Peach Crisp

Substitute frozen peaches, cut into 1-inch pieces, for mangos. Substitute combination of ⅛ teaspoon cinnamon and ⅛ teaspoon nutmeg for garam masala in filling, and cinnamon for garam masala in topping.

Rice Pudding

SERVES 2

TOTAL TIME 1¼ hours

- 4 cups unsweetened plant-based milk, plus extra as needed
- 3 tablespoons sugar
- ¼ teaspoon table salt
- ⅛ teaspoon ground cinnamon
- ¼ cup medium-grain white rice
- ½ teaspoon vanilla extract

Kitchen Improv

USE WHAT YOU'VE GOT

We prefer the consistency of pudding made with medium-grain rice, but you can substitute long-grain rice.

LEVEL UP

Sprinkle with fresh or dried fruit and/or toasted nuts. Dollop with store-bought plant-based whipped cream or our Whipped Coconut Cream (page 336).

WHY THIS RECIPE WORKS Rice pudding is one of those simple, unassuming desserts that, when done just right, can be truly sublime. Tasting of little more than sweet plant-based milk and good vanilla, the pudding has a short ingredient list, but the ratio of ingredients is key. We like the results we get from 4 cups of milk to ¼ cup of medium-grain white rice, which gives us completely cooked, tender grains of rice and pudding with a creamy, thick—but not stodgy—consistency. While any kind of plant-based milk will work here, we prefer to use an unsweetened variety so that we can precisely control the pudding's sweetness. Although this recipe requires a relatively long cooking time, it's low-maintenance time, requiring just a bit of stirring to prevent scorching. The flavor of the milk you use will come through, so use a milk you enjoy on its own; we particularly like the flavor of puddings made with oat or almond milk. Note that puddings made with soy- or pea protein–based milks may develop a skin during cooking and require more frequent stirring.

Combine milk, sugar, salt, and cinnamon in large saucepan and bring to boil over medium-high heat. Stir in rice and reduce heat to low. Cook, adjusting heat to maintain gentle simmer and stirring regularly to prevent scorching, until rice is soft and pudding has thickened to consistency of yogurt, 50 minutes to 1 hour. Stir in vanilla and adjust consistency with extra milk as needed. Serve warm or chilled.

VARIATIONS

Coconut-Cardamom Rice Pudding

Use coconut milk and substitute ground cardamom for cinnamon. Sprinkle with ¼ cup toasted coconut before serving.

Lemon–Bay Leaf Rice Pudding

Add 1 bay leaf to saucepan with milk; discard after rice pudding is fully cooked. Add 1 teaspoon grated lemon zest with vanilla.

Dark Chocolate–Avocado Pudding

SERVES 2

TOTAL TIME 25 minutes, plus
2 hours chilling

½ cup water

⅓ cup (2⅓ ounces) sugar

2 tablespoons unsweetened
cocoa powder

1½ teaspoons vanilla extract

½ teaspoon instant espresso
powder (optional)

⅛ teaspoon table salt

1 large avocado (8 ounces),
halved and pitted

1¾ ounces bittersweet or
semisweet chocolate,
chopped

Kitchen Improv

LEVEL UP

Top pudding with shaved chocolate, fresh berries, and/or chopped
toasted nuts. Dollop with store-
bought plant-based whipped cream
or our Whipped Coconut Cream
(page 336).

WHY THIS RECIPE WORKS Making a luscious chocolate pudding by substituting avocados for the cream and eggs has become an established vegan trend. But more often than not, these puddings are a far cry from the silky-smooth, ultrachocolaty pudding we crave, as they can have a grainy texture and lackluster chocolate flavor that fails to conceal the avocado's vegetal notes. Luckily, the right method can banish these problems for good. Rather than simply blending all the ingredients together at once, we start by creating a simple hot cocoa syrup in a saucepan, with a touch of espresso powder, vanilla, and salt to enhance the chocolate flavor. Meanwhile, we process the flesh of one large ripe avocado for a full 2 minutes, until absolutely, flawlessly smooth. Next, with the food processor running, we carefully stream in the cocoa syrup until the mixture is velvety and glossy. We finish by blending in a moderate amount of melted dark chocolate to give the pudding even more richness and wonderfully full chocolate flavor. Note that not all chocolate is vegan; check the ingredient list carefully to be sure.

1 Combine water; sugar; cocoa; vanilla; espresso powder, if using; and salt in small saucepan. Bring to simmer over medium heat and cook, stirring occasion-ally, until sugar and cocoa dissolve, about 2 minutes. Remove saucepan from heat and cover to keep warm.

2 Scoop flesh of avocado into food processor bowl and process until smooth, about 2 minutes, scraping down sides of bowl as needed. With processor running, slowly add warm cocoa mixture in steady stream until completely incorporated and mixture is smooth and glossy, about 2 minutes.

3 Microwave chocolate in bowl at 50 percent power, stirring occasionally, until melted, 2 to 4 minutes. Add to avocado mixture and process until well incorporated, about 1 minute. Transfer pudding to bowl, cover, and refrigerate until chilled and set, at least 2 hours or up to 24 hours. Serve.

Berry Granitas

MAKES 1 pint

TOTAL TIME 15 minutes, plus
3 hours freezing

- 8 ounces fresh or thawed frozen berries
- 6 tablespoons water
- ¼ cup (1¾ ounces) sugar
- 2 tablespoons lemon juice (2 lemons)
  Pinch table salt

Kitchen Improv

LEVEL UP

Add 2–3 tablespoons chopped fresh mint, 1–2 teaspoons grated fresh ginger, or 1–2 teaspoons grated lemon zest to blender in step 1. Serve with fresh berries, store-bought plant-based whipped cream, or our Whipped Coconut Cream (page 336).

WHY THIS RECIPE WORKS This mostly hands-off recipe for a refreshingly fruity granita with a light, crystalline texture requires no specialized equipment—just a blender, baking dish, fork, and freezer. We blend fresh or thawed frozen berries (either works equally well here) with just enough water to form a silky puree and enough sugar to give the granita its modest sweetness and the proper consistency when frozen. Lemon juice contributes acidity that brightens the fruit flavor. When scraped, this granita yields light, flaky ice crystals that linger briefly on the palate for a chilling pause before melting in the mouth in a flood of fruitiness. You can use fresh or thawed frozen blueberries, raspberries, blackberries, hulled strawberries, or a combination. If using fresh strawberries, weigh them after hulling. If using any type of thawed berries, do not drain them before adding them to the blender.

1 Process all ingredients in blender on high speed until very smooth, 1 to 2 minutes. Strain mixture through fine-mesh strainer into 8-inch square glass baking dish. Freeze, uncovered, until edges are frozen and center is slushy, about 1 hour. Using fork, scrape edges to release crystals. Stir crystals into middle of mixture and return dish to freezer. Repeat scraping and stirring, using tines of fork to mash any large chunks, every 30 minutes to 1 hour until granita crystals are uniformly light and fluffy, 2 to 3 hours.

2 Immediately before serving, scrape granita with fork to loosen. Spoon into chilled bowls or glasses and serve. (Any remaining granita can be transferred to airtight container and frozen for up to 1 week. Scrape granita again to loosen before serving.)

Nutritional Information for Our Recipes

We calculate the nutritional values of our recipes per serving; if there is a range in the serving size, we used the highest number of servings to calculate the nutritional values. We entered all the ingredients, using weights for important ingredients such as most vegetables. We also used our preferred brands in these analyses. We did not include additional salt or pepper for food that's "seasoned to taste."

	CALORIES	TOTAL FAT (G)	SAT FAT (G)	CHOL (MG)	SODIUM (MG)	TOTAL CARB (G)	DIETARY FIBER (G)	TOTAL SUGARS (G)	ADDED SUGARS (G)	PROTEIN (G)
BUILDING-BLOCK RECIPES										
Vegetable Broth Base (per 1 cup broth)	10	0	0	0	350	2	0	1	0	0
Umami Broth (per 1 cup broth)	35	0.5	0	0	240	4	0	0	0	3
Aquafaba Mayonnaise (per 1 tablespoon)	180	20	3	0	75	0	0	0	0	0
Cashew Ricotta (per 2 tablespoons)	60	5	0.5	0	40	2	0	1	0	1
Lemon-Herb Cashew Ricotta	60	5	0.5	0	40	2	0	1	0	1
Cashew Parmesan (per 1 tablespoon)	50	3.5	0.5	0	115	3	0	0	0	2
Chimichurri (per 1 tablespoon)	70	7	1	0	0	1	0	0	0	0
Pesto (per 2 tablespoons)	110	11	1.5	0	80	2	1	0	0	1
Chermoula (per 1 tablespoon)	45	4.5	0.5	0	50	1	0	0	0	0
Yogurt-Tahini Sauce (per 2 tablespoons)	20	1.5	0	0	35	1	0	0	0	1
Lemon-Herb Yogurt Sauce	20	2	0	0	35	1	0	0	0	1
Avocado Yogurt Sauce	30	2.5	0	0	35	2	1	0	0	1
Ranch Dressing (per 1 tablespooon)	90	10	1	0	120	0	0	0	0	0
Quick Lemon-Herb Vinaigrette (per 1 tablespoon)	110	11	1.5	0	90	2	0	1	1	0
Quick Ginger-Sesame Vinaigrette	110	11	1.5	0	90	1	0	1	1	0
Quick Tarragon-Caper Vinaigrette	110	11	1.5	0	100	1	0	1	1	0
Harissa (per 1 tablespoon)	110	11	1.5	0	150	3	1	0	0	1
Fennel Oil (per 1 tablespoon)	130	7	2	0	0	0	0	0	0	0
Rosemary Oil	130	7	2	0	0	0	0	0	0	0
Quick Pickled Red Onion (per 1 tablespoon)	20	0	0	0	90	5	0	4	4	0
Sumac Pickled Onion	15	1	0	0	90	1	0	1	1	0
Crispy Shallots (per 1 tablespoon)	20	2	0	0	0	2	0	1	0	0
Classic Croutons (per ¾ cup)	100	8	1	0	105	5	0	1	0	1
Umami Croutons	100	8	1	0	130	5	0	1	0	1
Garlic Croutons	100	8	1	0	105	5	0	1	0	1
Garlicky Tempeh Crumbles (per ¼ cup)	150	9	0	0	20	10	0	0	0	8
Chorizo Tempeh Crumbles	150	9	0	0	35	10	0	0	0	8
Italian Sausage Tempeh Crumbles	150	9	0	0	20	10	0	0	0	8

	CALORIES	TOTAL FAT (G)	SAT FAT (G)	CHOL (MG)	SODIUM (MG)	TOTAL CARB (G)	DIETARY FIBER (G)	TOTAL SUGARS (G)	ADDED SUGARS (G)	PROTEIN (G)
CHAPTER 1: BREAKFAST										
Black Beans on Toast with Tomato and Avocado	360	14	2	0	900	48	14	5	0	14
Pa Amb Tomàquet with Lemon-Basil Ricotta	370	20	3	0	680	38	2	4	0	8
Everything-Crusted Tofu Breakfast Sandwich	470	25	3.5	0	800	45	6	6	0	18
Breakfast Tacos with Scrambled Tofu	390	14	0.5	0	860	53	3	10	0	14
Breakfast Tacos with Scrambled Plant-Based Egg	490	23	5	0	970	52	3	10	0	19
Chickpea and Tofu Shakshuka	360	14	2	0	600	35	10	13	0	20
Hash Brown Omelet with Kimchi	450	31	3.5	0	610	43	3	2	0	6
Mangú Breakfast Bowl with Tempeh	530	28	4.5	0	600	61	8	24	0	16
Savory Breakfast Grits with Chili and Lime	340	8	0.5	0	420	60	2	21	0	7
Sweet Breakfast Grits with Maple and Pecans	330	8	0	0	260	57	2	19	0	7
Baked Oatmeal with Apple and Pecans	480	23	2.5	0	300	64	10	23	0	7
Baked Oatmeal with Banana and Chocolate	510	21	6	0	350	76	9	32	15	8
Chia Pudding Parfaits with Pineapple and Coconut	380	22	13	0	260	46	11	23	0	6
Chia Pudding Parfaits with Matcha and Kiwi	440	26	14	0	330	48	18	12	0	9
Classic Cinnamon French Toast	430	13	0.5	0	540	63	0	13	7	10
Crunchy Cinnamon French Toast	410	12	0.5	0	480	63	0	13	7	9
Whole-Wheat Pancakes	540	22	1.5	0	730	78	8	19	6	12
Banana-Walnut Muffins	380	16	1.5	0	260	53	2	24	17	6
Banana Muffins with Coconut and Macadamia Nuts	370	15	2.5	0	270	54	2	25	17	5
Chocolate Chip–Ginger Scones	370	17	13	0	310	53	1	17	5	5
Skillet Granola with Apricots and Walnuts	380	18	2	0	150	51	4	24	12	7
No-Bake Cherry and Almond Bars	240	12	1	0	100	29	4	19	0	6
CHAPTER 2: SOUPS, STEWS, AND CHILIS										
Vegetable and Barley Soup	380	15	2	0	1010	54	7	6	0	8
Soupe au Pistou	320	14	2	0	1130	40	9	10	0	12
Chilled Watermelon Soup	230	15	2	0	160	23	6	15	0	3
Italian Wedding Soup	320	8	4	0	910	46	6	4	0	17
Kimchi, Tofu, and Vegetable Soup	380	11	0.5	0	960	49	4	8	0	21
Miso-Ginger Udon Noodle Soup	460	12	0.5	0	850	69	3	6	0	21
Carrot Soup with Thai Curry Paste and Tofu Croutons	420	29	13	0	1260	27	3	6	0	13
Sweet Potato and Peanut Soup	470	23	3	0	1020	57	12	17	0	13
Vegetable Chowder with Dijon-Panko Topping	360	10	1.5	0	980	56	10	11	0	8

	CALORIES	TOTAL FAT (G)	SAT FAT (G)	CHOL (MG)	SODIUM (MG)	TOTAL CARB (G)	DIETARY FIBER (G)	TOTAL SUGARS (G)	ADDED SUGARS (G)	PROTEIN (G)
CHAPTER 2: SOUPS, STEWS, AND CHILIS (CONT.)										
Corn and Poblano Chowder with Tempeh Chorizo	460	18	3	0	890	61	5	8	0	20
Sun-Dried Tomato and White Bean Soup	320	12	1.5	0	1170	40	11	4	0	16
Skillet-Roasted Garlic and Chickpea Soup	270	11	1.5	0	1060	33	10	0	0	11
Moong Dal with Tomatoes, Spinach, and Coconut	510	21	0	0	750	58	11	5	0	26
Okra Pepper Pot	250	11	6	0	970	33	8	10	0	5
Summer Vegetable Stew	400	22	3	0	1020	46	8	16	0	6
Green Bean, Tomato, and Bulgur Stew	250	8	1	0	800	37	7	12	0	7
Weeknight Meaty Chili	390	15	4.5	0	1080	45	15	9	0	19
Green Jackfruit Chili	420	22	2	0	990	47	19	7	0	10
CHAPTER 3: SANDWICHES, BURGERS, AND FLATBREADS										
Packable Pita Sandwiches with Hummus, Arugula, and Tomato	230	4	0.5	0	880	40	1	2	0	9
Packable Pita Sandwiches with Ricotta, Basil, and Roasted Red Peppers	290	10	1.5	0	860	41	1	5	0	9
Chickpea Salad Sandwiches	460	26	3	0	970	44	9	9	0	12
Curried Chickpea Salad Sandwiches with Raisins	530	26	3	0	980	60	10	24	0	13
Grilled Cheese Sandwiches with Caramelized Onion and Apple	420	22	11	0	1120	52	2	9	0	7
Grilled Cheese Sandwiches with Tomato and Pesto	530	33	12	0	1200	52	2	9	0	9
Tofu Katsu Sandwiches	700	25	2	0	1130	90	1	114	1	23
Philly-Style Broccoli Rab, Portobello, and Cheese Sandwiches	580	30	12	0	1070	72	3	15	0	17
Buffalo Cauliflower Wraps	530	26	3	0	1150	61	5	13	3	13
Tempeh Larb Lettuce Wraps	340	17	3.5	0	1130	26	3	9	4	28
Grilled Kofte Wraps	520	21	7	0	760	58	5	6	0	25
Shawarma-Spiced Tofu Wraps with Sumac Onion	700	34	4.5	0	1110	69	6	17	15	34
Not-from-a-Box Weeknight Tacos	440	17	7	0	1010	54	6	6	0	20
Citrusy Jackfruit Tacos	460	17	1	0	980	71	9	21	17	5
Spiced Cauliflower Burgers	430	18	2.5	0	820	54	5	20	0	14
Make-Ahead Lentil and Mushroom Burgers	370	16	2.5	0	500	49	7	7	0	12
Portobello Mushroom Burgers with Sriracha Slaw	260	14	2	0	780	28	2	7	0	8
Garlic and Herb Burgers with Beet Tzatziki	380	17	7	0	970	35	4	8	0	21
Grilled Flatbread with Kale and Apple	660	35	5	0	910	70	5	13	3	15
Artichoke and Spinach Calzones	530	19	1	0	970	72	6	4	3	15
Broccoli and Roasted Red Pepper Calzones	500	21	13	0	1170	67	3	7	3	10

	CALORIES	TOTAL FAT (G)	SAT FAT (G)	CHOL (MG)	SODIUM (MG)	TOTAL CARB (G)	DIETARY FIBER (G)	TOTAL SUGARS (G)	ADDED SUGARS (G)	PROTEIN (G)
CHAPTER 4: SALADS										
Black-Eyed Pea Salad with Peaches and Pecans	360	19	2	0	850	54	12	16	0	16
Caesar Salad with Pan-Roasted Mushrooms	470	32	4	0	830	37	5	7	0	12
Chopped Salad with Kale and Pan-Seared Tofu	400	29	10	0	800	23	4	5	0	12
Hearts of Palm Ceviche with Tomato, Jicama, and Avocado	490	32	5	0	800	54	15	7	0	6
Beet Salad with Watercress and Spiced Yogurt	310	23	3.5	0	870	21	5	14	0	9
Meaty Taco Salad with Black Beans	500	22	7	0	1120	56	17	9	1	26
Carrot Noodle Salad with Harissa, Mint, and Apricots	290	17	2.5	0	930	33	9	19	2	4
Garlicky Broccoli and Chickpea Salad	410	28	3.5	0	930	33	11	8	0	13
Warm Escarole and Cannellini Bean Salad	450	21	2.5	0	550	55	15	24	0	12
Charred Cabbage Salad with Torn Tofu and Plantain Chips	390	23	3	0	890	35	6	12	2	14
Roasted Grape and Cauliflower Salad with Chermoula	420	31	4.5	0	960	33	8	19	0	7
Roasted Zucchini, Corn, and Tomato Salad with Maple Vinaigrette	420	27	3.5	0	900	40	5	14	5	8
Grilled Vegetable and Orzo Salad with Lemon and Basil	380	16	2.5	0	930	51	3	6	0	11
Rainbow Salad with Crispy Tempeh	400	20	4	5	500	47	9	25	2	13
Spinach Salad with White Beans, Corn, and Sumac	280	8	1	0	870	43	11	5	0	10
Spinach Salad with Black Beans, Chili, and Lime	280	8	1	0	980	44	12	5	0	11
Bread and Tomato Salad with Lima Beans, Feta, and Olives	510	32	10	0	890	46	6	5	0	11
Bread and Tomato Salad with Cannellini Beans, Mozzarella, and Basil	510	31	10	0	1060	46	8	6	0	10
Warm Spiced Couscous Salad	490	15	2	0	700	76	8	21	0	14
Freekeh Salad with Sweet Potato and Walnuts	560	28	3.5	0	770	66	14	3	0	14
Soba Noodle Salad with Edamame, Cabbage, and Peanut-Ginger Sauce	550	18	2	0	740	73	3	12	3	24
Soba Noodle Salad with Miso-Ginger Sauce	530	18	1.5	0	680	72	2	10	0	21
Bún Chả	570	26	7	0	940	66	4	9	6	20

	CALORIES	TOTAL FAT (G)	SAT FAT (G)	CHOL (MG)	SODIUM (MG)	TOTAL CARB (G)	DIETARY FIBER (G)	TOTAL SUGARS (G)	ADDED SUGARS (G)	PROTEIN (G)
CHAPTER 5: PASTA AND NOODLES										
Spaghetti with Garlic, Olive Oil, and Artichokes	600	28	4	0	800	77	9	3	0	15
Skillet Penne with Fresh Tomato Sauce	450	9	1	0	900	77	6	10	0	14
Skillet Penne with Fresh Tomato Sauce and Crispy Caper Crumbs	510	11	1.5	0	980	85	7	10	0	15
Fettuccine with Summer Squash, Ricotta, and Lemon-Parmesan Crumbs	600	25	3.5	0	650	79	6	7	0	18
Spaghetti with Broccoli and Avocado Pesto	580	24	3	0	770	80	13	5	0	18
Creamy Cashew Mac and Cheese	640	28	3.5	0	800	80	5	5	0	23
Creamy Cashew Mac and Cheese with Roasted Cauliflower and Plant-Based Sausage	800	37	7	0	1200	87	7	7	0	37
Cashew e Pepe e Funghi	580	24	3.5	0	980	76	5	6	0	17
Campanelle with Roasted Cauliflower and Garlic Sauce	670	31	4.5	0	1030	84	9	7	0	20
Rigatoni with Quick Mushroom Ragu	500	13	1.5	0	1000	77	5	9	0	16
Linguine with Weeknight Bolognese	620	19	7	0	1110	81	7	7	0	26
Spaghetti with Meatballs and Marinara	690	20	7	0	1120	96	10	13	0	30
Spaghetti with Pesto Meatballs	900	42	11	0	1280	98	11	13	0	32
Baked Ziti with Creamy Leeks, Kale, and Sun-Dried Tomatoes	660	17	2	0	850	108	9	11	0	17
Unstuffed Shells with Butternut Squash and Leeks	640	21	2.5	0	1000	93	7	8	0	15
Meaty Zoodles with Mango and Garam Masala	400	23	7	0	880	30	4	8	0	19
Stir-Fried Noodles with Mushrooms, Snow Peas, and Bell Peppers	480	11	1.5	0	950	82	6	11	0	16
Dan Dan Mian	760	37	9	0	1030	81	7	6	2	29
Japchae	400	23	2	0	1000	44	5	13	3	6
Spicy Basil Rice Noodles with Bok Choy	450	16	2	0	860	72	5	15	7	9
CHAPTER 6: VEGETABLE, GRAIN, AND BEAN MAINS										
Vindaloo-Spiced Green Beans, Chickpeas, and Potatoes	480	18	2.5	0	890	63	12	8	0	16
Panang Curry with Eggplant, Broccolini, and Tofu	720	27	10	0	1160	99	6	12	0	26
Curry Roasted Cabbage Wedges with Tomatoes and Chickpeas	460	26	3.5	0	940	48	17	11	1	14
Baharat Cauliflower and Eggplant with Peas	590	29	4	0	890	71	12	16	5	19
Grilled Potatoes and Vegetables with Pesto	500	33	5	0	1120	42	11	8	0	12
Grilled Squash and Vegetables with Chimichurri	370	25	3.5	0	950	34	11	9	0	9
Loaded Sweet Potato Wedges with Tempeh	410	16	2.5	0	800	54	8	14	0	12
Roasted Acorn Squash with Bulgur and Chickpeas	680	38	6	0	1020	77	15	13	0	15
Stuffed Eggplant with Lentils, Pomegranate, and Cashew Ricotta	560	31	4.5	0	950	58	16	17	2	16

	CALORIES	TOTAL FAT (G)	SAT FAT (G)	CHOL (MG)	SODIUM (MG)	TOTAL CARB (G)	DIETARY FIBER (G)	TOTAL SUGARS (G)	ADDED SUGARS (G)	PROTEIN (G)
CHAPTER 6: VEGETABLE, GRAIN, AND BEAN MAINS (CONT.)										
Sweet Potato and Black Bean Enchiladas	560	17	2	0	1170	97	16	12	0	16
Cauliflower and Chickpea Paella	510	18	2.5	0	1180	71	12	6	0	16
Green Fried Rice with Green Beans and Spinach	620	26	2.5	0	860	85	5	4	0	13
Kimchi Fried Rice with Seitan	740	15	2	0	870	132	2	2	0	23
Beet-Barley Risotto with Kale	440	16	2	0	1090	61	12	10	0	11
Risotto Primavera with Mushrooms, Asparagus, and Peas	440	23	3	0	1190	52	4	5	0	12
Pearl Couscous with White Beans, Tomatoes, and Fennel	480	17	2.5	0	920	73	11	11	0	16
Espinacas con Garbanzos	450	18	2.5	0	980	55	9	6	0	16
Red Beans and Rice	620	15	2	0	1150	109	14	6	0	18
Red Lentil Kibbeh	500	23	3.5	0	1030	59	11	7	0	17
Mushroom, Brussels Sprout, and White Bean Gratin	480	22	3	0	980	53	12	7	0	13
Tofu Mole with Zucchini Ribbon Salad	500	32	5	0	1000	34	8	14	0	25
Glazed Tofu with Pigeon Peas and Rice	760	31	13	0	970	97	11	28	0	31
Crispy Tempeh with Sambal	860	32	0	0	1140	98	0	5	5	24
Stir-Fried Seitan with Cashews	450	21	4	0	1210	35	2	6	0	34
Grilled Tofu with Charred Broccoli and Peanut Sauce	460	33	5	0	980	18	4	5	0	26
Crispy Baked Tofu Peperonata	470	33	4.5	0	900	33	5	9	0	12
CHAPTER 7: SMALL PLATES										
Pan-Seared Tofu	100	7	1	0	290	2	0	0	0	9
Pan-Seared Seitan	210	7	1	0	900	12	0	0	0	27
Pan-Seared Tempeh Steaks	270	15	1.5	0	330	20	0	0	0	15
Scrambled Plant-Based Egg	210	16	0	0	570	0	0	0	0	13
Easy Black Beans	250	8	0.5	0	790	41	1	3	0	12
Easy Black Beans with Chipotle and Lime	250	8	0.5	0	790	41	1	3	0	12
Easy Black Beans with Bell Pepper and Cumin	250	8	0.5	0	790	42	1	3	0	12
Garlicky Braised Chickpeas	270	17	2.5	0	400	24	7	2	0	8
Braised Chickpeas with Bell Pepper and Basil	280	17	2.5	0	400	26	8	3	0	8
Braised Chickpeas with Smoked Paprika and Cilantro	270	17	2.5	0	400	24	7	2	0	8
Curried Lentils	250	8	1	0	470	34	13	4	0	14
Lentils with Ras el Hanout and Lemon	250	8	1	0	470	34	13	4	0	14
Lentils with Carrots and Mint	260	8	1	0	490	36	14	5	0	14
Herbed Couscous	190	7	1	0	200	27	2	2	0	4
Couscous with Tomato, Scallion, and Lemon	210	7	1	0	200	31	4	4	0	5
Couscous with Saffron, Raisins, and Almonds	280	10	1	0	200	43	3	16	0	6

	CALORIES	TOTAL FAT (G)	SAT FAT (G)	CHOL (MG)	SODIUM (MG)	TOTAL CARB (G)	DIETARY FIBER (G)	TOTAL SUGARS (G)	ADDED SUGARS (G)	PROTEIN (G)
Hands-Off Baked Brown Rice	290	7	1	0	300	53	2	0	0	5
Hands-Off Baked Brown Rice with Peas and Mint	320	7	1	0	300	57	4	2	0	7
Hands-Off Baked Brown Rice with Pine Nuts and Basil	410	18	2	0	300	55	3	1	0	8
Bulgur Pilaf with Dried Apricots and Almonds	280	10	1.5	0	550	44	6	11	0	6
Bulgur Pilaf with Tomatoes and Kalamata Olives	210	8	1	0	290	32	5	2	0	5
Bulgur Pilaf with Shiitake Mushrooms and Edamame	240	9	0.5	0	500	35	6	4	0	9
Creamy Orzo with Boursin	350	15	6	0	690	47	1	2	0	8
Orzo with Pesto and Sun-Dried Tomatoes	420	21	3	0	680	50	1	2	0	9
Orzo with Shallot, Capers, and Dill	280	8	1	0	510	45	1	3	0	8
Celery Root Puree	240	10	1.5	0	630	34	6	5	0	5
Extracreamy Celery Root Puree	310	17	6	0	750	37	7	6	0	5
Celery Root Puree with Horseradish and Scallions	240	10	1.5	0	660	35	6	6	0	5
Roasted Red Potatoes with Rosemary	260	11	1.5	0	330	37	4	3	0	5
Roasted Red Potatoes with Fennel Seeds and Olives	280	13	1.5	0	570	38	5	3	0	5
Roasted Red Potatoes with Curry Powder and Ginger	310	16	2.5	0	330	39	5	4	0	7
Roasted Artichoke Hearts with Fennel and Tarragon	390	26	2	0	610	17	10	3	0	17
Roasted Artichoke Hearts with Bell Pepper and Olives	390	27	2	0	590	16	10	3	0	17
Lemony Skillet-Charred Green Beans	120	7	1	0	160	12	5	6	0	3
Skillet-Charred Green Beans with Crispy Bread Crumb Topping	210	14	2	0	170	18	5	6	0	4
Skillet Broccoli with Olive Oil and Garlic	180	15	2	0	340	9	4	3	0	5
Skillet Broccoli with Rosemary Oil and Orange	180	15	2	0	340	9	4	3	0	5
Pan-Roasted Brussels Sprouts	130	7	1	0	330	14	6	3	0	5
Pan-Roasted Brussels Sprouts with Gochujang and Sesame Seeds	220	15	2	0	500	19	6	6	0	6
Roasted Carrots with Yogurt-Tahini Sauce	270	17	2.5	0	670	27	8	12	0	6
Roasted Carrots with Chimichurri	330	25	3.5	0	460	25	8	11	0	4
Roasted Cauliflower	180	15	2.5	0	210	11	5	4	0	4
Roasted Cauliflower with Smoked Paprika and Shallots	230	17	2.5	0	220	17	6	7	0	5
Cauliflower Steaks with Chimichurri	450	43	5	0	380	15	6	5	0	6
Grilled Eggplant with Ginger-Sesame Vinaigrette	310	25	3.5	0	440	22	6	14	2	3
Grilled Eggplant with Lemon-Herb Yogurt Sauce	290	26	3.5	0	300	14	6	8	0	3

	CALORIES	TOTAL FAT (G)	SAT FAT (G)	CHOL (MG)	SODIUM (MG)	TOTAL CARB (G)	DIETARY FIBER (G)	TOTAL SUGARS (G)	ADDED SUGARS (G)	PROTEIN (G)
CHAPTER 7: SMALL PLATES (CONT.)										
Sautéed Baby Spinach with Almonds and Raisins	220	13	1.5	0	250	23	5	15	0	5
Sautéed Baby Spinach with Leeks and Hazelnuts	200	14	1.5	0	260	14	5	2	0	5
Chile-Rubbed Butternut Squash Steaks	240	14	2	0	880	27	5	7	2	3
Grilled Zucchini with Lemon-BasilVinaigrette	210	19	3	0	470	8	2	5	0	3
Grilled Zucchini with Curried Vinaigrette	210	19	3	0	470	8	2	5	0	3
CHAPTER 8: DESSERT										
Chocolate–Peanut Butter Truffles (per truffle)	150	10	3.5	0	85	15	0	12	7	2
Thin and Crispy Chocolate Chip Cookies (per cookie)	160	9	2.5	0	200	21	0	8	8	2
Chewy Peanut Butter Cookies (per cookie)	180	9	2	0	180	22	1	15	14	4
Fudgy Brownies (per brownie)	210	8	2.5	0	115	33	1	22	21	2
Fig Streusel Bars (per bar)	210	9	3	0	150	30	0	18	8	2
Individual Lemon–Poppy Seed Cakes	530	22	7	0	540	76	1	48	48	8
Individual Orange-Almond Cakes	540	23	7	0	540	76	1	48	48	8
Individual Funfetti Cakes	540	21	7	0	540	79	0	51	48	7
Melon, Plums, and Cherries with Mint and Vanilla	130	0.5	0	0	20	33	3	29	4	2
Plums, Blackberries, and Strawberries with Basil and Pepper	150	1	0	0	0	37	7	28	4	3
Roasted Pears with Dried Apricots and Pistachios	500	14	1.5	0	80	72	8	54	25	4
Grilled Pineapple with Coconut-Rum Sauce	320	10	7	0	15	58	4	49	27	2
Grilled Mango with Coconut–Five Spice Sauce	400	11	7	0	15	79	6	72	27	4
Strawberry Shortcakes	630	43	38	0	360	58	2	23	17	9
Peach Shortcakes	650	43	38	0	360	64	2	30	17	10
Blueberry Hand Pies (per pie)	330	16	7	0	300	53	3	21	14	5
Free-Form Summer Fruit Tartlets	570	28	11	0	590	72	4	29	19	7
Easy Apple Galette	240	9	4	0	160	36	3	20	4	3
Garam Masala–Spiced Mango Crisp	470	11	4.5	0	200	93	1	69	27	4
Peach Crisp	370	11	4.5	0	200	66	4	45	27	4
Rice Pudding	350	5	0	0	600	71	0	49	48	4
Coconut-Cardamom Rice Pudding	310	13	12	0	320	48	1	24	19	2
Lemon–Bay Leaf Rice Pudding	350	5	0	0	600	71	0	49	48	4
Dark Chocolate–Avocado Pudding	440	25	8	0	150	59	8	35	34	4
Berry Granitas (per ½ cup)	70	0	0	0	35	17	1	15	13	0

NUTRITIONAL INFORMATION

Conversions and Equivalents

Some say cooking is a science and an art. We would say that geography has a hand in it, too. Flours and sugars manufactured in the United Kingdom and elsewhere will feel and taste different from those manufactured in the United States. So we cannot promise that the loaf of bread you bake in Canada or England will taste the same as a loaf baked in the States, but we can offer guidelines for converting weights and measures. We also recommend that you rely on your instincts when making our recipes. Refer to the visual cues provided. If the dough hasn't "come together in a ball" as described, you may need to add more flour—even if the recipe doesn't tell you to. You be the judge.

The recipes in this book were developed using standard U.S. measures following U.S. government guidelines. The charts below offer equivalents for U.S. and metric measures. All conversions are approximate and have been rounded up or down to the nearest whole number.

example

| 1 teaspoon | = | 4.9292 milliliters, rounded up to 5 milliliters |
| 1 ounce | = | 28.3495 grams, rounded down to 28 grams |

volume conversions

U.S.	Metric
1 teaspoon	5 milliliters
2 teaspoons	10 milliliters
1 tablespoon	15 milliliters
2 tablespoons	30 milliliters
¼ cup	59 milliliters
⅓ cup	79 milliliters
½ cup	118 milliliters
¾ cup	177 milliliters
1 cup	237 milliliters
1¼ cups	296 milliliters
1½ cups	355 milliliters
2 cups (1 pint)	473 milliliters
2½ cups	591 milliliters
3 cups	710 milliliters
4 cups (1 quart)	0.946 liter
1.06 quarts	1 liter
4 quarts (1 gallon)	3.8 liters

weight conversions

Ounces	Grams
½	14
¾	21
1	28
1½	43
2	57
2½	71
3	85
3½	99
4	113
4½	128
5	142
6	170
7	198
8	227
9	255
10	283
12	340
16 (1 pound)	454

conversions for common baking ingredients

Baking is an exacting science. Because measuring by weight is far more accurate than measuring by volume, and thus more likely to produce reliable results, in our recipes we provide ounce measures in addition to cup measures for many ingredients. Refer to the chart below to convert these measures into grams.

Ingredient	Ounces	Grams
Flour		
1 cup all-purpose flour*	5	142
1 cup cake flour	4	113
1 cup whole-wheat flour	5½	156
Sugar		
1 cup granulated (white) sugar	7	198
1 cup packed brown sugar (light or dark)	7	198
1 cup confectioners' sugar	4	113
Cocoa Powder		
1 cup cocoa powder	3	85
Butter†		
4 tablespoons (½ stick or ¼ cup)	2	57
8 tablespoons (1 stick or ½ cup)	4	113
16 tablespoons (2 sticks or 1 cup)	8	227

* U.S. all-purpose flour, the most frequently used flour in this book, does not contain leaveners, as some European flours do. These leavened flours are called self-rising or self-raising. If you are using self-rising flour, take this into consideration before adding leaveners to a recipe.

† In the United States, butter is sold both salted and unsalted. We generally recommend unsalted butter. If you are using salted butter, take this into consideration before adding salt to a recipe.

oven temperatures

fahrenheit	celsius	gas mark
225	105	¼
250	120	½
275	135	1
300	150	2
325	165	3
350	180	4
375	190	5
400	200	6
425	220	7
450	230	8
475	245	9

converting temperatures from an instant-read thermometer

We include doneness temperatures in many of the recipes in this book. We recommend an instant-read thermometer for the job. Refer to the table above to convert Fahrenheit degrees to Celsius. Or, for temperatures not represented in the chart, use this simple formula:

Subtract 32 degrees from the Fahrenheit reading, then divide the result by 1.8 to find the Celsius reading.

example

"Cook burger patties until meat registers 130 to 135 degrees."

To convert:
$130°F - 32 = 98°$
$98° ÷ 1.8 = 54.44°C$, rounded down to 54°C

Index

Note: Page references in *italics* indicate photographs.

A

Aleppo pepper
  Harissa, 26, *26*
Almond butter
  Soba Noodle Salad with Edamame,
    Cabbage, and Peanut-Ginger
    Sauce, 174, *175*
  Tofu Mole with Zucchini Ribbon
    Salad, 254–55, *255*
Almond milk, about, 8
Almond(s)
  and Cherry Bars, No-Bake, 60, *61*
  and Dried Apricots, Bulgur Pilaf
    with, *286*, 287
  -Orange Cakes, Individual, 329
  and Raisins, Sautéed Baby Spinach
    with, *310*, 311
  Saffron, and Raisins, Couscous
    with, 282
  Warm Escarole and Cannellini Bean
    Salad, *154*, 155
Apple
  and Caramelized Onion, Grilled
    Cheese Sandwiches with, 106, *107*
  Galette, Easy, *342*, 343
  and Kale, Grilled Flatbread with,
    132, *133*
  and Pecans, Baked Oatmeal with,
    46, *47*
Apricots
  Dried, and Almonds, Bulgur Pilaf
    with, *286*, 287
  Dried, and Pistachios, Roasted
    Pears with, *332*, 333
  Harissa, and Mint, Carrot Noodle
    Salad with, 150, *151*
  and Walnuts, Skillet Granola with,
    58, *59*
Aquafaba Mayonnaise, 22
Aromatics, buying, 13

Artichoke(s)
  Garlic, and Olive Oil, Spaghetti
    with, 180, *181*
  Hearts, Roasted, with Bell Pepper
    and Olives, 294
  Hearts, Roasted, with Fennel and
    Tarragon, 294, *295*
  and Spinach Calzones, *134*, 135
Arugula
  Carrot Noodle Salad with Harissa,
    Mint, and Apricots, 150, *151*
  Hummus, and Tomato, Packable
    Pita Sandwiches with, 102, *103*
  Rainbow Salad with Crispy Tempeh,
    164, 165
  Roasted Zucchini, Corn, and
    Tomato Salad with Maple
    Vinaigrette, 160, *161*
Asparagus
  Mushrooms, and Peas, Risotto
    Primavera with, *242*, 243
  storing, 14
Avocado(s)
  and Broccoli Pesto, Spaghetti with,
    186, *187*
  Chilled Watermelon Soup, 68, 69
  –Dark Chocolate Pudding, 348, *349*
  Everything-Crusted Tofu Breakfast
    Sandwich, 34–35, *35*
  Mangú Breakfast Bowl with
    Tempeh, 42–43, *43*
  Rainbow Salad with Crispy Tempeh,
    164, 165
  storing, 14
  Tomato, and Jicama, Hearts of
    Palm Ceviche with, *144*, 145
  and Tomatoes, Black Beans on
    Toast with, 30, *31*
  Yogurt Sauce, 25

B

Baharat Cauliflower and Eggplant
  with Peas, 222–23, *223*
Baking sheet, 20
Banana
  and Chocolate, Baked Oatmeal
    with, 46
  Muffins with Coconut and
    Macadamia Nuts, 54
  -Walnut Muffins, 54, *55*
Barley
  about, 4
  -Beet Risotto with Kale, 240, *241*
  cooking chart, 270
  and Vegetable Soup, 64–65, *65*
Bars
  Cherry and Almond, No-Bake, 60, *61*
  Fig Streusel, 326, *327*
  Fudgy Brownies, *324*, 325
Basil
  and Bell Pepper, Braised Chickpeas
    with, 279
  Cannellini Beans, and Mozzarella,
    Bread and Tomato Salad with, 168
  Chilled Watermelon Soup, 68, 69
  Crispy Tempeh with Sambal, *258*, 259
  Green Fried Rice with Green Beans
    and Spinach, 236, *237*
  and Lemon, Grilled Vegetable and
    Orzo Salad with, 162, *163*
  -Lemon Ricotta, Pa Amb Tomàquet
    with, *32*, 33
  -Lemon Vinaigrette, Grilled
    Zucchini with, *314*, 315
  and Pepper, Plums, Blackberries,
    and Strawberries with, 330
  Pesto, 24
  and Pine Nuts, Hands-Off Baked
    Brown Rice with, 284, *285*
  Rice Noodles, Spicy, with Bok Choy,
    212, 213

Basil (*cont.*)
Ricotta, and Roasted Red Peppers,
Packable Pita Sandwiches
with, 102
Soupe au Pistou, 66–67, *67*
Spaghetti with Broccoli and
Avocado Pesto, 186, *187*
Bean(s)
about, 6
Black-Eyed Pea Salad with Peaches
and Pecans, *138,* 139
brining, 272
cooking chart, 272–73
freezing, 17
Lima, Feta, and Olives, Bread and
Tomato Salad with, 168–69, *169*
Moong Dal with Tomatoes,
Spinach, and Coconut, 88, *89*
pressure cooking, 272
Red, and Rice, 248–49, *249*
stovetop cooking, 272
Weeknight Meaty Chili, 96, *97*
see also Black Bean(s); Chickpea(s);
Green Bean(s); White Bean(s)
Beer, vegan, buying, 7
Beet(s)
-Barley Risotto with Kale, 240, *241*
Rainbow Salad with Crispy Tempeh,
164, 165
Salad with Watercress and Spiced
Yogurt, 146–47, *147*
Tzatziki, Garlic and Herb Burgers
with, 130, *131*
Berry(ies)
Blueberry Hand Pies, 338, *339*
Free-Form Summer Fruit Tartlets,
340–41, *341*
Granitas, *350,* 351
Plums, Blackberries, and
Strawberries with Basil and
Pepper, 330
storing, 14
Strawberry Shortcakes, 336–37, *337*
Black Bean(s)
Chili, and Lime, Spinach Salad
with, 167
Easy, *276,* 277
Easy, with Bell Pepper and
Cumin, 277
Easy, with Chipotle and Lime, 277
Meaty Taco Salad with, 148–49, *149*
and Sweet Potato Enchiladas,
232, *233*

Black Bean(s) (*cont.*)
on Toast with Tomatoes and
Avocado, 30, *31*
Blackberries
Free-Form Summer Fruit Tartlets,
340–41, *341*
Plums, and Strawberries with Basil
and Pepper, 330
Black-Eyed Pea(s)
cooking chart, 273
Salad with Peaches and Pecans,
138, 139
Blender, immersion, 20
Blueberry Hand Pies, 338, *339*
Bok Choy, Spicy Rice Noodles with,
212, 213
Bolognese, Weeknight, Linguine with,
196, 197
Bouillon, buying, 13
Bread(s)
Crumb Topping, Crispy, Skillet-
Charred Green Beans with, 297
freezing, 17
and Tomato Salad with Cannellini
Beans, Mozzarella, and Basil, 168
and Tomato Salad with Lima Beans,
Feta, and Olives, 168–69, *169*
vegan, buying, 7
see also Croutons; Toast; Tortillas
Breakfast, list of recipes, 29
Broccoli
and Avocado Pesto, Spaghetti with,
186, *187*
Charred, and Peanut Sauce, Grilled
Tofu with, *262, 263*
and Chickpea Salad, Garlicky,
152, 153
and Roasted Red Pepper
Calzones, 135
Skillet, with Olive Oil and Garlic,
298, *299*
Skillet, with Rosemary Oil and
Orange, 298
using up, 18
Broccolini
Eggplant, and Tofu, Panang Curry
with, *218,* 219
Grilled Potatoes and Vegetables
with Pesto, 224, *225*
Grilled Squash and Vegetables with
Chimichurri, 224
using up, 18
Broccoli Rabe, Portobello, and Cheese
Sandwiches, Philly-Style, *110,* 111

Broth
Base, Vegetable, 21, *21*
concentrates, buying, 13
Umami, 22
Brownies, Fudgy, *324,* 325
Brussels Sprout(s)
Mushroom, and White Bean Gratin,
252–53, *253*
Pan-Roasted, 301
Pan-Roasted, with Gochujang and
Sesame Seeds, *300,* 301
using up, 18
Buffalo Cauliflower Wraps, 112, *113*
Bulgur
about, 4
and Chickpeas, Roasted Acorn
Squash with, 228, *229*
cooking chart, 270
Green Bean, and Tomato Stew, *94,* 95
Make-Ahead Lentil and Mushroom
Burgers, 126–27, *127*
Pilaf with Dried Apricots and
Almonds, *286,* 287
Pilaf with Shiitake Mushrooms and
Edamame, 287
Pilaf with Tomatoes and Kalamata
Olives, 287
Red Lentil Kibbeh, *250,* 251
Bún Chả, *176,* 177
Burgers
Garlic and Herb, with Beet Tzatziki,
130, *131*
Lentil and Mushroom, Make-
Ahead, 126–27, *127*
Portobello Mushroom, with
Sriracha Slaw, *128,* 129
Spiced Cauliflower, *124,* 125
Butter, plant-based, about, 10

C

Cabbage
Charred, Salad with Torn Tofu and
Plantain Chips, 156, *157*
Edamame, and Peanut-Ginger
Sauce, Soba Noodle Salad with,
174, *175*
Soba Noodle Salad with
Miso-Ginger Sauce, 174
Tofu Katsu Sandwiches, *108,* 109
using up, 18
Vegetable and Barley Soup,
64–65, *65*

Cabbage (*cont.*)

Wedges, Curry Roasted, with
Tomatoes and Chickpeas, 220, *221*
see also Coleslaw mix

Caesar Salad with Pan-Roasted
Mushrooms, 140–41, *141*

Cakes, Individual
Funfetti, 329
Lemon–Poppy Seed, 328–29, *329*
Orange-Almond, 329

Calzones
Artichoke and Spinach, 134, *135*
Broccoli and Roasted Red
Pepper, 135

Caper(s)
about, 6
Crumbs, Crispy, and Fresh Tomato
Sauce, Skillet Penne with, 182
Shallot, and Dill, Orzo with, 288
-Tarragon Vinaigrette, Quick, 26

Carrot(s)
Buffalo Cauliflower Wraps, 112, *113*
Italian Wedding Soup, 70, *71*
Japchae, 210, *211*
Kimchi, Tofu, and Vegetable Soup,
72–73, *73*
and Mint, Lentils with, 281
Miso-Ginger Udon Noodle Soup,
74, 75
Noodle Salad with Harissa, Mint,
and Apricots, 150, *151*
Roasted, with Chimichurri, 302
Roasted, with Yogurt-Tahini Sauce,
302, *303*
Soup with Thai Curry Paste and
Tofu Croutons, 76, *77*
Spiced Cauliflower Burgers, *124*, 125
storing, 15
Vegetable and Barley Soup, 64–65, *65*
Warm Escarole and Cannellini Bean
Salad, *154*, 155
Warm Spiced Couscous Salad,
170, 171

Cashew(s)
e Pepe e Funghi, 190, *191*
Mac and Cheese, Creamy, *188*, 189
Mac and Cheese, Creamy, with
Roasted Cauliflower and
Sausage, 189
Make-Ahead Lentil and Mushroom
Burgers, 126–27, *127*
Parmesan, 23
Ricotta, 22
Ricotta, Lemon–Herb, 22

Cashew(s) (*cont.*)
Ricotta, Lentils, and Pomegranate,
Stuffed Eggplant with, 230–31, *231*
Stir-Fried Seitan with, 260, *261*

Cauliflower
Baharat, and Eggplant with Peas,
222–23, *223*
Buffalo, Wraps, 112, *113*
Burgers, Spiced, *124*, 125
and Chickpea Paella, *234*, 235
Creamy Cashew Mac and Cheese,
188, 189
and Grape, Roasted, Salad with
Chermoula, *158*, 159
Roasted, 304, *305*
Roasted, and Garlic Sauce,
Campanelle with, *192*, 193
Roasted, and Sausage, Creamy
Cashew Mac and Cheese
with, 189
Roasted, with Smoked Paprika and
Shallots, 304
Steaks with Chimichurri, 306, *407*
using up, 18
Vegetable Chowder with Dijon-
Panko Topping, 80, *81*

Celery, storing, 15

Celery Root
Puree, *290*, 291
Puree, Extracreamy, 291
Puree with Horseradish and
Scallions, 291

Ceviche, Hearts of Palm, with Tomato,
Jicama, and Avocado, *144*, 145

Cheese
Artichoke and Spinach Calzones,
134, 135
Boursin, about, 9
Bread and Tomato Salad with
Cannellini Beans, Mozzarella,
and Basil, 168
Bread and Tomato Salad with
Lima Beans, Feta, and Olives,
168–69, *169*
Broccoli and Roasted Red Pepper
Calzones, 135
Broccoli Rabe, and Portobello
Sandwiches, Philly-Style, *110*, 111
Chopped Salad with Kale and
Pan-Seared Tofu, 142, *143*
creamy, 8
Creamy Orzo with Boursin, 288, *289*
Extracreamy Celery Root Puree, 291
feta, about, 9

Cheese (*cont.*)
Grilled, Sandwiches with
Caramelized Onion and Apple,
106, *107*
Grilled, Sandwiches with Tomato
and Pesto, 106
melty, taste tests on, 9
plant-based, types of, 8–9
Rainbow Salad with Crispy Tempeh,
164, 165
see also Parmesan; Ricotta

Chermoula, 25

Chermoula, Roasted Grape and
Cauliflower Salad with, *158*, 159

Cherry(ies)
and Almond Bars, No-Bake, *60*, 61
Melon, and Plums with Mint and
Vanilla, 330, *331*

Chia Pudding Parfaits with Matcha
and Kiwi, 49

Chia Pudding Parfaits with Pineapple
and Coconut, *48*, 49

Chickpea(s)
Braised, with Bell Pepper and
Basil, 279
Braised, with Smoked Paprika
and Cilantro, 279
and Broccoli Salad, Garlicky,
152, 153
and Bulgur, Roasted Acorn Squash
with, 228, *229*
and Cauliflower Paella, *234*, 235
cooking chart, 273
Espinacas con Garbanzos, *246*, 247
Garlicky Braised, *278*, 279
Green Beans, and Potatoes,
Vindaloo-Spiced, 216–17, *217*
Salad, Curried, Sandwiches with
Raisins, 105
Salad Sandwiches, *104*, 105
and Skillet-Roasted Garlic Soup,
86, 87
and Tofu Shakshuka, 38, *39*
and Tomatoes, Curry Roasted
Cabbage Wedges with, 220, *221*
Warm Spiced Couscous Salad,
170, 171

Chile powder
Chile-Rubbed Butternut Squash
Steaks, 312, *313*
Easy Black Beans with Chipotle and
Lime, 277
Tofu Mole with Zucchini Ribbon
Salad, 254–55, *255*

Chiles
 chipotle, in adobo, freezing, 17
 Corn and Poblano Chowder with
  Tempeh Chorizo, *82, 83*
 Green Jackfruit Chili, *98, 99*
 Okra Pepper Pot, 90–91, *91*
Chili
 Green Jackfruit, *98, 99*
 Weeknight Meaty, 96, *97*
Chili powder
 Chorizo Tempeh Crumbles, 27
 Savory Breakfast Grits with Chili
  and Lime, *44, 45*
 Spinach Salad with Black Beans,
  Chili, and Lime, 167
Chimichurri, 24, *24*
 Cauliflower Steaks with, 306, *407*
 Grilled Squash and Vegetables
  with, 224
 Roasted Carrots with, 302
Chives, storing, 15
Chocolate
 and Banana, Baked Oatmeal with, 46
 Chip Cookies, Thin and Crispy,
  320, 321
 Chip–Ginger Scones, *56, 57*
 Dark, –Avocado Pudding, 348, *349*
 Fudgy Brownies, *324, 325*
 –Peanut Butter Truffles, 318, *319*
 vegan, buying, 7
Chopped Salad with Kale and Pan-
 Seared Tofu, 142, *143*
Chorizo Tempeh Crumbles, 27
Chowder
 Corn and Poblano, with Tempeh
  Chorizo, *82, 83*
 Vegetable, with Dijon-Panko
  Topping, 80, *81*
Cilantro
 Bún Chả, *176, 177*
 Chermoula, 25
 Freekeh Salad with Sweet Potato
  and Walnuts, 172, *173*
 Green Fried Rice with Green Beans
  and Spinach, 236, *237*
 Meaty Taco Salad with Black Beans,
  148–49, *149*
 Roasted Grape and Cauliflower
  Salad with Chermoula, *158*, 159
 Tempeh Larb Lettuce Wraps, 114, *115*
Cinnamon French Toast
 Classic, 50, *51*
 Crunchy, 50

Citrus
 juice, about, 6
 zest, about, 6
 zest, freezing, 17
 see also specific citrus fruits
Coconut
 and Macadamia Nuts, Banana
  Muffins with, 54
 and Pineapple, Chia Pudding
  Parfaits with, *48, 49*
Coconut milk
 about, 8
 Carrot Soup with Thai Curry Paste
  and Tofu Croutons, 76, *77*
 Chia Pudding Parfaits with
  Pineapple and Coconut, *48, 49*
 Coconut-Cardamom Rice
  Pudding, 347
 freezing, 17
 Glazed Tofu with Pigeon Peas and
  Rice, 256, *257*
 Grilled Mango with Coconut–Five
  Spice Sauce, 334
 Grilled Pineapple with
  Coconut-Rum Sauce, 334, *335*
 Moong Dal with Tomatoes,
  Spinach, and Coconut, 88, *89*
 Okra Pepper Pot, 90–91, *91*
 Panang Curry with Eggplant,
  Broccolini, and Tofu, *218*, 219
 using up, 18–19
 Whipped Coconut Cream, 336
Coleslaw mix
 Not-from-a-Box Weeknight Tacos,
  120, *121*
 Portobello Mushroom Burgers with
  Sriracha Slaw, *128*, 129
Collard greens
 Okra Pepper Pot, 90–91, *91*
Complete proteins, 6
Cookies
 Chocolate Chip, Thin and Crispy,
  320, 321
 Peanut Butter, Chewy, 322, *323*
Corn
 and Poblano Chowder with Tempeh
  Chorizo, *82, 83*
 Spinach Salad with Black Beans,
  Chili, and Lime, 167
 White Beans, and Sumac, Spinach
  Salad with, *166*, 167
 and Zucchini, Roasted, and Tomato
  Salad with Maple Vinaigrette,
  160, *161*

Cornmeal, about, 4
Couscous
 Herbed, 282, *283*
 Pearl, with White Beans, Tomatoes,
  and Fennel, 244, *245*
 with Saffron, Raisins, and
  Almonds, 282
 Salad, Warm Spiced, *170, 171*
 with Tomato, Scallion, and
  Lemon, 282
Creamers
 Celery Root Puree, *290, 291*
 Chocolate Chip–Ginger Scones,
  56, 57
 plant-based, about, 8
 Unstuffed Shells with Butternut
  Squash and Leeks, 202, *203*
 using up, 19
Croutons
 Caesar Salad with Pan-Roasted
  Mushrooms, 140–41, *141*
 Classic, 27
 Garlic, 27
 Umami, 27
Cucumbers
 Bread and Tomato Salad with
  Cannellini Beans, Mozzarella,
  and Basil, 168
 Bread and Tomato Salad with
  Lima Beans, Feta, and Olives,
  168–69, *169*
 Bún Chả, *176, 177*
 Chopped Salad with Kale and
  Pan-Seared Tofu, 142, *143*
 Garlic and Herb Burgers with Beet
  Tzatziki, 130, *131*
 storing, 15
Curry Paste
 Charred Cabbage Salad with Torn
  Tofu and Plantain Chips, *156*, 157
 Grilled Tofu with Charred Broccoli
  and Peanut Sauce, 262, *263*
 Panang Curry with Eggplant,
  Broccolini, and Tofu, *218*, 219
 Thai, and Tofu Croutons, Carrot
  Soup with, 76, *77*
 vegan, buying, 7
Curry Powder
 Curried Chickpea Salad
  Sandwiches with Raisins, 105
 Curried Lentils, *280, 281*
 Curry Roasted Cabbage Wedges
  with Tomatoes and Chickpeas,
  220, *221*

Curry Powder (*cont.*)
 and Ginger, Roasted Red Potatoes
  with, 292
 Grilled Zucchini with Curried
  Vinaigrette, 315
Cutting board, 20

D

Dal, Moong, with Tomatoes, Spinach,
 and Coconut, 88, *89*
Dan Dan Mian, 208–9, *209*
Dates
 No-Bake Cherry and Almond Bars,
  60, 61
Desserts
 Berry Granitas, *350*, 351
 Blueberry Hand Pies, 338, *339*
 Chewy Peanut Butter Cookies,
  322, *323*
 Chocolate–Peanut Butter Truffles,
  318, *319*
 Coconut-Cardamom Rice
  Pudding, 347
 Dark Chocolate–Avocado Pudding,
  348, *349*
 Easy Apple Galette, *342*, 343
 Fig Streusel Bars, 326, *327*
 Free-Form Summer Fruit Tartlets,
  340–41, *341*
 Fudgy Brownies, *324*, 325
 Garam Masala–Spiced Mango
  Crisp, 344, *345*
 Grilled Mango with Coconut–Five
  Spice Sauce, 334
 Grilled Pineapple with Coconut-
  Rum Sauce, 334, *335*
 Individual Funfetti Cakes, 329
 Individual Lemon–Poppy Seed
  Cakes, 328–29, *329*
 Individual Orange-Almond
  Cakes, 329
 Lemon–Bay Leaf Rice Pudding, 347
 Melon, Plums, and Cherries with
  Mint and Vanilla, 330, *331*
 Peach Crisp, 344
 Peach Shortcakes, 337
 Plums, Blackberries, and
  Strawberries with Basil and
  Pepper, 330
 Rice Pudding, *346*, 347
 Roasted Pears with Dried Apricots
  and Pistachios, *332*, 333

Desserts (*cont.*)
 Strawberry Shortcakes, 336–37, *337*
 Thin and Crispy Chocolate Chip
  Cookies, *320*, 321
Digital kitchen scale, 20
Dill, Shallot, and Capers,
 Orzo with, 288
Dressing, Ranch, 25

E

Edamame
 Cabbage, and Peanut-Ginger Sauce,
  Soba Noodle Salad with, 174, *175*
 Miso-Ginger Udon Noodle Soup,
  74, 75
 and Shiitake Mushrooms, Bulgur
  Pilaf with, 287
 Soba Noodle Salad with
  Miso-Ginger Sauce, 174
Eggplant
 and Baharat Cauliflower with Peas,
  222–23, *223*
 Broccolini, and Tofu, Panang Curry
  with, *218*, 219
 Grilled, with Ginger-Sesame
  Vinaigrette, *308*, 309
 Grilled, with Lemon-Herb Yogurt
  Sauce, 309
 Stuffed, with Lentils, Pomegranate,
  and Cashew Ricotta, 230–31, *231*
 Summer Vegetable Stew, 92–93, *93*
Egg(s)
 liquid plant-based, about, 10
 Scrambled, Breakfast Tacos with, 37
 Scrambled Plant-Based, 275, *275*
Enchiladas, Sweet Potato and
 Black Bean, 232, *233*
Escarole and Cannellini Bean Salad,
 Warm, *154*, 155
Espinacas con Garbanzos, *246*, 247
Everything-Crusted Tofu Breakfast
 Sandwich, 34–35, *35*

F

Farro
 about, 5
 cooking chart, 270
Fennel
 and Tarragon, Roasted Artichoke
  Hearts with, 294, *295*

Fennel (*cont.*)
 Vegetable Chowder with
  Dijon-Panko Topping, 80, *81*
 White Beans, and Tomatoes, Pearl
  Couscous with, 244, *245*
Fennel Seeds
 Fennel Oil, 26
 Italian Sausage Tempeh
  Crumbles, 27
 and Olives, Roasted Red Potatoes
  with, 292, *293*
Fig Streusel Bars, 326, *327*
Flatbread, Grilled, with Kale and
 Apple, 132, *133*
Flavor boosters, 6–7
Freekeh
 about, 5
 cooking chart, 270
 Salad with Sweet Potato and
  Walnuts, 172, *173*
Freezer storage tips, 16
French Toast
 Classic Cinnamon, 50, *51*
 Crunchy Cinnamon, 50
Fruits
 storage temperatures, 15–16
 see also Berry(ies); *specific fruits*
Funfetti Cakes, Individual, 329

G

Galette, Easy Apple, *342*, 343
Garam Masala
 and Mango, Meaty Zoodles with,
  204, 205
 –Spiced Mango Crisp, 344, *345*
Garlic(ky)
 Braised Chickpeas, *278*, 279
 Broccoli and Chickpea Salad,
  152, 153
 Chermoula, 25
 Croutons, 27
 freezing, 17
 Harissa, 26, *26*
 and Herb Burgers with Beet
  Tzatziki, 130, *131*
 Olive Oil, and Artichokes, Spaghetti
  with, 180, *181*
 and Olive Oil, Skillet Broccoli with,
  298, *299*
 Pesto, 24
 Sauce and Roasted Cauliflower,
  Campanelle with, *192*, 193

Garlic(ky) (cont.)
 Skillet-Roasted, and Chickpea
  Soup, *86, 87*
 Tempeh Crumbles, 27
Ginger
 –Chocolate Chip Scones, *56, 57*
 and Curry Powder, Roasted Red
  Potatoes with, 292
 freezing, 17
 -Miso Sauce, Soba Noodle Salad
  with, 174
 -Miso Udon Noodle Soup, *74, 75*
 -Peanut Sauce, Edamame, and
  Cabbage, Soba Noodle Salad
  with, 174, *175*
 -Sesame Vinaigrette, Grilled
  Eggplant with, *308, 309*
 -Sesame Vinaigrette, Quick, 26
Gochujang and Sesame Seeds,
 Pan-Roasted Brussels Sprouts with,
 300, 301
Grains
 boiling directions, 270
 cooking chart, 270
 list of, 4–5
 pilaf-style directions, 270
 storing and reheating, 270
 see also specific grains
Granitas, Berry, *350*, 351
Granola, Skillet, with Apricots and
 Walnuts, 58, *59*
Grape(s)
 and Cauliflower, Roasted, Salad
  with Chermoula, *158, 159*
 storing, 15
Gratin, Mushroom, Brussels Sprout,
 and White Bean, 252–53, *253*
Green Bean(s)
 Cauliflower and Chickpea Paella,
  234, 235
 Chickpeas, and Potatoes,
  Vindaloo-Spiced, 216–17, *217*
 Lemony Skillet-Charred, *296*, 297
 Skillet-Charred, with Crispy Bread
  Crumb Topping, 297
 Soupe au Pistou, 66–67, *67*
 and Spinach, Green Fried Rice with,
  236, 237
 Tomato, and Bulgur Stew, *94, 95*
 using up, 18
Green Jackfruit
 Chili, *98*, 99
 Tacos, Citrusy, *122, 123*

Greens
 storing, 15
 see also specific greens
Grits, Savory Breakfast
 with Chili and Lime, *44, 45*
 with Maple and Pecans, 45

H

Hand Pies, Blueberry, *338, 339*
Harissa, 26, *26*
 Mint, and Apricots, Carrot Noodle
  Salad with, 150, *151*
 Red Lentil Kibbeh, *250*, 251
Hash Brown Omelet with Kimchi, *40, 41*
Hazelnuts and Leeks, Sautéed Baby
 Spinach with, 311
Hearts of Palm Ceviche with Tomato,
 Jicama, and Avocado, *144*, 145
Herbed Couscous, 282, *283*
Herb(s)
 about, 7
 fresh, freezing, 17
 fresh, storing, 15
 -Lemon Cashew Ricotta, 22
 -Lemon Vinaigrette, Quick, 25
 -Lemon Yogurt Sauce, 25
 Ranch Dressing, 25
 substituting dried for fresh, 13
 see also specific herbs
Horseradish and Scallions, Celery
 Root Puree with, 291
Hummus, Arugula, and Tomato,
 Packable Pita Sandwiches with,
 102, *103*

I

Immersion blender, 20
Italian Sausage Tempeh Crumbles, 27
Italian Wedding Soup, 70, *71*

J

Jackfruit
 Green, Chili, *98*, 99
 Tacos, Citrusy, *122, 123*
Japchae, 210, *211*
Jicama, Tomato, and Avocado, Hearts
 of Palm Ceviche with, *144*, 145

K

Kale
 and Apple, Grilled Flatbread with,
  132, *133*
 Beet-Barley Risotto with, 240, *241*
 Creamy Leeks, and Sun-Dried
  Tomatoes, Baked Ziti with,
  200, 201
 Italian Wedding Soup, 70, *71*
 and Pan-Seared Tofu, Chopped
  Salad with, 142, *143*
Katsu Sandwiches, Tofu, *108*, 109
Kibbeh, Red Lentil, *250, 251*
Kimchi
 Fried Rice with Seitan, *238, 239*
 Hash Brown Omelet with, *40, 41*
 Tofu, and Vegetable Soup, 72–73, *73*
 vegan, buying, 7
Kiwi and Matcha, Chia Pudding
 Parfaits with, 49
Kofte, Grilled, Wraps, *116*, 117

L

Larb, Tempeh, Lettuce Wraps, 114, *115*
Leeks
 and Butternut Squash, Unstuffed
  Shells with, 202, *203*
 Creamy, Kale, and Sun-Dried
  Tomatoes, Baked Ziti with,
  200, 201
 and Hazelnuts, Sautéed Baby
  Spinach with, 311
 storing, 15
Lemon
 and Basil, Grilled Vegetable and
  Orzo Salad with, *162, 163*
 -Basil Ricotta, Pa Amb Tomàquet
  with, *32, 33*
 -Basil Vinaigrette, Grilled Zucchini
  with, *314, 315*
 –Bay Leaf Rice Pudding, 347
 -Herb Cashew Ricotta, 22
 -Herb Vinaigrette, Quick, 25
 -Herb Yogurt Sauce, 25
 Lemony Skillet-Charred Green
  Beans, *296*, 297
 –Poppy Seed Cakes, Individual,
  328–29, *329*

Lentil(s)
about, 6
with Carrots and Mint, 281
cooking chart, 273
Curried, *280*, 281
and Mushroom Burgers,
Make-Ahead, 126–27, *127*
Pomegranate, and Cashew Ricotta,
Stuffed Eggplant with, 230–31, *231*
with Ras el Hanout and Lemon, 281
Red, Kibbeh, *250*, 251
Lettuce
Buffalo Cauliflower Wraps, 112, *113*
Caesar Salad with Pan-Roasted
Mushrooms, 140–41, *141*
Meaty Taco Salad with Black Beans,
148–49, *149*
Wraps, Tempeh Larb, 114, *115*
Lime
Black Beans, and Chili, Spinach
Salad with, 167
and Chili, Savory Breakfast Grits
with, *44*, 45
and Chipotle, Easy Black Beans
with, 277
Liquid plant-based egg, about, 10
Loaf pan, 20

M

Macadamia Nuts and Coconut,
Banana Muffins with, 54
Mango
Crisp, Garam Masala–Spiced,
344, *345*
and Garam Masala, Meaty Zoodles
with, *204*, 205
Grilled, with Coconut–Five Spice
Sauce, 334
Hearts of Palm Ceviche with
Tomato, Jicama, and Avocado,
144, 145
Mangú Breakfast Bowl with Tempeh,
42–43, *43*
Maple
and Pecans, Savory Breakfast Grits
with, 45
Vinaigrette, Roasted Zucchini,
Corn, and Tomato Salad with,
160, *161*
Matcha and Kiwi, Chia Pudding
Parfaits with, 49

Mayonnaise
Aquafaba, 22
vegan, about, 10
Meat
bulk ground, buying, 11
bulk ground, taste tests on, 11
Bún Chả, *176*, 177
Creamy Cashew Mac and Cheese
with Roasted Cauliflower and
Sausage, 189
Dan Dan Mian, 208–9, *209*
Garlic and Herb Burgers with Beet
Tzatziki, 130, *131*
Grilled Kofte Wraps, *116*, 117
handling, tips for, 11
Italian Wedding Soup, 70, *71*
Linguine with Weeknight
Bolognese, *196*, 197
Meaty Taco Salad with Black Beans,
148–49, *149*
Meaty Zoodles with Mango and
Garam Masala, *204*, 205
Not-from-a-Box Weeknight Tacos,
120, *121*
plant-based, about, 11
precooked crumbles, about, 11
Spaghetti with Meatballs and
Marinara, 198–99, *199*
Spaghetti with Pesto Meatballs, 199
using up, 19
Weeknight Meaty Chili, 96, *97*
Meatballs
Italian Wedding Soup, 70, *71*
and Marinara, Spaghetti with,
198–99, *199*
Pesto, Spaghetti with, 199
Melon, Plums, and Cherries with
Mint and Vanilla, 330, *331*
Milk, plant-based, types of, 8
Mint
Bún Chả, *176*, 177
and Carrots, Lentils with, 281
Harissa, and Apricots, Carrot
Noodle Salad with, 150, *151*
and Peas, Hands-Off Baked Brown
Rice with, 284
Tempeh Larb Lettuce Wraps, 114, *115*
and Vanilla, Melon, Plums, and
Cherries with, 330, *331*
Miso
about, 7
Cashew e Pepe e Funghi, 190, *191*
-Ginger Sauce, Soba Noodle Salad
with, 174

Miso (*cont.*)
-Ginger Udon Noodle Soup, 74, *75*
Umami Broth, 22
Umami Croutons, 27
**Mole, Tofu, with Zucchini Ribbon
Salad, 254–55, *255***
**Moong Dal with Tomatoes, Spinach,
and Coconut, 88, *89***
Muffins
Banana, with Coconut and
Macadamia Nuts, 54
Banana-Walnut, 54, *55*
Mushroom(s)
about, 7
Asparagus, and Peas, Risotto
Primavera with, *242*, 243
Brussels Sprout, and White Bean
Gratin, 252–53, *253*
Cashew e Pepe e Funghi, 190, *191*
Japchae, 210, *211*
Kimchi, Tofu, and Vegetable Soup,
72–73, *73*
and Lentil Burgers, Make-Ahead,
126–27, *127*
Pan-Roasted, Caesar Salad with,
140–41, *141*
Philly-Style Broccoli Rabe,
Portobello, and Cheese
Sandwiches, 110, 111
Portobello, Burgers with Sriracha
Slaw, *128*, 129
Ragu, Quick, Rigatoni with, 194, *195*
Shiitake, and Edamame, Bulgur Pilaf
with, 287
Snow Peas, and Bell Peppers,
Stir-Fried Noodles with, 206, *207*
Umami Broth, 22
Mustard
Umami Croutons, 27
Vegetable Chowder with Dijon-
Panko Topping, 80, *81*

N

Nonstick skillet, 20
Noodle(s)
about, 5
Bún Chả, *176*, 177
Dan Dan Mian, 208–9, *209*
Japchae, 210, *211*
Rice, Spicy Basil, with Bok Choy,
212, 213

Noodle(s) (*cont.*)

Soba, Salad with Edamame, Cabbage, and Peanut-Ginger Sauce, 174, *175*

Soba, Salad with Miso-Ginger Sauce, 174

Stir-Fried, with Mushrooms, Snow Peas, and Bell Peppers, 206, *207*

Udon, Miso-Ginger Soup, 74, *75*

vegan, buying, 7

Nut butters

about, 6

see also Almond butter; Peanut Butter

Nutritional yeast

about, 7

Cashew e Pepe e Funghi, 190, *191*

Cashew Parmesan, 23

Creamy Cashew Mac and Cheese, *188,* 189

Creamy Cashew Mac and Cheese with Roasted Cauliflower and Sausage, 189

Umami Broth, 22

Umami Croutons, 27

Nuts

about, 6

see also specific nuts

O

Oat berries, cooking chart, 270

Oat milk, about, 8

Oats

about, 5

Baked Oatmeal with Apple and Pecans, 46, *47*

Baked Oatmeal with Banana and Chocolate, 46

Fig Streusel Bars, 326, *327*

Skillet Granola with Apricots and Walnuts, 58, *59*

Oils

Fennel, 26

Rosemary, 26

Okra Pepper Pot, 90–91, *91*

Olives

about, 6

and Bell Peppers, Roasted Artichoke Hearts with, 294

Bread and Tomato Salad with Cannellini Beans, Mozzarella, and Basil, 168

Olives (*cont.*)

and Fennel Seeds, Roasted Red Potatoes with, 292, *293*

Kalamata, and Tomatoes, Bulgur Pilaf with, 287

Lima Beans, and Feta, Bread and Tomato Salad with, 168–69, *169*

Omelet, Hash Brown, with Kimchi, *40,* 41

Onion(s)

Caramelized, and Apple, Grilled Cheese Sandwiches with, 106, *107*

Quick-Pickled Red, 26

storing, 15

substituting shallots for, 13

Sumac, 27

Sumac, Shawarma-Spiced Tofu Wraps with, 118, *119*

Orange(s)

-Almond Cakes, Individual, 329

Rainbow Salad with Crispy Tempeh, *164,* 165

and Rosemary Oil, Skillet Broccoli with, 298

P

Pa Amb Tomàquet with Lemon-Basil Ricotta, *32,* 33

Paella, Cauliflower and Chickpea, *234,* 235

Panang Curry with Eggplant, Broccolini, and Tofu, *218,* 219

Pancakes, Whole-Wheat, *52,* 53

Paprika

Harissa, 26, *26*

Smoked, and Cilantro, Braised Chickpeas with, 279

Smoked, and Shallots, Roasted Cauliflower with, 304

Parfaits, Chia Pudding

with Matcha and Kiwi, 49

with Pineapple and Coconut, *48,* 49

Parmesan

Beet-Barley Risotto with Kale, 240, *241*

Caesar Salad with Pan-Roasted Mushrooms, 140–41, *141*

Campanelle with Roasted Cauliflower and Garlic Sauce, *192,* 193

Cashew, 23

Parmesan (*cont.*)

-Lemon Crumbs, Summer Squash, and Ricotta, Fettuccine with, *184,* 185

plant-based, about, 9

Risotto Primavera with Mushrooms, Asparagus, and Peas, *242,* 243

Parsley

Chimichurri, 24, *24*

Herbed Couscous, 282, *283*

Pasta

about, 5

Baked Ziti with Creamy Leeks, Kale, and Sun-Dried Tomatoes, *200,* 201

Campanelle with Roasted Cauliflower and Garlic Sauce, *192,* 193

Cashew e Pepe e Funghi, 190, *191*

Creamy Cashew Mac and Cheese, *188,* 189

Creamy Cashew Mac and Cheese with Roasted Cauliflower and Sausage, 189

Creamy Orzo with Boursin, 288, *289*

Fettuccine with Summer Squash, Ricotta, and Lemon-Parmesan Crumbs, *184,* 185

Grilled Vegetable and Orzo Salad with Lemon and Basil, *162,* 163

Italian Wedding Soup, 70, *71*

Linguine with Weeknight Bolognese, *196,* 197

Orzo with Pesto and Sun-Dried Tomatoes, 288, *289*

Orzo with Shallot, Capers, and Dill, 288

Rigatoni with Quick Mushroom Ragu, 194, *195*

Skillet Penne with Fresh Tomato Sauce, 182–83, *183*

Skillet Penne with Fresh Tomato Sauce and Crispy Caper Crumbs, 182

Spaghetti with Broccoli and Avocado Pesto, 186, *187*

Spaghetti with Garlic, Olive Oil, and Artichokes, 180, *181*

Spaghetti with Meatballs and Marinara, 198–99, *199*

Spaghetti with Pesto Meatballs, 199

Unstuffed Shells with Butternut Squash and Leeks, 202, *203*

vegan, buying, 7

see also Couscous

Peach(es)
    Crisp, 344
    Free-Form Summer Fruit Tartlets,
        340–41, *341*
    and Pecans, Black-Eyed Pea Salad
        with, *138*, 139
    Shortcakes, 337
Peanut Butter
    –Chocolate Truffles, 318, *319*
    Cookies, Chewy, 322, *323*
    Grilled Tofu with Charred Broccoli
        and Peanut Sauce, *262*, 263
Peanut(s)
    Chewy Peanut Butter Cookies,
        322, *323*
    -Ginger Sauce, Edamame, and
        Cabbage, Soba Noodle Salad
        with, 174, *175*
    Panang Curry with Eggplant,
        Broccolini, and Tofu, *218*, 219
    and Sweet Potato Soup, *78*, 79
Pears, Roasted, with Dried Apricots
    and Pistachios, *332*, 333
Peas
    Baharat Cauliflower and Eggplant
        with, 222–23, *223*
    Green Fried Rice with Green Beans
        and Spinach, 236, *237*
    and Mint, Hands-Off Baked Brown
        Rice with, 284
    Mushrooms, and Asparagus,
        Risotto Primavera with, *242*, 243
    Pigeon, and Rice, Glazed Tofu with,
        256, *257*
    Snow, Mushrooms, and Bell
        Peppers, Stir-Fried Noodles
        with, 206, *207*
Pecans
    and Apple, Baked Oatmeal with,
        46, *47*
    Fig Streusel Bars, 326, *327*
    and Maple, Savory Breakfast Grits
        with, 45
    and Peaches, Black-Eyed Pea Salad
        with, *138*, 139
Pepper(s)
    Bell, and Basil, Braised Chickpeas
        with, 279
    Bell, and Cumin, Easy Black Beans
        with, 277
    Bell, and Olives, Roasted Artichoke
        Hearts with, 294
    Bell, Mushrooms, and Snow Peas,
        Stir-Fried Noodles with, 206, *207*

Pepper(s) (*cont.*)
    Breakfast Tacos with Scrambled
        Plant-Based Egg, 37
    Breakfast Tacos with Scrambled
        Tofu, *36*, 37
    Cauliflower and Chickpea Paella,
        234, 235
    Chickpea and Tofu Shakshuka, 38, *39*
    Chilled Watermelon Soup, *68*, 69
    Chopped Salad with Kale and
        Pan-Seared Tofu, 142, *143*
    Crispy Baked Tofu Peperonata,
        264, *265*
    Grilled Potatoes and Vegetables
        with Pesto, 224, *225*
    Grilled Squash and Vegetables with
        Chimichurri, 224
    Grilled Vegetable and Orzo Salad
        with Lemon and Basil, *162*, 163
    Not-from-a-Box Weeknight Tacos,
        120, *121*
    Pot, Okra, 90–91, *91*
    Roasted Red, and Broccoli
        Calzones, 135
    Roasted Red, Ricotta, and Basil,
        Packable Pita Sandwiches
        with, 102
    Savory Breakfast Grits with Chili
        and Lime, *44*, 45
    Sweet Potato and Peanut Soup,
        78, 79
    see also Chiles
Pesto, 24
    Broccoli and Avocado, Spaghetti
        with, 186, *187*
    Grilled Potatoes and Vegetables
        with, 224, *225*
    Meatballs, Spaghetti with, 199
    and Sun-Dried Tomatoes, Orzo
        with, 288, *289*
    and Tomato, Grilled Cheese
        Sandwiches with, 106
Philly-Style Broccoli Rabe, Portobello,
    and Cheese Sandwiches, 110, 111
Pickled Red Onion, Quick, 26
Pigeon Peas and Rice, Glazed Tofu
    with, 256, *257*
Pineapple
    and Coconut, Chia Pudding Parfaits
        with, *48*, 49
    Grilled, with Coconut-Rum Sauce,
        334, *335*

Pine Nuts
    and Basil, Hands-Off Baked Brown
        Rice with, 284, *285*
    Cashew Parmesan, 23
    Pesto, 24
Pistachios
    and Dried Apricots, Roasted Pears
        with, *332*, 333
    Spaghetti with Broccoli and
        Avocado Pesto, 186, *187*
Pistou, Soupe au, 66–67, *67*
Pizza dough, recipes using, 19
Plantain(s)
    Chips and Torn Tofu, Charred
        Cabbage Salad with, 156, *157*
    Mangú Breakfast Bowl with
        Tempeh, 42–43, *43*
Plums
    Blackberries, and Strawberries with
        Basil and Pepper, 330
    Melon, and Cherries with Mint and
        Vanilla, 330, *331*
Pomegranate, Lentils, and Cashew
    Ricotta, Stuffed Eggplant with,
    230–31, *231*
Poppy Seed–Lemon Cakes,
    Individual, 328–29, *329*
Potatoes
    Green Beans, and Chickpeas,
        Vindaloo-Spiced, 216–17, *217*
    Hash Brown Omelet with Kimchi,
        40, *41*
    Roasted Red, with Curry Powder
        and Ginger, 292
    Roasted Red, with Fennel Seeds
        and Olives, 292, *293*
    Roasted Red, with Rosemary, 292
    Summer Vegetable Stew, 92–93, *93*
    Vegetable and Barley Soup,
        64–65, *65*
    Vegetable Chowder with
        Dijon-Panko Topping, 80, *81*
    and Vegetables, Grilled, with Pesto,
        224, *225*
    see also Sweet Potato(es)
Proteins
    complete, 6
    list of, 5–6
Pudding
    Dark Chocolate–Avocado, 348, *349*
    Rice, *346*, 347
    Rice, Coconut-Cardamom, 347
    Rice, Lemon–Bay Leaf, 347

Pudding Parfaits, Chia
  with Matcha and Kiwi, 49
  with Pineapple and Coconut, *48*, 49
Puff pastry
  Blueberry Hand Pies, 338, *339*
  Easy Apple Galette, *342*, 343
  vegan, buying, 7

Q

Quick-Pickled Red Onion, 26
Quinoa
  about, 5
  cooking chart, 270

R

Radishes
  Chopped Salad with Kale and
    Pan-Seared Tofu, 142, *143*
  Kimchi, Tofu, and Vegetable Soup,
    72–73, *73*
  Loaded Sweet Potato Wedges with
    Tempeh, *226*, 227
  Rainbow Salad with Crispy Tempeh,
    164, 165
Raisins
  and Almonds, Sautéed Baby
    Spinach with, *310*, 311
  Curried Chickpea Salad
    Sandwiches with, 105
  Saffron, and Almonds, Couscous
    with, 282
  Spiced Cauliflower Burgers, *124*, 125
  Tofu Mole with Zucchini Ribbon
    Salad, 254–55, *255*
  Warm Escarole and Cannellini Bean
    Salad, *154*, 155
  Warm Spiced Couscous Salad,
    170, 171
Ramekins, 20
Ranch Dressing, 25
Refrigerator storage, 14–16
Rice
  about, 5
  Brown, Hands-Off Baked, 284, *285*
  Brown, Hands-Off Baked, with Peas
    and Mint, 284
  Brown, Hands-Off Baked, with Pine
    Nuts and Basil, 284, *285*
  Cauliflower and Chickpea Paella,
    234, 235

Rice (*cont.*)
  cooked, freezing, 17
  cooking chart, 270
  Green Fried, with Green Beans and
    Spinach, 236, *237*
  Kimchi Fried, with Seitan, 238, *239*
  and Pigeon Peas, Glazed Tofu with,
    256, *257*
  Pudding, *346*, 347
  Pudding, Coconut-Cardamom, 347
  Pudding, Lemon–Bay Leaf, 347
  and Red Beans, 248–49, *249*
  Risotto Primavera with Mushrooms,
    Asparagus, and Peas, *242*, 243
Rice milk, about, 8
Ricotta
  Basil, and Roasted Red Peppers,
    Packable Pita Sandwiches
    with, 102
  Cashew, 22
  Cashew, Lemon–Herb, 22
  Cashew, Lentils, and Pomegranate,
    Stuffed Eggplant with,
    230–31, *231*
  Grilled Flatbread with Kale and
    Apple, 132, *133*
  Lemon-Basil, Pa Amb Tomàquet
    with, *32*, 33
  plant-based, about, 9
  Summer Squash, and Lemon-
    Parmesan Crumbs, Fettuccine
    with, *184*, 185
  Unstuffed Shells with Butternut
    Squash and Leeks, 202, *203*
Risotto
  Beet-Barley, with Kale, 240, *241*
  Primavera with Mushrooms,
    Asparagus, and Peas, *242*, 243
Rosemary
  Oil, 26
  Oil and Orange, Skillet Broccoli
    with, 298
  Roasted Red Potatoes with, 292
Rum-Coconut Sauce, Grilled
  Pineapple with, 334, *335*

S

Saffron, Raisins, and Almonds,
  Couscous with, 282
Salads
  Beet, with Watercress and Spiced
    Yogurt, 146–47, *147*

Salads (*cont.*)
  Black-Eyed Pea, with Peaches and
    Pecans, *138*, 139
  Bread and Tomato, with Cannellini
    Beans, Mozzarella, and Basil, 168
  Bread and Tomato, with Lima Beans,
    Feta, and Olives, 168–69, *169*
  Bún Chả, *176*, 177
  Caesar, with Pan-Roasted
    Mushrooms, 140–41, *141*
  Carrot Noodle, with Harissa, Mint,
    and Apricots, 150, *151*
  Charred Cabbage, with Torn Tofu
    and Plantain Chips, 156, *157*
  Chopped, with Kale and
    Pan-Seared Tofu, 142, *143*
  Couscous, Warm Spiced, *170*, 171
  Escarole and Cannellini Bean,
    Warm, *154*, 155
  Freekeh, with Sweet Potato and
    Walnuts, 172, *173*
  Garlicky Broccoli and Chickpea,
    152, 153
  Grilled Vegetable and Orzo, with
    Lemon and Basil, 162, *163*
  Hearts of Palm Ceviche with
    Tomato, Jicama, and Avocado,
    144, 145
  Meaty Taco, with Black Beans,
    148–49, *149*
  Melon, Plums, and Cherries with
    Mint and Vanilla, 330, *331*
  Plums, Blackberries, and
    Strawberries with Basil and
    Pepper, 330
  Rainbow, with Crispy Tempeh,
    164, 165
  Roasted Grape and Cauliflower,
    with Chermoula, *158*, 159
  Roasted Zucchini, Corn, and
    Tomato, with Maple Vinaigrette,
    160, *161*
  Soba Noodle, with Edamame,
    Cabbage, and Peanut-Ginger
    Sauce, 174, *175*
  Soba Noodle, with Miso-Ginger
    Sauce, 174
  Spinach, with Black Beans, Chili,
    and Lime, 167
  Spinach, with White Beans, Corn,
    and Sumac, 166, 167
  Zucchini Ribbon, Tofu Mole with,
    254–55, *255*

Sambal
    Crispy Tempeh with, *258, 259*
    vegan, buying, 7
Sandwiches
    Chickpea Salad, *104*, 105
    Curried Chickpea Salad, with
        Raisins, 105
    Everything-Crusted Tofu Breakfast,
        34–35, *35*
    Grilled Cheese, with Caramelized
        Onion and Apple, 106, *107*
    Grilled Cheese, with Tomato and
        Pesto, 106
    Packable Pita, with Hummus,
        Arugula, and Tomato, 102, *103*
    Packable Pita, with Ricotta, Basil,
        and Roasted Red Peppers, 102
    Philly-Style Broccoli Rabe,
        Portobello, and Cheese, *110*, 111
    Tofu Katsu, *108*, 109
    see also Burgers
Saucepan, 20
Sauces
    Avocado Yogurt, 25
    Chermoula, 25
    Chimichurri, 24, *24*
    Lemon-Herb Yogurt, 25
    Pesto, 24
    Yogurt-Tahini, 25
Sausage and Roasted Cauliflower,
    Creamy Cashew Mac and Cheese
    with, 189
Scale, kitchen, 20
Scallion(s)
    and Horseradish, Celery Root Puree
        with, 291
    storing, 15
    Tomato, and Lemon, Couscous
        with, 282
Scones, Chocolate Chip–Ginger, *56, 57*
Seeds
    about, 6
    see also specific seeds
Seitan
    about, 6
    Kimchi Fried Rice with, *238, 239*
    Pan-Seared, 274
    Stir-Fried, with Cashews, 260, *261*
    using up, 19
Sesame-Ginger Vinaigrette
    Grilled Eggplant with, *308, 309*
    Quick, 26

Sesame Seeds
    and Gochujang, Pan-Roasted
        Brussels Sprouts with, *300, 301*
    Tofu Mole with Zucchini Ribbon
        Salad, 254–55, *255*
Shakshuka, Chickpea and Tofu, 38, *39*
Shallot(s)
    Capers, and Dill, Orzo with, 288
    Crispy, 27
    and Smoked Paprika, Roasted
        Cauliflower with, 304
    substituting onions with, 13
Shawarma-Spiced Tofu Wraps with
    Sumac Onion, 118, *119*
Shopping strategies, 12
Shortcakes
    Peach, 337
    Strawberry, 336–37, *337*
Skillet, nonstick, 20
Small plates
    list of recipes, 267
    mixing and matching, 268–69
Smoked Paprika
    and Cilantro, Braised Chickpeas
        with, 279
    and Shallots, Roasted Cauliflower
        with, 304
Soups
    Carrot, with Thai Curry Paste and
        Tofu Croutons, 76, *77*
    Corn and Poblano Chowder with
        Tempeh Chorizo, 82, *83*
    Italian Wedding, 70, *71*
    Kimchi, Tofu, and Vegetable,
        72–73, *73*
    Miso-Ginger Udon Noodle, 74, 75
    Skillet-Roasted Garlic and
        Chickpea, 86, 87
    Soupe au Pistou, 66–67, *67*
    Sun-Dried Tomato and White Bean,
        84, *85*
    Sweet Potato and Peanut, *78*, 79
    Vegetable and Barley, 64–65, *65*
    Vegetable Chowder with
        Dijon-Panko Topping, 80, *81*
    Watermelon, Chilled, *68*, 69
    see also Stews
Soy milk, about, 8
Soy sauce
    about, 7
    Umami Broth, 22
Spices, about, 7

Spinach
    and Artichoke Calzones, *134, 135*
    Espinacas con Garbanzos, *246, 247*
    and Green Beans, Green Fried Rice
        with, 236, *237*
    Japchae, 210, *211*
    Salad with Black Beans, Chili,
        and Lime, 167
    Salad with White Beans, Corn,
        and Sumac, *166*, 167
    Sautéed Baby, with Almonds and
        Raisins, *310*, 311
    Sautéed Baby, with Leeks and
        Hazelnuts, 311
    Tomatoes, and Coconut, Moong
        Dal with, 88, *89*
Squash
    Butternut, and Leeks, Unstuffed
        Shells with, 202, *203*
    Butternut, Steaks, Chile-Rubbed,
        312, *313*
    Grilled Vegetable and Orzo Salad
        with Lemon and Basil, *162, 163*
    Roasted Acorn, with Bulgur and
        Chickpeas, 228, *229*
    Summer, Ricotta, and Lemon-
        Parmesan Crumbs, Fettuccine
        with, *184, 185*
    summer, storing, 15
    and Vegetables, Grilled, with
        Chimichurri, 224
    see also Zucchini
Sriracha Slaw, Portobello Mushroom
    Burgers with, *128, 129*
Stews
    Green Bean, Tomato, and Bulgur,
        94, 95
    Moong Dal with Tomatoes,
        Spinach, and Coconut, 88, *89*
    Okra Pepper Pot, 90–91, *91*
    Summer Vegetable, 92–93, *93*
Strawberry(ies)
    Plums, and Blackberries with Basil
        and Pepper, 330
    Shortcakes, 336–37, *337*
Sugar, vegan, buying, 7
Sumac
    Onion, 27
    Onion, Shawarma-Spiced Tofu
        Wraps with, 118, *119*
    White Beans, and Corn, Spinach
        Salad with, *166, 167*

Sweet Potato(es)
  and Black Bean Enchiladas, 232, *233*
  Okra Pepper Pot, 90–91, *91*
  and Peanut Soup, *78, 79*
  and Walnuts, Freekeh Salad with,
    172, *173*
  Wedges, Loaded, with Tempeh,
    226, 227

T

Tacos
  Breakfast, with Scrambled
    Plant-Based Egg, 37
  Breakfast, with Scrambled Tofu,
    36, 37
  Citrusy Jackfruit, *122,* 123
  Not-from-a-Box Weeknight, 120, *121*
Taco Salad, Meaty, with Black Beans,
  148–49, *149*
Tahini
  -Yogurt Sauce, 25
  -Yogurt Sauce, Roasted Carrots
    with, 302, *303*
Tarragon
  -Caper Vinaigrette, Quick, 26
  and Fennel, Roasted Artichoke
    Hearts with, 294, *295*
Tartlets, Free-Form Summer Fruit,
  340–41, *341*
Tempeh
  about, 5
  Chorizo, Corn and Poblano
    Chowder with, *82,* 83
  Crispy, Rainbow Salad with, *164,* 165
  Crispy, with Sambal, *258,* 259
  Crumbles, Chorizo, 27
  Crumbles, Garlicky, 27
  Crumbles, Italian Sausage, 27
  Larb Lettuce Wraps, 114, *115*
  Loaded Sweet Potato Wedges with,
    226, 227
  Mangú Breakfast Bowl with,
    42–43, *43*
  Steaks, Pan-Seared, 274
  using up, 19
Thai Curry Paste
  Charred Cabbage Salad with Torn
    Tofu and Plantain Chips, 156, *157*
  Grilled Tofu with Charred Broccoli
    and Peanut Sauce, *262,* 263

Thai Curry Paste (*cont.*)
  and Tofu Croutons, Carrot Soup
    with, 76, *77*
  vegan, buying, 7
Toast
  Black Beans on, with Tomatoes and
    Avocado, 30, *31*
  Classic Cinnamon French Toast,
    50, *51*
  Crunchy Cinnamon French Toast, 50
  Pa Amb Tomàquet with Lemon-
    Basil Ricotta, *32, 33*
Toaster oven, 3, 20
Tofu
  about, 5
  and Chickpea Shakshuka, 38, *39*
  Croutons and Thai Curry Paste,
    Carrot Soup with, 76, *77*
  Eggplant, and Broccolini, Panang
    Curry with, *218,* 219
  Everything-Crusted, Breakfast
    Sandwich, 34–35, *35*
  Glazed, with Pigeon Peas and Rice,
    256, *257*
  Grilled, with Charred Broccoli and
    Peanut Sauce, *262,* 263
  Katsu Sandwiches, *108,* 109
  Kimchi, and Vegetable Soup,
    72–73, *73*
  Mole with Zucchini Ribbon Salad,
    254–55, *255*
  Pan-Seared, 274, *274*
  Pan-Seared, and Kale, Chopped
    Salad with, *142, 143*
  Peperonata, Crispy Baked, 264, *265*
  Scrambled, Breakfast Tacos with,
    36, 37
  Shawarma-Spiced, Wraps with
    Sumac Onion, 118, *119*
  Torn, and Plantain Chips, Charred
    Cabbage Salad with, 156, *157*
  using up, 19
Tomatillos
  Green Jackfruit Chili, *98, 99*
Tomato(es)
  and Avocado, Black Beans on Toast
    with, 30, *31*
  and Bread Salad with Cannellini
    Beans, Mozzarella, and Basil, 168
  and Bread Salad with Lima Beans,
    Feta, and Olives, 168–69, *169*
  Buffalo Cauliflower Wraps, 112, *113*
  canned, 6

Tomato(es) (*cont.*)
  Chickpea and Tofu Shakshuka, 38, *39*
  and Chickpeas, Curry Roasted
    Cabbage Wedges with, 220, *221*
  Chilled Watermelon Soup, *68,* 69
  Crispy Baked Tofu Peperonata,
    264, *265*
  Everything-Crusted Tofu Breakfast
    Sandwich, 34–35, *35*
  Green Bean, and Bulgur Stew, *94,* 95
  Hummus, and Arugula, Packable
    Pita Sandwiches with, 102, *103*
  Jicama, and Avocado, Hearts of
    Palm Ceviche with, *144,* 145
  and Kalamata Olives, Bulgur Pilaf
    with, 287
  Loaded Sweet Potato Wedges with
    Tempeh, *226,* 227
  Meaty Taco Salad with Black Beans,
    148–49, *149*
  Pa Amb Tomàquet with Lemon-
    Basil Ricotta, *32, 33*
  paste, freezing, 17
  and Pesto, Grilled Cheese
    Sandwiches with, 106
  Rainbow Salad with Crispy Tempeh,
    164, 165
  Red Beans and Rice, 248–49, *249*
  and Roasted Zucchini and Corn
    Salad with Maple Vinaigrette,
    160, *161*
  Sauce, Fresh, and Crispy Caper
    Crumbs, Skillet Penne with, 182
  Sauce, Fresh, Skillet Penne with,
    182–83, *183*
  Scallion, and Lemon, Couscous
    with, 282
  Soupe au Pistou, 66–67, *67*
  Spaghetti with Meatballs and
    Marinara, 198–99, *199*
  Spaghetti with Pesto Meatballs, 199
  Spinach, and Coconut, Moong Dal
    with, 88, *89*
  Summer Vegetable Stew, 92–93, *93*
  Sun-Dried, and Pesto, Orzo with,
    288, *289*
  Sun-Dried, and White Bean Soup,
    84, *85*
  Sun-Dried, Creamy Leeks, and
    Kale, Baked Ziti with, 200, 201
  Weeknight Meaty Chili, 96, *97*
  White Beans, and Fennel, Pearl
    Couscous with, 244, *245*

Tools and equipment, 20
Tortillas
    Breakfast Tacos with Scrambled
        Plant-Based Egg, 37
    Breakfast Tacos with Scrambled
        Tofu, 36, 37
    Citrusy Jackfruit Tacos, 122, 123
    Meaty Taco Salad with Black Beans,
        148–49, 149
    Not-from-a-Box Weeknight Tacos,
        120, 121
    Sweet Potato and Black Bean
        Enchiladas, 232, 233
Truffles, Chocolate–Peanut Butter,
    318, 319
Tzatziki, Beet, Garlic and Herb
    Burgers with, 130, 131

U

Umami Broth, 22
Umami Croutons, 27

V

Vegan cooking for two
    building block recipes, 21–27
    equipment and tools, 20
    flavor boosters, 6–7
    food storage guidelines, 14–17
    grains, 4–5
    identifying vegan food products, 7
    ingredient hacks, 13
    pantry foods, 4–7
    plant-based dairy, 8–10
    plant-based meat, 11
    proteins, 5–6
    recipe improvisations, 2–3
    shopping strategies, 12–13
    using up ingredients, 18–19
Vegetable(s)
    and Barley Soup, 64–65, 65
    Broth Base, 21, 21
    Chowder with Dijon-Panko
        Topping, 80, 81
    Grilled, and Orzo Salad with Lemon
        and Basil, 162, 163
    storage temperatures, 15–16
    Summer, Stew, 92–93, 93
    see also specific vegetables

Vinaigrettes
    Ginger-Sesame, Quick, 26
    Lemon-Herb, Quick, 25
    Tarragon-Caper, Quick, 26
Vindaloo-Spiced Green Beans,
    Chickpeas, and Potatoes,
    216–17, 217
Vinegar, about, 7

W

Walnut(s)
    and Apricots, Skillet Granola with,
        58, 59
    -Banana Muffins, 54, 55
    and Sweet Potato, Freekeh Salad
        with, 172, 173
Watercress and Spiced Yogurt, Beet
    Salad with, 146–47, 147
Watermelon Soup, Chilled, 68, 69
Wheat berries
    about, 5
    cooking chart, 270
Whipped Coconut Cream, 336
Whisk, 20
White Bean(s)
    Bread and Tomato Salad with
        Cannellini Beans, Mozzarella,
        and Basil, 168
    Corn, and Sumac, Spinach Salad
        with, 166, 167
    Green Jackfruit Chili, 98, 99
    Mushroom, and Brussels Sprout
        Gratin, 252–53, 253
    Soupe au Pistou, 66–67, 67
    and Sun-Dried Tomato Soup, 84, 85
    Tomatoes, and Fennel, Pearl
        Couscous with, 244, 245
    Warm Escarole and Cannellini Bean
        Salad, 154, 155
Whole-Wheat Pancakes, 52, 53
Wild rice, cooking chart, 270
Wine
    boxed, buying, 13
    freezing, 17
    vegan, buying, 7
Wraps
    Buffalo Cauliflower, 112, 113
    Grilled Kofte, 116, 117
    Shawarma-Spiced Tofu, with Sumac
        Onion, 118, 119
    Tempeh Larb Lettuce, 114, 115

Y

Yogurt
    Avocado Sauce, 25
    Banana Muffins with Coconut and
        Macadamia Nuts, 54
    Banana-Walnut Muffins, 54, 55
    Chia Pudding Parfaits with Matcha
        and Kiwi, 49
    Chia Pudding Parfaits with
        Pineapple and Coconut, 48, 49
    Garlic and Herb Burgers with
        Beet Tzatziki, 130, 131
    Meaty Zoodles with Mango and
        Garam Masala, 204, 205
    plant-based, about, 10
    Sauce, Lemon-Herb, 25
    Sauce, Lemon-Herb, Grilled
        Eggplant with, 309
    Spiced, and Watercress, Beet Salad
        with, 146–47, 147
    Spiced Cauliflower Burgers, 124, 125
    -Tahini Sauce, 25
    -Tahini Sauce, Roasted Carrots
        with, 302, 303
    using up, 19

Z

Zucchini
    and Corn, Roasted, and Tomato
        Salad with Maple Vinaigrette,
        160, 161
    Grilled, with Curried Vinaigrette, 315
    Grilled, with Lemon-Basil
        Vinaigrette, 314, 315
    Grilled Vegetable and Orzo Salad
        with Lemon and Basil, 162, 163
    Meaty Zoodles with Mango and
        Garam Masala, 204, 205
    Ribbon Salad, Tofu Mole with,
        254–55, 255
    Soupe au Pistou, 66–67, 67
    storing, 15
    Summer Vegetable Stew, 92–93, 93